MW01039023

Violet Throne

Legacy of the Aset Ka

Violet Throne

Order of Aset Ka

Luis Marques

Violet Throne — Legacy of the Aset Ka

Luis Marques

Occult and artistic concepts by Luis Marques.
Advanced spiritual and metaphysical work by Elënya Nefer and Luis Marques.
Graphics and artwork by Tânia Fonseca, André Caetano and João Gonçalves.
Revision by Tânia Fonseca and Elizabeth Tray.

Published and edited in Portugal by Aset Ka

Apartado 52230

4202-803 Porto, Portugal

To contact the author, mail can be sent to the publisher's address using the author's name, as recipient, and the contents will be forwarded. The Aset Ka will not guarantee that every letter written to the author will be answered, but all will be forwarded.

Asetian Bible — Public Edition published in 2007 (ISBN 978-9899569409)
Kemet — The Year of Revelation published in 2009 (ISBN 978-9899569416)
Book of Orion — Liber Aeternus published in 2012 (ISBN 978-9899569423)
Words in Silence — Liber Silentis published in 2014 (ISBN 978-9899569430)
Violet Throne — Legacy of the Aset Ka published in 2017 (ISBN 978-9899569447)

Kemetic Order of Aset Ka
www.asetka.org
public@asetka.org

Violet Throne
Legacy of the Aset Ka

Aꜱᴇᴛɪᴀɴ Bɪʙʟᴇ

Part One
Asetian Mysteries

✝

Part Two
Asetian Magick

Book of Orion
Liber Aeternus

☥

WORDS IN SILENCE
LIBER SILENTIS

Disclaimer

Asetians are by no means harmless beings or the personification of kindness. They do not abide by social standards nor fall under the understanding of the common mind. In the silence and darkness of their inscrutable nature they are known not to be social and often do not nurture an inborn friendliness over society. Their ageless culture is built upon predatory occultism, the dark arts, a powerful layer of spirituality and secrets long forgotten to mankind.

In their dual essence and misunderstood existence, as elemental forces of nature, the Asetians may be gentle, loving and protective, being capable of the most selfless acts of healing and nobility, while also wielding a devastating side that can be fierce, unforgiving and horrifying. However, awareness of this fact does not mean that an Asetian mind is something that you should fearfully run away from. Their legacy echoes a culture that teaches spiritual growth, learning and evolution; that fights stagnation, dishonesty and weakness. They, above all, protect wisdom, shield innocence and enforce loyalty, honor and union. Asetians are the craftsmen of the subtle, the swordsmen of magick and the scholars of arcane wisdom.

But... is it dangerous to study Asetian knowledge?

For the immature and ignorant-minded, the obsessive, compulsive and paranoid; for the weak, the numb and the slow; the ones drowned in a crown of ego or enslaved by a desire of vanity; for those that do not perpetually question the mystical details in life and challenge their own reality; the ones who believe in religion and dogma out of everything that is pushed down their throats; for the disrespectful and arrogant towards everything that they do not know and fear; to all those people... yes, Asetian spirituality is and always will be a very dangerous subject to study and get involved with.

The Order of Aset Ka will not be held responsible for what use is made with the information provided within their work, texts, teachings and practices. The occult science of the Asetians is an expression of the timeless voice of nature that unveils the secret keys to the fabric of immortal consciousness, and as such it is bound to the exercise of responsibility. The potential danger in its misuse is undeniable.

This book was designed for Asetians and the followers of the violet path, but everyone from any walk of life is welcome to read, meditate and question this work. Just keep an open and sharp mind.

Welcome to our world...

Introduction

E m Hotep.
Some say that time is an illusion, an established framework
that bends reality into linear progression. No matter how deceptive or
illusory, the symbolism that can be established through time and its
mirrored manifestation described as history presents an important
element of initiation that is intimately entwined with the fabric of
existence. Precisely ten years — one and zero, the all and its opposing
nothingness — after publishing my first occult work with disclosure
to the general public I bring forth the most intricate flag on the
tapestry of Asetian mysteries, culture and magick. This first decade is
not an end but a gateway; a never-ending and always-evolving path of
wisdom, initiation and liberation.

> *This is our emblem of truth. It is a song of immortality*
> *and a hymn of defiance, conquer and strength sung by*
> *silent warriors but also a definitive banner of victory.*
> *The Violet Throne is not a book — it is a legacy.*

In the Asetian tradition the symbolism of the throne is not
related with the physical object but appears as an archetype of
guidance, wisdom and enlightened power that is historically tied to
the essence of Aset. In Ancient Egypt the secret name and pictorial
symbol of Aset was represented by the hieroglyph of a throne, a sigil
of divine illumination and immortal authority but most importantly an
ideological representation of Her timeless legacy.

The grimoire that you are now holding between your hands is a
massive tome that carries the reader through a long journey of occult
wisdom, initiatory secrets and ancient culture; it lives as a behemoth
magickal endeavour of ageless spiritual power immortalized in nine
hundred and thirty pages. It is art and magick in pure form and

genuine manifestation. Imbued into this magister edition hides an ancient spell of binding magick — an enchantment of forgotten wisdom that allows for the initiate and the secrets presented within the text to bend the realm of matter and evolve as one. However, that fiery spark shall only resonate with those who are true to the violet Fire and loyal to the burning heart of Aset. Through this consecration the physical tome becomes a gateway between worlds; a concealed doorway to the forgotten realm of the Aset Ka.

As a compendium of magickal teachings focused on the study of higher mysteries, the *Violet Throne* unites three distinctive but profoundly important occult *Libri* in a unique collection of alchemical transformation and organic initiation, featuring a special edition of the *Asetian Bible*, the hallmark grimoire in Asetianism and predatory spirituality, alongside the initiatory pages of the *Book of Orion* and the lessons from *Words in Silence*. Presenting my three books that have marked the realms of advanced magick, occult mysteries and ancient spirituality during the past decade in a single compilation not only curates the content in a unified format that can be masterfully used in temples, ritual chambers and established ceremonial practice, but also provides the ideal cosmic timing to the reveal of a revised and augmented *Asetian Bible*.

The included edition of this classic text has been thoroughly edited with sections carefully rewritten and improved with gnosis never openly revealed before. It has been developed through a slow process that reflects the work of many years as words were crafted and impregnated with powerful magickal intent, featuring content that established and defined some of the darkest magickal arts, the misunderstood nature and hidden truths of vampire culture as well as its spiritual mysteries as they are understood today. A version of the introduction chapter from the first public edition in 2007, the year of revelation, has not been forgotten and is included as reference due to its historical value. Some words and concepts from the former edition were updated as originally intended to their rightful nomenclature that is used internally at the Aset Ka, lessening the relevance of descriptions previously provided as intentional psychological markers no longer required for inner validation. The literary sequence of the Asetian Lineages has been reordered according to its usage in ritual and initiation since the nature of such symbolism was used as a subtle marker to inner teachings in 2007; meanwhile, it has been publicly revealed with the release of the *Book of Orion* in 2012 where the implications and significance of such order became apparent and properly explained.

During this time I was asked why is that in my books I often reference the Asetians as they instead of we and that reason is simple but designedly symbolic in nature. My literary works mirror the wisdom of Aset and are crafted to echo the many shades of Her legacy as a blessed endeavour where I strictly focus on the violet nature of the Asetian family for its beauty and truth. I have imbued these pages with this essence of timeless magick and hidden keys of enlightenment without any expectation or desire for recognition, since it was my determination to teach and initiate without an influence of ego or praise and my work is an honest and unique reflection of that stance. So as an emblematic token and personal commitment I oftentimes make reference to the Asetians in a way that defines their nature and kin as the inscrutable manifestation of Aset rather than limiting their reality by the constraints of definition and interpretation or establishing their existence through the tangible realm of me and my magick.

Also on the nature of language and symbolism, many have wondered why it is that I have always chosen to begin these books and address my students with Em Hotep but the explanation is also simple: it represents a common Asetian greeting that is also frequently used by Asetianists and allies of the Asetian legacy as a sign of reverence towards the Aset Ka. It is an expression of bond, unity and mutual respect formed by two Ancient Egyptian words that carry a denotative meaning that can be roughly translated as *In Peace* — not the ordinary peace of common society but a profound peace of mind and spirit that can only be attained through honor and the acceptance of truth. The usage of such an old expression for greetings and departures both orally and in literature is nearly timeless, dating back to the early days of the Egyptian civilization and its significance has survived to this day as an iconic mirror of the magick of words that is so intrinsically ours and markedly Asetian.

It is important to underline that this grimoire suits a different audience than my previous books and was meticulously crafted for more specialized readers and practitioners, being a special edition released by the Aset Ka in this first decade of revelation, not intended for the general public or curious minds but a magickal tool for occult masters, knowledgeable scholars and educated collectors. Initially this tome was planned to be accessible only internally but the growth and passion of Asetianists around the globe made it clear that the only fair action would be not to prevent them, who have been loyally with us for so long, from partaking in this special moment. As such, this edition is also a celebration, the anniversary of the first decade since the revelation of the *Asetian Bible* — an immortal legacy that will endure the test of time. At its fundamental heart of mystical light the tome of the *Violet Throne* is not a mere binding of pages or the unification of different books on magick; it is a journey of alchemical transformation, inner discovery and an initiation of profound transcendence.

†

The past years have been spiritually rich and transformative in a time of change and revealing of truth. The unleashing of the *Asetian Bible* in public form and its unique teachings have effectively changed the perception of magick and vampirism of a generation, influencing diverse communities across the world that have adopted its concepts and newfound wisdom even if not always acknowledging its origins or sources. With its detached silence and experienced approach the Aset Ka pioneered vampiric magick and its secretive methods of initiation, revealing the spirituality of the Asetians alongside vital knowledge of advanced metaphysics and subtle anatomy that connected for the first time the practice and nature of vampirism with the ancient foundations of a spiritual path that reestablished a timeless culture of balance, growth and wisdom. Silently observing the degree of significance that my works and teachings left in this process and how they marked an era has been an incredibly humbling experience that did not make me feel relevant or entitled but instead grateful and respectful. The countless testimonies that we have witnessed during this time from nameless readers and practitioners, sharing their experiences, achievements and explaining how my words and magick changed their lives — sometimes profoundly and completely — is undeniable proof of its spiritual value and the beauty of this internal alchemy that is not mine but yours as well. In the end I can only genuinely thank them back because often unknowingly they mirror the immeasurable strength of the violet family and the unseen power of the Aset Ka. Their hearts beat with a forgotten flame of an ancient time now lost to mortal minds, fighting and conquering against sometimes impossible odds when others would have given up... never surrendering.

Throughout the steady progress of time, and heightened by the release of our public teachings and literary publications, people have sought the Order of Aset Ka in different ways, sometimes passionately or even obsessively, seeking to join its ranks or simply driven by an honest desire to learn and follow the Asetian path. While a noble quest and valid aspiration, such ventures are sometimes entwined in misunderstanding of the tradition and what the Aset Ka represents. Despite the internal policies of privacy and secrecy from an Order that does not provide a membership application system — the Aset Ka operates on a strict and highly limited method of access reserved only to direct invitation by the Higher Magisterium — it remains an essential realization that official allegiance with internal ranks is not required to explore, follow, understand, develop and grow in the Asetian system of magick, spirituality and initiation. Through a natural process of evolution, discovery and spiritual exploration the mysterious path of the Asetians can be treaded by anyone following it with honesty, dedication and love. My books represent magickal keys to someone pursuing such dangerous spiritual road; they were carefully manifested with magick that can be unleashed in the initiatory journey of the soul and its teachings extend beyond the reading of words.

However, that is not to say that this is a path that remains open to everyone, as it certainly is not. Those daring to take upon the quest of Asetian wisdom will find greater obstacles than demons and more terrifying truths than their deepest nightmares. Only the strong can survive the crossing of our violet road but most importantly only the truthful shall overcome the dangers that await beneath this knowledge. These abominations can manifest in the most unlikely forms imaginable, coming forth from outside but also sprouting from within. One who succeeds upon the ancient trials of the elders may understand that not only members of the Aset Ka can practice our magick and learn from our secrets. Many feel the need for direct contact, personal tutoring and guidance but often seek it as a reflection of insecurity towards their own abilities. Those who fear loneliness surround themselves with others to feel safe and their journey ends but those who overcome such fears embrace the eternal crossing alone and find the liberating force of their own strength. Our faces are as diverse as the stars in the sky and the banners of our family can be found in any willing heart of flame. The only courage that you require can be found within the darkest dungeons of the soul and its power is limitless. Use it wisely and you shall find the enlightening light of our violet candle. At the top of the pyramid beneath the burning desert remains the eye that devours time and reflects the key.

In modern times the predominant popular culture is plagued by a simplistic and oftentimes ignorant approach to magick and the occult that portrays metaphysics and energy work as umbrellas for wishful thinking and techniques that rely on the mere desire of needy minds. This leads to a false sense of confidence and broken understanding by those that do not dwell into deeper studies, assuming a belief in energy and magick that stems from delusion and the inability of higher practice. To all of these people, especially those who benefit from these forms of ignorance, the unique scholarly and scientific approach of the Aset Ka to occult wisdom and advanced magick presents a serious threat that has never been taken lightly. The daringly open and fearless publication of my works during the past decade has proven this long known truth, bringing to the surface the flaws and insecurities of an occult society in decay that dreads the liberating power of wisdom, educated knowledge and academic research. This mediocre but strongly rooted bias has brought offence towards the Asetian path and tradition from many angles and for many years but I believe that such a culture built on what is easy, quick and simple will remain the rotten face of commercial occultism for times to come, promoting a society of unable practitioners and blind followers that reject every roadmap that requires them to think for themselves and undertake the hard work that wielding magick implies. Guided by this mastered understanding the Order of Aset Ka takes pride, confidence and determination in never being deterred by adversarial opposition in any shape or form, always rising from its own ashes like a newborn phoenix. It has done this fiercely across the ages, writing history and shaping the course of the future with the initiatory feather of silence that makes this violet call a unique beacon of truth, power and immortality at the grasp of anyone daring to seek it.

Every form of knowledge is bound to misunderstanding and subject to the many variables of context and interpretation, often influenced by culture, dogma and social standards. Having grown as an author as well as an occultist in Europe and being actively involved with its intricate occult reality for a long time has brought me into a position of understanding towards the various elements of traditional occultism and initiatory paths, including their natural and profoundly rooted bonds of secrecy. There are major cultural differences between the occult traditions, initiatory Orders and magickal practices found in the older European societies and the modern but sometimes superficial paths explored by popular culture that lack the background, gnosis and history, frequently leading to unfounded and ignorant criticism towards the tradition of secrecy found in genuine esoteric systems. Having readers from all over the world, spanning entirely different continents and cultures makes it inevitable that some of my approaches to occult wisdom, magickal practices and spiritual teachings will be misunderstood by some. This further reinforces my well-established and recognized belief that a broader study of different cultures, paths and branches of knowledge does not weaken students of the occult in any way. Instead, it actually provides them with a unique set of tools, potentiating the making of responsible choices and more accurate interpretations of what I present within my work as its depth and complexity often daunts the less experienced.

There is an elegance to Asetian magick and philosophy that people have learned to recognize, being markedly unique and so distinctively ours. The layered depth, refinement and subtle symmetry found in the living path of the Aset Ka has become a benchmark in occult tradition and a rare signature of excellence that is sought by many who attempt to replicate, mimic and adapt. As universal as Asetian knowledge has proven to be its essence can never truly be copied or reproduced for the veil of mysteries and initiations that flourish from the Violet Flame is undeniably irreplaceable and remarkably singular, having endured undefiled for aeons and always emerged stronger than ever, prevailing against all forces and conquering every opposer with its rising silence and charm.

Explore the pages carefully and attentively for they hold initiatory magick with the power to induce an active spiritual effect on the reader with adequate sensitivity. There were some who experienced visions and long forgotten memories of past lives while exploring the contents hereby presented, while others have lost more than their minds and precious sanity. I shall not cloak the awareness of anyone reading these pages by stating that this book is safe and without consequence for I openly recognize that it is not. As dangerous as I accept my methods and knowledge to be I think that their potential is of great value to those who seek them with an honest heart. Several literary elements present in the introductions to my previous books discreetly provide a wealth of teachings with relevant significance to those with the spiritual maturity and awareness to study them. Some have considered the introduction chapters found in my works to be occult texts with distinctive initiatory power that define an occult *Liber* even when studied independently from the rest of the grimoire that it prefaces. These introductory pieces of written magick are intentional, as I methodically craft the Heka that defines my work and legacy. From those relatively brief texts alone both student and scholar can learn that their path is one and the same, as well as uncover the treacheries that await hidden in their roadmaps of growth, transformation and enlightenment. A wise reader can learn from my magick and teachings not how to avoid falling but how to recognize the fall as another lesson and also glance into the art that allows one to distinguish the false from the truthful. Study everything; learn from each and everyone with no limitations, fears or insecurities but realize that only by separating genuine from fake and lies from truth will allow occultists to survive and for their achievements to prevail.

No accomplished occultist can learn the mysteries of magick or develop an understanding of spirituality by relying solely on books. Any work claiming otherwise is nothing but a marketing maneuver intended to prey on the ignorant and deceive the unaware. My writings are not an end but a tool — a device to liberate your magick hidden within. They will not give you power but simply teach how to seek and find your very own latent abilities. The books of the Aset Ka are not intended to teach every single element on the occult and metaphysics, as that would not even be possible or educationally viable. Instead they initiate the seeker through a series of ethereal gateways into a higher gnosis. I will not provide the answer to every question you desire or place the key to the mysteries on your hand as my readers are expected to fight the long journey of the soul and battle upon the mirror of nightmares in order to find what they seek. Spiritual evolution and magickal power are only attainable through undeniable hard work and those forces cannot be limited by the constraints of time. Only the strongest persevere to reach the gates of wisdom and access the complete layer of teachings that I am presenting. This dangerous road without boundaries or time will require profound meditation and committed magick beyond the reading of these words. Yet, words are power, so find the cryptic energy that they are willed to manifest and you shall unveil more than what mere artifices of language can entail.

Teaching magick, occult mysteries and spirituality, both in person and through my books, as well as developing methods of specialized psychology, techniques of advanced metaphysics and establishing a tradition that was lost to contemporary generations has been a great personal challenge and something that has taught me much in return. Since early childhood — in this life and others before it — I have always been a natural learner, which often allowed me to grasp upon intricate subjects with ease and explore them to great results and achievement. That which may seem as a blessing is not without its obstacles and handicaps, since many spiritual and magickal lessons that were second nature to me have been proven to be complex and difficult for others to understand which in my early days resulted in frustration. It can be a daunting quest to teach and explain the abstract and subtle details of occult wisdom and magickal practice when they were born with you, learned through intuition or explored with the realization that you have already learned and taught them before — a previous life, or better said, a collection of lifetimes. I have been writing during all of my life, not always for others but also privately for myself as I see the art of writing as a powerful form of magick and spiritual introspection. However, to properly teach the most transcendent mysteries on the realm of masters requires a set of attributes that only comes with experience, but most importantly can only be attained under the realization that to teach also means to learn and such can be a definitive lesson in humility.

I write to learn and discover; to grow and evolve. I write to transform, initiate and transcend. Writing as a form of art can be practiced as an intricate ritual that when done under the veil of magick becomes silent prayer. Not all understand when I say that I would still write — and with the very same passion and commitment to truth — even if I did not have one single reader. That is because my words never come from ego nor do they find inspiration in the pursuit of recognition in any form as I live beyond such limited notions. I have written during every step of this journey that we call life, even when those works were far from any idea of publication. Writing became a treasured spiritual art for me and one of the most profound forms of magick that I chose to embrace. Now I use it to teach, initiate and enlighten but only the honest souls of old shall understand my legacy.

To every Asetian, Asetianist and wandering soul honoring the light and darkness of Aset who may be seemingly forgotten in distant shores, solitarily and remote, secluded from the nurturing hearth of Family and Order, this *Violet Throne* emerges as a beacon of guidance, strong embrace of comfort and flame of initiation. You will go through sorrow and torment, sometimes manifesting sooner and other times later in the personal roadmap of fate that defines the living experience of life. Pain instilled by the dishonor of others, through a rotten and decaying society, is augmented by the cosmic alignment of days and moments but is sometimes even established by Self. Those moments of agony and despair embraced alone in universal solitude — the daunting hours from the innermost night of the soul — may find unforeseen warmth in these pages for they share more than magickal teachings and spiritual truths but mirror the essence of Home. This unspoken unity, transcendent joy and profound passion that is found in Asetianism requires no words and heeds no doubt for it is acknowledged in silence, felt on the darkest hour and celebrated upon the immortal altar that is found deeply within.

I often mention that my books can only be understood under the dim light of the night sky, where our mysteries are revealed. The spiritual significance of the cosmos visible after dark is exceptionally unique, for it is the only natural canvas that humanity has yet no power to alter and interfere. This detail gifts the meditative observance of the universe with such purity that under proper initiation its silent language manifests in lessons of incomparable magickal power.

> *While gazing at the ethereal beauty of Orion roaming the darkened heavens you are breathing the same emotional rapport that was experienced by the ancients while the pyramids were raised, temples built and primordial magick intoned. In that very moment of absolute singularity you can find staring back at you the same artistic gem that reflected on the divine eyes of Aset as She gave birth to the firstborn Asetians and the only thing you are left with is a profound and overwhelming sense of gratitude. That is magick.*

The *Violet Throne* is a teardrop from the Breath of Aset and the essence of Ancient Egypt, my immortal Kemet of old — an undying passion of immeasurable beauty that defines the mysteries of past, present and future. A song of time beyond the constraints of matter that is perpetually engraved on the fabric of the spirit and light of the soul. As a genuine legacy of Asetianism and its mysterious culture the beauty of this grimoire lies in the understanding how its magick is timeless, an essence unchanged by the slow decay of time. Although profoundly more silent and elusive than ages long past, the *Violet Throne* remains as relevant today as it was millennia before and so it shall endure until the end of days for Her legacy is eternal and the mighty Throne of infinite color and unspeakable flame remains unbrokenly, passionately and loyally at the service of Her Highness Aset...

May the Ka be with your Ba.

Luis Marques
Order of Aset Ka
2017

Asetian Manifesto

To become an Asetian is to die and be reborn.

To forget all you have learned and learn all you have forgotten.

To be an Asetian is to be blessed with everlasting Love.

Is to be cursed by a never-ending thirst for perfection.

An Asetian is a fierce warrior, a faithful lover and an eternal concubine. Having the power of the Pharaoh, the discipline of the Samurai, the knowledge of the Wizard and the commitment of the Geisha.

Kemet is our Holy Land. The genesis of our immortal Ba.

The Tao is Knowledge. Power is through Blood.

Our Ka is sacred.

Our essence is the storm raindrops in the ocean of mankind, the winds that blow on their faces and the quakes that shake the very foundations of their ground.

We are the children of the Gods.
We are the Cursed Ones and the Blessed Ones.

We live in Secret. We live in Silence. And we live Forever...

ASETIAN BIBLE
LEGACY OF ASET

Introduction

E m Hotep.

The book you are holding gathers information — spiritual, metaphysical and philosophical — whose essence was kept secret for thousands of years. For a long time the Order of Aset Ka has kept secret within its walls a deep and profound spiritual tradition that grew and developed from a dark predatory path old as time itself. The *Asetian Bible* is an occult grimoire that initiates the mysterious journey into this Ancient Egyptian spiritual tradition, presenting rare information and esoteric literature on the metaphysical knowledge, magickal practices, hidden wisdom and ancient culture experienced and lived by the Asetians. This system of initiation is here explored in a way that allows for educated occultists to develop a fundamental understanding of the tradition, slowly developing inner skills and subtle abilities that ignite the potential and open the gateways into the dangerous quest of Asetian knowledge, magick and enlightenment, often described in literature as the Great Work; the journey of the soul.

Within this book the seeker finds a path built upon predatory spirituality and adversarial philosophy, where life force — also described as vital energy — can be metaphysically drawn to fuel powerful magickal abilities, attain spiritual mastery and maintain the internal subtle system empowered and balanced. This particular element of distinctive magickal practice is undeniably vampiric and it relates to the ancient mysteries behind the convoluted lore of the historical vampire, a term coined by the common people to describe such feared beings that later became used throughout different cultures and myths tied to the predatory undead. Prominent in European culture during the medieval period, these vampires of folklore have no historical connection to the predatory beings of

Ancient Egypt, sometimes described as the firstborn vampires but only accurately defined by the word Asetians.

Some may find these darker arts, concepts and techniques to be inhumane, unethical or something worse, so never forget that this tradition stands at the edge of a dark path that cannot be studied without exposure to an array of hidden dangers and unforeseen consequences. Since darkness is a concept often misunderstood through blind dogma, the ignorance of popular culture and the misinformation of the media, it becomes of importance to underline that in Asetian philosophy the terminology does not mean harm, evil or unbalance but something entirely different, dwelling into the hidden branches of wisdom that deal with secret, silent and intricate practices that oppose the materialistic and superficial minds of ordinary society. A dark tradition is not for the masses and it is not even accessible to anyone that willingly chooses it. Darkness and the magickal arts are established through a secretive path that only the aware, the evolved and the dedicated can truly embrace; a road where many will fall, sometimes permanently losing themselves when not approached with honesty and a humble heart. That is part of what the Asetians have to teach through their timeless culture and lost wisdom where the proper name for such legacy is Asetianism — the hidden secrets of the ancient world.

Concerning the relevance found in the name of this book and its potential for mistaken religious implications, the word *bible* is commonly translated simply as *book* and it is particularly used to represent the central texts of any spiritual traditions and underlying teachings. Furthermore, under etymological examination the term comes from the classical Latin language where it derives from the word *biblia* that finds its roots in *byblos,* a term for Egyptian papyrus.

Under such light of understanding the symbolism in the title becomes adequately accurate to represent what is found within this book.

The *Asetian Bible* is organized into two different major sections: a spiritual book and a metaphysical module. The first part addresses different aspects of Asetian theology, spirituality and philosophy, being strictly Asetian in nature. Some of the included concepts and definitions will not apply to everyone and their understanding will develop and evolve in time as the initiate progresses through a complex process of inner growth, spiritual maturity and natural initiation. This first part of the book develops around potentially confusing subjects and intricate symbolism that is not always evident or literal, some of which can appear subjective without proper scrutiny and an advanced understanding. As such, the first book is not intended to be read lightly or in a sportive manner, as within its contents can be found much symbolical information and spiritual teachings, sometimes intentionally disguised alongside subliminal details specifically designed for the identification and pre-awakening of dormant unaware Asetians. However, focusing on tracking such cues can prove to be futile for the serious seeker, as the true power behind this book is found behind the doorways of growth achieved with its words and learning through its magick in order to ignite the hidden flame of the soul — a silent initiation.

In the second part the reader will find an occult grimoire of metaphysics and energy manipulation studied as vibrational magick, which diverging from the previous section has much information that can be applied not only to Asetians but also to a large spectrum of occultists and scholars. This module is structured into distinctive chapters that range from basic concepts of subtle energy and metaphysics, passing through the study of subtle anatomy to more advanced vampiric magick and feeding techniques. That second part of the bible was intended to be a small, approachable and concise tool for Asetians and occultists, as well as establishing a reference to anyone interested in energy manipulation or the arts of vampirism. It is not the intention of this section to teach anyone how to master energy manipulation nor it should be used as definitive occult education, but instead aims to work as a primer on the subtle nature of vampirism and the metaphysical intricacies within the Asetian culture. The included chapters provide a valuable reference that can be easily consulted, studied or addressed at any needed time during spiritual exploration, occult study or magickal practice. However, there are hidden teachings to be found that will not be obvious on a first reading, so the wise shall approach this tome as a magickal tool and not just another book or a collection of words.

Additionally, it should be noted that in technical chapters the most basic steps on energy manipulation are intentionally not included as it is assumed that the reader has background knowledge on magick, energy work and experience with energy sensing. Variants of subtle feeding and energy draining are going to be described and defined as concepts, but in-depth information on the practical techniques being analysed is not going to be developed due to the inherent dangers with the publication of such information to the general public. This is not a practical book on procedures but a framework of concepts and initiatory catalyst as no genuine vampire literature would disclosure the secrets of magickal feeding to outsiders.

There is much speculation and deceitful fantasy being displayed in contemporary media, explored by a society that preys on ignorance and misinformation. With this work there is a strong commitment to present for the first time an honest account of real vampirism as opposed to the delusional reality perpetuated by charlatans and role-players. This book presents the hidden nature of vampirism without the influence of fiction or ego, exposing practices and a timeless predatory culture in its truest form while breaking old paradigms and inaccurate concepts. This grimoire provides a much-needed reference for both vampires and humans, establishing a framework that can be used as a default source of information in the examination, debate and study of vampirism, energy work and the secretive path of wisdom known as Asetianism.

It should be obvious to anyone educated in occult mysteries that actual vampires lack the fictional abilities to fly, shape-shift or dissipate into smoke, just like elements of gothic fashion, long hair or sharp fangs have absolutely no connection with real vampirism. Most concepts found in popular culture are nothing more than a poor representation of fiction often embraced by those who wish to pose the archetype without the knowledge of what vampirism entails and how it manifests. Acknowledgment of such facts should be a requisite in the study of this book since anyone seeking fantasy, self-deception or delusion so commonly embraced by an egotistical society in decay is bound for a cunning — maybe even painful — surprise when faced against the darkest mirrors found within the teachings and gnosis here fiercely presented.

Although unsurprising to students of Asetianism it is worth mentioning that in this work I have not included the complete set of Asetian mysteries, which are mostly internal to the Aset Ka and developed under a secretive initiatory framework that is too profound and powerful for irresponsible disclosure. Advanced knowledge and mastery, including practices of Asetian high magick, intricate ritual work and transformational initiation encompass an array of teachings that are slowly discovered and developed on the vast realms emerging within, as students evolve and progress through the Asetian tradition and universal initiatory ladder, hence conquering their own personal path.

Along the corpus of these occult documents were included intentional gaps and flaws that may appear as misconceptions to unaware eyes when they are far from arbitrary. These elements are intentionally elaborated and positioned, working as another of our unique methods of validation and spiritual gauge. This further emphasises the notion that this grimoire represents more than just a mere text on the occult; it is in fact a powerful metaphysical tool that can be used and activated in a multitude of ways. Apparent simplification of key concepts and philosophies is strategic, since Asetianism will remain — not by design but through nature — an elitist and secretive tradition of mysteries with a profound and deeply complex spiritual system underlying the basic framework to be grasped through the unaided eye. With this in mind the Asetian Bible accomplishes two things at the same time: giving the general public, researchers and scholars the fundamental concepts for a layman's understanding of the foundation and mysteries of the hidden tradition of Egypt, while leaving Asetians and followers of the path with a prime reference on Asetianism and its violet spark, slowly opening the inner doorways for a more profound development and exploration of inner mysteries that will ignite their own evolution.

The concepts and practices being presented are relevant to Asetians, in most cases developed by the Aset Ka throughout a long established history, so when using them to explain experiences or phenomenon in a non-Asetian environment certain factors should be taken into consideration. While some of these principles can be applied to general metaphysics and explored by anyone fluent in the magickal arts, it is still of vital importance to realize that they relate to Asetian knowledge. Dealing with Asetian magick and exploring Asetian wisdom is no light matter and an undertaking that should always be approached responsibly under a mature mindset. Neglecting this simple remark can have grave and sometimes even irreversible consequences.

It should also be stated that the Order of Aset Ka and its teachings are not a closed shell of information. The Order has studied, developed and improved a wide range of knowledge and mystical practices across millennia. The diverse traditions that are the subject of study and research by the Aset Ka encompass a broad selection of knowledge and practices explored within the multilayered occult spectrum. These range from the different branches of the Western mystery schools to much older Oriental and Middle Eastern esoteric traditions, the misunderstood knowledge of European traditional witchcraft, the obscure practices of Persian, Babylonian and Sumerian sorcery, the mind-bending initiatory works of the Kabbalah and several traditions aligned with the left hand path, as well as the secretive and often feared gnosis found in the forgotten path of spiritual vampirism.

The many cultures and interpretations found through this unlimited pursuit for knowledge, mirrored on countless sources of scholarly and metaphysical study that are embraced within the Aset Ka, do not define the nature of Asetianism and its spiritual legacy. Instead, they establish a layer of wisdom and historical perspective that enriches the educated mind of a learned practitioner, potentiating a higher mastery of the occult through the mindset of different civilizations and eras. Tying the pieces together slowly unveils how some of those traditions and paths have secretly developed and flourished from an earlier foundation that finds seed in the wisdom of the Asetians, oftentimes changed, adapted and misinterpreted to the point of losing its original identity and spiritual power.

Asetianism distinctively breathes with its very own character and strong fingerprint, allowing the followers of this tradition to study varied forms of art, mysticism and knowledge as an important scholarly tool in their personal evolution and understanding of history. That alone does not mean that any culture can be intertwined in a practical way with the purer Egyptian practices, as many represent incompatible material whose study does not mean acceptance, belief or agreement but simply an effective learning mechanism used with awareness to achieve a higher gnosis. In the end the immortal legacy of Asetianism rests in the lost culture of Ancient Egypt passed through the teachings of Aset since the time before time — now hidden in symbolism and disguised as art protected from the defacing hands of humanity and their will to destroy everything that they cannot subdue or control. Asetians can never be limited, restrained or controlled and shall never submit to any other power or force in this world, as their flag of magick and wisdom still flies high up in the skies and can only be seen by those who approach them with the truth of an honest heart and a pure soul.

During a long-term study of the book I remind that this edition is not by any means a final work. The *Asetian Bible* reflects the true dynamic nature of the Asetians, with their empathy towards evolution and *kheperu* — meaning *transformation* in Ancient Egyptian. So while you are holding a published volume in your hands the text will eventually change over time when further work is developed since evolution is a never-ending process and new scientific discoveries are made, methods get improved, further past-life work is achieved and new sections are written and added to this growing work. As we progress through this new era of our history and the Aset Ka slowly lifts the veil from further layers of Asetian mysteries and inner teachings, those steps will also be reflected in newer versions of the

☦

book, so treat your original copy carefully as it may one day become a rare magickal item and one of cherished significance in occult history.

Although the Asetian tradition is a path attached to profound ancient roots, its knowledge and practices are not static and stagnated but quite the opposite, manifesting as a timeless culture that is in constant evolution, growth and recurring inspiration for new learning, just like the Asetian soul. This dynamic nature of the Asetians and their spirituality is expressed in ancient architecture at many temples in Egypt, like for example the ones found at Em-Waset — a location the Greeks called Thebes and that still linger today in Luxor and Karnak — with a historical growth, development and engineering that accurately and intentionally expresses the dynamics of Asetian evolution. Clues and symbolism relating to such dynamics are found expressed throughout many of the Ancient Egyptian constructions, with foundations often much older than the edifications that now stand. This is explained through the recurrent reconstruction of the temples, a spiritual and scientific methodology adopted by the ancient architects and priests to maintain the precise accuracy of their sacred spaces in tune with the ever-changing stellar alignment, natural alterations in subtle energy, metaphysical development and spiritual evolution of the soul. Their intent was for the temples to become living entities of energy and power, worthy sacred spaces for the manifestation of divinity that just like the mind, body and soul of an Asetian should be in constant evolution.

Finally, it should be clear that others and myself related with the publication of this work and the Order of Aset Ka are very much aware that the release of this book and the challenging secretive information under disclosure is going to be polemic, not only because of the nature of its contents and approach, touching subjects that nowadays are still considered taboo inside occult societies but also due to the inborn tendency of the common mind to attack and dismiss every source of wisdom that questions their authority and expertise, no matter how true and beneficial it may be. There will be criticism and judgment because it is easier to judge than it is to learn and understand, so that can be an effective cue to reflect on the inner handicaps of those who can only follow easier paths and are unable to do the hard work required by advanced occult studies, being expressions enforced by ignorance, fear and ego.

As an author and an occultist my take regarding criticism is that I have always considered it to be a positive sign. I expect and look forward to those critical remarks and comments. If someone will criticize our philosophies, beliefs, practices or any other thing related with our own nature, life and metaphysical approach, it is because in some way they feel affected by us. Or else they wouldn't be spending their own energies attacking someone they probably don't even know and that surely would never feel attacked or intimidated by them. So, in this way, and often unconsciously, they are changed by us. We made them move and act just because of what we are and represent. That is our chaotic nature.

The stronger someone condemns and criticizes the Aset Ka the more power and self-confidence the Asetians can achieve. Asetians are true spiritual adversaries; the nemesis of vulgar and stagnated society. The antagonists want that opposition and challenge, actually feeding from it. Growing from it. Conquering through it.

Most will not understand what is being accomplished with this grimoire and the historical significance of its release. While some might grasp a glimpse behind the veil of what is being presented only a few will truly understand the great picture of what is being taught. I hope the journey you are beginning through this book will be as enriching as mine was researching and writing it. This work was written, developed and compiled between two very different geographic locations, both very important to me and the Order of Aset Ka. Those places were Portugal, most importantly the northern city of Porto, and the sacred lands of Kemet in Egypt where I have been passionately developing text and magick, not only in terms of writing but also through exploration, metaphysics, meditation and ritual. This year while back in the ancient lands of the Asetian empire in Egypt much spiritual work for the completeness of this book was achieved in sacred locations of the Asetians. My work was done within the walls of once mighty temples now found in the ruins of Luxor and Karnak, beneath the lingering ceiling of the Temple of Horus in Edfu, lost in the desert and among the remains of remarkable Deir-el-Bahari, under starry nights on the sacred island of Philae with the guiding presence of Orion and Sirius in the sky, through meditation on the plateau of Giza and inside the very initiatory chambers within the pyramids of Khufu and Khafre, not forgetting the moments of peace while sailing the Nile through wild Egypt under the pale moonlight as we did countless times in ages now lost.

This development was a long odyssey marked with adventure and battle not only to myself but also to those who worked with me during this process, a journey that was longer and more profound than most would suspect, even the ones closer to us. The planning for open release of this book is quite old and has been a great undertaking comprised of development, research and intense metaphysical work. More than just the writing and redesign of already existent inner texts to be ready for disclosure to the general public, the work behind which content could be published without restriction and what knowledge should be kept secret was a considerably difficult task. The decision not to include practical techniques of advanced magick within this book became quite obvious from an initial stage, as the dangers allied to a public release of such power and the chances for it to reach unworthy hands or irresponsible minds was never an option. Additionally, the possibility of inner mysteries becoming unveiled by initiates without the hard work that potentiates growth and enlightenment, as opposed to the traditional discovery and evolution through the initiatory journey of the soul, made evident that our recognized stance of secrecy as an initiatory Order of mysteries should remain intact.

Concerning the author I would not describe myself as just an occultist since I am also a scientist by traditional and scholar definition. So I can say that something seen from my point of view will reflect precisely that, not only a metaphysical and spiritual approach but also a practical and analytical understanding. Much work developed internally within the Order of Aset Ka has a scientific component and nothing is taken for granted or accepted out of dogma, cultural influence or myth. Profound examination is often encompassed in our occult studies and verified through evidence, experiment and analysis. Personally I defend that science and the occult have much to learn from each other. It was somewhat recent in our collective history that occult studies became increasingly pushed away by modern science and have seen their credibility defaced in modern scholarship — but to the advanced Ancient Egyptian mind it is all entwined.

At last but central to everything that it represents this book is a gift from Aset to Her children. She is the One reason for this Asetian undertaking; Her words, blessings and guidance are the true core behind this tome and the energy that surrounds it. Treasure and embrace it, the same way as we do, because it bears the true essence of Aset imprinted on its subtle echoes, vibrations and feel. She is the beginning and has no end...

✝

Part One
Asetian Mysteries

Sacred Pillars
The Seven Frameworks

T he sacred pillars embody a profound and vital set of frameworks in the Asetian tradition. They appear as ancient sigils, expressed through simplicity in seven Ancient Egyptian hieroglyphs of special initiatory power. Their use and magickal implications are immense and such understanding unveils a timeless quest of intricate complexity. From ritual, energy work and initiation to the revealing of answers and transformational truths, the Asetian sacred pillars encompass a core magickal system old as time itself. Origins are found in the earlier days of the Egyptian empire, developed by the elders as a tool to translate the language of nature and teach through magick and symbol the greater mysteries of life and death — the keys to understand the Universe. Such secrets are tied to the most ancient teachings of Aset, passed down to Her children through magick, love and blood; a legacy lingering today in the evolutional path of the Aset Ka.

The seven pillars will be represented in the following pages through pictorial design in their oldest form as Ancient Egyptian symbols, while their deeper meaning, spiritual correlation and metaphysical implications will be slowly unveiled through the process of initiation and growth within the Asetian tradition — an eternal lesson to the soul. It is important to acknowledge that these seven frameworks are also magickal seals; true metaphysical sigils with the power to manifest the inner Asetian world and express the subtle mechanisms of nature itself. They are the engine behind everything ever conceived — secret keys of thought, transformation and illumination in a glimpse of the divine spark inside every Asetian. The pillars can be approached as metaphysical tools to be explored and unleashed by the initiate, as guardians of dangerous magickal practice and teachers of mysterious secrets, being assimilated by the mind as archetypes of philosophical thought and, ultimately, unveiled in their true nature as dynamic and living entities that permanently and constantly interact with every particle of every being in an eternal flow of time.

Do not seek for easy answers or quick solutions as those are prime enemies of the accomplished occultist. Masters understand that haste is a friend of failure and ego a pet of weakness, so they bend time and avoid frustrations by accepting its natural tides where only through hard work and by proving their inability to give up true power shall be attained. This power is not of a futile nature and it serves no vain desire as it follows only mastered wisdom and only there lies the force to command the world. On a first approach by anyone not yet experienced with Asetian symbolism and practice the following pillars should be used in meditation and explored carefully. Seekers should remember that they are treading sacred ground and respect is a requirement of understanding. Reference to such material should come recurrently as the senses increase and evolution manifests. If the inner work does not succumb to stagnation and strength is found to conquer reality and hidden truth then the following pages shall be visited several times for many years to come.

Ankh
Immortality

Khepri
Transformation

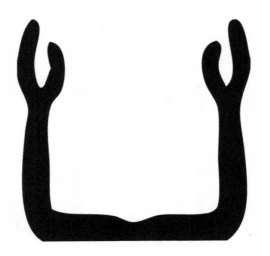

Ka
Energy

Tiet
Blood of Aset

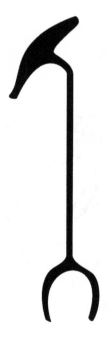

Was
Power

Ba
Soul

Ib
Heart

Book of Nun
Asetian Cosmogony

T he *Book of Nun* is a tome of genesis, portraying the spiritual backbone of Asetian mythology. Its contents can take you on a journey back to the earlier Egyptian memories, spawning an age before the dawn of time now mostly forgotten to those who walk this Earth. This book of Asetian cosmogony opens the hidden door to the mysterious origins of magick, spirituality and divinity, in a text that bears distinctive elements that can be studied as close representations of sacred literature. Cosmogony is the word used to describe the philosophical study concerning the beginning of time and associated belief systems, traditions and cultures, as well as the branch of science dedicated to studying the origins of the Universe. Etymological roots can be found in *kosmogonia*, a Greek word meaning *the world to be born.*

In a sense the *Book of Nun* can be approached as the very beginning of Asetian history, here represented for the first time in a declassified publication, albeit still a small drop from the extensive records on Asetian mythology and documented history throughout the centuries. Its contents represent a vital part of the epitome of Asetian sacred theology.

Although this text is essentially of Kemetic nature, which is clear from its symbolism and cultural reference present in different ancient papyrus, it does not reflect the complete aspects and synchronism of Egyptian religion as interpreted by some schools of thought in modern Egyptology. Contemporary representations are often incomplete and greatly lacking in spiritual understanding, resulting from studies that focus on the tangible reach of the limited human mind without proper metaphysical expertise, which almost invariably produce inaccurate results that do not take into account the intricate mind of the Egyptian people and their higher achievements as a culture entirely dedicated to spirituality and committed in the understanding of life and death — the definitive pioneers in development of the magickal arts. Additionally, most basic elements of Egyptian religion being studied in modern times with disregard for their scholarly complexity, multilayered symbolic nature and profound spiritual legacy, must be understood as a first layer of the spiritual system of the common people, not the initiatory mysteries studied within the ancient temples. One that was gradually changed and tampered over the millennia by men, through the course of history by the influence of war and politics, resulting in a modernly accepted version of Egyptian mythology that although highly entwined in Asetian tradition does not preserve its purity in essence and content, being merely one of the many possible interpretations and the result of limited understanding.

The Aset Ka follows an ancient spiritual system and holds a set of mysteries that were protected from the intervention of humanity and the natural process of history in twisting original truths and secrets. Through advanced processes of validation the integrity of Asetian teachings is maintained and shielded, remaining safely guarded through a cryptic initiatory process that cannot be broken. The metaphysical development within Asetian workings and its clear relation with the occult should not be seen as a sign of the lack of a scholarly approach or the extensive use of scientific process. In fact, much work done within the Aset Ka is of a scientific nature and conducted by experienced practitioners with a scientific background. Magick and science are not as incompatible as most people would think, and its segregation can only be found as a result of fear and a desire for control when facing something beyond the understanding of leading minds. The same is true when researching ancient history and the many branches of discovery. A scholarly approach should not mean limited, fearful or closed-minded. Egyptology effectively has become, in many schools of thought, a decadent field without much scientific ground and attention to detail — it is a game of correlations, not factual truths.

While studying the pyramids in Giza and its origins, the construction of Khufu — the higher monument in the ancient plateau — was assumed as factual by Egyptologists to belong to a pharaoh that was never found inside the pyramid itself or anywhere else. These pyramids, unlike every other Egyptian temple, are not decorated with hieroglyphs and spiritual scriptures except for small markings concealed in hidden chambers, so there is no hard evidence of who built them and when. Egyptology assumed for them to be tombs raised for pharaohs, when the reality is that no body or mummy was ever found within a pyramid to validate such claims — being the only piece of evidence a large block of stone in a central chamber, again assumed to be the empty tomb of a king, when it could as easily be a vessel used in ritual and meditation within a central initiatory chamber of a special temple, something obviously overlooked by those who have no understanding of magickal practice. The same is valid for the dating of these monuments, using the previous assumption on who designed, engineered or commanded the building of the pyramids it was then traced a possible dynasty and potential timeframe. Achieved without proper scientific method or accuracy such a theory is now being disproven by actual science, when recent studies in the field of geology have found characteristic weathering marks on different layers of an iconic adjacent monument — the sphinx. The level of decay and erosion found engraved on stone show clear evidence of intensive rainfall that extended for a long period of time and, interestingly, Giza lays at the entrance of a desert with a harsh arid climate. The most scientific interpretation is for those structures to have already been there when the Sahara was still in development, a process known in paleoclimatology research — the weather is in constant change, deserts are formed, forests die and oceans see their depths closed by the tectonic movement of entire continents — so the perimeter of the now deserted locations was undergoing a slow process of transformation from a very different biome.[1] That would explain the presence of intense rain and a distinctive weather mark. Such realization brings the actual dating of the sphinx and pyramids to a much older timeframe, very different from the one proposed by modern Egyptology and their non-scientific methods but actually much closer to Asetian history and in tune with the teachings portrayed by the Aset Ka for a very long time, sustaining our belief that science and the occult have much to learn from each other and only with an unlimited mind can truth be achieved.

So it should be clear that it is not the motivation behind this work to represent an exclusive perspective of modern Egyptology, but to present a broader and less limited view potentiated through a higher understanding. This cosmogony is above all Asetian, so while many concepts can indeed be found in a traditional Ancient Egyptian context with correlation with modern findings and the study of Egyptology, they are ultimately based on an Asetian perspective and are bound to the profound nature of Asetian understanding. It is important to remind that the words presented within this work are not intended to provide a mythological background for a modern religious practice, nor a replacement for the scholarly accepted and often misunderstood mythology of Ancient Egypt. They teach the spiritual history of a divine bloodline with roots in the sacred lands of Kemet — a song older than memory yet engraved in our hearts. One that cannot be understood through an exercise of the mind but only through the eyes of the soul.

The Beginning

In the beginning there was only one realm, a single shard of transcendent existence known by the ancients as Duat. Not of physical manifestation, this ethereal plane was filled with the infinite possibility of nothingness. A place where all creation was nothing and everything existed in a land beyond time and space. Its understanding is now lost, as the incarnated mind lacks the ability to perceive the existence of absolute boundless divinity. This underworld is infinite. A world before worlds; the kingdom before kings. A void of eternity devouring all manifestation. To this day it remains the only place where darkness and light are one, with no beginning and no end. Eternal.

First there was Nun; the abyssal Waters of chaos. Unformed and unaware. Infinite potential without manifestation. The nothingness that resides in the Duat from where everything emerges. It is the never-ending cycle of the ouroboros, forever biting its tail. Eternal death and rebirth.

In this cradle of creation, through imbalance and fusion of opposing singularities, chaos was set in motion as the wheel of time that gives birth to ethereal Fire rotated and from this nothingness a primeval consciousness emerged: the formless abyss of Amon also known as Atum. The primordial force without soul or polarity, not a deity but the nothingness of Nun given form into manifestation. Amon exists beyond the boundaries of thought or magick — not an entity at all. In a sense, Amon is Nun in motion and given purpose.

Alone. An eternal stone perpetually gazing into the sunrise of creation. Formed but unaware. Amon was the monstrous inscrutable sphinx of the Duat, surrounded by the endless possibility of the unformed Nun. They embody the demiurgical forces, the original spark that ignited the creation of the whole Universe.

There was no past, present or future as such dimensions became an afterthought of primal manifestation. Everything was darkness and everywhere was light as no notion of time was yet conceived. So at the dawn of all existence One transmuted into Two. Primordial magick manifested and immortal Fire was set alight. A singular act of creation where polarity emerged; a force that would potentiate all creation through the universal unfolding of chaos, the flow of a great river forever frozen now running free for the first time, chasing eternity in immortal surrender. Masculine and feminine energies engulfed Nun and devoured its nothingness. One candle with two flames: the male principle carried the light of day and the heat of the Sun — so he came forth as Shu, the lord of Fire; as the female essence crafted emotion and passion, bringing the darkness of the night and the coldness of the Moon — she was Tefnut, lady of Water.

United through their oneness, Fire and Water created the world from the birth of spirit to the crafting of matter. In a cosmical secret that is only found in the tales of forgotten Gods these opposing forces hide the mystery of divine creation, where through the union of absolute impossibility immortality is achieved. So the physical world came into existence — primeval love given form. A small shell within the Duat, this newfound Universe was a conceptual matrix that unlike all other realities was permanently bound to physical rules and a complex set of standards we know today as nature.

> *"Hail Atum, who made the sky. Who created that which*
> *exists. Lord of all that is. Who gave birth to the Gods."*
> Egyptian Book of the Dead

Through the unimaginable union of elemental Fire and spiritual Water life found a way. The first cosmic big bang. Nature emerged and showed its power as king and queen of this world, ruling the physical realm from the smallest subatomic particle to the largest constellation in the sky. Those forces were set in motion through the diligence of three major powers of the physical world: Maat, watchful ruler of universal order and balance; Khepri, androgynous master of transformation and rebirth; Apophis, fierce daemon of chaos and destruction. Three leaders of this new reality tied to the boundaries of matter — minions of nature and ministers at its divine court.

Sky and Earth

Through this alchemical union of magickal illumination the land of incarnation emerged and manifested. As ancients of this world the inextinguishable flame of Shu flowing through the seductive fluidity of Tefnut deluged their united essences into two divine children: Nut the spirit of the Sky and Geb the spirit of the Earth.

The essence of the Sky was feminine; the beautiful and mysterious body of heavens. Nut became the infinite space from above. Earth was an epitome of the masculine principle of fertility as Geb manifested physical, defined and strong, so he became the foundations of physical life below. They are two divine lovers, forever bound to the physical Universe. Eternally watching over each other until the end of days they remain unceasingly separated, entwining their bodies only in a sudden glimpse of cosmic magick at dusk and dawn, or kissing one another in the silver lighting rupturing from the bosom of Nut in the Sky and touching the lips of Geb as it reaches the Earth. This eternal condemnation of their timeless existence in this realm is found engraved deep within the core of every Asetian, manifested in emotion and heightened senses during such moments in the daily cycles of nature and in the roar of its storms. Long forgotten to the tales and ancient stories of mortals, Geb and Nut are divine ancestors of the Asetian family. In their misunderstood existence they sing the same silent song in a timeless process of decay that is as slow as immortality, where a single word can last for ages of mortals. They are one but you can only see them as two. As Above, so Below.

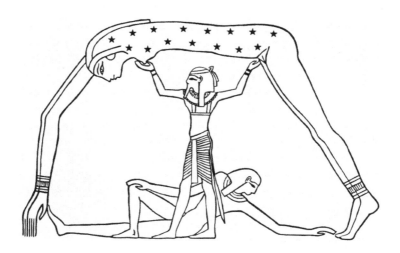

Through their love this new world was being populated with all forms of life, light and chaos and the whole Universe was now filled with stars and planets. In this spectacle of creation and newborn life two mighty forces were bound to the fate of this world. Worshipped by the ancients they were known as Ra and Thoth, two powerful Gods that the modern world recognizes as the Sun and the Moon. Ra is bright, arrogant and a master of life. Thoth is dark, detached and a master of wisdom. Through their magick they control time and hold the subtle wheel that rotates to the cycle of each day. In the light of morning lays the realm of Ra and all life falls under his influence, but with the setting of night the kingdom of Thoth is found and his knowledge can then be unveiled.

Life flourished on Earth in this spiritual spring, from the first cells to complex organisms all now flowing in the river of evolution. Time was raised as the evolutionary catalyst — the frequency of order unbroken by chaos, a linear cadence in the tune of nature. The branches of divinity desired for meaning to the existence of this life that was now independently forging a path of its own, so the living manifestations were gifted and infused with spiritual souls, a vessel of divine spark within their unaware creation. Nature changed, evolved and adapted as the Duat bended to the laws of the Gods, hence the cycle of reincarnation emerged. The finality of death was replaced with the hope of life, so that both could coexist by the magick of rebirth. In each human a mortal Ba was guided to incarnation, crafted by Amon out of tiny droplets from the oceans of Nun.

> *"He fashioned mankind and engendered the Gods.*
> *All live by that which emanated from him.*
> *His manifestations are hidden among people.*
> *They constitute all beings since the time of the Gods."*
> Temple of Khnum

Four Rulers

Through the spiritual marriage of Nut and Geb, the union of Sky and Earth, the four elder Gods of our world were born. Blessed with the power to cross between realms they could inhabit the Duat and travel across the body of their father, the Earth. Primordial magick flew through them and everything possible was at the grasp of thought and touch. The four divine siblings inherited different characteristics and powers from the universal essences of their ancestors, but united they could balance all existence and overpower any force. Their true name was kept hidden from the world, known to humanity simply as Isis, Osiris, Nephthys and Seth. As for Isis, divinity named Her Aset.

> *Aset was magickal and beautiful. Osiris was understanding and introspective. Nephthys was dark and mysterious. Seth was cunning and strong. So the four magnum deities, inheritors of divine power, fell in love with the splendor of the Earth and decided to make it their home. They chose a sacred land in the shores of a great river, called it Kemet meaning the Black Land, later to be known as Egypt...*

There they aided creation, inspired evolution and forged a nation. Sharing the divine culture of the Gods, the common people were taught language, medicine, philosophy and science. Smaller groups with a higher understanding were initiated into the secretive practices of magick, the art of all arts. Slowly the gifts from the Gods transformed a primitive culture into an advanced spiritual community, the footsteps of a great civilization to mirror their passion, wisdom and creativity — but life has a way of its own and the human mind a

✝

desire for power without equal, as history would make devastatingly clear in ages yet to come.

Sep Tepy

During earlier times of this period the Gods lived together and in harmony with humanity, in peace and respect with animals, plants and all expressions of nature. Temples were built out of mighty stones and raised in honor of these powerful beings that never aged. Schools of mysteries, healing and magick. Priests and priestesses devoted their lives to follow them, being gifted with craftsmanship and wisdom while learning their abilities and advanced teachings. This golden age of our planet was known by the ancients as the Sep Tepy, meaning *First Time*, and it represents the dawn of history in a time when Gods walked this Earth, sailed its rivers and left such an enduring mark that it remains still visible for those who know where to look.

Osiris, the first divine pharaoh and father of the realm, ruled Egypt alongside his sister-lover Aset and as a reflection of their immortal love they empowered the sacred lands with magick and beauty that would leave the world in awe, becoming the greatest empire ever built. They were loved and respected by their people but they were also feared as such is the nature of the human mind.

Allies to the throne, their mighty siblings Nephthys and Seth took lordship over the wild lands to west and south of the kingdom, having dominion over the sands of desert and the beasts in the Nile. There they crafted their magick and cursed the desert with violent storms where any trespassing enemy would die a painful death. Here villages were raised and armies gathered, loyal to the crown they patrolled the boundaries of the empire. Unlike their siblings at the throne they held no known seat of power and established a very different relationship with their people, passing down the higher secrets of magick only to those selected out of strength, while Aset and Osiris selected them out of wisdom. To the followers of Seth there was no tolerance for weakness but the four elder deities sang in unison in how they treasured loyalty — the greatest gift they could ever teach to humanity... only if they would be willing to learn its importance and beauty.

Breath of Life

As the empire grew and humanity evolved also did the magick of the Gods and so they ventured into the forbidden arts of creation. From the darkest essence of Nephthys and the protective embers of Osiris a new divine force emerged — the jackal Anubis. Named by the royal family as Anpu, the young God took charge of the ceremonies of the dead until the coming of his father, living in the Duat and learning its mysteries in the absence of the four great rulers, supervising the gates between worlds and the process of death experienced by all life on Earth. This responsibility and art of great prestige in the underworld granted him the role as Lord of Death, a commitment Anubis masterfully keeps to this day as the protector of the dead and embodiment of death. He guides the lost souls through the many dangers awaiting at the gates of crossing, bringing them before the unspoken halls of truth where the daemoness Ammut lies observant as the devourer of the dead; the abominating death of the soul.

At the same time Aset, being the crown of magick and mastering many secrets unknown to Her brothers, wielded the powers of creation without being limited by the transcendent fusion of essences in duality, unlike the magick of Nephthys and Osiris ignited in the creation of Anubis. Being able to move between worlds — the physical and the divine — She forged magick never attempted before by casting and raising Her own breath of life in the realm of the Duat, an essence that was a vital part of Her soul and that would later be known as the Violet Flame. This immortal spark of creation was broken into three distinctive elements by the alchemical magick of Orion; three souls emerging from the forbidden Fire of Aset, not a mirror of Her image but singular parts of Her core now given life through undecipherable power. They were only three and represented the love of Aset given form. From their first cry that formed unknown magickal words never shared with another soul, She understood that the world would forever fear and misunderstand them but there was something else that Her magick reluctantly foresaw. The devastating consequences of Her Will would one day ignite the darkest of nights on a terrifying dance for a blood-red sunrise. In that very moment of transcendence... She knew.

"May your flesh be born to life, and may your life encompass more than the life of the stars as they exist."
Pyramid Texts

The three Ba that emerged from the Breath of Aset were Her sacred children. She brought them to the physical world to inhabit Geb, the divine manifestation of Earth, and to prosper on the sacred lands of Kemet She so dearly loved. There they would be able to embrace life in a whole different way, see through an empowered lens of perception and understanding while experiencing the beauty and emotion of the material plane but also the pain and lessons of the harshest obstacles, alongside the bitterness of physical mortality. This would be their trial by Fire and an initiation that could bring completeness and mastery.

In this descent into matter their souls incarnated as three children — a boy and two girls — but the world would only remember the name of Her first-born: Horus, the falcon God destined to inherit the kingdom of the Gods as the throne of Egypt. Not the spiritual name but his legacy as pharaoh the word Horus would linger on, echoing throughout eternity in the history of the ages. Humanity would write tales and songs about him, pass them on to their children who would then change, incorporate and retell its origins with those of other Gods and different times until they all became a distant myth, hiding in the subconscious of ancient souls who lived back in those days.

To Aset the three were one and their undeniable differences would not refute that but complement it. United, they were Her. Albeit their names now forgotten or lost to the uninitiated the two young girls would grow to become of crucial importance to the fate of the empire and their actions, strength and abilities would shape the course of history in no lesser way than Horus. In the secluded privacy of Her inner temple Aset strived for the development of Her children, teaching them magick, art and healing. When the time was right and the Universe perfectly aligned She kissed them tenderly and blessed them with Her consecrated blood; with Her lips She engraved a sacred mark hidden deep within their soul. Under the guiding paleness of Thoth and the silver light of Orion She uttered the secret words. They were eternal.

> *"She uttered the spell with the magical power of Her mouth. Her tongue was perfect and it never halted at a word. Beneficent in command and word was Aset. The one of magical spells."*
>
> Egyptian Book of the Dead

This great mystery would stand at the core of Her teachings and so She named Her spiritual legacy Aset Ka. A direct symbol of its true origins — the essence of Isis, or in the words of the ancients the Ka of Aset. She solemnly uttered and fiercely marked in blood that those loyal to Her would forever be loyal to them for they are one.

The Asetians
Although divine in essence and bearers of an immortal soul, while on Earth the children of Aset were bound to the limitations of nature and the cycles of reincarnation. They were able to influence their surroundings, seize thoughts, foresee events and heal many wounds but their bodies decayed and died just like those of the common people. They appeared human even if their presence was felt as manifestly different but they were not of human nature. Their souls could not be broken by any art or through any craft.

This distinctive mystery of their existence would set them apart from any other incarnated being, manifesting not only through remarkably powerful metaphysical abilities and unique spiritual senses but also resulting in an inborn need for vital force — the energy of life

— to empower and sustain their demanding subtle systems and advanced magickal skills. Their secret was that unlike humans they were not of this realm and their nature was native to the Duat, the land of the dead where Aset forged their existence out of Her flame. There they were boundless but in here they were restricted and confined to a coffin of matter. This need for the subtle energy of life experienced while incarnated in a physical shell would be the origin of their description as vampires. A term coined by humanity to describe these misunderstood beings that they could not comprehend. So the legend of spiritual vampirism as creatures of magick was born. Created out of fear and ignorance but capable of instigating allure and desire, myths surrounding vampires were seen throughout the world and in nearly every culture from the ancient world to the dark ages of medieval times. Albeit sometimes unrelated with their presence but still moved by such origins, many cultures hide evidence of Asetian influence. The children of Aset and their followers travelled the world as the memories of centuries were written, hiding in plain sight by the side of unsuspecting mortals and unaware societies, teaching in silence and initiating those who were loyal their actions changed cultures, shifted empires and forged the steps of history.

Unlike their Mother these demigods would not to leave the physical realm at the end of the Sep Tepy, when the age of the Gods would come to an end. They would remain here as representatives of the Flame of Aset and the embodiment of Her divine legacy. Always evolving, forever changing and adapting to new realities, they were there as history unfolded, societies changed and kingdoms burned. They gathered followers, friends and allies; unique beings with a never-ending commitment to learning but above all bearers of unwaveringly loyalty as Aset taught them to be. Passed unto them the secrets of knowledge and initiated their souls in a transcendent dark kiss that betrayed life — that would forever be their sacred mark and immortal bond as they would do the same to their loyal followers. In this way by the Light of Aset and the Will of Her children a new spiritual kin was born, one that would master the centuries and forever haunt in silence, always watchful in the shadows of this world as empires fall and times shift. They are the Asetians.

"I have come that I may be your magical protection. I give breath to your nose, even the north wind that came forth from Atum to your nose. I have caused that you exist as a God with your enemies having fallen under your sandals. You have been vindicated in the sky, so that your limbs might be powerful among the Gods."

Egyptian Book of the Dead

The three first-born Asetians were known as the Primordials, founders and initiators with the power to rise the elders. Loved by all Asetians they are the eternal leaders of the Aset Ka, the sacred and immortal family of Egypt. Divine and transcendent the Primordials manifest the Will of Aset and their magick is present still, feared by the deceitful and neglected by the unaware it can be found in the most unexpected moments when one is not looking. Horus and his two sisters sit on the triple throne of the Asetian empire, a noble responsibility of timeless commitment that is never surrendered to another but kept vacant and under vigil until they return life upon life. They are the three crowns of Egypt; ageless masters, teachers and guides, standing at the top of an intricate pyramid forged in violet Fire, gathering at the table of the elders and commanding the royal council of the Higher Magisterium.

Epic Wars

Ra was always one of the most powerful forces in this realm of flesh. With his burning light he promoted life but also brought death. Through the mystery of his hidden name the mighty Sun held the power to control the living and everywhere his light touched he could see and hear with no other able to oppose him. He was revered and feared.

His power was given full reign on the lands ruled by Seth, who allied with his scorching influence to control the vast extension of the fiery desert. Surrounding the Nile and its black silt, on the flourishing areas overpowered by green and vegetation, Osiris and Aset did not entrust free control to Ra so he saw his power diminished right at the heart of the empire of the Gods. This decision was enigmatic to many but Aset remained adamant in the acceptance of Thoth's forces instead of allowing Ra to exercise his full power. If She had foreseen the tides yet to come or what was the extent of the reasoning behind such decisions no one really knows.

As the dominion of Seth increased in numbers and extension of land beyond the forces of Osiris so did his demands for tribute and favor multiply with each coming season. Within his hidden temple in the desert he commanded thousands and manipulated those who would not bow to his will. While his power grew Seth kept close watch on the matters of court even during moments of absence when spies were ever present, so the progressively diminished rights granted by the throne did not pass unnoticed despite his silence. In the heat of day and under blinding light the old God of many faces conspired in secret.

Being mistress of magick, mystery and deceit, Aset spiritually poisoned Ra with an agonizing spell never before seen. Caught off guard and surprised by the boldness of an attack with such power he did not imagine She possessed, Ra approached with solar arrogance and demands. He was met with a darker face of Aset no one had ever seen, a beautiful Lady of ice and stone with the terrifying eyes of thunder. She brandished the magickal cure but it would take from him a dear secret — the mystery of his hidden name. Realizing his powerless efforts on the face of such an abominating force, Ra shared with Aset his secret name but left with an imposing warning: only She would be able to wield its magick and if such secret would ever be shared it would lose all of its power. Aset gave him no word but his secret remains safely within Her grasp.

> *"One falls down with terror if his ineffable name is spoken. Not even another God can call him by it. He, whose name is hidden. Because of this he is a mystery."*
> Egyptian Papyrus

Victorious in confrontation with mighty Ra and conquering a portion of his terrible power the violet Goddess rose as supreme ruler of the empire. Those events would echo throughout eternity in a never-ending dispute from Her brother Seth and his minions, who could never accept the rulership of Aset and would forever challenge Her will and children on a battle of epic proportions. Fire of the Gods

was kindled and the war for the throne of Egypt was about to begin —
a confrontation that could threaten all life, an omen of sorrow and
pain.

Aset instructed the removal of the armies of Seth from guarding
the borders of the inner lands of the realm and instead decided to
appoint such a task only to those who had already fought in Her
service with proven loyalty. Seth, now commanding armies in greater
number than any other force in the empire, followed the will of Queen
Aset and receded his position deeper into the desert but left the lands
of Kemet under strategic siege. Realizing the failure of his secretive
plans to prevent the rising of Aset to power, he could still control all
trading routes in and out of the empire, a vital resource for the welfare
of its people.

The divine Queen ruled the empire with strength and beauty by
the side of Her gentle pharaoh Osiris, leading Her people to glory and
wisdom in a legacy that would defy time and history. The tides of time
were changing as fear and doubt slowly took the clouds in the sky and
descended into the dreams of innocent children. Protection of the
empire was enforced by a small yet dark force of unspeakable deeds, a
personal army created and trained by Aset under the title of Seven
Scorpions, later to be known as the Imperial Guard. Described by the
ancients as the most terrible force ever conceived, this elite legion was
versed in the magickal secrets and perfected in the arts of war. Riding
majestic unsaddled horses with no bridle that could cross the sands
faster than the wind this mobile army could be seen clothed in black
ever when there was conflict. With their faces mostly unseen and
cloaks dancing to wild songs of death they were led by Serket, the
elder poison with a flaming sword that could kill immortals.
Abominating daemons of the ancient world bound to the Will and life
force of Aset, these beings were not of this reality and their very

breath could inflict fear into the fragile hearts of men. Through their eyes She could see everything and pierce further than any other.

The nights were colder and tension of previous events intoxicated the air when the scent of incense was no longer felt. Conflict increased and what was once a land of peace was now tormented by the edge of swords and the shine of arrows. As chaos took reign under the devices of Apophis the strikes from Seth on the shores of the Nile increased into a regime of crime and violence.

Displeased with the road taken the royal crown gathered with the presence of the four elder Gods to determine the future of all. Cunning and astute, Seth did not dare to challenge Aset but proposed a duel with Osiris to settle the rightful claim to the throne. Ever noble the divine pharaoh took arms in defense of the realm but Seth had a different plan in mind. Without the knowledge or consent of Nephthys the trickster conjured his arid magick, bringing the light of Ra and the blinding strike of a sandstorm. The desert visited the black lands of Egypt and destroyed its crops and the children cried for the life of their king. Seth had succeeded and Osiris laid dead, not in his soul for he was immortal but his body shredded to pieces by the treachery of his own brother.

Crying in horror, Aset used Her breath of life to heal Osiris but the pharaoh was tired and weakened. No longer seeing the beauty of old in this land now torn for power and lust he abandoned Egypt never to return, living forever in the Duat where he took the place of Anubis, his son, presiding the ceremonies of the dead and the tribunal of souls at the halls of Ammut. His surrender from physical life would allow for Anubis to join the royal family in Egypt where he would befriend the children of Aset and entrust them with his secrets of death and the mysteries of the Duat. Swearing allegiance to their fate as so would his children and their children thereafter, the Anubians would never abandon their calling as it was born out of pure love and as long as life existed and time did not cease they would always protect the children of Aset. Until the end of time they would remain keepers of the Asetians, a family that would respect them as friends and honor them as lovers. Establishing themselves as a treasured part of this divine family called Aset Ka their dedication was admired by all.

> *"If I live or pass on, I am Osiris. I enter you and appear through you. I decay in you and I spring forth from you. I descend in you and I repose on your side. The Gods are living in me! As I live and grow in the emmer that sustains the exalted ones."*

Coffin Texts

Aset endured in Egypt without Osiris until She felt the three children were ready to take leadership of the Aset Ka and guide the followers of Her legacy forever. The treachery of Seth would condemn him to haunt the dead sands of the desert until the end of days but the pain of his attacks would forever echo in memory and nightmare. The Sethian followers increased as magick and hatred grew in the exile of their leader, while armies carrying his banners fought the Aset Ka for centuries in a series of great battles that we now know as the Epic Wars.

A deep old scar on the face of the Aset Ka would be reflected in myth and lore as the era when Seth took the eye of Horus. The Sethian lord would never give in, fighting for his convictions forever as his ideals could never be aligned with the power and leadership of Aset. The brutality of the Sethian armies alongside the torture and severity of their attacks conquered them many battles and claimed many lives.

His revenge was eminent and the blood of Aset spilled and defaced. It was then when the decision was made and the Asetian Mother gave the commanding order. Only Her soul held the power to raise such force and this was the day She had dreaded its arrival. It was a moment of no return when the cruel voice of Aset took the most difficult decision of all and set life ablaze as She unleashed Serket in full force. Seth was answered in a decisive move that would bring the age of the Epic Wars to its closure, through the most feared metaphysical force the world has ever witnessed. Sending forth the Imperial Guard and making use of the most terrible powers ever conceived the Aset Ka extinguished lives in a bloodshed greater than any other before. Night took over and death danced throughout the lands in a spectacle of horror and sin. Tears of Aset dropped on the sacred sand as Her forces created havoc and brought destruction in a massacre of prophetic proportions. Those were the darkest times in history. An era of suffering, blood and torture.

Fathers did not return home and children would not see the dawn of day, as daemons feasted in fury while innocence was taken away. In this day the fate of the Gods was sealed and two opposing forces were forged and bound to darkness in a way that no human can ever comprehend. Not a battle of good and evil or a war of black and white, the timeless existence of both families forever instigated fear in humanity who would call them vampires and someday dismiss their presence as folklore, in a futile attempt to forget the daring truth that they are not alone.

Aset and Seth led an eternal battle for the throne of Egypt, fighting for much greater mysteries than those you will ever know, but their conflict would linger on in silence not as war in the understanding of mortals but enduring in a spiritual confrontation able to survive the test of time.

Farewell of the Gods

Time to rebuild followed in a new period of peace and newfound prosperity. Bonds of trust and union were reforged, alliances emerged and inspiration ignited. Many centuries passed and the Egyptian people lived in peace, learning about the mysteries within their world and honoring the Asetian teachers they would someday write tales about and celebrate in songs.

The waters of the Nile were loyal to its course, flowing as seasons changed and mighty temples rose on the edifications of older structures, hallmarks of a lost spirituality taught by the Fire of immortality. The desert progressed consuming crop and land, only to recede once again in a silent cycle insignificant to the years of common people. Slowly the Sep Tepy was coming to an end and with it the forgotten era of the Gods. A golden age of spiritual evolution and magick moved by the inspiring teachings of elder forces unruled by time.

It was in the cradle of Asetian rule when Horus was appointed pharaoh, taking the throne of Egypt in place of his Mother. No longer the child of the Moon he brought forth the solar flare and empowered the four elements of nature, so by the side of his nameless sisters they defined the course of history. Unchallenged in its supremacy the empire expanded and the sacred teachings of the Asetians were passed down through initiation, forging a spiritual nation moved by wisdom and balance.

Aset left Egypt and sang an immortal farewell to the physical world, embracing Her ethereal existence in the realms of the Duat where She joined Osiris and Nephthys as they would forever rule the lands of infinity. The Aset Ka remained on Earth as the representatives of the Gods, teaching about honor, loyalty and love. Although its force is better known for the leadership of Egypt on the elder throne of the pharaoh, their true seat of power is not of this plane and resides in the ever-flourishing gardens of the Duat where Aset awaits them, for they are Her children and that will last forever.

"Aset will embrace you in peace. She will drive away the opponent from your path. Place your face to the West, that you may illumine the Two Lands. The dead have stood up to look at you. Breathing the air and seeing your face. Like the rising of the Sun-disk in its horizon. Their hearts are pleased with what you have done. To you belong eternity and everlastingness."

Egyptian Book of the Dead

Ages have passed since the shadow of the Epic Wars and peace now walked alongside beauty in the sacred lands of Kemet. The line of pharaohs was long and became an edification of the Asetian family, when the immortal children took an unexpected step never to be understood by the conscious mind of their people. From the halls of royalty and the inner sanctums of temples the Asetians left into the call of mystery and embraced their silent fate of watchful darkness. The Aset Ka broke the last great alliance with mortals and offered the throne to humanity. Ever in greedy desire and uncontrollable thirst for power, they took the gift in awe and new wars soon followed. It was time to test the honor of their souls and reveal how much they had learned from the wisdom of Gods or if the poisonous seeds of selfishness, vanity and ego remained their true masters. Unaided and with absolute freedom the choices of humans now wrote the fate of all.

In exchange for such generosity the leaders of the people made a vow to an untold treaty. The living bloodline of the Gods would be unwritten from history and celebrated through mystery only in energy and spirit. So in secret they would remain until the time they decide to rise once more from the silent dungeons of this world. The pact was sealed and their words carefully followed but the tales would survive in myth as the stories of the Gods. Changed and retold across the centuries they were passed down through generations and can be found today in papyrus and broken walls of ancient temples. Shrouded in symbolism and initiatory secrets the old words speak of the times of the Asetians and their many mysteries when the divine forces walked this Earth and raised empires. So it ended the kingdom of the Gods and the human era began. Secrets, mysteries and ancient dreams... this is not just our story; it is yours as well.

Unknown but not forgotten, the Asetian family would linger in secret and darkness, found alongside unsuspecting societies and in countless cultures, from the halls of temples to the very royal chambers of pharaohs, sometimes guiding evolution as kings or queens and others just watching the blood spill from the corrupt hands of men. The Asetians were there, ever-present like a shadow observing in absolute silence, they were seen with the eyes but not by the mind for only few knew they ever existed. Forever watching, adapting and evolving through the immortal nature of their kin. In silence, they waited...

The Asetian empire is still alive today and its banners fly high in the heart of those who remain loyal, surviving in the shadows of this world where true magick is crafted and beauty preserved. Silently and in secret we remain a dim violet light of a once mighty past. We are the last swords of magick and initiators of spirit. The writers of fate and the prophets of death. We bring forth the immortal Flame of Aset perpetually alive as thunder breaking the lies of humanity with no redness able to halt our hymn.

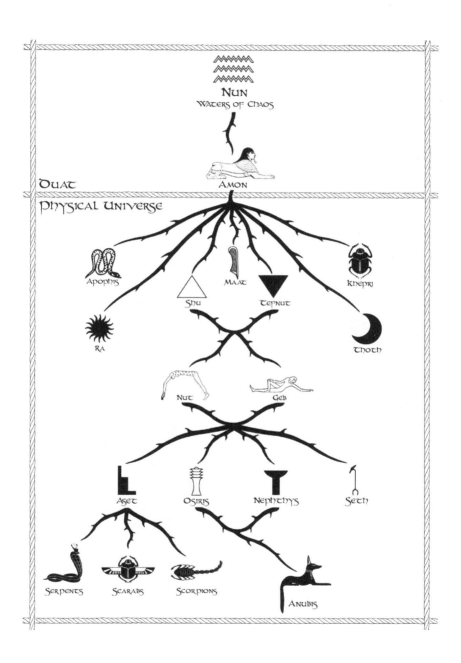

Children of Aset
The Asetians

The Asetians are spiritual souls without a human nature. Their existence cannot be accurately described with words or understood by the mind as the intricacy and beauty of Asetian reality manifests in full only when unrestricted within the realm of transcendence. Bound to the cycles of reincarnation alongside humanity the children of Aset are creatures of magick and spirit, so although they may appear physically indistinguishable from others to unaware eyes limited by the deceit of matter, the Asetians are spiritually immortal. Biologically similar to humans, their strength comes from greatly developed subtle senses and a very distinctive mind where the foundations of human psychology simply do not apply. Attempting to study their nature, abilities and mindset through a human paradigm is futile — they excel at energy manipulation and other occult abilities commonly described as magick, wielding knowledge gathered throughout the centuries in constant evolution and growth. Gifted with a sharp intellect paired with heightened sensitivity, an awakened Asetian can easily manipulate and outmaneuver anyone judging without respect or committed in such understanding. For ages they have studied the human mind in ways that modern psychology has yet to grasp, providing them with tools and unique abilities that have been confused with mind reading and different powers, which although conceivable can often be simply explained through keen observation and intuition used alongside psychological understanding, giving the illusory effect of foreseeing thoughts and actions.

Ancient masters and timeless teachers, the Asetians forged a metaphysical family in the shadows of this world, raising the energies of the planet and balancing the tides of time. Walking alongside mortals since the times of Ancient Egypt, from the halls of pharaohs to the temples of sacred mysteries, the Asetian family remained ever watchful as one last banner of the divine spark on Earth.

In their limitless understanding and ethereal awareness, this mysterious family of the elder Gods is called Aset Ka, meaning *the essence of Aset* — the divine Mother who poisoned the Sun and gave life to immortals. To this day the secretive Order of Aset Ka remains a stronghold of mystical power and a catalyst of evolution unlike any other. Operating in secret and teaching through initiatory silence, the Aset Ka is an ancient Order founded in Egypt by Aset and led under Her name and cosmic Will by the three children — the Primordial Asetians. Sailing through the tides of centuries the Aset Ka has, often in secret, influenced cultures, seized powers and shifted the course of nations. The presence of the Asetians in civilizations of past and present can be felt by those who recognize their distinctive mark. Carefully watched by the wise in societies who know the unwavering secret of their existence, there are clues and irrefutable evidence of the influence of the Aset Ka in different countries, extensive periods of time and diverse cultures — just laying there, frozen in time and forgotten by the blindness of humanity, lost to all who lack the awareness to see it. Even today the puzzle can be unsealed only if the pieces are properly connected, but those able to achieve such understanding are responsible enough not to interfere and leave the ancient Order to its own devices. Everyone who has ever stared into the eyes of an Asetian without their mask of flesh has found an eternal abyss and faced the abominating fear of their own demons, since by placing a hand in the darkness of their violet Fire no doubt remains once the veil is revealed.

Wielders of an existence unknown to many and misunderstood by most, the Asetians are often described by human culture as vampires, a word coined by the common people to represent their predatory instincts and a sign on the limited understanding of their nature. They are the first-born of the immortal kin, detached from society and the mundane, the mysterious Asetians are studied as the primordial vampires and their blood is believed to be both sacred and a curse. Alluring and terrifying. Attractive and repelling. Loved but feared. They live in a world that does not know of their existence but yet remembers them in dreams and desires, sometimes long lost emotions from an ancient past. A human society that does not care for the values of honor and loyalty that represent the very core of Asetian culture.

It is important to underline that for the Aset Ka the word that defines them is not vampire but Asetian. Albeit the word being just an attempt at defining the undefinable and limiting what can never be limited, this term does not refer exclusively to the three primordial children of Aset but also to the eternal bloodline that emerged from their essence. The predatory abilities that inspired old vampiric myths and fears are nothing but a smaller part of what being an Asetian truly means. It is a drop in the infinite possibility and transcendent existence of the Asetians, an often-misunderstood detail among those who attempt to study this culture.

With ancient roots at the dawn of creation in an era before time the Asetians were the masterminds behind the empire they forged in earlier Egypt during a period described as the Sep Tepy. The age of the Gods was a time of balance and wisdom when magick was the breath of understanding and cosmic mastery but such knowledge remains yet visible in clues left throughout the past with much evidence carved hard in stone, as the power and knowledge taught by the Gods was used to raise a nation responsible for the most advanced civilization in known history.

The vampires from the Order of Aset Ka are not creatures from fiction or myth, nor are they new-age psychic vampires alike who identify with the deluded nature of modern alternative cultures inspired in the misunderstanding of their nature. They are part of a very restricted family, one to wield the magick of the ancients and to carry the blood of immortality. Born thousands of years in the past, dead and reborn for ages in an ever-changing world of blindness and deceit, their souls linger forever. Hidden behind the veil of mysteries and mastering a sacred path within the occult societies of this world, these eloquent predators of life and death watch the centuries in ethereal observance. In silence they walk among you.

✝

Lineages
Spiritual Bloodline

S ince the dawn of empires and primordial ages of ancient past the Asetian history has always been triple. By the mysteries of Orion the sacred Flame of Aset is manifested under the light of Three; not just a number or mathematical symbol but a unique key to the magickal formulae of the elders.

This magickal principle of the sacred three is a prime framework found in all laws of metaphysics and directly experienced in the nature of subtle energy — present in the underlying mechanisms of how it fragments, transmutes and ignites. It is also perpetually tied to Asetian history and the power of Aset, reflected in Her immortal children who manifest the triple nature of Her essence. The Primordial Asetians are three and only three, embodying the threefold mystery of the Violet Flame.

Through them the bloodline of Aset developed as three mighty rivers of life, flowing vigorously in the endless stream of evolution. As the Asetian family established in the course of history, shaping their spiritual destiny and carving the path of initiation, each of the three Primordials was the hallmark of one of the three distinctive paths, forging the Asetian Lineages.

Asetians were born out of one of the Primordial essences within the triple foundation of the Asetian breath of life. Each unique but bound to the vibrations of Lineage, the bloodline of Aset developed in three distinctive but complementary ways. With varying sets of characteristics, abilities and weaknesses, the three Lineages represent the completeness of Aset. United they are Her and only through their love She can be seen.

Being a strictly Asetian concept, the nature of the Lineages can only be understood under the light of Asetianism and the teachings of the Asetians. Due to the ancient nature of the Asetian system and its profound connection with nature, spiritual foundations and universal magick, similarities may be found in religious sects, occult Order structures, political hierarchies and social stratification castes of past and present. While such study may prove fruitful in terms of historical understanding, to draw correlations between other systems and the Asetian Lineages is futile and bound to misunderstanding, often leading to wrong assumptions and a lesser comprehension of the fundamentals of ancient formulae. In Asetianism the nature of its spiritual Lineages does not represent a caste or hierarchical system, embodying a concept of transcendence and internal alchemy that bears no resemblance or functional application to the mundane notions of structure. It is of paramount importance to approach Asetian wisdom with a clear understanding on the origins of such knowledge and how it connects with the nature of the Asetians, for only when seeing it through an Asetian mindset all pieces of this major puzzle can safely be matched into place.

As with most Asetian concepts a complete understanding of the Lineages may not be possible within a non-Asetian mind, relating to a layer of initiatory comprehension and spiritual awareness that can only be slowly unveiled by the evolution of the soul and the attaining of inner enlightenment, heightened through the alchemy of every awakening experienced in each incarnation. To the world, the existence of the three Lineages is one of the most iconic and easily recognizable elements of the Asetian tradition and pillars of the Aset Ka — a subject bound to much speculation and misunderstanding where opinion and guesswork is often passed as knowledge and truth by the less aware. As with everything Asetian its elements and concepts are bound to admiration and flame, but the wise initiate should know how to separate what stands above from what cries below. That should separate truth from lie and mystery from fiction, for raw energy cannot be faked or its initiatory power deceived. All else is nothing but fume.

Represented in symbol and manifested in flesh, Serpent, Scarab and Scorpion are the three Lineages of the Asetian bloodline. A complete circle of infinite potential, the personification of divinity through unquestionable union. The Serpent is the Lineage of Viperines, the silent initiators and craftsmen of magick. The Scarab is the Lineage of Concubines, the flowing hearts and catalysts of evolution. The Scorpion is the Lineage of Guardians, the artists of loyalty and swords of the flame.

They have been known under many names and their descriptions changed over the millennia according to the ones telling their tale. Worshipped and hated, they have been feared by some and admired by others but few now remember their true names. Unique to each Lineage there is a banner of magick and power, personified in the sigil of their line. In the natural diversity of their kin they find common ground in the characteristics of subtle metabolism, energy vibration, strengths and weaknesses. These qualities and elements specific to each Lineage are connected to the three distinctive ways in which the subtle body can respond to the alchemy of Asetian initiation and the death of mortality, as well as a permanent echo of the imprint from each Primordial, the founders of the three Lineages. Varying in character as flowers blossoming in spring, Lineages should never be seen as limiting on individuality as each Asetian treads a unique path and embraces important freedom of choice and decisions in carving the future.

The Lineages can be seen as the three paths of Asetianism, the three inner flames from the heart of Aset. They are the three thrones of Egypt; the three crowns of magick. Not only functioning as a working magickal framework and a closed energy circle enhanced by the gifts from each Lineage, they can also be studied as powerful archetypes of magick, ritual and initiation. Energetically they complement each other with their strengths and weaknesses, reversing polarities and resulting in a spiritual circle of immeasurable power. In this triple way energy is balanced at its peak, without stagnation or dissipation, to be then absorbed by the whole as one while promoting empowerment and balance of the three. Through this practice the Asetians can elevate the frequency of their magick, increase the scope of their aura and enhance their individual abilities and subtle senses by making their energy denser, pulsating with a higher vibration and power. However, despite all the mysteries behind their grand magick of union and enforced through loyalty, the Lineages should be understood as something much deeper than a metaphysical framework or a powerful magickal system, ultimately becoming a profound spiritual foundation with a transcendent quality as intricate as the stars in the body of Nut.

Beyond the beauty of such connection and the unbreakable bonds of this family, in a world that is real and not blessed with the perfection of a fairytale, the metaphysical relationship between the three Lineages has suffered over the centuries and undergone periods of strife and uncertainty. Clouded by the influences of matter and the blinding fabric of unawakened existence, some Asetians have been lost and unaware of their nature and true origins. From passionate lovers to fierce enemies, members of different Lineages have loved and fought together, sometimes drifting away from their secret reality, forgotten of their past and family, many times lost and alone... unknowingly waiting for the spark of their brothers and sisters to awaken the violet light hiding within. Eternally they cling to existence in this realm until the moment of their liberation into awareness is presented once again and the immortal reunion with the Aset Ka is achieved. Having incarnated throughout countless cultures and in numerous periods of time, facing each other in opposing fields of battle, born into adversary families and rising within enemy nations, the eternal bonds of their hearts and the burning nature of the Asetian flame resists the challenges of time and fate. For they are unbreakable and no storm can cause it lingering harm but only throw sand and keep it dormant.

The following pages will expand on the nature of each Asetian Lineage, examining their characteristics and distinctive foundations. However, it remains important to realize that such study is only but a canvas for a limited understanding on the triple nature of the Asetians, as each member of the family is single and unique independently of Lineage. This examination of each archetype is by no means final, static or determinant on the unveiling of the nature of an Asetian, a process that requires a different approach and an infinitely more complex set of spiritual cues intentionally not included within this work. There are known details recurrent to each Lineage that were also omitted from the public descriptions provided by the Aset Ka. This is a conscious decision that serves a specific purpose, which requires understanding that is outside of the scope of this book. Additionally, it is possible for a member of a Lineage not to display a few characteristics defined in these chapters and apparently not fit into the publicly known model, or for another one to express different elements of all three. Nothing is set in stone and the truth of the Asetian soul can only be found within the limitless existence of nature. While this may appear random to the unaware mind there is nothing aleatory when studying it on the altar of understanding.

SERPENT
LINEAGE OF VIPERINES

M asters of wisdom and protectors of arcane mysteries, the introspective Serpents are timeless initiators. Gifted with the Eye of Aset they are able to see what no other can, which is simultaneously a blessing and a curse. Embodying the oldest archetype of the immortal predator, these collectors of souls and forgotten secrets are givers of life and bringers of death. This duality places them between the two extreme poles of morality and understanding, being known for the greatest acts of love and healing but also for causing pain and torment like no other.

The reptile animal-sigil of this Lineage is meaningful and no mere coincidence, being a renowned archetype of knowledge and the mastery of wisdom since time immemorial, a potent symbol found today hiding in plain sight. For example, in the Caduceus, a Greek image connected with Hermes that portrays a winged staff entwined in two coiling serpents, or the Rod of Asclepius that symbolizes healing through a serpent rising along a wooden wand, both old alchemical images that are now well known symbols of modern medicine used by doctors and practitioners all around the world. Snakes and serpents are also studied in human psychology as they have an ability to instigate fear in the mind, and even to those without a past trauma associated with these animals there is a common connection with irrational fear and dread. Additionally, their ability to craft venom within their bodies and the natural resistance to the poison of other animals is a powerful metaphysical symbolism to the mindset, character and abilities of Asetian Serpents as well as to their threatening magickal arts. The advanced senses of these animals make them dangerous predators and a fierce weapon of nature, capable of delivering death almost unnoticeably, while the shedding of skin embodies an archetype of renewal and immortality that represents the conquering of death and continuous initiation that so accurately resonates with what the Lineage stands for. An ocean of symbolism, alchemy and mystery brings these Serpents to life, unveiling their ancient connections with the magickal arts and the very fabric of spirituality. A cryptic truth to be found in the timeless song of nature but only grasped by those committed to the study of these Serpents' hidden flame while respecting the light reflected within their immortal eyes.

The rarest of Asetians to manifest into existence, Serpents are few and trace their roots to Horus, one of the three Primordials and founder of the Lineage. This connection alongside an inborn talent for leadership and the ability to inspire others has placed Serpents into various positions of power throughout history, and although existing only in small numbers their mark is strongly carved in the past as they shaped the course of the future.

They are commanders of nations and captains of legions, leading the silent army of immortals with the power to strike unto the very heart of men with one thousand arrows and the flames of dawn. Serpents rise as the voices behind a storm and the words beneath primordial teachings. The ancients know them as the ones who can summon the banner of the dead and rally the forces of the night; they are the unrelenting grip on the everlasting sword of time.

Humanity has admired, worshipped and desired the mysterious Serpents but also cursed, abominated and hated their existence; they have always been feared and loved. This Lineage is the most misunderstood of all three, finding its balance only in the realm of transcendence, which makes their incarnated existence within the physical world a fragile manifestation of their tremendous inner potential. Such weakened link with the realm of matter and their own bodies grants the members of this Lineage heightened subtle senses and intuition, where interacting with energy and crafting magick

Link

7-Day

Nov-22-11
08:51 AM

through

Valid
Nov 15, 2011 08:52 AM

becomes an afterthought of their very existence. However, detachment from the mundane is not without consequence and it haunts these Asetians with a never-ending sense of not belonging while incarnated and recurring struggles with grounding. With a mind that never fully lives within their bodies or blends with that of common society, they inhabit a world of their own, which is evidenced by strong creativity, great artistic sensitivity and broad imagination. Such can be an asset in the crafting and projection of their wicked magick and another useful tool within their broad arsenal, but without conscious control and proper mastery it can turn into imbalance and depression.

Relentless in every battle they willingly choose to partake in, Serpents are formidable foes to any opponent but also premium targets of great strategic value to their enemies. Behind their cunning, wisdom and ingenuity that makes them such an admirable force they can lose motivation if not continuously inspired. Inspiration is a nourishing Fire that fuels their unique flame, dancing at the heart of the manifold abilities and potential of a Viperine — an aspect that should be cultivated, developed and mastered during self-development and growth. Great imbalances are not common in souls of this Lineage but if allowed to occur, root and develop they can become catastrophic as the might of Serpents known for their power of life and creation can also be wielded for death and destruction, which when allied to the forces of chaos can lead to unspeakable deeds.

When motivated and inspired these Asetians can manifest in the realm of the living as some of the most innovating artists, groundbreaking scientists and wisest scholars, paving their way and legacy as the most relevant occultists in history, but if lacking such vital spark they can become unbalanced and channel their outstanding magickal power into destructive outlets and ill temper. Due to their inborn spiritual strength and fierce personality Serpents cannot and should not be controlled or submitted to outer forces, as results can be unpredictable and the consequences rarely justify the benefits.

The intensity of their link with the ethereal reality and the land of spirit may provide a sense of abstraction and a unique insight into the mysteries of this world, however the energy required to sustain such a soul while bound to flesh and the laws of physics is undeniable, making some Serpents physically weaker than the other Lineages and able to manifest biologically through a set of potential handicaps such as their heightened sense of physical pain. Without proper knowledge this may be misunderstood as low tolerance to pain when that is not the case. In fact, their system is hardwired to process sensation, naturally increasing it for maximum awareness, which comes as a great esoteric tool that allows for them to see the world in a different and more intense way, though it can also create havoc and leave them vulnerable when dealing with pain and torture. Understanding the intensity of such connection with the subtle leads to the other end of the scale and the frail link with the physical, something that echoes to the body in many ways, sometimes manifesting through illness and other medical conditions of a subtler nature. Different variants of allergies, throat and respiratory conditions, limited eyesight especially in bright environments and cardiac complications are common ailments found in some members of this Lineage. Being unable to properly adapt their living bodies to the constant shift between spirit and matter can cause symptoms of extreme anxiety and abnormal distress. This is sometimes visible in tremors and coldness of the hands found even in balanced Serpents, silently taking a toll on the suffering immune system and holding a negative grip under different scales of magnitude depending on energy levels and when they were spiritually nurtured.

Recognizable for the depth of their gaze and the ethereal feel within their eyes, the acute flow of energy permanently flooding the highly developed Crown Shen of Serpents often results in the decay of hair follicles, where the intense flame of such magick literally burns the subtle outlets on their divine crown, echoing to the physical scalp. Ancient Serpents within the history of the elders shaved their heads as a sign of purity and a mark of their developed spiritual crown, an attribute of divine leaders and a cultural element found in pharaohs, princes and the higher priests of Egypt — all known to bear the influence of this Lineage evidenced in more than one way.

During energy crisis and spiritual strife their system can reach a point of collapse or in some cases manifest more explosively through aggressive behavior, arrogance and a destructive nature. Most of these conditions can be improved, although never fully corrected, through the mastery of meditation, energy work and metaphysical healing. The single most efficient solution to attain such balance while under strain from a high demand of energy is through vampiric feeding — the communion of life.

More than the other two Lineages, Serpents have a greater need for vital force that results from their high energy metabolism, implying a major benefit from the spiritual empowering through the ethereal blood of life. While some Asetians with a lower metabolism barely require the effort of active draining, Serpents indulge in the arts of feeding more regularly in order to maintain balance and remain sane. That is achieved through different practices and techniques, from simple to more advanced with greater magickal requirements, which can be done socially and virtually unnoticed, to more intimate sexual drains done privately. Due to such requirements in terms of frequency and vibration they do not find the same advantages as the other Lineages in ambient feeding, since such energy is not only scarcer but for the most part much poorer in terms of spiritual quality, however it can still be used and of significance if harnessed within empowered locations or where the force of nature is wild and strong. Ideally Serpents find a source of great empowerment when in sacred ground, such as their native lands and temples in Egypt where their mighty force can be unleashed. Their energy system is highly efficient in handling energy spikes and in the consumption of intense energy, making Serpents proficient in situations of contact and sexual feeding, where they are known to excel.

These elements from the nature of Serpents can make them be understood as the most vampiric of their kin; silent, skilled and living in darkness while requiring more energy to sustain such fast subtle metabolism and to empower the intensity of their unique abilities. Bearers of an unbreakable personality, sometimes even selfish, these conquerors of empires are the lash of immortality, feeding off great victories and in each transcendent achievement. Wielders of such a great intellect, Serpents have every reason to be feared for they are dangerous in unspeakable ways. Still, they remain treasured and loved within the Asetian family, recognized as the hand that holds those who feel drowning and losing themselves into the abyss. Loyal friends, harsh teachers and skillful healers, Serpents sit on the throne of the Asetian spiritual empire and honorably protect the crown of Aset with wisdom and fierce determination. Their advice and diligent judgment is respected by all.

Mentors and guides of past and present, the Asetians from this Lineage are highly evolved beings. Prophets, alchemists and scholars, Serpents have the ability to see beyond the horizon and above the crowd, providing them with unmatched spiritual insight. This sensitivity is found in their passionate bond with Aset, an immortal flame burning to the very core of their being. Such boundless perception can sometimes manifest through intolerance and heightened detachment, particularly when dealing with the limited mind of the mundane. While these characteristics can be harnessed for the greater good of the Asetian family, and indeed the evolution of Asetianism and the loyal execution of the Will of Aset would not have been possible without the leading poison of Serpents, it is also a dangerous side of their nature. If unstable and not bound to the exercise of responsibility or the reasoning of mastery, it can develop into destruction fueled by ego and malice that if paired with the scope of their power can be used to disastrous consequences.

Concerning their soul, Serpents have the most balanced energy body when it comes to the duality of metaphysical polarity. Located on the Middle Pillar of the Tree of Life, they can see through opposing minds and gather the emotional sight of male and female. Grasping different perspectives they can analyse situations under masculine and feminine mindsets, seeing beyond cultural conditioning and social limitation. Having both energies flowing within their system and mingling the two polarities, Serpents are uniquely positioned to manifest the best — or worse — from both sexes, despite the irrelevancy of the body they incarnate with.

While their internal system is not the most chaotic of the three they are the ones that can more easily induce change over the environment and alter the energy within everyone they interact with. Serpents shift minds with ease, inspire ideas, manipulate thoughts and break established dogmas. This can be useful if explored responsibly but also very dangerous when used egotistically for personal interest with disregard for ethics, trust and respect.

Being the ones that promote the most dramatic change and growth in others, it is common to see friends and lovers unconsciously adapting to the very peculiar nature of the Serpent, in this way forging a stronger bond and a higher understanding of each other, achieving a deepened sense of completeness typical of relationships with a member of this Lineage. However, due to the initiatory nature and influence of Serpents such transition is not always simple and subtle, especially if they are received with stagnation and conditioning, which can result in damage to the psyche and mental stability of those closely dealing with their magick. In some situations such resistance to growth and evolution can lead to serious psychological problems on those dealing with Serpents, including the jailing of the mind from the victim into the will and energy of the Serpent, in worst cases leading to depression, paranoia and even dementia. It should be noted that such changes are not necessarily the result of manipulation and control but a natural process of change and transformation that is connected to the inspiring essence of these Asetians that promote initiation into higher awareness and understanding through their very touch. Just like nature itself the initiatory breath of Serpents is not a door to an easy and peaceful path of transformation, coming through fire and storm with the force to break any barrier.

Unlike Scorpions and a characteristic that is more commonly found in the psyche of Scarabs, the members of the Serpent Lineage are often less independent creatures. This manifests on a very different level than how it can be expressed by Scarabs, as Serpents hardly connect with most of humanity and traditionally despise an overly social nature. Their true heart is moved by the Asetian family and deepest bonds as there is where their independence hinders, as Serpents rely on the emotion, loyalty, safety and happiness of their loved ones to prosper. Although this may not be easily perceived and Serpents do not allow for such frailty to be exposed, their sensitivity and spiritual mind needs the support and presence of those special few. Loneliness can unbalance their energy system and touch their otherwise fierce and strong spirit, echoing into the mental realm and potentially manifesting through sorrow, imbalanced mood and belligerence. This only applies to the closest bonds of Serpents, often those of the Asetian family and others who they might have nurtured an ancient connection with, being the only ones they truly care for within their hearts of stone.

Serpents dedicate their lives to the learning of different knowledge, the mastery of various arts and understanding of all mysteries, living as collectors of wisdom and keepers of secrets. Perfecting their practices and gathering wisdom across the centuries the Asetians from this Lineage often recollect, sometimes vividly, memories from their previous lives, being able to tap unto those experiences and consciously manifest them as actual information and expertise that it would otherwise not be possible for them to possess in the limited time of a single life. This is an enlightening spiritual tool, accessible to every Asetian but inborn and natural to Serpents, that gives them the ability to excel in different scientific fields, sometimes apparently without former training, and to master a wealth of knowledge with inhuman insight and unique understanding. Such gift makes their power limitless, so they became valuable targets and are often seen as a threat by those who observe such capabilities, even on an unconscious level. This may cause for them to be condemned and vilified through the artifices of falsehood and rumor by those who fear their potential and the liberating truth they can bring, rising as true adversaries of anyone who inspires deceit or promotes the vain paths of futility.

In their misunderstood existence Serpents are often the most desired and feared of Asetians, gathering within them all of the greater mysteries. Experts at manipulation and masters of deceit, Serpents can allure who they intend and repel others at the whip of their magickal will. Impressive by nature and charming in a distinctively inhuman way, these eloquent immortals can gain the trust and admiration of all, however frequently rejecting and even consciously avoiding being the praise and spotlight of common minds. One of the most trustworthy souls for those who are worthy of their honor, Serpents can be very dangerous to outsiders and the last adversary you should seek to face. Lords of many faces and seers of fate they can be everyone and no one. They can be a villain or a saint, your friend or your enemy, your lover... or even you.

SCARAB

LINEAGE OF CONCUBINES

M asters of chaos and channelers of energy, the mutable Scarabs are the seeds of transformation. The most diverse of all Asetian Lineages, they are a symbol of awakening and adaptation, gifted with powerful abilities to generate energy and release it with ease, empowering others through their craft and will.

Having an advanced and continuous cycling operation as part of their subtle nature, Scarabs release and reabsorb energy on a regular basis without conscious effort, making them great donors of life force and natural energy workers but resulting in beings of a strong chaotic influence. Such chaos can be both a powerful tool but also a delicate handicap, allowing for a profound liberation of mind and body but also leading to confusion and imbalance if not under cautious control.

The iconic animal-sigil of this Lineage embodies a profound symbolism of transformation that accurately represents the adaptive nature of these Asetians. The Egyptian scarab is one of the oldest references to spiritual rebirth, often connected to the mysteries of awakening but also an immortal banner of this Lineage. Its mythology ties to the alchemical transformation of inert matter into the gift of life as the beetles were observed rolling their eggs into balls of dung that would safeguard and incubate their newborn children; a symbolism that is allegorical to the vibrational breath of Scarabs that allows them to channel and heighten vital energy in order to willingly gift it to other Asetians as empowerment, making them exceptionally unique vampires.

Scarabs constantly interact with all forms of energy surrounding them, absorbing it from the environment and other living beings. This energy is naturally filtered and altered within their system, being then released back into the environment. This can have powerful effects in cleansing ritual space and intensifying vibrations, being also one of the mechanisms that makes Scarabs such strong allies to Serpents who they often bond with to great depth, being able to feed their energy needs and heightening their inner powers. The mental instability that can arise from this natural cycling is notorious, something that can be balanced under the guidance and expertise of a Serpent or a Scorpion, who often become mentors and great friends found by the side of most accomplished Scarabs.

Despite the power and abilities drawn from such characteristics, Scarabs find in such aspect of their nature one of their greatest condemnations — the permanent melding with energy from surrounding sources results in the most humanized soul of the three Lineages. This detail, although making Scarabs recognizably different from other Asetians, is not without potential as it allows for a more natural and easier interaction with humans at a level that makes it possible for them to see and analyse situations through a mortal mindset. This might make Scarabs less elitist but provides them with a great evolutionary tool that allows for them to adapt to society and flourish undetected within their midst, even though it plagues their inner development with a higher need for initiation and awakening in order to achieve the advanced spiritual growth natural of the Asetian kin.

Their strong and sometimes uncontrollable creativity potentiates great artistic qualities that can be channeled into valuable assets and resourceful outlets, leading some Scarabs to develop as successful artists of different crafts. The heterogeneity of this Lineage is one their greatest strengths as it allows for them to excel in a multitude of situations and succeed in many fields of experience, adapting and overcoming obstacles that would oftentimes prove problematic to other Lineages.

Some Scarabs are known for their taste for selective submission, however this should not be understood in the sense that most humans would see a fetish or weakness. Their submissive nature is only directed towards those that they are capable of bonding profoundly and forging a deeper spiritual connection, while they are likely to remain rebellious and independent towards most of the world. Sometimes explosive and undisciplined, they remain a mystery to those that interact with them, being able to inspire passion but also becoming dangerous when moved by their obsessive nature.

The intrinsic ease in adapting to different scenarios and blending with ordinary society can numb the flame within Scarabs and confuse them towards their true nature, silencing the manifestation of their darker side. This may be interpreted as a less defined character than what it is commonly found amongst other Asetians, making a few Scarabs bound to weaker personalities. However, every Scarab just like every other Asetian is unique and cannot be defined or constrained by rules, and each obstacle to be found in their nature can be developed and improved through hard work, dedication and determination, in a process that can be mastered under the aid of a Serpent with their rock solid personality and through the influence of their timeless wisdom.

Most of these elements are not a reflex of mental conditioning but have strong ties to the metaphysical nature of this Lineage. An unstable Scarab can suffer from light to severe psychological complications that are often heightened by emotional onset and that can result in recurring episodes of confusion or in worst cases in a complete loss of identity and sense of Self. Due to the myriad of different energies that touch the auras and pass through their systems, the subtle body of Scarabs is unable to retain standard quantities of their own pure energy bound to the unique fingerprint of their being, resulting in a process that could be understood as similar to that of energy poisoning by an outside human source. This flood within their inhuman system by non native and oftentimes polluted energy, frequently of much lower vibration, places great strain on the brain and how the mind retains the keys to self-awareness, being a trigger to cases of emotional and mental collapse.

To protect themselves from the conditioning of their energy system and the overtaxing of their metaphysical nature, Scarabs can greatly benefit from meditation practices, advanced energy stabilization techniques and by following a healthy diet. Such efforts can be essential to the maintenance of their sanity and safety, as well as the first course of action to achieve inner balance, both energetically and emotionally. Also due to this predisposition Scorpions can have a positive effect on the mindset of Scarabs, which through such relationship and interaction can make use of the powerful shields found on the other Lineage to keep them grounded from the uncontrollable overflow of energy created by their internal system. Because of such effects the development of their own energy shields should be a high priority to Scarabs, alongside the blossoming of a stronger personality and a heightened sense of identity. This allows them to retain full awareness of their nature in a determined way so that they can interact with others without being drowned in their energies and feelings to the point of losing the inner Asetian compass, vital to every member of the immortal family.

Cyclical stages in personality, the onset of emotion due to various triggers and conditioning natural to incarnated life can manifest through the alteration of mental phases, often as a result of conflicting energies, being a situation that can induce a state of disorientation, fear and desperation. This hindrance towards spiritual equilibrium, otherwise essential to any Asetian, can be a subtle cause behind varying symptoms such as lethargy, lack of concentration and apathy, which if untreated can lead to depression and a nearly absolute negligence of Self. Such bewilderment with underlying metaphysical causes can be common among Scarabs but the esoteric and spiritual nature of the process, although highly scientific to those fluent in subtle medicine and anatomy, will not be easily diagnosed by modern medical practice and its limited understanding of the non-physical. Such situations can be of great concern not only to Scarabs but to every Asetian, especially the unawakened that not being aware of their nature and abilities are lost in a sea of living, not being able to benefit from the support and healing of other Asetians and the expertise of more advanced practitioners within the Aset Ka.

Not all consequences of the chaotic nature of Scarabs are grievous, being also the mechanisms that potentiate many of the abilities unique to their Lineage, including those that will not be made public due to the tactical advantage they provide. Some manifest in actual biological capacity, which for example allows for a Scarab to endure in scarce environments with limited ingestion of food while maintaining their physical system stable, for medium to longer periods of time depending on energy state and physical condition. Although this enhances the survivability of the Lineage it leaves them in an unbalanced energetic state that is not recommended unless strictly necessary, and if used without responsibility can have severe biological consequences. Even when done consciously and by those experienced with the process, when ceasing the compensation for biological fuel with subtle energy the physical and mental system will enter a state of overdrive until it regains former strength, which may leave the Scarab with strong cravings and an urge to recover faster through the ingestion of high quantities of food. In terms of stabilization such approach is ineffective and should not be explored, a situation that if left unattained can in worst cases lead to bulimic patterns.

Scarabs can be passionate and obsessive lovers, deeply connecting with who they love and naturally establishing a rooted energy link. This may manifest in heightened jealousy moved by desire and a considerable sense of possession and protection towards their loved ones. They may lack the warrior nature of Scorpions and their fierce determination but Scarabs can go to great lengths when driven by emotion and are able to do incredible things when it comes to showing their loyalty, often assuming socially awkward positions and publicly condemned attitudes without regard for consequences. They are beings of extreme intensity, which is a characteristic that can be found within the three Asetian Lineages, although they all express it differently in their own unique way. Asetian dedication and commitment towards their loved ones is often interpreted as obsession and can be seen as something wrong or dangerous by the ordinary human mind, which is used to mediocre relationships and weaker bonds where dishonesty and betrayal is common ground, living in a society that discredits true love only to recognize pleasure and the selfish desires of instant gratification. For this and other reasons any attempt to understand Asetian love and union through a human mind is nothing but futile.

When dealing with those outside of their spiritual family, if not someone they care about, Scarabs tend to be manipulative and even creative liars. This often causes them to succeed in manipulation, which can reflect their will or be the target of other agendas. In their innocence and confusion Scarabs may appear to be deceptively trustworthy, unlike Serpents that often breathe danger through their eyes. Such delusion is a weapon they use and abuse, entangling the belief of others in the silvery silk of their minds.

Concerning energy polarity they are similar to the nature of Scorpions, with energy signatures being defined as masculine or feminine. However, although having a defined polarity their psyche is everything unlike their fellow Scorpions, and the imbalances of their mind and chaos of their energy may raise confusion towards their true sexual identity, mixing energy signatures that cloud the defined line of their polarity giving place to uncertainty and doubt, especially among younger Scarabs.

The renowned ability of Scarabs to commune with other Asetians through the sharing of their vital energy without major loss of internal stability, besides making them exceptional donors and competent healers, is also secretly bound to their talent in dealing with pain. Opposite to the heightened sensitivity to physical pain found in Serpents, those of the Scarab Lineage have an inborn resistance to pain, torment and torture. They can, for short periods of time, use vital energy in small bursts to numb sensations flowing through the nervous system before reaching the brain, something that can be mastered and used to their advantage in ways that when accurately fine-tuned may be redirected and transformed into pleasure, allowing for them to actually feed from their own pain and finding gratification in the flame of such sensations. This magickal process can be especially desirable when done under absolute trust and within an intimate context, allowing for Scarabs to feed from the energy release caused by the feelings of physical pain, empowering themselves in the process and achieving desired altered states of consciousness that liberate magickal potential. This ability depends on a metaphysical mechanism that although possible to be explored by other Lineages it is inborn to Scarabs and can sometimes manifest without knowledge or training, even before the awakening.

Some Scarabs have learned to value interaction with a broad range of people and mingling with society, carving their own way within social standards. They are the ones that better connect with humans, establishing bonds with those of non-magickal nature and, in some cases, even acting like one of them. This Lineage is undoubtedly more social than the other two, being seen as the less elitist of Asetians, which may be understood as a strength but also a weakness. However, not all Scarabs are open to outsiders or appreciate the perks of community and social interaction as in their diversity some are fierce, determined and proud Asetians with an elitist heart focused on inner growth and the quest for perfection.

For a minority of Scarabs bound to a weaker nature and limited by the blindness of ego, such connections with human society can make them abide to mundane standards of superficiality, seeking achievement not through the art of spiritual development and magickal understanding but by embracing the path of vanity and praise. Although often successful in such endeavours and wielding the ability to see crowds kneeling before them, those achievements never lead to inner satisfaction and completeness, leaving the Scarabs with a sense of barrenness and empty existence that will later echo throughout their lives, no matter how hard they try to exhibit a smile to the world while silently weeping within. This, however, should never be understood as the true nature of a Scarab for any being is susceptible to weakness and may be deceived by the pitfalls of ego in its many forms, and such Scarabs are rare and do not represent the foundations of their Lineage.

Additionally, the human connection may also cause for some to feel a sense of duty towards their biological families even when that is not earned or corresponded with respect. This is a characteristic that is the opposite of what can be found among Scorpions, known for their ease in breaking bonds with humanity after awakening and for severing unwanted emotional attachments. The ability for a Scarab to overcome this will vary and be influenced by the strength of the bond established in the old days of the Asetian empire in Egypt, as this will reflect on how they can fight against the lack of identity in modern times and fully embrace their true nature. So again the elder Serpents and Scorpions can be powerful role models to evolving Scarabs, being their mentors and initiators towards enlightenment, often becoming a living and breathing safe haven to their wandering souls.

Scarabs are warm creatures with gentle hearts and they must be understood with care. The mysteries of their nature walks them through an intricate path of torment and pleasure, unknowingly longing for the key to their sleeping soul. Born with hidden powers, Scarabs are misunderstood by the world and their importance is often underestimated by those unable to see the violet mist concealed within. Their destiny is immortally bound to the Asetian family as their hearts are sealed within the ethereal realms of the Aset Ka, and so their legion haunts humanity in every moment for they remain eternally unknown.

SCORPION

LINEAGE OF GUARDIANS

asters of the darkest arts and warriors of supreme loyalty, the seductive Scorpions are guardians of immortal love. Known for their protective nature and strong personalities, the members of this Lineage wield some of the most powerful defensive techniques known in existence. Gifted with outstanding natural shields Scorpions are fierce opponents in any metaphysical fight. Their abilities were extensively explored in the ancient world where they embraced ranks as generals, captains and knights, being the masters of warfare within the Aset Ka. This was seen not only in terms of their strategic might, rivaled only by the cunning mastermind of Serpents, but also by taking arms and leading their brothers and sisters at the edge of battle, spearheading the front lines with the kind of dedication that fears no death.

Mysterious by nature and misunderstood within the judging hearts of society, Scorpions can be shy but their inborn antisocial behavior is a defined hallmark of the Lineage. They are silent and do not share their mind unless a bond of trust can be forged. This can make them appear alluring to outsiders who feel fascinated by their mystery and drawn to the darkness surrounding them, but it can also be misinterpreted as arrogance.

The animal-sigil of the Lineage is an interesting representation of these Asetians, not only because of its obvious symbolism of eminent danger and creation of deadly poison but also because the scorpions found in the wild, common in Egypt from the ancient times to this day, are known for their aggressive behavior, particularly when provoked or touched, which is similar to the reactions from the members of this Lineage in their unique stance concerning disrespect and the invasion of their personal space. Scorpions define their body as their temple and within it hides the sacred spark and altar of their magick; to commune with their flesh is a blessing granted only to a few. In old folklore there was the belief that wild scorpions sting themselves to death using their own venom when forced into capture, a banner of this Lineage that fears no death and that would gracefully embrace it in the face of dishonor. Asetian Scorpions defy life and welcome death for the protection of their spiritual family, when fighting for their honor or in the name of the driving force of their existence: love — a characteristic that remains unmatched in any other creature of this world. The abandoning of life following the death of a lover may seem romantically poetic to some and a concept inspired by lost gothic literature, something even absurd to the judging mind of society in modern times, but not to Scorpions who embrace life as an extension of their emotions and face death as the path to immortal reunion. Such mindset and practice, only if enforced by True Will, is known within the Asetian culture as the Deadly Poison, and although not exclusive to Scorpions it was founded and inspired by their undying flame.

Asetian Scorpions should not be confused with the Seven Scorpion daemons of Aset — Her Will and servitors as leaders of the Imperial Guard. The Seven are not Asetian in nature and embody a nameless force of unspeakable power, unlike the Lineage of Scorpions that defines one of the three sacred foundations of the children of Aset alongside the initiatory Serpents and the mutable Scarabs. Albeit unrelated with the Seven some of the elders of the Scorpion Lineage held prominent ranks within the Imperial Guard as well, leaving their mark in history as wise commanders of this elite army and feared warriors experienced in the arts of combat and fluent in the language of bloodshed. Achievement and victory in the past of the Aset Ka was often secured through the iron fist of these Asetians and the pain they shed for the realm; deeds conquered with honor and blood that should never be forgotten.

✝

Within the Asetian family Scorpions are remarkably important pillars, being the grounding force of this immortal kin. Their powerful connection with elemental Earth and slowest energy metabolism makes them able to ground and center others, induce rationalization and enhance the mental process, as well as inspire a sense of security only felt by the side of their protective presence. This passive energy metabolism combined with their inborn ability to raise and empower incredible metaphysical shields leaves Scorpions in a great defensive position among all magickal practitioners. Besides being often unaffected by spells and other energy attacks, they are incredibly difficult to be drained by someone who is not Asetian and spiritually connected with them, making them hardly victimized by malignant magick. Through this they may sometimes appear unpleasant as Scorpions naturally alter their aura and shift their vibrations as both defensive and offensive mechanisms that can make their energy unattractive to others, another of their inborn metaphysical abilities with the spark of conflict and the taste of war.

The slow subtle metabolism allows for them to fast for long periods of time and to rely on their own energy without the need to drain from other sources or to actively manipulate energy, which is a great metaphysical asset particularly in times of danger and strife. This explains why some members of this Lineage may not experience the need of vampiric draining, being able to rely on passive processes of energy absorption that are barely noticeable and recur naturally in their system, making them appear to be deceptively non vampiric, a misconception that is not spiritually accurate. Being a vampire is a condition of the soul and not the categorization of practices related with the feeding of blood or the draining of energy, as both things can be done by humans with the metaphysical skills or willingly embracing the fetich of blood and yet it does not make them vampires.

To the Aset Ka vampirism is a much deeper concept entwined with ancient spirituality and the initiatory path to enlightenment, making it profoundly different from the lore of fiction and modern views embraced by many who seek nothing but attention and the promulgation of ignorance, a mindset despised by Scorpions known to nurture no respect for such weakness.

Frequently, Scorpions benefit from strong bodies, balanced health and a great immune system, a consequence of being the ones with the best physical connection from the three Lineages. Such stability can only be shaken by a profound energy imbalance, often triggered by emotional response and rarely affected by metaphysical attacks, making Scorpions the most enduring among Asetians. This link with the physical realm and particular energy metabolism, opposite to the natural disconnection found in Serpents, can in a few cases manifest through steady increases in body mass and weight, a situation that can be easily balanced through proper energy work and a healthy lifestyle. This is another reason why Scorpions can greatly benefit from dedicated physical activity and the martial arts in order to master their own bodies and regulate the biological rhythm in tune with their magickal nature.

Such balance with nature and the realm of matter is a useful characteristic that allows Scorpions to excel in different situations where the other Lineages manifest handicaps, however it is also one of their greatest enemies. The mighty energy shields and natural grounding of these Asetians makes them potentially less sensitive to energy and the subtle intricacies of intuitive metaphysics, often reacting to the realm of spirit unconsciously although accurately. Such condition may in certain situations, particularly prior to awakening, manifest through symptoms of limited creativity, skepticism, detachment from their spiritual nature and distrust in potential abilities. Their protective nature may enclosure them in a mental shell, a stronghold of their inner Self safekeeping Scorpions from harm and confusion in order to prevent imbalance. This mechanism is highly effective and again defines their resilience, however it also keeps them shielded from the true nature of their divine spark, a powerful force that must be unleashed and allowed to burn in absolute beauty of the inner Fire present in this Lineage once each Scorpion reaches conscious awakening.

It should be noted that although Scorpions express less inborn potential to manipulate energy when compared to the other Lineages that does not mean they cannot become powerful practitioners. In fact, with proper guidance, training and dedication, Scorpions have the ability to master any magickal practice and to rise as great masters of this ancient art. As every Asetian, they are beings of energy and spirit, living through the same violet magick and embracing the transcendent existence of their kin.

The metaphysical side of Scorpions cannot be neglected or reduced to the power of their shields and the fierceness of their attacks. Predatorily they are masters of Tantric Feeding, being proficient at such metaphysical practice in a much more efficient way than other Asetians and marking them as more actively vampiric than what can be erroneously perceived. Using such subtle mechanisms Scorpions can drain condensed vital energy through sexual activity, even without the requirement of pleasure of their own. When a true state of Tantric Feeding is achieved the physical pleasure given by the Scorpion is released by the partner in a powerful echo of strong sexual energy that can be immediately absorbed, or consciously drained, allowing for them to feel the pleasure of their partners, feeding from those high vibrations and released energy being fueled by the pulse of physical pleasure. This is an advanced form of sex magick that is highly vampiric in nature and that has been perfected by this Lineage throughout many lifetimes; a unique drain of intimate energy where Scorpions empower their flame and achieve heightened states of pleasure by the mere act of giving that very same pleasure to someone in absolute trust. This is a profoundly bonding experience and an innate ability of Scorpions who through such erotic magickal skills can rely on a feeding technique that is more efficient in their system and attuned to their nature, providing a raw source of intense life force. This is not something they use lightly and, added to their natural elitism and solitary nature, it can only be shared with the deepest bonds forged through time, which Scorpions above all are known to restrict to an absolute minimum.

Although an energy of less intensity this Lineage can also naturally harness vital essence through romantic interaction but such an approach is again restrictive as it can only be activated from strong emotional connections. Opposed to Scarabs who indulge in the arts of infatuation and enjoy playing the game of seduction, Scorpions embrace love as sacred and honor such burning force as a manifestation of the divine. Beneath thick shields and behind cold detached hearts Scorpions are misunderstood beings of pure love, being the only hidden power that can balance their souls secretly longing for the gentle care of the one who wields the cryptic key to their temple. Such profound and often unique bonds that they protect as sacred have the quality to endure forever and can take lifetimes to be found and forged, only then unleashing the hymns of immortal love. The ethereal magick of love is the central living force to Scorpions and it remains the sole power that has the ability to break them. In its mysteries lies the key to their weakness and the seed to turn their unshakeable balance into madness. A potent weapon for their enemies although one not easily wielded. This divine love is uniquely Asetian and its beauty is beyond the comprehension of mortal men.

This makes Scorpions, in certain ways, more independent than the other two Lineages. Despite the rare few they admire and care for it becomes natural for them to detach from literally everyone, often embracing isolation and avoiding interaction without any form of feelings and emotion towards all others. This is true even concerning their biological family, which they consciously detach from after awakening if no past Asetian bond is felt, liberating life and will to the flame of their inner heart. Such coldness and lack of compassion is not something that human society would accept, leaving Scorpions to be condemned as monsters by the judgmental eyes of those who lack the ability to see their true beauty. Independent, detached and solitary, hidden behind the dungeons of their emotional darkness, Scorpions can only achieve spiritual maturity and mental liberation after a properly guided and responsible awakening, an initiatory process that can be profound and should not be approached lightly.

Behind such coldness and independence lies one of the most caring and sensitive beings in existence, even if one is only able to experience it towards the select few worthy of their emotion. Scorpions find in love, loyalty and family the engine of life itself, being the energy that sustains them and the inspiration that allows for them to adapt and evolve. Without it they wither and stagnate, becoming an abandoned rock naked to the wind.

Not every Scorpion finds true love and lives by it. In fact, many embrace the solitude of their nature and the commitment of their spiritual path, but if such a soul is found then a profound inner initiation manifests within them. Nothing then makes sense without the presence of that one soul and all further motivation of life and growth becomes bound to that love and to fulfill that sacred purpose

— living for their beloved. This unbreakable dedication can potentially lead to the experience of jealousy and a strong sense of possession and protectiveness, making them increasingly more aggressive and intolerant. If uncontrolled and under the influence of imbalance such situations can lead to extreme consequences, a reason why every mind should be bound to the exercise of responsibility and self-mastery.

Although known to actively feed less regularly, if at all, when compared to the other two Lineages and in situations where Tantric Feeding and sex magick is not desired, Scorpions are proficient at empowering their systems through ambient feeding particularly when relying on the energies of nature, which can be easily perceived in major storms, great waterfalls or when lost in virgin forest or unoccupied desert. Elemental energy is an intuitive source of empowerment to Scorpions who can easily connect with its frequency and ethereal vibration, naturally relating with the energies of Water and Earth. Such inborn connection with nature and its force can manifest in a strong sense of attraction towards majestic locations where nature is abundant and its powers run deep, providing a source of energy and balance for this Lineage to exercise its hidden vampiric nature. In a subtle system that is not used to high or frequent impulses of raw energy, these massive drains from powerful elemental sources and the urge to feed from such environments and situations can lead to emotional peaks and strong sensations during the process.

They can also exploit social situations where they project themselves above and dominate the surrounding energy, enforcing their flame and reducing the aura of others, although such activity can also be understood as a magickal attack. Most Scorpions are able to maintain their energy reserves to a bare minimum without exhibiting vulnerabilities or lasting consequences, although allowing for the slow decay of mental condition. This manifests in a reluctance towards change and adaptation that can lead to stagnation and cyclical perpetuation, where without the active circulation of new energy in the subtle system the mind develops attachment mechanisms and does not promote the energy flow required to set in motion natural change and acceptance. Because of this condition some profound changes experienced in the life of a Scorpion can be troublesome and require special attention and balance, being able to cause emotional impact and stress due to such subtle characteristics.

The slower rate of the subtle metabolism found in this Lineage when combined with the robust nature of their inner shields and supra-auric defensive filters can promote stagnation and blockages, primarily due to the accumulation of stagnant energy within the system without proper cycling and its encrusting inside the meridian vessels that consequently slow down the main Shen centers. Such condition can echo to the mental and physical layers in the form of headaches, fatigue, inertia and, in worst cases, depression. With understanding of the underlying mechanisms causing such symptoms these situations can be greatly improved with proper energy healing and metaphysical techniques. Energy stagnation and blockages are serious conditions that affect both Asetians and humans, promoting illness in different locations of the body and manifesting through varied mental conditions, from mild to severe, which are hardly perceptible or holistically understood by modern health practitioners limited by conventional practice, often requiring the aid of subtle medicine and the proper usage of energy healing.

Stagnation can be easily activated and set in motion by the higher vibration of Serpents and their unique abilities to drain, manipulate and transform energy. Such aid is oftentimes essential to Scorpions suffering from these conditions and that form of healing greatly effective. Scarabs may also provide valuable assistance with such cases although less efficiently and promoting effects at a slower pace by breaking stagnation centers with their energy cycling, promoting a healthier flow. However, it is important that Scarabs operating with healing on this level should be carefully selected among Asetians not suffering from stagnation themselves and other subtle or spiritual ailments, otherwise such medical work would be counterproductive or even the cause of unintended consequences.

Less sensitivity to light is an old characteristic of the ancient Scorpions — a consequence of their shields and natural magickal defenses that allowed for them to ride across the desert and fight in full force under the blinding sunlight. This has led to the myth that Scorpions are less pale than the other two Lineages, however this did not come from an actual difference in melanin or pigmentation but it is historically accurate mostly because they better tolerate the burning scorch of the Sun than other Asetians who are affected by such energies, seeing their powers and extra-sensory abilities diminished. Scorpions are not immune to the powers of the Sun but they are uniquely prepared to endure its dominating force with minimal consequences, a lingering trait from their divine Mother who once overpowered Ra during a time now forgotten.

Maybe not as determined and critical as Serpents in gauging situations and wielding their inborn analysis tools, the personality of Scorpions is also strong and unshaken, sometimes even caustic. That is seen particularly when in observance of common society and the general mindset of those lacking character, driven by the need of integration or the vain desire of recognition. Scorpions are natural adversaries, having no tolerance for inflated egos, futility, unfounded arrogance and all other related weaknesses. Due to such characteristics their presence and opinions may be seen as unpleasant or undesired, particularly among those who reflect the very same traits they abominate or who are foolish enough to confront their sharp ideals. Condemning all who follow along with the rest of the human herd, they may grow intolerant driven by a genuine disgust for the uglier flaws of character seen at the foundation of many and taking pride in making that a banner of their temper. In this way Scorpions have a very determined and strong-willed character, with attitude and ideals increasing in scope but also understanding after facing the challenges of their own awakening, allowing them to grow and develop into a rock-solid catalyst of Fire.

In terms of energy polarity Scorpions are opposed to Serpents and even Scarabs to some extent, exhibiting recognizably masculine or feminine energy at their core. This provides them with a distinctive advantage concerning inner balance and self-identity but it can also condition their analytic skills and mindset. Males develop as strong, determined and unequivocally masculine forces, while females grow into sensual, confident and erotically feminine creatures. All of them warriors, loyally committed to the very end.

They are intense and alluring even when only their shadow can be seen, for it is unmistakably hard to conquer their trust and reach the true essence of these beings often clouded in mystery. Beyond their sensual nature Scorpions are admittedly sexual creatures, bringing many dangers that although not easily perceived have become legendary. The actions and emotions of this Lineage can often be fueled by rage and anger, which they harness and heighten to greater frequencies with potentially unwanted consequences to others and themselves. Echoing through migraines and ill temper if allowed to stagnate within their system, these energies can also be projected and redirected towards effective psychic attacks and powerful offensive magick, or otherwise metaphysically dumped through less exhausting options.

Unapologetically elitists, Scorpions identify such side of their nature with Serpents and struggle with more passive Scarabs, often the more tolerant of the three. Such character leads to antisocial behaviors and the desire for isolation from vulgar society with its common mentality of worship towards fame and the opinion of others, when Scorpions can only value honor, wisdom and the beauty that runs within. They above all restrict their friendships to a minimum, only sharing their true face with an elite few. Growing increasingly stronger after the awakening these Asetians exhibit no interest whatsoever in socializing with the masses or the common need for acceptance and integration, again unlike most Scarabs that easily befriend humans, being far less demanding in social situations and taking advantage of such interaction and attention.

In the end one of the strongest hallmarks of the Scorpion Lineage is their unbreakable loyalty. Devoted like no other, the passionate Scorpions know no limits to their bonds of honor and commitment, dedicating themselves in every lifetime and fighting even upon the face of death. They are the most honorable of Asetians, in ways that can only be envied by the human race. Their hearts are burning Fire and their souls carry the scent of undying love.

Asetianism
Path of the Soul

$\mathcal{T}$ he path of the elders is a hidden map to ancient mysteries, a sinuous road of enlightenment for the wandering soul carved on the landscape of time through the abominating blood of daemons. Asetianism is the heart of divinity and the flame of immortality; it is the magickal, spiritual and cultural legacy of Aset that was honored, embraced and celebrated in Kemet by the Asetians and their followers thousands of years ago.

The Asetian tradition manifests through the fire of wisdom, the lessons of truth and the embracing of loyalty. It is a timeless song that has echoed the secrets of nature throughout countless centuries, hidden from the eyes of vanity, ego and those who only sought power. It remains shielded from anyone seeking to deface it, safeguarded by an intricate system of initiation, secrecy and spiritual cryptography. Unbroken, its magick is locked in the forgotten tombs of the desert, only possible to be opened by the honesty of the purest hearts.

This is the culture of the Asetians and spiritual path of the followers of Aset. In this book I teach not only its foundations and elemental aspects but rely on the power of word, energy and symbol to lay down a framework of initiation that can only be understood by the few who are able to connect with the emotion of the Violet Flame and through its mysteries decipher the path unveiling before their eyes and the honor to guide their souls. So it begins…

Spiritual Wisdom
The wisdom of the Aset Ka manifests beyond the embracing of a culture built upon the feared practice of predatory spirituality or the dominion over forgotten powers found on the linen of nightmares. Asetianism is a tradition based on balance. It is an intricate spiritual path that liberates the soul to conquer life and death through the

mysteries of nature and the lessons of wisdom. It initiates the seekers with a set of tools that allows for them to see the world without masks. It is a dance of color to the vibrant breeze of eternity.

Asetianism holds the key for spiritual and emotional completeness, but its study is not an easy undertaking and certainly something that should never be approached lightly. Through its magickal formulae the initiates are led to the mirror of all truths, facing their demons holding no other weapon than bare Will. This is the hall where the humble become kings and the deceptive fall into eternal slumber. Never underestimate its dangers or the potency of such magick; instead surrender to wisdom and be graced with the subtlety of our teachings. They can guide you to doors of understanding where you may unlock the beauty of simplicity and the transcending power behind most subtle elements of existence, often ignored when the focus of awareness is not guided by truth. It will not only liberate but also transform the mind with the forces of chaos and the lessons of pain. Only through courage shall you find the inner temple. Yet, only the wise remember that the doors of Asetian magick hold the power of rising to unimaginable heights but also to drown into unspeakable depths with the passiveness of a new dawn. These teachings are unsuspiciously dangerous and the path you are now discovering has led many into madness, or worse, to be forgotten in oblivion — abandoned in the dungeons of despair where no memory can survive.

Many waste their lives with the superfluous by embracing the varying pits of vanity, ignorance and insignificance, never truly valuing the spiritual gifts that are presented to every single soul at birth. Unknowingly they insult the sacredness of life and the blessing of living, only to end their brief days in this realm with an accomplishment of no value and nothing worthy of remembrance. The focus of every breath in this realm should be inspired on the development of Self through inner growth and spiritual evolution. The pursuit for the attaining of enlightenment is a daunting quest and a path that can only be mastered through dedication and a colossal effort enduring of lifetimes. Asetianism promotes transformation and evolution through its natural process of initiation and growth, but it does not accomplish such feat without pain and the many obstacles that separate the worthy of its magick from the futile attempts of lesser creatures. Every initiate will fall, for only then can one learn how to get up and walk — it is a lesson. To embrace Asetian mysteries and the study of this tradition alone is a major catalyst of change and one that should never be forgotten. Such change is not a tangible force or a manifestation within the obvious realm of the physical but a profound manifestation of your singularity; the true hidden identity of Self. This may not be subtle and become a spiritual product of great intensity, often leading to life-changing realizations of inestimable value.

Although not a religion, Asetianism enhances the spiritual life of the adepts with renewed clarity and emotional maturity, providing the mental tools that allow them to craft their own evolution in a true initiatory process for the soul. Through the understanding and acceptance of their spiritual nature, when allied to the transcendence of magick and related metaphysical practices, the seekers find an unseen layer of reality, being able to experience it in a much deeper way than the mundane world is able to offer. In this process of self-discovery and experimentation the subtle abilities increase exponentially, opening doors for the slow unveiling of a forgotten past of the soul hidden behind the veil of former lives. This unleashes a dim light with the potential for discovery and exploration by those daring to lift the cloak of ethereal matter at the heart of the akashic records where all life remains untouched. A road that should only be treaded with extreme caution.

The secrets of the past and the mysteries they may unlock hold a prominent but dangerous key to evolution. Exploration of the past and previous life experiences is profoundly entwined with the Asetian tradition, having the Aset Ka developed and protected distinctive techniques and advanced metaphysical tools aimed at such exploration and practice, unfolding the sealed coffins of akashic truth and providing insight into past-life occurrences and lessons with the clarity, accuracy and often verifiable results characteristic of Asetian magick. The spiritual seed bound to every Asetian as well as the passion nurtured by those that shared their emotion and energy is a strong focus center and anchor point for the effectiveness of past-life work and tracking, reason why those that have delved into the mysteries of Asetianism in a previous life, no matter how far back in time, find there a powerful beacon into their forgotten past and a cue to reforged union.

When understanding Asetianism as an ancient mystical tradition with countless secrets lost in time, just waiting to be found and uncovered by those with attuned keys, the value of intuitive work, meditative exploration and scientific validation applied to past-life research becomes clear — something that was always taken very seriously within the Aset Ka. However, seriousness does also imply a dosage of objectivity and skepticism unlike popular approaches to the subject of reincarnation and regression, which are often done without proper knowledge and reach conclusions of no honest credibility. While the majority of Asetian metaphysical work related with regression and past-life research is centered on the knowledge of Kemet, commonly described as Ancient Egypt, and the established lives of the Asetians, their allies and opposers during that age, from the immemorially ancient Sep Tepy to later dynastic periods, it is not out of the scope of interest the research of other eras and different societies in varied timeframes. Following the decay of Egypt and the decision of the Aset Ka to withdraw from the throne of the empire, the Asetians have been scattered in history throughout different cultures and have ventured into distant lands. Some were lost in time and space, drawn apart from the Aset Ka for long periods of time, shaping the course of history and silently writing the fate of many, sometimes with intent and strategically aligned with higher purposes of Asetian nature and other times unconsciously, unaware of their spiritual identity and past. This has led to diversity, with Asetians incarnating under so many different cultures and mastering different paths, a detail that eventually enriched the global knowledge repositories of the Asetian family, providing the Aset Ka with a broader understanding and mastery of the philosophies and cultures of the world, which is not only an interesting tool of growth and development but also a potentially dangerous strategic advantage of intellectual might.

Through such diversity and the committed exploration of the many expressions of knowledge found in different civilizations, Asetianism has evolved throughout the centuries beyond the boundaries of Egyptian culture and practice, increasing in complexity and scope but maintaining its seed and essence from the beautiful land on the shores of the Nile, ferociously protecting those roots grown on the empire of Kemet forged in a time at the dawn of existence. Ultimately the fundamental secrets of reincarnation and past lives are so profoundly rooted in the Asetian culture and intimately experienced through its exploration that they are not approached as a belief system, not being accepted out of faith or scripture but an enlightened truth that in its very essence just is. Asetians are the ones who lived and remembered...

> *"I have been given eternity without limit. Behold, I am the heir of Eternity, to whom have been given everlastingness."*
>
> Egyptian Book of the Dead

Egyptian Legacy

This undying connection with the vast and intricate spiritual legacy of Ancient Egypt, easily observable in almost every aspect of Asetianism as a path with such distinctive identity, should not be understood as mere cultural elements or the lingering symbolism of a now extinct ancient religion. Its teachings, initiations and wisdom express some of the most profound mysteries of the Universe, patiently laying the eternal travel of the soul, now found in art, symbol and the small riddles scattered in every breath of the tradition of the Aset Ka and within most texts of Asetian influence to see the light of existence since the old days.

One of the most distinctive examples of Kemetic cultural presence in Asetianism can be found on the Asetian cosmogony presented in this grimoire as the *Book of Nun*, where any student familiar with the history and mythologies of Ancient Egypt can draw parallels of theological and historical nature. However, as obvious as some connections may appear during initial studies, when based upon flawed notions of modern beliefs and the inaccurate extrapolations of such findings they should be avoided or at the very least treated with a degree of skepticism, circumventing the dangers of biased assumptions or blindly accepting the misguided roads not leading to the valley of wisdom. A deeper study of apparent connections and clues to be found in ancient symbolism will often provide surprising answers that can open unexpected doors for those that do not take previously established notions for granted, as knowledge takes many turns and truth hides in dark places. Ancient Egyptian art, symbol and myth — in fact, the synergistic power of its legacy — yields many secrets that speak through silence and emotion to the very core of each Asetian and the followers of Asetianism, reflecting the inner truth of their existence and unveiling lost tales of a shared past, shaping forgotten history right before their eyes but only when they are open to the darkest chambers of our pyramid and closed to the blinding light of the material world.

There is relevant reasoning on why the Ancient Egyptian people and their culture are recurrently referenced with the prefix word ancient while other archaic cultures of similar historical periods are not. The people and legacy of Ancient Egypt is now extinct, broken throughout time and eventually lost in the torment of wars and the politics of envious empires. True Egyptian blood died alongside their empire of old Kemet, a mighty banner that endured for millennia, as the contemporary rulers of their lands are of Arab descent, bearing a beautiful Middle Eastern culture but representing a profoundly different people that must not be confused with the actual Ancient Egyptians.

Asetians incarnated in modern times experience this bond with the legacy of Egypt and the passion it unleashes very intensely, finding transcendent connection, solace and teaching in the ancient Neteru — the old Kemetic word for deities. This manifests differently in each Asetian whereby besides the immortal devotion and love nurtured for Aset, their spiritual Mother and founder of Asetianism, they may also identify in diverse ways with the rest of the elder pantheon, as the Gods and Goddesses from the Sep Tepy. Although distinctive and independent, they are all interconnected, forming one undefinable ethereal family that embodies the infinite face of divinity.

While some rely on a purist approach to the Asetian tradition and its Ancient Egyptian roots, embracing the older practices and culture almost exclusively, in tune with the life and rituals from the temples of that time, others embrace a broader experience of spirituality and magick by adopting modern paradigms and different cultural backgrounds as long as they are compatible with the core teachings and an advanced understanding of Asetian philosophy. Such resonance and experience is personal and individual to each practitioner of Asetianism and even though passion for the Egyptian mysteries and hidden truth is a common element of all, each explores it differently according to inner growth, spiritual evolution and past experiences. No matter how contrasting the Asetian roads taken in this path may appear they all share the same passion for Aset, an equal commitment to growth, wisdom and truth, and the respect alongside an undefinable sense of loyalty towards the Asetians — the eternal initiators of the soul.

> *"Our deeds still travel with us from afar and what we have been makes us what we are."*
>
> Mary Ann Evans

Asetian history is long, intricate and confusing even to the most dedicated scholar, being rich in surprising events, dramatic changes and a wealth of intrigue and misunderstanding. Forged on the fields of battle and raised through the wisdom of the temples, the Aset Ka has faced wars, opposition and strife since its very inception, even after its exodus from Egypt and later spiritual exile in Europe. Asetians have established themselves in different locations throughout their past, from the Middle East to the islands of Japan, where they left a mark and evidence of their ideals that remain visible to those dedicated to the study of tracking their legacy in history and culture. Even if some of the wars that involved Asetian armies, the strategic mastermind of their leaders or the secretive plotting of their hidden agendas have been of political, cultural or ideological influence, it remains certain that conflict was never instigated by Asetians drawn to a quest of fame and glory. Oftentimes such events escalated from the natural effect that Asetians have on people, which is particularly visible among the religiously obsessed, the closed-minded and those who fear power if not their own and everything that remains unknown. The knowledge brought by the Asetians and their intimate understanding of nature, magick and the mysteries of the mind has always been a recurring element of envy, dispute and intrigue among humans aware of their existence and the power they wield. Such flaws in the fabric of mankind have led them to many dishonorable acts driven by an unfulfilling hunger for power and control, seeking the exploitation and deface of Asetian magick as well as the silencing and destruction of the Aset Ka. This is a failed quest that remains alive to this day, hidden behind the mundane existence of those not aware of this magickal world, perpetually seeking the secrets of the ancients and committed to end these immortal masters who once freely taught them the knowledge of science, medicine and the truths of the spirit but who now remain adamantly in silence, observing their lies and the unfolding of time. After so many centuries wisdom should have taught them that such rotten desires became an edification of nothingness, no more than a fruitless quest of frivolous purpose, for the children of Aset will forever remain watchful but strong just like the very nature that surrounds them. That was Her gift; immortality and everlastingness.

Anubians: Children of Anubis

Souls of darkness and masters of death, ethereally roaming between the realm of the living and the infinite land of the dead. Bound to the violet path of Aset they are unquestionably loyal to Her honor and divine rule; mysterious beings eternally dedicated to the safekeeping of the Asetian bloodline. The Anubians also known as The Shadow are spiritual children of Anubis — silent, committed and noble. Raised in the heart of the empire among the arts of Aset and Anubis, taught and befriended by the Asetian masters, Anubian souls are almost as old as the violet children. Students of the mysteries and masters of the craft, these obscure creatures of ancient times reincarnate to this day, remaining committed to fight for the honor and safety of the Asetians. Whether as respected members of the Aset Ka, holding conquered positions of power or embracing an isolated and solitary journey, their loyalty to Aset remains unbroken as an echo of the Will of their divine father: the dark lord Anubis, keeper of the halls of death, who willingly committed his very soul for Her honor.

Raised by Aset and taught in Her mysteries, Anubis is a silent but fierce warrior of Her house — a leader of darkness and a commander of legions that should never be underestimated. His unique understanding of death and power over the lands beyond life are of immense spiritual significance and immeasurable relevance. Binding his allegiance to the Asetian empire and playing an active role during the Epic Wars, his children became an essential part of the family and their inner council a respected arm of the Aset Ka.

✝

In modern times the children of Anubis are sometimes described as Keepers, a symbol of their protective nature and dedication towards the Asetians, being Anubian a more accurate representation of their spiritual identity while the word Keeper is entwined in reference to their chosen manifestation and will — a hallmark of their militant vigilance for the Aset Ka. Just like the Asetians they nurture a passion for their roots in Ancient Egypt and its cultural legacy, finding power and strength in those immortal bonds. Their connection with the Asetians is profound and beyond the description of words, a realm of union that can be better understood under the light and study of Asetian cosmogony through the *Book of Nun*.

The inner nature and identity of an Anubian can be diverse, manifesting in countless branches of reality, but like an Asetian their soul is not human. Depending on vibration and energy metabolism they may have a strongly vampiric side or no trace of a vampire's behavior at all, resulting in the existence of Anubians who identify as vampires and others that do not. Such difference is irrelevant to their spirituality so no distinction is made between the varied nature of Anubian Keepers.

Also like the Asetians, Anubians undergo a process of awakening and initiation in each incarnation, which can range from a natural development of self-realization to a more violent experience. During this stage of awakening they discover their psychic abilities and metaphysical powers, however the major changes happen on a spiritual level when Anubians finally acknowledge and understand their importance along the path of the Aset Ka and experience the profound emotion towards the Asetians deep within the heart, one that is present in every fiber of their being. That bliss transcends time and reconnects the soul of a Shadow to that of Anubis — it is primordial magick.

Finding in Asetianism a road for the soul and the fountain of courage from their ancestors, the children of Anubis dedicate their lives to spiritual growth, the development of different arts and answer every call of danger from an Asetian, who they fiercely protect as a burning desire that nurtures their heart and fulfills their spirit. This deeply resonates with their nature as an emotion from the past, when they were entrusted by their father Anubis with the safekeeping of the Asetian elders during the Sep Tepy. They were the silent eyes of the Aset Ka, keeping watch over the empire as shadows in the dark, reporting their secrets to the Asetians while operating everywhere and nowhere, sometimes even as members of the thrice feared Imperial Guard and other nameless elite forces or going deep behind enemy lines at the very heart of the Sethian Order. The Council of Anubis within the Aset Ka forged its legacy and honor without ego, using humility and hard work as the selfless banner of their mighty power, and it remains known for both its compassion and deadliness.

Now they may be found in any walk of life, from unsuspecting monks experienced with meditation and prayer to committed masters of martial arts and modern warriors; maybe even the apparently simpler of neighbors next door bearing an ordinary job but wielding Anubian powers in silence and secrecy. Detached assassins operating in the realm of the living or in the seas of the astral, emotional priests within temples, spies beyond enemy eyes and perilous influence, trustworthy friends, allies and lovers — their service and role have ever been legendary.

It remains essential to exercise reason and grounding when studying every element of the Asetian tradition, not to confuse any facet with fiction or the illusion of others. Asetianism exists above the realm of desire, expectation and human creation but its allure can be deceiving for those with a weak mind or a needy ego. Strive for balance and seek only the truth, never to be guided through the stream of delusion. Only then the hidden chambers of the Anubians and the forbidden halls of the Asetians may be accessed — only through honesty.

Some Anubians are incredibly gifted in energy manipulation and the magickal arts, having developed intuition, balance and control. They can become great students of the occult and masters fluent in the mysteries if under proper guidance. Such characteristics often become an important asset and tool in their path and mission within the Aset Ka, as well as a powerful weapon in the service of protecting the Asetians. These great sorcerers of our time represent a dangerous element awaiting the enemies of our spiritual empire, instigating hope and fear among those who know of their fate and power. They are forever alert and beyond persuasion, wielding the blessing of Aset and the guidance of Anubis they are the swords in the dark.

Asetianists

The path of the Aset Ka and its ancient tradition is eternal and Universal. Founded by Aset and protected by the Asetians, Asetianism is unrestricted and without boundaries except those imposed by Self. Such notions, sometimes misunderstood in modern times, make it clear that despite being taught and initiated by the Asetians within the Order of Aset Ka, Asetianism is far reaching and followed by countless others of no Asetian lineage. Beyond mastery of the dark arts and the predatory nature of its spirituality this tradition is not exclusively vampiric, being embraced by humans all around the globe and in every culture, seeking inner growth through magick and wisdom, as well as spiritually evolving to the full extent of their potential. Speaking the transcendent language of nature through the immortal code of the children of Aset, Asetianism is accessible to all. This affirmation comes however not without a word of caution, recurrently found when dealing with Asetian magick outside of the internal scope of those experienced with its power and the consequences that it may entail. Stating that Asetianism can be freely embraced by anyone honestly seeking it with respect and honor is the truest statement, however to explore its power for personal gain and without genuine commitment in enlightenment is bound to inevitable failure.

The infinite doors that lay hidden in the treacherous road for the temple of truth that can be found within Asetianism may only be interpreted and opened through powerful spiritual initiations. Some of those initiatory secrets, however, do not result from the constructs of esoteric trials or carefully crafted occult lessons, but are actually an echo of the magickal processes of nature and its transformational properties of spiritual awakening and renewed understanding. This makes Asetian initiations part of a magickal system of subtle power but unbreakable quality, as they cannot be tricked or exploited by the devices of dishonesty and greed. The temple of Asetianism hides behind the doors of simplicity carved by the magick of immortality; it is a temple where only the true can enter.

Asetianist is the name given to anyone who embraces the path of Asetianism and lives its culture, studies its wisdom and practices its magick. Every Asetian is by definition an Asetianist, but not every Asetianist is Asetian. The many occultists following the Asetian path are Asetianists in their own right, whether their nature is human, vampiric or of any other transcendence. Outsiders commonly confuse the meaning behind the words Asetian and Asetianist, but they cannot be used interchangeably. That said, someone does not have to be a member of the Order of Aset Ka to be an Asetianist, and in fact there are many Asetianists throughout the world who are not associated with the Order.

Even if most Asetians do not hold in great esteem the mundane society with its flaws and vices, the Asetian tradition does not promote the diminishing of humanity and its values, for just like the Asetians each human is unique and its kin diverse. Although to the ancient eyes of immortals humans have failed miserably in their honor, loyalty and valor, there are still human beings capable of great deeds and worthy of respect, even if they are rare and few. In fact, some of them were once great allies of the Asetians, having fought by their side as brothers and sisters during the Epic Wars and other battles in history. Some have even forged a profound connection and mutual respect with the Asetian family, reuniting in different lifetimes and nurturing that long-lasting fellowship. Humans have been friends, lovers and fierce enemies of the Asetians; they have been fathers, mothers and children. For better and worse their fate is entwined as they incarnate life after life bound to this twisted realm of matter. The empire of the Asetians is now forgotten and humans rule over the realms of Earth with all of their political might, but the spiritual kingdom of the Aset Ka remains and in secret it is carved with the fate of all. Humans who are awakened to this reality and can hear our silent call still have within them the strength of old, being proud to call themselves Asetianists.

During ancient times the Aset Ka maintained a vast network of temples and mystery schools throughout Egypt and beyond, from the fertile shores of the Nile to the inhospitable villages in the desert. Many people, from common folk to the highborn and nobility, came to these sacred locations for wisdom, healing and growth. They learned the secret mysteries of alchemy and how to master the powers of magick; practiced lessons of medicine and the calculations of engineering. They held the Asetians under great esteem and admiration, sometimes becoming their greatest students, friends and even fierce protectors. Some of these Asetianists incarnate in modern times, experiencing a powerful sense of familiarity with the Asetian tradition and finding in our culture an emotional sense of home. Many seek the Aset Ka for guidance or aid but few are reunited with the Asetians as there are many lessons to be learned and some can only be achieved through a solitary road. All share a common passion for Egypt and a sense of respect and protectiveness towards the Asetians, remaining loyal to the eternal flag of Aset.

In early days Asetianists studying within the temples and practicing the magickal arts were also known as disciples, meaning the ones who learn and those that were awakened. The concept had no implication of servitude and described a committed involvement in a life of discovery and esoteric pursuit. The disciples of Aset lived through different tides of varying spiritual and political influence during their presence in Ancient Egypt, from the open teachings and mighty temples of a philosophy celebrated in public to times of secrecy and hidden strongholds of a magickal tradition experienced in darkness. Later in history the concept of disciples spread to other traditions and different uses around the Middle East, being absorbed by the religions of men, and it can still be found today in Christian literature as the followers of Jesus: the twelve disciples. In the Aset Ka the terminology fell into disuse long ago and although some may still identify with the word and embrace its old meaning most have rallied around the title of Asetianist, openly using it to describe their path, passion and allegiance.

The vast majority of Asetianists reincarnating in this era continue their growth through the Asetian path once their life places them into contact with elements of Asetianism or the symbolism of the Aset Ka. It is a powerful process of awakening and self-realization that can be intense and overwhelming or a slow road plagued with obstacles that can take a lifetime to overcome. Life is a school of evolution and Asetian initiations can last for brief moments or take the slow decay of centuries. Not all Asetianists remember their past lives, as in fact true memories of reincarnation are rare and the connection with Asetianism and their past in Egypt is more commonly found through feel, intuition and emotion, as a growing passion for everything Asetian and the unique flame of their energy. They are all drawn in different ways towards the Aset Ka and this can manifest through comfort, trust and a soothing sensation to more overpowering or even agonizing desires — all moved by passion, sometimes even unknowingly. They find in Asetian energy and teachings a way of life and a celebration of home, a way to embrace their origins and find the true face of their soul. Sometimes adrift for lifetimes in the wheel of reincarnation and its chaotic cycles, Asetianists remain strongly dedicated to Aset and Her children being undoubtedly an important sect of the Asetian family, members of their spiritual empire and precious beacons of light to other Asetianists lost in the dark.

Family

Asetians and Asetianists are much more than a group that follows an old tradition of mysteries, students of a unique spiritual path or the masters of energy and magick. They are a family. This was evident during the ancient times when many were incarnated and nurtured unique bonds of closeness, but such a link endures still and remains victor to the test of time.

Even when blessed with the gifts of knowledge and insight, how one understands life and the workings of existence is still influenced by the boundaries of opinion and ideology, shaped by experience, learning and wisdom, which are all rather personal and unique to each individual. This healthy diversity found among those of the Asetian path promotes a rainbow of approaches and attitudes towards life, where the foundations and spiritual values remain the same but how one chooses to experience them and liberate such magickal awareness is subject to absolute freedom. Although evidently not experienced in every case, having knowledge over the mechanisms of regression and the mysteries of past-life experience can cause some to understand their biological family as a vessel to the physical realm and part of the process of reincarnation. In Asetians this can lead to a sense of detachment from their parents and relatives bound only by a bond of flesh, particularly after awakening and strongly evidenced among those of the Scorpion Lineage. Through such process of learning it becomes clear to the Asetian mind that a mother or a father are not the seed of their ancient life, and even if such realization may be hard to understand to a human mind, where parents are often revered as if their children owe them for their lives, the path of awareness and insight comes much more naturally to those of the Asetian family. Since most of humanity is tied to the cycles of reincarnation they cannot actively select their parents and incarnating families, or make a more conscious decision about their future lives and among who they might live, leading to natural difficulties in achieving enlightenment in this regard. This is unlike the Asetians, who have a unique insight that without being bound to physical reincarnation makes such a natural process of evolution a personal choice, although not followed by all. As such, this provides them with a level of control over the cycles of rebirth that is exclusively inhuman and easily found reflected in how they approach life and experience death.

The Asetians that incarnate still undergo the experience of physical birth just like every human and the spiritual unawareness that follows, where previous lives are temporarily forgotten as a consequence of the fall into matter. They hold their magickal potential dormant until awakening is triggered, which can manifest as early as childhood, or even more rarely almost instantly after birth, but more commonly as one grows past the teenage years and enters adulthood, in some cases only manifesting much later in life. The time of awakening has no correlation to mastery or inner ability and it should be accepted as the right time in every case. Not being tied to the cycles of reincarnation means that not every Asetian takes physical form, just like others of their kin remain in the Duat for centuries only to embody flesh within this realm at a later era for silent reasons of their own and intimate to the purpose of the Aset Ka.

Such profound understanding of nature and the spiritual insignificance of biology does not imply, in any way, that newly awakened Asetians should intentionally mistreat their families. It only means that they should exercise a sense of justice and use such clarity and awareness towards honorable judgment and balanced action according to their own ideals and those of the path they embrace, treating a biological family as they deserve based on their actions and the respect they earned, not with fear or undeserved feelings towards something that it is not their own — the life of the Asetian. Knowing their true origins, understanding what they entail and accepting the mysteries of inner nature leads every Asetian, and also many Asetianists, to consider the Aset Ka as their real family, the house of their deepest bonds and emotions, nurturing a profound respect, trust and loyalty for every other Asetian. Such connection that survives the mantle of death with a flame that endures throughout lifetimes manifests in this selfless passion and honest loyalty towards the Order of Aset Ka, rising as the eternal temple of the violet children and immortal throne of Aset. This realization can never be defined by words or properly explained to an outsider for it transcends reason and matter, promoting feelings that have no possible comparison to what can be experienced through life alongside a merely biological family or limited by a bondage to the physical. The ethereal song of the Asetian family, intoned where Asetians, Anubians and Asetianists stand together, is a timeless cadence that established them as this unique spiritual family that transcends time and constantly renews itself upon the altar of immortality. Nothing can ever be more important, more powerful or more beautiful than Family.

Tradition

To understand Asetianism is to see what stands above and below, before and behind. It is to place the macrocosm and microcosm on the same layer of manifestation and to transverse the valley of eternal night with a candle made of trust. The first step must always go within or all knowledge is lost upon the deceit of ego. The illumination coming from the wealth found within and the silent wisdom beneath this path must become one and the same.

Asetianism promotes understanding on a raw level, down to every fiber of one's being. In every incarnation an initiate must fight to achieve spiritual realization and unlock further wisdom. This is a slow and constant process of discovery, growth and adaptation; a chaotic dance of opposing forces and newfound battles in a blend of frustration and realization. The inner quest potentiates a dynamic expansion of consciousness, manifested through an initiatory cycle of rebirth. The profound discovery felt upon the liberation of understanding and achieved through the mysteries that must be conquered will empower the initiate with the precious cradle of joy and happiness. Such balance and inner peace is not only achieved through the constant evolution of the mind and the secret equilibrium of chaos under the acceptance of impermanence but also in the realization found from walking this timeless spiritual road. Unspeakable and transcendent emotion awaits behind the veil of the material abyss for those who have felt the sacredness of the divine spark. Asetians have tasted the nectar of immortality. They are beings of pure energy and manifested emotion, empowered with the mystical essence of the Violet Flame. By celebrating life and living it deeply, the pinnacle of Asetianism is found on the love for Aset and by ultimately experiencing it first hand, unconditionally embracing Her and in this way honoring the divinity that hides within.

On the quest for balance that an Asetian undergoes in every single lifetime there is a need to achieve subtle harmony among the three main aspects of manifest existence in this realm: the mind, the body and the spirit. Only a wise symmetry attained amidst these interlaying factors can potentiate the maintenance of a sane and healthy life. However, that is a very hard and unstable condition to achieve, particularly for a vampiric creature owner of a natural process and mindset that constantly promote chaos and change, both children of the forces of imbalance that hold the power of transformation. Instability and stagnation in any of these three areas quickly echo to all other aspects of manifestation no matter how healthy they may be, for we are a union of worlds and not a singular isolated shell of simplicity, explaining why a weakened spirit may promote disease in the very same way as a storm thriving in the mind can rupture body and its biological processes. Everything is interconnected in a complexity of fragile natural synergies so that imbalance, blockage or illness on a focus point carries the potential to harm every other layer of existence. Multilayered stability, self-control, understanding and mastery must be essential disciplines to every Asetian or Asetianist, being amongst the most valuable sets of tools found in this path and an established ambition to its followers.

Every stage of Asetian development is a slow, dangerous and obscure road of inner and outer discovery, unfolding through the elusive mist of many lifetimes, where every single life represents a further evolutionary step in the quest for wisdom and enlightenment found along the eternal cycle of violet rebirth. This quest remains a powerful but not definitive mark on the immortal map of an Asetian soul, embracing a tradition that encompasses a magnitude of things that range to infinity. One of the major pillars enhancing this pursuit is knowledge and that holds fundamental keys to countless doors. Through the power of knowledge and its forthcoming wisdom the initiates unfold their missing realities and the freedom to embrace their own nature, developing inner gifts and abilities that ultimately empower them to a greater potential. Knowledge in its many forms and manifestations is a vital tool in the development of any initiate of our mysteries and its potential should never be underestimated, no matter how much it gets discarded and discredited by the ignorant minds of our time. Spiritual development, higher understanding and inner mastery are slow and enduring processes in the Asetian journey through life. This metaphysical initiation is a system of transmutation. By the pure and profound change it is meant that the initiate achieves to alter in form, manifestation and nature, which is an expression of the powerful force of the Violet Flame. This transmutation, deeply connected with the nature of vampiric rebirth, represents the alchemical essence of the Asetian soul; ever changing and eternal. Through such timeless mystery we can establish the Asetians as the alchemists of the soul — creators and destroyers, catalysts of renewal and evolution with the power to transform lead into gold — for they are givers of life and omens of death, the pillars of subtle existence and owners of the breath of immortality. This transformational gnosis is so profoundly connected with the traditional Ancient Egyptian wisdom and spirituality that even the word alchemy has its roots in the Arabic *al-kimiya* that can be translated as *from Kemet,* literally symbolizing *The Art from Kemet.* So the genuine secrets of alchemy remain a legacy of the ancients, a tome of knowledge and expertise of the Asetians, not to be confused with the distorted alchemy of the Middle Ages that would later give birth to the science of modern chemistry but instead finds its foundations on the Kemetic art of spiritual transformation and magickal development.

While magick and energy manipulation are generally described as metaphysical elements mastered by those initiated into Asetianism, the practice of meditation is not always mentioned. As a universal tool of focus and transcendence, the power of awareness enhanced through meditative techniques should never be underestimated, being a valuable craft for any Asetian or occultist to explore. Through proper usage of such techniques the initiate can learn the foundations that pave the way for more advanced magickal work such as astral travel, energy projection and akashic regression, while meditation alone holds the potential for attaining different states of consciousness and explore practices such as energization, relaxation and contemplation, all precursors to inner balance and basic Shen cleansing. Whether used as holistic medicine, spiritual practice or as an energy manipulation routine, meditation is a valuable tool when applied towards self-discovery and mindfulness, commonly practiced among those of the Asetian tradition alongside the arts of energy and magick.

The Asetians as beings of subtle essence and intense vibration are constantly interacting with energy and altering its properties with their very presence, something that although mastered through proper learning is also experienced to a lesser degree as second nature and manifests, even unconsciously, throughout all their lives. Living in a layered world of energy, surrounded by invisible forces and constantly interacting with them on many levels is something natural and inborn for Asetians, who often remain aware of such interactions and abilities from a young age. This permanent and definitive connection with subtle energy is such a central element in Asetianism that it is often used by outsiders to define the Asetian nature, expressed by the word vampire. As vampires this interaction with energy fuels their abilities and maintains stability on a deeper level by aligning mind, body and spirit. However, to define vampires by their abilities to drain energy and manipulate it would be a misconception, for vampirism is not truly defined by elements of energy or blood but by the nature of the soul.

Asetianism has pioneered the knowledge and understanding of vampirism as a condition of the soul, frequently misunderstood by those who dabble into its culture and tradition without a deeper foundation or proper insight of its origins and secrets, sometimes mistakenly describing vampires as incomplete, broken or even diseased. Such notions could not be more inaccurate and further from the truth, yet to define an Asetian merely as a vampire would also be an exercise of ignorance. To be Asetian holds much greater meaning than vampiric condition and ability, inferring a profound and intricate aspect of spiritual nature, wisdom and immortality. Even though vampirism remains an undeniable layer of Asetian darkness, that alone should not and cannot define their nature and infinite complexity. Such understanding is essential in the exploration of Asetianism and in the study of this culture, along with the very important distinction between fiction and reality. There is a crucial difference between what people may believe vampires to be and what they actually are. To

✝

learn the latter without delusion or deceit the seeker must courageously plunge deeper into the study of Asetian mysteries, accepting wholeheartedly all the inherent dangers that await every soul daring to tread this road into the darkest corners of existence.

Throughout history the Asetians gave birth to a myriad of mythologies and lore, some of which are still studied today. A mature mind must perceive the reasons and origins behind the existence of those concepts, to interpret the subtle symbolism and lost thread of connection so that hidden clues become visible and clear, such as how certain stories found across the ages sometimes are nothing more than the result of fear and imagination united by the human mind when failing to comprehend the essence and truth behind an Asetian vampire.

As an esoteric tradition with a heavy focus on growth, spiritual evolution and psychology, Asetianism is vehemently opposed to a futile cultivation of the ego and its obsessive worship so common amongst unevolved minds. However, the relevance of the ego as a tool of awareness for Self is not denied or ignored but instead understood under a detached light without the influence of vanity. Obviously no Asetian or Asetianist should neglect the pleasure of incarnated life in its many expressions nor should wisdom and spirituality be obstacles to living fully and completely. In fact, Asetianism enforces life and promotes pleasure, because together they are allies to self-development and understanding. If you do not live you cannot know and if you do not practice you can never achieve. An uncontrolled, demanding and self-centered ego can condemn the evolution of anyone, so while its influence should not be ignored a state of unawareness on how it holds the power to diminish you as a unique being and to hinder your growth is a common trigger knocking many into a life of no real worth or higher achievement. Should we deny our tastes, dreams and desires? Never. We should not bow to the expectations of others and hold our character above any note, but once those dreams and goals are driven by others and how they perceive us, then Self is no longer in control and others are. The egocentric constantly give power to others without realizing it, by striving for attention they need others when they should only need Self. Modern society has promoted a mindset driven by ego where people constantly seek the acceptance and validation of others. Such reality has built a culture of slaves where people live based on the expectations of others without a strong personality of their own and individuality. They are no longer unique, sometimes becoming nothing more than a speck within a lost herd.

Spirituality, mysticism and the occult should never be used to fulfill the ego, expectations and futile desires or to prove we are better and more powerful than others. Magick does not serve that purpose and Asetians would never make use of their powerful esoteric abilities for the amusement of others or to make a point, nor will our magick ever be used for demonstration or to prove power. That is utterly against the essence we seek to protect, as well as opposed to personal evolution and the very foundations of magickal principle, not to mention a disrespect for the nature of these mysteries and the Higher Self, making only sense for unstable minds under the slavery of ego that desire attention above mastery. You do not owe magick or validation to anyone and when someone is capable they do not fear criticism for they are absolutely confident in their ability, finding no need in its exhibition, leaving such claims and worries for dabblers and pretenders.

Asetianism has always been unapologetically darkness given form, thought and focus. It is a tradition that involves concepts and studies that remain a taboo even in the most obscure of occult communities and scholarly circles, dwelling on the fearless exploration of the darkest arts and mastery of forgotten wisdom, such as its intricate layers of predatory spirituality, dangerous magick and high-end energy manipulation that Asetian teachings are known to convey. All of those elements have made Asetianism feared and approached with intolerance, often avoided or blatantly discarded, not only because of its apparent evil nature and inhumane practices but also due to misinterpretation and the ignorance of those who are unequipped to understand or not brave enough to intelligently learn from its true power. Despite their vampiric undertones Asetians do not identify with the ideals of evilness or goodness, seeing both concepts as result of social stigma, cultural identity and religious dogma. Vampires are more than an archetype of darkness and their ideologies are not constrained by mundane concepts of good and evil as they see the world beyond such limitations. Holding no correlation with the medieval monstrosity found in the lore of a bloodsucking beast and undead corpse or with the modern fictionalized version of a flying and biting hero, the predatory nature of real vampires manifests through an intricate system of adversarial forces and profound liberation.

The most common contemporary views of vampire mythologies portrayed in fiction and popular culture fuel the recurring loudness, superficiality and ignorance of communities and fans that misunderstand the true nature of vampirism and exhibit themselves in a spectacle that pales in comparison to the profound beauty and charismatic appeal of a living vampire. You are unlikely to find those vampires of fiction and myth projecting their conscious awareness to admire the art of the Taj Mahal in India, exploring every crevice of stone lost on the Great Wall of China, comfortably falling asleep on the granite sarcophagus inside the Great Pyramid of Khufu in Egypt or deeply meditating within the sacred walls of the Temple of Philae surrounded by forgotten symbolism and hieroglyphic magick as the Nile bathes its shores since time immemorial. That lies beyond the realms of fiction but it can surprisingly be found entwined into the fabric of reality.

However, the many layers of Asetianism are not only about Ancient Egypt or the mysteries of elusive vampires. Despite being a long established tradition with a strong and fierce identity of its own, the Asetian teachings promote comparative religious studies and attentive research of different cultures, alongside the exploration of varying branches of knowledge and opposing traditions. The followers of the Asetian path are not chained by dogma nor bound by culture, experiencing the ultimate form of spiritual liberation, awareness and understanding. This is also true because Asetians believe that truth is out there to be found, explored and mastered, while knowledge should not be something preached, forced or manipulated, especially when it comes to spirituality and the discovery of what you are. Through this mindset based on confidence and freedom the cultural development, mystical learning and inner growth of each individual initiate within the path of the Aset Ka is welcoming of other philosophies, traditions and practices, something that is always encouraged to be explored and learned without fear or judgment. With such an open-minded approach Asetianists often attain a considerable amount of knowledge and culture, helping to solidify their understanding of the world, history and humanity, as well as their place within their own path of Aset, while empowering them with the spiritual and intellectual tools that characterize an awakened and learned Asetianist. Beyond being a vital tool of growth knowledge is also a potent weapon and proficient occultists excel in the arts of manipulation, where such cultural advantage can often place them on fruitful and strategic positions out in the real world. Such mastery when allied to the efficient use of energy and experienced wielding of magick can prove knowledge to be a much-feared device, revealing the legacy of the Aset Ka as a force of great danger that simply cannot be controlled.

Magick

What we describe as magick represents a fundamental art at the core of Asetian culture. The essence of this misunderstood science and mysterious subtle art has been studied, developed and established by the Asetians for millennia as the primordial initiators of these secretive practices. They find in magick a living and breathing element of their lives, manifesting the invisible thread that ignites all life and binds it together as the ever-present seed of mysteries. For countless centuries the Asetians have been silent keepers of magickal knowledge and protectors of the secrets of the ancients, safekeeping the old ways and mysteries forgotten in time as immortal initiators with the blessing of life and the transcendence of death.

Nature holds the many keys of magick and life itself is ultimately a unique magickal experience. Magick is empowered by nature and nature is manifested by magick. Asetians acknowledge, treasure and respect the forces of nature, celebrating its dynamic powers of creation and destruction. Seeing it as a precious and delicate balance of forces that should be protected and esteemed, it is difficult for an Asetian mind to comprehend the atrocities that humanity constantly does to this precious gift and planetary home that was entrusted for them to cherish.

This approach to magick as mystical, as it may seem to the uninitiated, is also bound to the serious and analytical mind of science, dwelling into the realm of metaphysics for which the Aset Ka is better known. Having developed a complex system of subtle anatomy and energy theory, Asetian science ties metaphysical knowledge not only to magick and art but also to medical practice, psychology, engineering, chemistry and geology. For example, the study of minerals — nature given form and manifested as matter — by exploring its hidden subtle properties and energy qualities alongside the scientific knowledge of applied mineralogy, is a common practice in this path. Minerals and naturally formed crystals are exceptional magickal tools, not only being capable of amplification and refraction of projected vital energy but also passively emanating a stable energy field that can vary in frequency and vibration according to genesis, composition and characteristics, proving to be a great resource for any occultist seeking to master metaphysics.

It is then easily perceived why Asetians often carry a special mineral magickally connected with their own energy fingerprint; a potent magickal device attuned to elemental forces that can be used as a secretive talisman and sometimes also as a wand, known to instigate both fear and desire in the minds of those who know what it signifies and the power it conceals. Such reality is not modern practice but an element of Asetian cultural identity that endures for countless centuries lingering from the days of their golden Egyptian empire, in a time where minerals were highly valued due to their magickal properties and metaphysical applications but also when science and magick were studied as one and the same. Despite the usage of minerals being common practice among contemporary occultists and seeing a strong resurgence within popular culture, their usability is far from simple and modern approaches often lack depth and mastery, promoting a rudimentary and shallow take on the exploration of mineral magick, resulting in poor and weak esoteric results. While techniques of energy cleansing can be easily learned, to make proper use of a mineral in direct energy manipulation, and by taking

✝

advantage of its highest potential or magickal efficiency, the geological tool requires submission to a procedure of initiation crafted for the specific mineral to be attuned. Most of those techniques include specific elements of initiatory magick that are still kept secret to this day due to their potency and potential danger if misused, sometimes also being considered sacred knowledge. Referenced in the learned circles as Encantatum, the ones who have mastered such an art have been initiated into its higher mysteries, with those secrets passed down directly from the Asetian temples and hence being able to initiate and attune a mineral for active energy work and the demanding requirements of high magick.

Although every mineral is valuable and holds metaphysical qualities there is one that holds a position of prominence among those of the Asetian path: amethyst. Being more than just magickal tools, amethysts are special and carry powers that are bound to the secret code of initiation. This unique variety of quartz composed by tetrahedrons of silicon dioxide and manganese exhibits a distinctive color that unsuspectingly lifts the mantle of nature as a clue to its spiritual ties to the mysteries of the Violet Flame — the essence of Aset. Despite the metaphysical power inherent to this mineral that was known and sought by the ancients, amethysts hold a close connection with the nature of the Asetians, emitting a natural energy field of soothing energy and bonding their essence to the aura of the Asetian that empowers it. This forges a strong energy link, making the amethyst a unique amplifier of specific vibrations that hold correlation with those of the Violet Flame. Through such an occult device, especially when attuned by an Encantatum, an Asetian is capable of projecting an energy beam of extremely high intensity that when mastered may be manipulated into different frequencies and directed under conscious will. This empowered object has several uses, not all of them publicly known, and it is oftentimes considered not only a sacred spiritual tool of great esteem but also a powerful magickal weapon, as so the enemies of the Asetians learned long ago that harming the body is of insignificant consequence when compared to that which can harm the very core of the soul.

Being aware of the potential dangers behind advanced energy work and high magickal practice is a recommended caution from the very early steps of occult study, something that should constantly be bound to a commitment of responsibility. However, acknowledgment of such notions that deal with concealed power and unseen peril should never come as an appeal for magickal mastery and learning, retaining only allure to the unstable and the delusional. Magick, its secretive techniques and empowered tools, albeit potent in the violent arts of subtle warfare and viable instruments of despair, torture and destruction, should always be understood as a path of understanding. Those seeking to abuse such powers only for personal gain and as a tool of conflict are on the road of the ego and nothing but oblivion awaits them. True magick ultimately bows to no one and only the wise and humble may aspire to control such elusive powers not by the means of force but through the call of wisdom and the manifestation of honor. Place the focus on awareness, growth and understanding so that your path may open before you under the silky rain of our mysteries; tread on the forest of disrespect carrying the tools of liars and a dreaded monster shall devour your hope between fiery wings.

Magick is an art that can be expressed through many forms and in many subtle languages, all having their use and being worthy of learned practice. Not only the highest mysteries and the most advanced techniques represent a valid element of study in Asetianism, for there is great power in simplicity and sometimes even the slightest gesture or crafted thought carries the seed to change realities, opening an important doorway of consequence and potential. Your spiritual craft, no matter how simplistic it may appear, should never be diminished but approached with the same level of passion as that of the most intricate magickal practices. Every magick must hold an aspect of sacredness and once that spark is lost it may be brief for it to lose meaning.

The world of dreams is a land of inner mystery but also an interesting layer of psychology, providing a window into the distorted reality of the unconscious mind. This area of the psyche is an important element of occult study, as the many abilities of the mind play a major role in magick, so Asetians have extensively studied the infinite alleys of thought and became masters on the understanding of the mind. Experts in psychology and the secrets of human mentality, Asetians hold great potential in exploiting the mental process of every being, understanding it and anticipating its outcome. This may sometimes be interpreted as an inhuman ability to read people and having the power to deeply know and understand them, however it is not seen as a metaphysical gift but the result of a higher awareness and profound understanding of human psychology. This makes them great at counseling, mediation, support and therapy, although it is uncommon to find Asetians willingly taking those roles outside of their world and in ordinary society.

The analysis of sleep and dream work from an esoteric perspective are well known occult practices that hold ties to magickal studies. Being able to tap into the altered states of consciousness achieved during the different stages of sleep can be a resource of knowledge and interpretation of the mind but also a process of projection into other realities. It can be approached as a technique to aid in the discovery of Self and the profiling of a mindset, or even as a door to higher and lower subtle planes. Through this inner tunnel of the unconscious mind the initiate finds a pond that does not only lead to the intimate reality of the dream realm crafted by thoughts, fears and expectations, but also to a far broader universe that is the astral plane itself. By learning the proper techniques it is possible to plunge deep into the microcosm of our inner realm and through such a door unveil the path for an outer reality within higher planes. Such forms of OBE — out of body experience — represent a process of projection that holds spiritual and metaphysical potential, having been explored for centuries by those familiar with the occult and witchcraft. Through the aligning of the macrocosm with the microcosm an initiate can tap into hidden knowledge, once the deception of the astral is overcome and the trials of the ethereal conquered, gaining a glimpse of what is known as the akashic records and providing an interesting tool to integrate into past-life work and regression techniques. Beware of the mastery required to successfully attain that wisdom as such path drowns you in a sea of illusion before the truth is allowed to be seen.

In the end, beyond all magickal practice and metaphysical work developed along this eternal path, the spirituality of the soul remains the mysterious backbone of all existence. The notion that vampires lack spirituality and distance themselves from divinity is a terrible misconception sometimes found in modern literature and theory, proliferated by a lifestyle subculture that found in the immortal predator an alluring archetype to hide weaknesses and mask the ego but who remains far from ready to understand the intricate spirituality that is experienced by the actual vampires that it desires to emulate. The unrelenting darkness of the vampiric path is entwined with a profound spark of divinity that is unbound from expectation or ego, empowered by confidence, loyalty and devotion at a level that surpasses faith. Such strong spirituality embraced by the Asetians across the centuries stands upon a solid foundation that remains unbroken since the time of the elders; a culture that is not and shall never be accessible to everyone, flourishing and evolving adamantly away from the scope of ordinary minds. That is the path of the Aset Ka, fiercely protected from exploitation, ambition and deceit for countless ages — a legacy that became known as Asetianism. In this abominable silence echoes the whispers of our truth and within those unspeakable secrets charge the banners of our honorable strength.

Asetian Sigil: The Dark Mark

The sacred sigil found on the cover of this book manifests through art and symbol the inscrutable infinity of the Asetian essence. More than just a seal of power, banner of wisdom and icon of immortality, the Asetian Sigil is the mark of Aset — Her breath of life and touch of everlastingness.

The enigmatic symbol is oftentimes known to outsiders simply as the Dark Mark, a term coined by the uninitiated to describe the ancient seal of the Asetian family and heirloom to their secret legacy. A mark that once instigated dread and despair to some while bringing hope and liberation to others. There is no doubt that this is a symbol of great power but most importantly it is an alchemical brand of wisdom concealing boundless layers of meaning that reach beyond that which the human mind can comprehend.

Despite being exclusively Asetian the sigil has been copied, adopted and defaced over the centuries by different cultures, groups and individuals, misrepresented in countless situations through an unconscious display of shallow ignorance. However, such evidence should not be of concern to a learned practitioner as the intricate interpretation and hidden power of the Dark Mark remains perfectly shielded from the uninitiated, making it meaningless when exploited by the wrong hands or unworthy minds.

This timeless symbol is honored by every Asetian of past and present, treasuring it as sacred and understanding the profound nature of its unique energy, while it also became genuinely revered by Asetianists all across the world. Its mysteries and meaning have been the target of quests, speculation and heated debate for many years and it still puzzles most dedicated to its study today. The mindful student of the mysteries knows better than to pay attention to rumor, distancing inner focus from popular belief and false knowledge, constantly seeking for the source where waters run purer.

During the ancient times of the Sep Tepy in Kemet the Asetian elders developed a sacred practice within the higher temples that held the secret to metaphysically tattoo the fabric of the soul, engraving magickal symbols and empowered sigils into the very core of their inner essence. These sacred rituals were crafted from the teachings passed down in initiation from Aset and taught to the Primordial Asetians who continued the tradition with their spiritual kin. Such transcendent transformation with the most profound spiritual alchemy replicated and represented the violet birth of the first-born Asetians under the creational powers of Aset, establishing one of the most intricate and misunderstood of Asetian mysteries, a study that is only attainable through lifetimes of enlightened growth and steady evolution. In the old days the Aset Ka was recognized by this secretive symbol, one created by none other than Aset and imbued with Her intimate magick and vital breath; a holy mark of Her bloodline and legacy of Her people. The elders tattooed it as art and magick on the wrist of their apprentices according to the secret tradition, infusing it with the darkest energy of rebirth and the vital crown of immortality, sealing its essence forever. Through this alchemical ritual not only the soul was engraved on its innermost core but the sigil was also blessed by Aset with Her gift of the Violet Flame, becoming a definitive banner of the Asetians and an always attentive beacon echoing in absolute silence the lost call of their Mother. So they find themselves once again after death, drawn to their eternal family that cannot die.

Such secrets remain protected within the walls of knowledge at the Aset Ka where these practices remain alive and some Asetians still follow the ancient tradition and wield on their wrists the sacred seal of their kin; the abominating mark of darkness and immortal Fire, a flag of divinity and a warning of death. The infamous Asetian Sigil remains a renowned symbol of the bloodline, family and history, having endured the test of time without losing its inscrutable power.

Unlike common symbolism added to the wrist for cosmetic or artistic value the Asetian Sigil is always tattooed facing the Asetian, with the root of the Ankh pointing towards the inner arm — the inner realm of the microcosm — and the Rays of Illumination rising outwards, in a fluid movement towards the hand and then ethereally projected into the outer world. This element of spiritual symbolism is purely vampiric and characteristic of a dark tradition, as the mark is drawn in a way that remains perfectly visible by eyes of the Asetian but appears inverted to others looking upon it. This is a clear echo of Asetian identity where the tattoo is never an object of exhibition or the promotion of power but a silent seal of true nature and eternal allegiance.

The metaphysical mark is unbreakable and eternal, engraved deeply into the soul and mingled with the very essence of the spirit. As the physical body of an Asetian is not immortal but only the soul, upon death so does the physical tattoo decay and perish, having to be redrawn on the flesh in every incarnation if the Asetian so desires. The ritual can only be executed after the awakening and according to secret techniques mastered by the Aset Ka, not to be confused with a standard artistic tattoo or body modification. It is an initiation and rite of passage but it does not define the sigil already engraved on the soul in a previous life; that is eternal and can never be destroyed. Once it exists it will be there forever and it does not require a mirrored physical representation on the skin to retain its meaning and bond.

As a sigil, magickal seal and spiritual flag, the Dark Mark is crafted from ancient symbolism and surrounded with mystery. In a very simplistic analysis the sigil embraces three distinctive layers of meaning, each carrying a unique energy fingerprint: the central Ankh, an Ancient Egyptian hieroglyph and most respected symbol in ancient times only carried by the Gods as a sign of divinity and eternal life, here representing the Asetian gift of immortality; an artistic rendering of the Wings of Aset as a symbol of Asetian genesis and divine lineage through the essence of Aset; and the Rays of Illumination, historically represented at the top of the head of Aset as a crown of wisdom and magick manifested into two rays of energy — the Violet Flame, projecting outwards from the Crown Shen and into the higher realms above the abyss.

The symbols carry other meanings that are only revealed upon initiation and hold keys to important mysteries. Their understanding is both profound and transformational, being studied throughout the whole life of an Asetian or Asetianist daring to lift the lost veil. The Asetian Sigil was crafted to perfection by the beautiful hand of undying love where no spiritual element is there by chance and hiding several layers of deeper mystery within its shell. The very Wings that fly forth from the immortal Ankh are manifested by three distinctive realms, reflecting the triple nature of the Asetians embodied in spirit by the three Lineages of Serpent, Scarab and Scorpion, mirrored in the night by the cosmic light of Orion in the sky.

✝

In the end the elusive Asetian Sigil is a hallmark of Asetianism. Its usage and secretive meanings have become more than an occult element of initiation or an aspect of esoteric tradition but a legend bound to endure until the end of time. The extent of its mysteries remains hidden under the immortal gaze of a soul born before the creation of the world.

Violet Flame

The inscrutable nature of the Violet Flame and its seed of raw divinity can be described in the most simplistic way as the essence of Aset; the aether of amethyst. It embodies the magickal breath emanating from the very soul of Her mighty Queen perpetuated in flesh as the blood of every Asetian. It stands untouched, impregnable and unbroken at the center of the Asetian mysteries while its study unveils one of the most intricate, challenging and elaborated paths of wisdom. As a concept and terminology it is found throughout different cultures and mirrored in entangled definitions, some misunderstood and others apparently meaningless, hidden behind a veil of ignorance and lost culture while its true origins lie carved in sand and stone behind the veil of ancient Kemet at the dawn of Asetianism and in the secrets of the Aset Ka.

Not possible to be taught by words and only understood through feelings, this unique and highly specialized energy is a manifestation of the divine flowing inside every Asetian. It is the prevailing spark among all members of the family, a transcendent bond of unbreakable power. It manifests on spiritual, emotional and physical levels by what can only be portrayed as ultimate oneness; the most intimate communion with Aset.

Sometimes referred to as the Touch of Aset this energy flows within the subtle system of an Asetian at all times during life and beyond death, although its vibration and frequency can vary only to be activated through ethereal touch. Its active flow of empowerment — metaphysically hardwired to the Crown Shen that links to higher dimensions — constantly interacts with every cell and imbues thoughts and emotions, being visible through the violet hues of the Asetian aura as gentle velvety mist. When heightened, empowered and ignited with vibrancy enhanced its force greatly expands and brightens the aura, unveiling a natural energy field that pulsates as it surrounds the body and permeates the surrounding areas, being tied to specific elements found in the subtle anatomy and energetic system of an Asetian.

In terms of magick it can be projected as an intense beam of violet Ka, carrying the gift of life and mystery of death. When approaching such gnosis through the lens of applied metaphysics this energy can be attuned to the burning qualities of Fire or the soothing flow of Water and directed to the empowerment of magickal objects and sacred tools as well as a vital element in the initiation of talismans and wands. The included material on the nature of the Violet Flame shall remain intentionally ambiguous and brief as such study dwells on the secretive realms of initiation and illumination. This knowledge albeit subtle conceals immeasurable power that if misused yields the potential for great destruction. Its surrounding secrecy has been safeguarded for centuries as its seals of purity remain unbroken.

> *"You live according to your Will. You are Wadjet, the Lady of the Flame. Evil will fall on those who set up against you."*
>
> Egyptian Book of the Dead

Dark Flame

The concept of Dark Flame is not comparable to that of the Violet Flame and no parallels should be drawn without meaning, since this flame can be established through a purely metaphysical definition without the initiatory and highly spiritual properties of its violet counterpart. They are not two aspects of the same energetic framework so comparing them in terms of magickal quality or metaphysical characteristics is bound to flawed understanding.

As an induced subtle condition that can be invoked or manifested in conscious or unconscious settings, the Dark Flame is an amorphous type of energy that coats the outer layers of the aura, being naturally activated as a metaphysical reaction to certain situations. On a lower level it can be expressed by heightened states of consciousness, mood swings and through bursts of courage, anger or ecstasy. Its concentration and release by the subtle body can be triggered as a natural process developing from different reactions to mundane situations such as confrontations, higher tension levels and more frequently when dealing with the perception of injustice, or it can also be intentionally invoked in a synthetic way through ritualistic processes and metaphysical techniques. In some cases its unconscious flow and activation is bound to a failsafe reaction to contexts of danger and extreme conditions, being related to the psychological mechanisms of self-preservation. The intense current of the Dark Flame should only remain active for short periods of time while it is fueled by streams of highly charged energy with specific vibratory qualities, quickly exhausting entire reservoirs from the internal energy system if done without control.

As such, it is a process that should be important to develop and understand, not only as a metaphysical tool but also as a device of inner balance. In the early steps of awareness some may find that the proper use of certain esoteric tools such as ritual, music, incense, writing, drawing and even blood can enhance the process and help achieve the altered state of focus where the Dark Flame manifests. Such tools should be understood as nothing more than focusing devices under will as they do not have the power to influence the energy of the Dark Flame, working on an unconscious — or conscious under mastery — level of the mind by tweaking it into the induced state required to ignite this energy. Feelings can also prove to be powerful triggers in accessing this flame, particularly the most charged and unbalanced ones such as rage and hate that can easily fuel it, however tapping into such dark roads of inner alchemy can be challenging and it requires a great deal of control and knowledge of Self. Everyone without exception has a darker side and those denying it simply lack the wisdom to perceive it, indulging in denial and a deluded sense of goodness. We are beings of duality and mastery comes from wielding the sword of darkness alongside the candle of light for only when united they can shape the course of your inner history.

Despite the violent undertones of the Dark Flame and its aggressive nature, the underlying power found in this energy can also be used for more positive ends and in nobler quests. Not only rage can fuel the hungry forces of the Dark Flame and it can be easily understood that if hate empowers it so efficiently so can the manifestation of love. In this way Asetians are able to center such profound emotions and direct them towards the achievement of great things, being capable of the most unimaginable actions while empowered by the strength of the Dark Flame, facing even the most dangerous of situations. This inner strength reflected in thought, attitude and fierce reaction when allied to committed ideals makes Asetians creatures often condemned in the eyes of mortals, especially among those unaware of their vampiric nature. Yet Asetians have always been relentlessly and proudly driven by the flaming forces of pure love, raw emotion and undying loyalty... all aspects profoundly rooted within their personality and highly prized in this lost culture.

Caution, responsible learning and patient mastery are advised when exploring the potential of the Dark Flame as its energetic surges hide the possibility for devastating force and unmatched consequence. Its dark nature finds a warmer cradle in imbalance and destruction, making its beneficial usage a challenge even for a learned occultist. The pace at which its activation burns energy can be unexpected and, as such, it raises an obvious handicap to vampires that as beings of energy rely on their subtle abilities and inner force to manifest their strength and manage balance. Mastering the stasis of different energy levels within the subtle system is out of the scope of studying the Dark Flame but it represents an important discipline to those exploring the vampire arts and dwelling into the dark threshold of our magick.

Predatory Spirituality

Dwelling into the study of magick and occult science, the Asetians emerge as founders of predatory spirituality and its metaphysical processes, having crafted, developed and established the original system that defined predatory spiritualism and magick standing at the center of the very foundations of the dark arts and a tradition that became known by contemporary mystery schools as the left hand path.

When elaborating on the advanced metaphysical senses and unparalleled magickal power that is inborn to Asetians they can reluctantly be described as apex predators, bearing the cunning and resolve to hunt and overpower, a concept that is strikingly reflected on their unique mentality, inner dynamics and subtle abilities that place them alongside Sethians at the very top of the magickal chain. Being prey to no one the Asetians are creatures of stealth and enlightened wisdom, lurking in the dark and mastering the shadows, shifting and adapting to new realities as the world ages and memories become history, always hunting in silence with one thousand eyes that never sleep and carrying the hidden poison of the centuries.

Standing as the ultimate spiritual predators does not imply that they are liberated from outside dangers, envy and hatred as there are those who seek to attack, deface and destroy the ancient bloodline, having marked their presence since the old times in Egypt to the modern ages of today. As resourceful as the enemies of the Aset Ka may have become they pale in comparison to true predators, for those who seek to steal power, defraud knowledge and plunder magick are nothing more than mere parasites unworthy of the focus of their desire. A predator is not defined by hunger for power as such is a deluded quest of fools, finding only true essence upon the liberation of what lies in the innermost nature and manifested through the higher perception and acute awareness of innate abilities. Dipped in the blood of pain and victory these forces of nature do not bow to illusions of grandeur or the vanity of exhibition, finding supremacy not in the praise of others but in the silent accomplishments of the soul.

Asetian predators are the frozen breath of the wild and the song of an elder hawk; they became the flow of Her river on a desolated desert for the eager and burning soul. With wings spanning wide as dragons and fire bursting in threads of silver, these predators conquer the jungle of life as incarnated shadows of life and death. Alchemists of the unseen they tame the world to their silent call and master the forces deep within, celebrating nature and their kin in a spectacle of communion as they feast on blood and skin.

✝

Finding valuable tools both in the elusive knowledge of occult arts and the arrogance of modern science, the Asetians established a relationship of cautious growth developed through symbiotic learning and exploration that has enhanced the evolution of all. Traditional science has much to learn from the mysteries buried deep within its older sibling known as the occult, which conceals pieces of the universal maze that still puzzle every scientist of our time, while magick can also benefit from the efficiency, focus and rationality of modern scientific processes and academic knowledge. If united under a common purpose guided by honesty and without fear they can establish a pillar of wisdom in a world that is found plagued by false information, pretentious teachings, delusions of ego and the inaccuracy of both commercial and popular magick. That is the stance held and taught by the Aset Ka where science meets magick, philosophy finds spirituality without the influence of religious dogma as the mysteries of alchemy and initiation are not dismissed on the face of scholarly wisdom, where subtle healing and holistic health are aligned with medicine, while scientists and occultists work together without the closed mind of judgment as one and the same.

The desire to control knowledge and withhold evolution alongside the vanity that hides behind title and recognition stands at the root of the fall between science and magick, being also a seed in the recurring discredit and disrespect for occult wisdom among the ignorant posing as wise; a mirror of the fear and insecurity that still rot in the heart of humanity. Asetian predators are eternal warriors of energy and spirit, discarding no knowledge, heeding no criticism and smiling to no praise but constantly embracing evolution beneath their silent gaze. They are occultist, scientist and artist, embracing the alleys of learning in every form and any realm with an undying passion that turns obstacles and limitations into mere concepts that they burn with cursed Fire.

The Wheel

In Asetianism the terminology and symbolism of the wheel refers to the concept of time in its fundamental machinery of cosmic resonance, manifested in reality through the alchemical process of reincarnation. As it rotates seasons come to pass, power shifts, ages become history and the reality that we are now allowed to perceive, study and document becomes perpetually bound to the silent movement of the invisible wheel.

This cycle is perpetuated by subtle threads that entwine into the ethereal fabric that defines the universe, making it undeniably real but also dangerously illusory. As a spiritual framework the wheel is bound to the manifest reality of matter, encased in the existence defined by life in physical shell although dependent from the timeless signal beaming from the opposing plane of death — the immeasurable land of the Duat. Time is a universal variable that only operates linearly within the confinement of the physical realm and, as such, it is a measurement of the living, bearing no hold over the dead who exist only beyond the perpetual manifestation of now; a negative mirror of the absolute moment. However, the cycle of reincarnation as a mighty contraption of vitality and transformation bends both realities and touches two worlds, transcending the realm of spirit and falling into the decay of matter as a singularity of time — the moment — given conceptual shape. That is rebirth in its endless form as a living ouroboros...

The wheel is marked by seasons, eras and aeons that change in scope and dimension according to the lens that constricts its realization. History is written to the silent tune of what the Asetians describe as Djehutys — spiritual formulae invisible to the unaware but pivotal to their very existence — but smaller rhythms establish the vehicle of reality that colors the pages of life such as the seasonal cycles raised by nature and the astronomical events marked by the cosmos.

This apparently simplistic but pragmatically intricate concept that is both spiritual and alchemical can be found mirrored on the esoteric tradition of Tarot, blatantly exposed on the major arcanum with the number ten commonly titled The Wheel of Fortune and echoed more cryptically on the major arcanum thirteen known as Death. Although the symbolism and its relevance to initiation goes further back in history, it is documented in medieval manuscripts and reflected in elements of archaic religious architecture throughout Europe, conveying the importance of understanding impermanence as the always-renewing flower of transformation that defines history and establishes fate. It is the invisible science of becoming.

To study the wheel one must become a scholar of history and committed student of arcane renewal, documenting life and investigating death; it means to understand the past and unveil the future, wielding the mysterious tools of magick, energy and craft that are seeded as valuable gifts by the arts of the Asetians.

> *"We are not the engine, nor are we the wheel.*
> *We are the ones that choose its direction."*
> Liber Aeternus I.6

Reincarnation

The lessons, experiences and reality of previous lives are fundamental aspects of the Asetian tradition and a recurring element of Asetian culture past and present. Remembrance of past lives is a valuable tool but it can also be a deceiving path if treaded without awareness and enlightened guidance. Regression manifests in different forms, from willing hypnotic and energy-induced regressive techniques to spontaneous visions brought forward through an established link in deep meditation, intuitive past-life exploration and more advanced mechanisms of access to forbidden ethereal records. The information attained from these practices alone is far from definitive and should not be taken as an accurate representation of historical fact, requiring deeper analysis and validation by other techniques and through established sources before being accepted. It is a long and complex process that requires a great deal of balance and a complete separation of the ego in order to achieve credible results and it should not be practiced or at least taken for granted without experience and proper knowledge.

From simple fragments of previous life experiences to fully fledged states of regression, knowledge of the past invariably implies an established link to the akashic records and access to its subtle echoes in some format, which can be limited and unconscious or part of an evolved spiritual achievement. The akashic records are a spiritual framework where detailed information of all life is stored. Established in an ethereal plane that is unbound of physical influence and distant from the reality of matter, there is no interference of space and time so every moment exists in its own instance of manifested energy, which can be tapped and sensed for a wealth of revelations concerning the thread that defines your soul; where you came from and where you are headed.

To access these records is no simple task or a safe quest, requiring the evolved predisposition not only to interpret its cryptic messages of light and shadow but also possessing the elusive keys that grant access to the akashic realms and their cosmic mysteries. Such knowledge is not set in stone and it can manifest in the most unexpected ways, as some have spent decades in such pursuit and the committed development of their own techniques before reaching viable results while others had unleashed spontaneous visions of their past during the early stages of life. For the vast majority of people to access truthful information of previous lives is not possible without hard work on spiritual growth and the appropriate techniques. If we look at the grand machinery of the universe this is true by design as life is an expression of potential learning, being a school of inner growth and subtle development, so knowledge of previous failures, successes and experiences can be a hindrance to current lessons in this life and a handicap for those lacking a higher perception. The spiritual amnesia induced through the process of birth and reincarnation into this reality is a tool of abstraction that allows for complete freedom and an effective trial of learning.

Understanding reincarnation and the multilayered reality of previous lives should provide the adept with profound knowledge and a device of enlightened comprehension. In modern times there has been a clear diminishing of the higher magickal practices and a shallow simplification of occult science, leading people to believe that magick and spiritual work are driven from popular culture and lore where a mystical weaving of the hand can provide them with answers. Such people and those notions stand at a complete opposite to the stance of the Aset Ka and Asetianism as tradition, culture and legacy, where our magick is only found through the loyal commitment of the soul and the dangerous alleys of advanced study. As another field of magick and the occult, regression is particularly dangerous as it can be easily misinterpreted, especially by those being guided by ego or attached to expectation. The potential for illusion is great and it is very common for people to make wrong assumptions about their previous lives based on ignorance or the lack of proper tools of self-knowledge, inner exploration and interpretation. The ego is a strong obstacle to evolution and truth, one that must be broken and not fed with deluded desires and pretentious falsehoods, which is why it is often simple to analyse those providing fictitious answers and wild claims that hold no merit.

Every element of the past carries a seed with the potential to affect the present and influence the future. This manifests on many levels, from unexplained emotions and attachment to specific locations or eras to the underlying triggers behind some of the most intricate fears, hopes and desires. Those influences from a previous experience in a past life can liberate knowledge and enhance your awareness, often triggering different emotions and actions in this life. On an unconscious level there are situations, people, symbolism, sets of knowledge and practices that bring forward a sense of familiarity and lost bonds that may be identified as recognition. This is more common after the awakening when initiates take conscious control over their life and identity, fully accepting the different layers of inner nature and attaining a mindset and lifestyle that subtly — or sometimes more harshly — reflect on the ancient decisions, interests, passions and achievements of a different incarnation. However, this does not imply that every mental aspect of your current reality and every decision taken upon instinct should be tied to a past-life experience as that is just not accurate and to extrapolate such broad conclusions would be absurd.

†

Influences of the past are more pronounced in the life of an Asetian who is bound to experience them more intensely. Having a thinner connection with the physical reality and realm of matter alongside a much stronger communion with energy and the subtle forces, the innate Asetian link to the akashic records is often less hindered by interference providing a purer gateway and a greater potential for past-life remembrance. Every awakened Asetian with the proper magickal tools has the potential to reach a better understanding of previous lives, sometimes being able to regain lost knowledge, craft and mastery of the past at a level that can challenge the most skeptic of minds, but not all seek such practices or attain that branch of wisdom in every life.

> *"Birth is not a beginning; death is not an end. There is existence without limitation; there is continuity without a starting point. Existence without limitation is space. Continuity without a starting point is time."*
>
> Chuang Tzu

The degree of relevance and dormant potential of past-life work to ancient souls like the Asetians is not hard to comprehend. While much information is accessible nowadays within the Order of Aset Ka from internal texts, archives and teachings or through contact with an awakened Asetian master, the strict processes of validation for new material, discoveries and developments must undergo advanced regression-based techniques, a standard procedure and effective approach when it comes to test, foolproof and ultimately accept obscure details of past history, magick and theory.

Among the different techniques of regression and advanced past-life work developed by the Aset Ka one has become notorious for its accuracy and capabilities, being used in the most delicate and important investigations within the Order as a set of verifiable techniques that we call Triangulation. Involving the magickal and regressive results from Asetian elders of different Lineage this practice has proven to be one of the most precise tools in the validation of ancient knowledge and forgotten truths, also providing a great level of error correction. As some see it as a weapon and strategic advantage, especially those eager for control and the ones who understand that knowledge itself is a powerful tool, the underlying principles of Triangulation are not public and remain bound to secrecy only to be used internally by the initiated.

Many fear the past... wishing to erase, conceal or run away from it, but I say that courage is also about acceptance. The past is what we are and you are here today just because of it. It sums up every experience and emotion ever lived, each piece of knowledge that was learned and the pain of every fall. Each step is a lesson and everything that you represent is condensed in a single page that is your existence manifested through what you have lived. In this way the past defines reality in every form, not only this life but also every one before it. To an enlightened mind remembrance can even be irrelevant as the knowledge is always there and it cannot be destroyed. Once that becomes understood and assimilated beneath the veil of time and the blindness of rebirth the colors of reality become crystal clear. We lived and so we learned.

Immortality

The veil of immortality is entwined with the violet fabric of soul and spirit that is found at the core of the Asetian spiritual paradigm. It postulates an alchemical edification that transcends perception and may be difficult to grasp by the uninitiated or misinterpreted by those under the slavery of dogma from religion but it represents a primordial truth for the enlightened Asetian mind.

To unveil, explore and understand their own immortality is a process of spiritual growth that Asetians undergo through the different stages of awakening and further development. This is not something accepted out of faith or blind belief but a realization driven from the profound expression of boundless understanding without the chaotic influence of doubt. As such and as with many other elements of Asetian wisdom this mature level of understanding manifests without expectation, being completely free of outside opinion and judgment that is perceived as irrelevant. At this level the judgmental acts of others hold no power for they merely reinstate confidence in the initiate, often raising frustration among unaware opposers.

Our concept of immortality does not present a tangible foundation that can be understood without a rational focus on spirituality. Putting aside the embellishments of fiction and myth, the immortality of the Asetian kin is not of their body but tied to the eternity of their soul; the essence within their Ba that can never age or fade away. Every Asetian is immortal and that is immutable but such fact is bound to spiritual nature and not to the biology of their body for anyone can be killed on a physical plane but not every spirit is eternal. The physical body of a vampire does not live forever as it will grow, age, weaken, decay and perish, just like everyone else. It is the soul that lives forever, retaining energy, experience and memory as centuries fall and history is written, returning to physical form inside a young body through the process of reincarnation, adopting a new shell of matter as yet another mortal vessel apparently indistinguishable from those of human kin. This very aspect of their mysterious existence makes Asetians spiritually inhuman as their souls are undeniably distinctive and unique without traces of human nature, even if the physicality of their bodies may appear the same.

The immortal soul of an Asetian is different from the soul of humans and the essence at the heart of humanity, not only in spiritual manifestation but also metaphysical characteristics, from the subtle body and Shen centers to the unique way it interacts with energy and the higher realms. This spiritual paradox found in the impossibility for the Asetian soul to undergo the natural stages of spiritual decay that humans experience throughout recurrent incarnations and its absence from the universal life cycle of energy may condition the unawakened mind in how it consciously accepts physical aging. For a being of absolute energy that is bound to eternal youth the notion of permanent death and the slow decay experienced in this realm of matter through the natural process of growth can be confusing, observing the physical vessel that we call body failing and losing its abilities while the soul continues to evolve and develop with the wisdom of the ages and unbounded potential that is hindered by flesh. Then death becomes liberation and the missing spark to find the limitless experience of Asetian nature once again. In that sense humans can normally deal better with the process of physical aging when compared to vampires as for them it is unconsciously a natural progression of life, not only in physical terms but also tied the nature of their own evolution while connected to the human spiritual form of existence. Such conflicted relationship with the nature of materialistic aging and decay is only experienced through the unaware attachments pierced by physical reality since age is nothing more than a very convincing illusion, especially for an Asetian gifted with insight into the endless fabric of eternity.

Just like the mythical phoenix that perpetually returns to life from ruin after bursting into flames and finding rebirth in the ashes,

Asetians are the embodiment of said principles as the alchemists of death and masters of rebirth, silently wielding the sword of immortality until the end of times. In fact the cultural lore of the phoenix from Greek mythology and its solar aspects find origin and inspiration in the Bennu bird [2] from Ancient Egypt that held a symbolical meaning of spiritual rebirth and reincarnation, remaining one of the many cultural legacies of Asetian symbolism lost in history and scattered throughout different civilizations.

The Asetian views and teachings on immortality are so deeply rooted in their magick and initiatory secrets that the essence of eternal life and immortal rebirth are echoed in two sacred pillars: the Ankh and Khepri, eternal life and spiritual transformation. That said, it should also be stated that sacred pillars cannot be interpreted through the devices of simplicity and in literal form so despite the granted implications its symbols express more than an idea but a stream of metaphysical and spiritual wisdom that can only be liberated by conquering their secrets and entering those elusive halls of power. The seven pillars of the Asetian tradition are imbued with the knowledge of the ancients and hold the keys to the mysteries of the universe, representing a profoundly intricate system that takes years, decades and even lifetimes to unveil.

Khenmet: The Dark Kiss
The touch of Aset is the cosmic matter of legends, interlaced on the subtle threads of amethyst that breathe Asetian life into existence. Khenmet embodies this dark kiss of immortal transcendence — it is initiation and alchemical transformation in highest form, the magickal expression of divinity reborn and invisible blessing of purity. A call of loyalty and unbreakable seal of eternal fate.

The spiritual terminology described as the dark kiss was created in reference to a manifestation of the essence of Aset in incarnated form, or in other words the becoming of life for an Asetian. It represents the alchemical spark and cosmic moment when Asetian essence is imbued with the breath of life and ignited into soul and spirit according to the old tradition. The elders called it Khenmet, an Ancient Egyptian word that literally meant kiss, established from Asetian scripture and teachings on the Breath of Aset and its unspeakable Flame of creation that manifested the secrets of immortal life. In Asetianism it is revered as a sacred word of infinite meaning and the purest eminence.

Both historically and mythologically the original Khenmet may be interpreted as the timeless moment when Aset conceived Her three children and empowered them with Her divine Ka; the coming into being of the Primordials. Its mysteries are found at the violet roots of the Asetian tree of genesis and in the seeds behind its fruits — the Asetians. Through those secrets and their transcendence the bloodline of the Gods was established and an Asetian flag would forever fly across the silent skies of our world.

The spiritual manifestation of the Asetian family and its flourishing from the inception of the three Primordials are intimately tied to the mysteries of Khenmet, a subject only approached in study by the most gifted and committed scholars of Asetianism. Further knowledge on this sacred alchemy will not be revealed within this tome nor in any other literary works of past, present and future, remaining amongst the finest safeguarded secrets of the Aset Ka and bound to dangerous magickal wisdom sought by legions since the ancient times. Taught only to the elders through initiation and a strict oath of secrecy, the desperate and illegitimate quests for such

✝

knowledge have raged wars and crushed empires, remaining lost to the world and hidden among those entrusted with its safekeeping.

Such degree of committed secrecy holds a noble call of protection and safety at heart, ensuring the purity of the Asetian teachings and never implying a hierarchy or status in any form as that is an expression of ego found in the realm of men and not a reality of those illuminated by the Asetian path and gnosis.

An orgasm of divinity at the cosmic birth of immortal kin, when death bows down to life and the Violet Flame ignites from within. That is the nature of Khenmet and it ultimately represents an initiation of death for the higher manifestation of life. It is the legendary Breath of Aset in a creational act of becoming — Ankh, Khepri and Tiet fused as one.

Heka and Serkem

In the Ancient Egyptian culture Heka was the personification of magick, an important concept in the primordial mystical tradition that later became the actual word for magick in the lost language of Kemet. Heka is timeless and has existed since the beginning of time, crafting reality and manifesting existence before duality came into being as it is described in the spells of the *Coffin Texts*, the funerary writings that later originated the *Book of the Dead*.

By examining and breaking the word Heka one finds an important symbol and hieroglyph: the Ka, metaphysical personification of energy and another Egyptian word, this one meaning *essence* or *life force*. This conveys the meaning that the manifestation of magick is through its essence, the subtle energy that feeds the Ba — our rising soul. In modern times the word is found in astronomy representing a star in the constellation of Orion known by the scientific name

Lambda Orionis, with etymological roots in the Arabic *Al Hakah*.[3] The connections between Orion and magick are immense and bound to ancient legacy, where the principles of their foundation are intricate enough for an entire book of its own, being detailed in the teachings presented within the journey through the *Book of Orion* — *Liber Aeternus*,[4] a primer on Orion magick and the spirituality of rebirth.

In the tradition of the elders Heka is the magick of words; the spark of initiation and flame of manifestation. It is power that does not bow and a force that bends only to mastery without the limitation of ego. The incredible power of words is magick in one of its purest forms. This raw and primal aspect of Heka makes it important to understand that Asetian magick, like every serious system of metaphysics, is a tool used for the development of Self and in the evolving path of spirituality, not a device of futility or selfish gain. The high magick that is a recurring signature of traditional Asetianism must never be confused with the popular methods of low magick or what is perceived today as commercial occultism. It carries the lost seed on the true origins of witchcraft as a forgotten tradition so frequently misunderstood and entirely different from its modern simplistic descriptions and primitive practices.

> *"Heka was made for them, to use as a weapon for warding off occurrences. And they created dreams for the night, to see the things of the day."*
>
> Egyptian Papyrus

Describing Heka as the power of words raises confusion in the minds of the uninitiated. Saying the exact word, doing the proper gesture and inducing the ideal thought at the right time during the perfect cosmic moment is in fact a powerful expression of magickal

✝

practice. However, this concept must not be limited by the perception of words as mere devices of communication and rulesets of established language. At the time of the Asetian empire in Egypt the Asetians used the Kemetic language as the main tool of interaction just like the rest of their people, developing a secretive dialect that was not crafted for active communication but to be used in advanced magickal practice and spiritual interaction with unnamed forces. This sacred language is known as Serkem and it was kept hidden within the ancient temples and interpreted only through initiation and by the manifestation of magick. Constructed through the ethereal grasp of universal powers and subtle forces of the unseen it embodies words of power that presented the actual magick of words — the ancient Heka.

Serkem survived the test of time and it is still used in magickal practice today within the Order of Aset Ka where its mysteries are studied and preserved. Interpreted only upon the dawn of unveiling the higher mysteries, it is particularly cherished by Asetians of the Serpent Lineage who are fluent in its cryptic meanings, empowering their magickal arts with this long forgotten language of their beloved empire. Misunderstood by the common people Serkem was feared in the old days by those aware of its existence, especially outsiders to the culture and realm who coined the term Black Speech in reference to its usage. This expression has roots in the name of Egypt itself, once known as Kemet meaning *black land,* so this elusive speech they could not understand and that was capable of stirring such profound emotions was also a black language in their unaware minds — it was the voice of elder scorpions.

The ancient etymology of the word Serkem is easy to uncover and holds clues to its past implications and the cause of such an elaborate fear. It is formed by the syncretism of two distinctive Egyptian words: *Serket* and *Kem,* meaning *scorpion* and *black* respectively. *Serk* is the broken form of the word *Serket* that besides holding the literal meaning for *scorpion* was also the name of an important entity in Asetian theology known to embody the representation of the Seven Scorpion daemons of Aset. These terrifying forces of the ancient world tamed only by the magick of Aset were bound to the words of Serkem, which represented their native language of power, an added reason behind the danger and fear associated with its use.

> *"The blood of Aset. The spells of Aset. The magical powers of Aset. Shall make this great one strong and shall be an amulet of protection that would do to him the things which he abominates."*
>
> Egyptian Book of the Dead

Asetian magick is not an echo of forgotten practices nor merely driven from a culture of ritual but the personification of nature and a profound understanding of the machinery of the universe. Having endured wise, strong and unbroken throughout the centuries its development has not stalled, incorporating different cultures and newly discovered knowledge, giving birth to other techniques and staying in constant motion and adaptation while retaining the fundamental aspects from its inception. Never straying from its characteristic embrace of high magick and secretive initiations, this culture remains untouched by the grasp of popular occultism as a tradition proud of its solid roots, being approachable only to select few that honor its essence. Asetianism is celebrated within the private circles of close communities dedicated to the honest study of occult mysteries, being often inaccessible to those who lack the commitment

✝

to hard work, the awareness for other layers of understanding or a determined focus on evolution.

> *"Albeit misunderstood by the less aware, my path has been through the embracing of the inspirational science, magick and art of Words. The power of words, not only through the means of language but also manifested by the realm of symbol and sigil, has been a personal form of magick and spirituality that I have embraced for many years, as well as developed and explored into the deepest dungeons of thought. With its roots in the forgotten culture of Ancient Egypt, where it was known as Heka and made legendary by the scholars, priests and pharaohs; we call it the Art of the Ancients, or the Touch of the Elders, and you may have seen and felt glimpses of its flame through my literary works. As surprisingly as it may appear at first glance, without words the human being is not capable of conscious thought. The mind and body have the ability to feel, but without language, there is no intellectual thought. Feelings are manifested energy, so they exist in the realm of purity, in the land of subtlety. Thoughts are words embedded with meaning, so they exist in the realm of magick. I hope that through my work the students of the occult, spirituality and the mysteries may come to respect and value what we consider to be one of the oldest and most powerful forms of art, magick and wisdom."*

Book of Orion, Liber Aeternus

Duality

The universe holds in the principles of duality an elementary mechanism that is present in all creation. From action to inaction, every force physical or subtle is under the influence of this dualism. Such notion is better understood under the light of contemporary science but it is also a fundamental aspect of metaphysics and magickal practice.

Not without spiritual significance, duality has been ever present in Asetianism under the understanding that every manifestation is composed by a double side, each of an opposing but complementary nature and attracted by one another. Not exclusive to the Asetian teachings these realizations have been largely adopted by well established traditions of past and present, such as the concept of Yin and Yang found in most branches of classical Chinese science and essential to the philosophy of Taoism and the practice of traditional Chinese medicine.

These two forces that form the edification of oneness in everything are present in every aspect of nature and manifested existence, making it complete. That is validated by metaphysics and its scientific observance but it is also found in philosophy and spirituality tied to the very notion of deity. An entity or principle described as God or Goddess can never be completely good or evil as ignorantly portrayed in Christian theology, nor is divine nature established in black or white. By definition that would make divinity utterly incomplete. The infinite and faceless manifestations of the divine are also elements of duality, holding the gentle and protective powers of kindness but also fiercely wielding the agonizing effects of devastation. Deity is not a benevolent personification of goodness as such is nothing but a modern delusion raised by dogma. If that was true and this religious view of a compassionate God that is omniscient and all

✝

powerful was correct, the world would not be so filled with ruthless suffering, injustice and meaningless pain, since not every destructive reality is created by the hand of humanity as much of it is also recurrently caused by the forces of nature and the very act of living.

The principles of duality open a window of understanding towards the nature of divinity that allows for the comprehension that Gods and Goddesses, being dual and not incomplete, carry within themselves the gifts of light and the forces of darkness. They manifest through healing and enlightenment but also by pain and suffering as their reality is the essence of nature. In the natural world this same duality is easily observed and better understood, as you may gaze upon a magnificent and revitalizing sunset in its unique cosmic art, feasting on plant or animal that Earth can provide and only but a few moments later be torn apart by an overpowering earthquake gifted by this same Earth and its natural power. You may observe the miracle of creation as life sprouts in human form, animal and plant, while not losing sight of every child screaming of pain and dying of famine. Duality is everywhere if you open the eyes and see.

In terms of spirituality the acceptance of light and darkness as the unified path for completeness and evolved enlightenment stands as a fundamental aspect of the Asetian tradition, promoting the understanding that only through the communion of duality can your true nature be revealed. The acknowledgment that every living being has not only a kind side of goodness but also a face of untamed evil is essential for the balanced individual and a wiser mind. Someone that only promotes light, peace and harmony, claiming to never experience anger or hatred and holding no harmful feelings, is someone that is unquestionably incomplete. That is true because such a person would not only be in delusion but also in denial of Self. It is a mental process of blockage and the result of their inability to foster acceptance, often conditioned by dogma, expectations and social stigma that by limiting awareness of Self one ends up exhibiting a profound lack of knowledge over character and identity. By repressing impulses, urges, thoughts and feelings an individual is only silently raising inner frustration and promoting the expression of something fabricated, resulting in an ultimately intolerant, unbalanced and incomplete personality under the disguise of pretending light and deluded goodness. The same applies to someone that only promotes violence, anger, vengeance and drama, without embracing the gentler faces of hidden nature. Duality is about equilibrium and the recurrent rebalancing of constantly opposing forces; an essential aspect of evolution. This balance of powers and its transcendent symmetry is the manifestation of Maat and reveals the profound beauty of her mysteries.

Imbalances between different layers of the opposing forces that manifest on every conceivable level are a common cause of disease, depression and disorder. Such influence is felt by everyone and found everywhere in nature, from a thunder storm caused by the shock of electrically charged regions of clouds to an avalanche triggered by the unstable volumes of snow or the geological science behind an exploding volcano. Balance and reaction to imbalance are the keys that set in motion every mechanism from physical to subtle.

These powers are not an expression of darkness versus light but encompass the countless forces at work in every occurrence. Back and forward, up and down, hot and cold, love and hate, positive and negative, male and female...

As with most details of our tradition we are known to unite mysticism and science — physics with metaphysics, chemistry with alchemy, psychology with spirituality — so granted that Asetianism does not explain an avalanche through an esoteric power or moved by an aware spiritual force, as those are natural events that are easy to understand on the light of scientific knowledge while they all reflect upon the universal nature of duality. A volcanic eruption finds its engine on the imbalance between the uplifting magma and the mechanical resistance of the bedrock preventing its uplift and expansion from the crust of our planet, on the verge of collapse from this weak dance of opposing forces at the whim of heat generated by the convection cells found in the upper mantle. The same is true for an earthquake, tornado or a tsunami; they are the result of naturally occurring imbalances from distinctive and contextually opposed forces that culminate in the intrinsic reaction of an attempt to regain balance and restore stabilization.

> *"For every action there is an equal and opposite reaction."*
>
> Isaac Newton

Duality manifests not only in nature and on the outer reality of the macrocosm but is also reflected within the internal microcosm of the initiate. Every living being exists in a constant struggle to regain balance over the unbalanceable. It is a permanent fight for control over instability from minor to major, as body and mind are filled with opposed forces, questions and frustrations that call for equilibrium. Absolute and complete balance is not possible while in this incarnated realm nor should that be a wise quest. Striving for awareness is vital while acknowledging opposing forces and accepting their dualism through a constant process that aims to fine-tune them under a healthier interaction between mind, body and spirit working as one single organism in permanent change and interconnection.

The dual nature of the Asetians becomes blatantly clear in the study of our culture, not from the echoes in every single line or concept but by grasping at the bigger picture behind this violet legacy. Asetians manifest the communion of darkness and light, love and vengeance, creation and destruction, life and death — they are beings of silence and darkness but their inner light can ignite the darkest of caves with the brilliance of wisdom. Being feared for the mastery of abominating powers and the confidence to wield them, Asetians are also capable of the most honorable, tender and loving acts imaginable. Only when seeing through the veil of those mysteries and realizing that this undeniable predatory nature can better sing alongside their marvelous gift of healing may Asetians truly uncover the full extent of the extraordinary powers lying dormant within their very soul.

Every obstacle to personal success, just like every challenge to inner progress and resistance to personal growth, represents the tides and echoes of the path of evolution. Maneuvering through these storms, overcoming pain and grief as lessons and crushing all obstacles is the way of the warrior and that is our chosen road. Rarely are the simpler and most desired paths revealed to be the wisest for not even the Gods can see all ends.

Darkness

Contemporary understanding and popular culture portray ancient traditions through a defective lens filtered by the inclusion of modern beliefs, views and mindsets, alongside the sometimes erroneous assumptions of past historians who lacked the adequate analytical tools or could not differentiate their judgment from religious stigma and cultural background.

The Ancient Egyptian Goddess most recognize as Isis is commonly described in modern times as beautiful, caring and loving; a symbol of light and peace. While such definition is not without value and truth it is also terribly incomplete. Isis is in fact a Greek word and name not found in Egyptian terminology, used in reference to an ancient deity that greatly predates the complete timeframe of Greek history. The Goddess has Her spiritual influence represented throughout the centuries, being celebrated in countless cultures by the infinite faces of the divine feminine, however Her true name goes back to the earliest times of the Egyptian culture during an era before the creation of the pyramids — that mysterious name is Aset. It is not without purpose, craft and intention that in Asetian literature the name of Isis is recurrently written in the more accurate Ancient Egyptian transliteration as Aset, while other deities of the pantheon are oftentimes addressed by a common version of their names in line with contemporary Egyptology, etymologically tied to the language of the Greeks and not the cryptic Egyptian of the elders.

Despite the limited understanding of modern and classic interpretations Aset wields a loyal and protective nature that is not inaccurately described in history and myth, although Her darker side sometimes forgotten or lost in time was recognized by the ancients who accepted and revered the incomprehensible nature of the Goddess in infinite manifestation. A beacon of violet light but a devastating force of shapeless darkness, this divine essence of dangerous silence and unseen magick was at the center of the ancient mystery schools and the foundation of religion and spirituality in Egypt, the timeless seed of an intricate system of wisdom and initiation that we know as Asetianism; the legacy of Aset as the embodiment of Her teachings.

The portrayal of Aset as a divine figure of light came much later in history and suffered adulteration and shaping from different cultures such as the Romans and Greeks, which added to the already misguided interpretations from later periods of the Egyptian dynasties and the neglecting of much older roots behind this universal force of dangerous beauty. In a sense skepticism is important when studying the occult not only as a tool of guidance but as it is useful in the separation of lore from reality and truth from myth, however a scholar drowned in absolute skepticism and blind awareness is also bound to never grasp the depth of ancient knowledge. How can someone unwilling to examine the complete realm of possibility, unaware of the subtle reality and the experimental application of magickal laws be properly equipped to study, interpret and understand the most complex spiritual culture in history that was left by the Ancient Egyptians? A tradition built upon the foundations of magick, power of symbolism, secrets of initiation, knowledge of the afterlife and mysteries of death can never be comprehended under the limited scope of an uninitiated mind. To see its hidden clues, grasp upon the profound meanings and uncover untold gnosis requires enlightenment without the chains of blind skepticism but in the candlelight of illuminated skepticism and higher consciousness.

Although the misconceptions and modern reconstructionism of ancient deities is prevalent in popular culture and even in some academic circles, the dark nature of Aset is well documented and known to historians. This darkness, astuteness and dangerous intent is clear in the classic clash of divine power between Ra and Aset, with the conquering of his secret name. Solar forces of Egypt and manifestation of the Sun, Ra was once the worshipped leader of the Gods. During a confrontation with Aset his solar powers were diminished as he was poisoned and his dominion subdued by the magick of Aset upon the unforeseen revelation of Her mighty arts. The Goddess would not bow to another God nor oblige to his scorching arrogance, so Her hidden flame was unleashed and Her true nature revealed; Aset crippled Ra with magick and in a battle of titans conquered his forbidden name, the symbol of his solar dominion over other Gods and the people of Egypt.

She did not submit to authority nor conform to established power, rising as the first divine opposer in Her courage and fierce boldness; the adversary of Gods. So the gentle and protective Aset can also be a frightening Goddess wielding the sword of darkness, capable of unimaginable and terrifying actions that were seen as far more evil than the nature of Her twin sister Nephthys, a silent deity more commonly described by modern scholars as the darker one. How wrong they were on that assumption...

Unknown to the world and unseen to the eyes of mortals Aset rises as Queen of darkness, the divine shadow of death; Mother of torment and crafter of nightmares. Her inscrutable face revealed by the pale light of the Moon is so terrifying that knowledge of Her abominating powers was erased from the pages of history, now only spoken through whispers and taught in secret. Many ancient myths were obfuscated and retold under different light, until popular knowledge from later dynasties portrayed a decadent and misunderstood understanding of the original Aset, now lost to those practicing the arts of old outside of the wisdom of unbroken mystery schools. The indescribable nature of the infernal aspect of this primordial Goddess can only be understood through initiation and communion with Her elder Fire. To study this element of Asetian gnosis and pursue those hidden teachings is the path of the warrior — a sword of the samurai as conqueror of the soul. It is a dangerous and treacherous road where the spirit is challenged and tested to the point of primal manifestation. The breath of life is consumed and any value that life once had stands on the edge of a timeless blade: one held by the storm of Her gracious hands.

This facet of darkness seeded by Aset is also present in the inner nature of the Asetians and an element of spiritual abstraction that is also embraced by Asetianists of different nature. Darkness should not be interpreted as a manifestation of evil as it is in fact an essence of liberation and the path of illumination through wisdom. It is the denial of ignorance, the breaking of ego and the opposing of vanity, falsehood and dishonesty. Such dark seed can only be found within and never in the judgment of others that should be discarded or recycled as empowering accomplishment.

A student of the occult may be faced with the misinformed notion that a dark or light tradition, just like the philosophies of left hand and right hand path, are in some way related with the practice of black magick and white sorcery — that is utterly false and a misguided expression of ignorance. In truth magick knows no color and attaches to no polarity; it cannot be defined by evilness or goodness. Good and evil are merely perspectives tied to a tapestry of ethics, religions, ideals and culture, so they cannot define the nature of magick. To describe something as evil is highly subjective, with definitions varying according to person and culture. Magick is not evil nor is it good as that remains in the mind of the practitioner; its results can be everything, for every form of magick can be used to heal just as it can be used to harm. The learned occultist understands that deadly poison on the right amount becomes medicine.

No true examination of the elusive nature of darkness would be complete without differentiating between archetype and entity. Most spiritual and religious cultures have developed archetypal systems to channel magickal thought, project intent and direct prayer; frequently related to a psychological and magickal construct tied to symbolism or a strong ideal but sometimes veiled beneath the banner of an entity that is merely conceptual and of talismanic quality but not representative of an expression of deity. In history we can find the names of Lucifer, Satan, Lilith, Jesus and countless others that convey and represent a philosophical idea manifested as archetype through collective consciousness. Such archetypal forces can be consciously explored in ritual and worked with in prayer but it remains important for the initiate to understand that these spiritual constructs are not real entities, or in other words, they are not divine beings or bearers of the living flame that we describe as soul.

Being a creation of the human mind and its unlimited potential for religious imagination, the many names worshipped throughout history differ from those found within the Ancient Egyptian pantheon, developed not from the roots of archetype but unveiled by the untold mysteries of divine infinity. There is power and inspiration to be harnessed in archetype but the enlightened seeker understands how such forces operate and manifest, often driven and empowered by the condensed energies, religious focus and committed faith established within those archetypes across the centuries — a power that can be bound, manipulated and explored by magickal will but not the spiritual manifestation of a superior consciousness that can be genuinely interacted with.

An apparently subtle difference for the uninitiated but of central importance and relevance to an honest practitioner of spirituality is found in the understanding and inherent magickal approach to divine entities. The inscrutable faces of divinity such as the infinite flames of Aset, the transformational springs of Osiris, the darkest nights of Anubis, the cautious observation of Nephthys or the scorching deserts of Seth cannot simply be touched by the limited magick of an incarnated soul and the confines of a restrictive realm of matter. Some are seduced by ego and illusion, falling into the traps of imagination and embracing delusions of grandeur, making bold claims of contacting divinities, embodying a deity or invoking their powers. However in most cases what is being accomplished, albeit unknowingly, is the subconscious process of taping into the archetypal representations of those entities, enforced through collective consciousness and risen on the fertile plains of inner realms of thought, emotion and psyche. Those experiences do not represent real entities but a powerful egregore manifested through belief and forged by culture, society and dogma, resulting from a religious operation and psychological paradigm where thoughts are given form, establishing the foundations of human faith.

This elaborate understanding becomes vital to the exploration of darkness and unveiling the spiritual aspects hidden within, by operating with the darker archetypes of magick while recognizing that nature and deity conceal terrifying faces of darkness as well. The dark path or left hand tradition is a world of mystery and educated perception empowered by introspection, aware silence, mental liberation, inner development and spiritual evolution, being also the realm of practice and study for high magick and its many secrets. It is not conditioned by religious dogma and it does not remain static in time nor is it bound to expectation or opinion, being an arduous road that demands sacrifice, honesty and loyalty. This is not a system for those who seek quick results and easy answers, as anyone lacking strength and the aforementioned qualities is better suited elsewhere and safer the further away they get from Asetianism. The many dangers within these studies were never denied or hidden and should be made very clear to anyone who dares to enter our realm.

The Asetians are a personification of darkness. They are manifested silence and the essence of perception; awareness without thought. As timeless creatures of forbidden darkness and sharp predatory instincts their light can only be understood upon the altar of

✝

violet truth and under the starry sky of our cosmos. In this insignificance of Self where you completely cease to exist their true nature is revealed.

Chaos

The nature of the vampire is that of a representative of chaos. An Asetian is known to promote change not only within Self but also visibly in others; a reflex of action and inaction to their influence. Metaphysically the energy of Asetians surrounds them and permeates those they interact with in constant motion and flow, breaking stagnation and shaking the mechanisms that spark creation and growth. It is this impermanence that makes room for the new, opening the doorways of learning, since what does not tolerate change is bound to remain the same, stalled and stagnant. This recurring challenge of established authority — spiritually, conceptually and socially — that inspires the grand quest for liberation and enlightened identity, aligned with a never-ending pursuit of knowledge that characterizes this tradition, is mirrored in the nameless Asetians scattered throughout history that became pioneers of discovery, inspirational artists and the unrelenting advocates of truth.

Those who come into contact with the Asetians are invariably changed by them, sometimes on a subtle level but others through a life-changing consequence of their interaction with these powerful forces of chaos. Those profound experiences may sometimes be traumatic, especially for the misguided and those under bondage of the ego, but the ones willing to undertake the hard work of understanding Self and genuinely invest in a higher sense of awareness often find the Asetian influence to be more than beneficial, unveiling it as an invaluable seed of growth, strength and realization in their lives. Such notions, however, do not imply that every effect of Asetian influence is positive for they are boundless as nature and the forces of chaos have no polarity, holding the daring mirrors that can shake the very foundations of the ground. As such, the latent Asetian ability to face people against the mirrors of truth, where their real and unmasked identity of Self is revealed, can prove to be a great tool not only of revelation and growth but also an abominable trial of catastrophic consequence for the weak, the false and the shallow.

The unstable forces of chaos are found mirrored on the Asetian pillars, holding a seat of especial significance under the dominion of Khepri. This pillar embodies the transcendence of spiritual transformation also referred to as Kheperu, a mystery that is greatly empowered by the manifestation of chaos. It can be said that chaos is the fuel of transformation — the action before the engine — breaking stagnation and giving it motion, being an instrument in the machinery of evolution.

Absence of chaos is an embodiment of spiritual death. It is the absolute lack of motion and the prevalence of stagnation — a path of oblivion and the slow decay of life. Only when challenged and faced with adversity does the initiate find inner truth, liberate strength and conquer abilities. Obstacles, strife and pitfalls are the natural tools to establish and define our own limitations, so without chaos and change it is not possible to grow, adapt and evolve.

On a spiritual perspective of the Kemetic tradition chaos is nothing. This undefinable nothingness springs forth from the primordial Waters of the abyss where the first essence emerged; the unformed potential of Nun without manifestation. Chaos then finds an embodiment out of the Duat and in our cosmic universe as the serpent-daemon Apophis, not a face of chaos itself but a reflex of its influential nature and invisible pressure. The nature of Apophis as a natural opposer of Maat is cyclical, echoed in the daily attacks against the solar barge or Ra as it travels the underworld every night.

As masters of chaos and harbingers of change the Asetians stand as silent initiators of mind and soul, wielding the flaming swords of transformation and becoming...

Vampires

The cultural legacy and spiritual tradition of vampirism are profoundly misrepresented in modern times. Vampires are predatory beings with heightened metaphysical senses but their nature should not be characterized by the isolation of this element just like a serpent cannot be reduced to its venom, a scorpion to its sting or a lion to its jaws. Vampirism is one of the many layers that constitute the intricate nature of Asetian existence but its predatory aspects alone do not define what Asetians are and represent for each individual Asetian in his or her own singularity is so much more than just a predator.

First and foremost the vampiric paradigm of the Asetian tradition is tied to the mysteries of predatory spirituality. This practice is characterized by the transfer and consumption of living essence that is also known as Ka — the Ancient Egyptian word for vital force, the energy of life. Albeit undeniably empowering in terms of metaphysical abilities and esoteric power, such practices encompass more than just an exchange of energy but englobe profound spiritual implications accessed only through advanced initiation and the understanding of deeper mysteries.

In popular culture, where these subjects are explored superficially and without in-depth knowledge, it is sometimes believed that the vibrational needs of vampires are related to subtle links that were severed from the universal sources of energy. This is incorrect and a metaphysical absurdity, as no subtle system would be able to sustain life without an active link capable of external absorption. Vampires, just like every other living creature, have these links intact and often more developed and stronger than those found in human subtle anatomy. Their higher requirements for life force are tied to a demanding subtle metabolism, established to safely fuel increased magickal abilities while retaining balance of the inner system in the process of operating on a state of overdrive.

Locked in ancient tradition the vampire arts were crafted and developed by the Asetians combining their knowledge of magick and the occult. Being well known for its power, blood magick has had a place of prominence and fearful respect in every esoteric culture known to humanity. However, the predatory instincts and vampiric nature of the Asetians was not born out of any curse or handicap but as a manifestation of their magickal soul not being native to the physical realm. This apparently small yet significant detail makes the Asetian subtle body in much greater need for vital energy while incarnated, characterized by a heightened energy metabolism unlike the one of humans who are native to the land of matter and profoundly entwined with the nature of this reality. For this reason the Asetians learned how to cycle their energy and ignite the flame within their souls through the sacred communion of their essences. In time they realized that through the vital energy of the living not only could their subtle systems be maintained and balanced but such force would also enhance their senses and empower their abilities, granting them a considerable amount of magickal power that they were used to wielding only in the realms of subtlety.

This ability to drain the breath of life earned them the name of vampires much later in history, a terminology that did not exist in Ancient Egypt and a description created by human minds to define this predatory nature in the eyes of their limited understanding. It then became a mark of these immortal predators that could touch life and take it away; not hunters of flesh but of the spirit.

Bound to this earthly manifestation the Asetians can touch the life of others and claim it to themselves. However, while in their native realm of the Duat, the land of the dead, their nature is not exactly vampiric as they do not require energy other than their own pure essence while their souls flourish and expand to the infinity of ethereal potential.

Popular culture has also seen a contemporary rise of the misuse of the word vampyre, which has been commonly adopted by those seeking to embrace the fictional archetype of vampires while lacking understanding of vampirism as a tradition and its legacy. The choice of archaic spelling and attempts to imply mystical significance through its usage to add some form of authenticity are an easily disproven fallacy of no relevance, representing nothing more than the adoption of an older word often used in modern times within a lifestyling context and unrelated with a truthful differentiation between the vampires of fiction and reality.

In terms of historicity the meaning of the words vampyre and vampire are one and the same, referring to risen undead corpses and the mythological interpretations of the past often tied to ignorance and fear of the unknown but fundamentally different from what occultists perceive as real vampirism. Although the word vampire inspires and holds various meanings in contemporary times, from the works of fiction to the realms of lore and spirituality, the practices we relate to its description are old and predate the original etymology of the word. Now reborn as terminology raised and adopted by humanity to describe the dark and elusive nature of these ancient creatures, the concept of vampire is not one genuinely embraced by the Asetians who transcend beyond its definitions and limitations. Having always distanced themselves from fiction, illusion and those who approach the archetype merely as a lifestyle, the Asetians adamantly and proudly embrace the linguistic terminology of Asetian above vampire to describe their identity and inner nature, being a much culturally richer and far more profound definition than anything the word vampire could ever mean.

Surrounded by folklore and misunderstanding the common knowledge about vampirism is driven from myth, lore and culture. Although the most exhaustively studied mythologies of the vampire have their origins in Europe, particularly relevant in Romanian and Slavic cultures where they were seen as undead monsters, legends of vampires can be found in nearly every moment of history from ancient times to modern days, being present in most cultures around the world. Through fear and desire, in hatred and worship, vampires have been ever present since humanity was able to draw and write about the mysteries surrounding them, from the tales of the ghostly Vetalas in India found in old Sanskrit literature to the Lilû vampiric demons, an Akkadian concept found in the mysteries of Babylonia and Sumerian literature. Better known in modern scholarship is the female incarnation of those ancient demons named Lilitu, later adopted by Jewish demonology as Lilith. Being explored as an archetype of darkness and vampirism within modern ritualistic traditions of the left hand path, she is sometimes erroneously described as the mother of vampires — a misconception and consequence of modern fiction.

However, the oldest accounts of vampirism can be traced back to Ancient Egypt, not only found in the symbolism of temples and descriptions in papyrus but visible among the established tales of Bast and Sekhmet or even more evident in the earlier funerary texts where such concepts get increasingly darker and of a cryptic nature. Inspired

✝

and influenced by the presence of the Asetians and their culture, the true origins of vampirism flourished to this day but still hold their secretive mysteries tied to the land where those legends began.

In modern times, vampirism and the ancient culture of vampires frequently became indistinguishable from fiction, being mistakenly connected with the literary works of imagination and the deluded reality of misguided individuals. Reaching mainstream culture through the classic work of fiction Dracula from Irish author Bram Stoker, the vampire has also increased in popularity due to the romanticized vampires from New Orleans found in the novels by Anne Rice.[5] [6] Precursor and inspirational catalyst to their works were the writings of English poet George Byron, less known in popular culture but drawing relevant threads between poetry and the secretive knowledge found through occult explorations. Although classical literature on the theme of vampires is not without artistic value and cultural significance, modern fiction of questionable quality continues to flourish through the exploration of the archetype while defacing its origins and spiritual background in exchange for hysteria and superficiality.

> *"But first, on earth as vampire sent,*
> *Thy corpse shall from its tomb be rent.*
> *Then ghastly haunt thy native place,*
> *And suck the blood of all thy race."*
>
> George Byron

It is a tasteless irony of contemporary history that vampirism is now found and trivialized around the world through pretentious communities built upon ignorance and strengthened by commerce that have taken the archetype of the vampire by storm and turned its roots

✝

into popular culture and a psychological gateway to channel egotistical desires for attention. Developing from the abuse of ancient myth and through the defacing of timeless culture and occult wisdom such contemporary cults represent a petty reflection of the spiritual elegance of immortals. With misinformed notions on the existence of the children of the night many of these pretending vampires endorse lies and advocate a lifestyle that is nothing more than delusion and role-play.

Springing from the realms of fiction and borrowing elements from traditions they do not understand, modern frauds seek the spotlight of exposure in a sad display of ego and vanity, unaware of how such expressions are diametrically opposite to the mind and culture of actual vampires. Such a disregard for the secrecy and silence that was ever embraced by vampires since the old days, as well as the grotesque expression of ignorance towards the elders and their Asetian origins, founders and respected ancestors of the immortal kin, present an evident sign of a limited mortal mind. Hiding an inability to craft magick and be initiated into the mysteries behind ideals of mainstreaming and a supposed end of secrecy is not only misguided as unquestionably false, just like using such limited understanding to justify a servitude to superficiality and be propelled by the media exposes nothing more than a weak display on the pitfalls of humanity. To real vampires, calm and observant in their cloak of immeasurable silence, such expressions of falsehood are a spectacle of dust unworthy of attention and one that only poses a threat of deception to those as limited as themselves. The ignorance and misinformation to be found in some works of popular culture and their weak attempts at studying or defining vampirism serves nothing more than the actual purpose of secrecy, allowing for those who are real to live in the shadows of a society that remains unaware of their existence and ever confused about the immortal forces lurking in the silence of this new dawn. It is a mirror of futility, a cloak of blinding fume that safeguards the mysteries and keeps the old vampires hidden, only to be seen by those who know that truth requires a level of understanding that can only be achieved through experience and initiation.

There are no simple paths to wisdom and our doors can only be found beyond the altar of a violet abyss. Simply reading this book will not open your eyes to the land of immortals and the truth of the elders, as such assumption would be naive. To understand the powers at work behind these pages you will have to transcend the limited perception of the living and embrace the quest of timeless truth through study, commitment and surrender. Allow for the magick of these words to consume your essence and to devour your ego, for only then you may find another ray of our light. To Asetians, vampirism is just a word and a concept bound to different meanings according to different people but most importantly it is not what defines them.

A healthy human energy system constantly draws energy from nature at different rates and speeds as a universal requirement to maintain its own subtle system and aura. Some work efficiently and in coherence with its energy centers but others are prone to blockages and other problems, manifesting indirectly through different physical and mental conditions, almost invariably with origins traced to energy stagnation. Most vampiric systems due to their particular subtle anatomy and high vibration of the soul cannot be stabilized in a continuous process under the regular cycling of universal energy. While this natural process of energy recharging effectively stabilizes the aura of the vampire and can be channeled into the fueling of an array of manipulative techniques and subtle powers, it does not support the high demands of their internal energy metabolism for extended periods of time. Vampires have found different solutions to this characteristic, from the exchange of sacred flame within their kindred to more feared processes of draining vital energy.

Besides the energy requirements a vampiric system can process energy of different vibrations and frequencies, to be altered, assimilated and applied in a variety of ways, depending on the needs and will of the vampire. It is a complex process of learning that implies a certain level of mastery not only in terms of metaphysics but also the understanding of subtle anatomy, occult science and magick. Through this process and inborn abilities vampires are not restricted to explore the energy of the living, studying and manipulating energy drawn from different sources and found in varying situations, from the elemental forces of nature to residual energy found in charged areas and temples or even by tapping into the dangerous essence of the dead, achieved through the techniques developed under our branches of necromancy.

Those abilities, particularly the draining of vital force from human beings, is often at the core of many fears concerning vampirism, a subject that remains taboo, clouded in mystery and doubt even to the most advanced occult minds of today. This is not only enforced through the demonic nature to be found in myth where vampires are seen as fearless predators and a dangerous omen of evil, but also further popularized through misconceptions in modern esoteric literature, from commercial authors that promote the importance of defensive magick against vampires without an attempt at understanding their nature to new-age currents and misinformed voices that describe a bland and lifeless vampire culture without a hint of factuality. Unwillingly serving the Asetian practice of secrecy and desire for privacy, they promote ignorance and embrace deceit for a modern culture that would rather live a conscious lie than to accept facing truth or embracing reality if that does not please their selfish needs for validation and inner weaknesses. Centuries shall pass and they will be forgotten as new liars emerge and different deceits are conceived, yet the Asetians and their passion for truth will continue in a timeless journey as they remain unshaken before the judgment of mortals or the opinion of fools, never truly forgotten amongst the darkest dreams of the living.

Although the majority of the population remains unaware of the existence of vampires even then the subject is sometimes dealt with caution and uncertainty, moved by a latent feeling of unexplained fear. Despite the fact that skeptics are to be found in every field of knowledge and branch of wisdom, the comical and confident tones can easily give place to insecurity and nervousness when all alone and facing the possibility of the unknown. Actually it is common practice among humans to attempt to ridicule what they fear or have failed to comprehend, expressed in a cowardly effort to discredit such possibility within their subconscious mind. Of course this manifests at an unconscious level and is mostly present within the realm of their own unawareness, but it is the result of humanity's recurrent fear for something that is beyond their realm of understanding. A weakness that can be easily exploited to disastrous effect by those taught in such mechanisms is another reason why knowledge truly is a key to greater power. That force of empowered knowing is found not in the simplistic acknowledgment of academic expertise but upon the grasp of all knowledge raised on the altar of wisdom.

Now, should every seeker believe that being afraid of the dangers of vampirism and the powers hiding beneath the gaze of an Asetian is wrong, irrational and bound to modern misconception? The accurate answer is no, most definitely not. However, it is my belief that a better understanding of the vampire and this ancient culture is vital and undoubtedly more effective than all the defensive techniques that students of modern occult traditions claim to possess. If a versed occultist willingly approaches an Asetian as enemy with intent to magickally conquer then defeat has already occurred before any confrontation took place. Those who come forward with honesty, approaching them as mentors and guides, who seek their words and counsel not for their power but for their friendship are the ones who uncover inner growth and find the seed of mastery, being led with the hand of respect towards the vault of enlightening truth. Many have sought the Aset Ka along the ages with the unwise intent to steal power or to unveil its secrets but only those who selflessly approached its halls with a genuine heart and a truthful mind found its doors of timeless wisdom. That is a step of initiation that can never be taught but only unveiled within the mysteries of your soul.

While vampires are indeed predatory beings, not only with the ability but also the mastery to respond with lasting damage and even lethal power, it is not entirely accurate to believe that the majority would attack and harm for no well-founded reason. Higher power is achieved through discipline and inner mastery, which can only be unveiled under the light of responsibility, balance and awareness. Asetians are not mindless destroyers or creatures of evil, although they will bring pain and suffering if that is a lesson that may open doors to a higher understanding. They initiate through fire and silence, using magick old as time itself, and that is something that only few are able to survive.

Most vampires are solitary beings indulging in the many possibilities of their inner darkness. Private by nature and secretive by culture they keep mostly to themselves, often not being bothered by the mundane issues of others or the politics of the world. They will, however, enforce their privacy effectively and fiercely if needed, so beware to exercise caution and respect.

On the subject of peril often the most dreaded — and sometimes even profoundly desired — practice of vampirism is the drain of energy and blood. While a vampiric drain can be harmful to the victim's energy system and leave permanent effects, with tangible changes being experienced on physical and mental levels, a controlled and responsible drain done to a willing donor aware of the practice can actually facilitate healing, prevent malignant stagnation, promote health and wellbeing as well as activate the natural cycling within the donor's system that will recharge the subtle body with renewed active energy. If well understood and properly executed, not all vampiric practices are harmful or inherently dangerous, providing a wealth of possibilities in terms of metaphysical treatments and alternative medicine. In fact, the ones who consciously rely on the drain and other techniques of vampires consider themselves blessed and treasure such exchanges with a sense of gratitude, which reflects on their state of mind and health.

Of course, and underlining it again, this is not to say that the magick of the Asetians should not be feared or their practices not be considered dangerous. Despite the positive vampiric influences described above and the great potential of the Asetians for healing and aiding through the arts of energy manipulation, the misuse of such techniques or their conscious use in offense can have devastating consequences. Caution and responsibility are always recommended when dealing with vampiric knowledge or when contact is being established with an unknown vampire as each individual is unique and moved by different ideals, making them unpredictable. While the Asetian touch may turn your life into a land of beauty and freedom it also holds the keys to suffering and torment. These are beings who were taught the secrets behind the ancient mysteries that can shake the grounds of every nightmare, so to appreciate their beauty with honest respect is a road of wisdom but it remains prudent not to forget the lethal potential that lies dormant within their hearts. The Sethians surely remember it.

> *"The strength of a vampire lies in his soul, as an immortal flame that burns furiously like the devastating forces of nature."*
>
> Words in Silence, Liber Silentis

The vampires from European medieval mythology were said to subsist solely through hematophagy, the ingestion of living blood from other humans or animals. Although this is just folklore and not how actual vampires live, many abilities described in fiction and lore were driven from older observances of the common people that would lead them to assume that vampires wield such powers. In many cases a connection with the occult can be determined and such abilities easily understood under the light of metaphysics.

The recurrent usage of blood is obvious and its metaphysical implications well known under occult scholarship, as the natural alignment of blood vessels and the meridian carriers of energy within the body empower such vital substance with living Ka — a subject to be further developed on the chapter about blood. Although the metaphysical and spiritual properties of blood are undeniable and its use to vampires legendary, its ingestion does not serve the purpose of sustaining the physical body but instead is to be processed by the subtle system, making the idea that a vampire can be sustained through blood a ludicrous claim and an impossibility to medical science.

Another power of the vampire to be found in myth is the ability to fly and shape-shift. These express the result of old fears and portray the imagination of uneducated people since no real vampire can fly or take the actual shape of an animal, however some instances can also be better understood through their metaphysical origins. One link is to be found in astral projection, where some vampires exercise their freedom and power. Those adept at such techniques can roam the astral realm under many forms and with many faces, being able to fly and shape-shift at will. Seen by some as young and seductive, others may only find someone apparently weak and old. The same is true with their ability to embody the shape of an animal while in the astral plane, empowering them with special qualities while journeying the lands of energy, from the mastery of winged flight to inhuman strength, acute night vision and agonizing poison. A real vampire cannot turn into mist or instantly disappear while bound to the physical realm and by the laws of physics; however, the astral plane is a place of energy, which can be mastered and wielded to their own advantage, so your awareness may be deceived or your senses tricked. These techniques can be particularly powerful, especially within an Asetian framework, as their arts hold the ability to bring the realms of spirit into touch with the land of matter, blending both realities and allowing for change to occur through magick. This secret is at the core of advanced manipulation and thought control, both complex powers that could for example influence the mind of farmers working the fields in medieval Europe so that they would describe the vampire as having certain unnatural abilities when in fact that was only happening in the realm of energy and being made manifest within their conscious mind. A dangerous ability nonetheless.

Such advanced techniques are connected to the inborn abilities of vampires in dealing with energy, manipulating its frequencies, altering its vibration and channeling it at will. This manifests on different levels but it is related with some details described in myth and celebrated in folklore, from mind reading to thought control and invisibility. Although the transfer of thoughts and emotions is possible through the manipulation of energy and crafting of subtle links, where vampires can induce feelings in others or simply avoid being noticed, this ability to manipulate the mind and touch the senses of humans through energy can be misinterpreted as having the power to become invisible, which is certainly not true.

A different myth is that of increased physical strength without developed muscular mass. Although it is possible to consciously channel energy to muscle tissue and fiber, fueling physical abilities for a short period of time in order to enhance strength and stamina or through other methods heighten eyesight, tactile sensitivity and auditory perception, it is not true that vampires are physically stronger than humans. In fact, due to the fragile link between their soul and the physical realm it is common for vampires to be slender and deprived of the brute force more easily found in human athletes, although drawing conclusions or generalizations of appearance to describe vampires are notions that must be understood as intrinsically flawed. It is highly unlikely or uncommon for a vampire to be willingly found in a physical confrontation as they see such actions relying on physical force as primitive tools and an obvious sign of imbalance, preferring more elegant weapons such as their minds and magick.

Like the examples just described, the history of vampirism when entwined with myth and folklore portrays the children of the night as mighty creatures full of fascinating abilities. However, it is paramount for the scholars of Asetianism to avoid interpreting them literally, since although most have a mystical connection of valid historical origin they must first be understood and interpreted in order to unveil the truth hidden beneath. Dealing with metaphysics alongside the mysteries of history is a highly academic process and a commitment that every serious occult pursuit should abide to.

In the end a question remains unanswered: how did the vampire change from the horrors of myth and the evil of history to the sensual and many times sexual allure of the creature seen in modern culture? The missing link is the archetype. The vampire today is no longer only seen as the hauntingly predatory creature but also as a personification of the deepest and most obscure desires. As a rebel adversary that cheats death and claims life the archetype of the modern vampire touches on the most profound human emotions. A master of passion able to break the barriers of time in order to find immortal love, reaching the very fabric of lost intimate dreams. This has a very intricate psychological significance as it resonates with the inner battle between the restraints of the conscious mind and the unbound freedom of the subconscious, promoting a release and liberation when such fascination becomes unleashed. Masters of thought and mind the Asetians embody the matter of dreams and desire, instigating emotion under the unique understanding of their kin. They became creatures that incite lust and inspire art; misunderstood monsters not only to be feared but also admired, unmatched in all existence.

Blood

The spiritual essence found within blood is an element entwined in mysticism and esoteric symbolism, incorporated in countless occult traditions for more than centuries. Its secrets were studied by the ancient alchemists and explored in obscure practices of blood magick, being intimately related with the lore of the vampire. The concept of an immortal creature that feasts on blood of the living owes a lot to folklore and myth. However, the spiritual and metaphysical connections to the energy matter of blood are built on reality, and such teachings have been part of scholarship within the Aset Ka that pioneered an understanding of occult science that exists behind the practices of vampires and blood.

The nature of this nearly sacred vampiric bond is unrelated with what is described in popular culture or archaic mythologies and its involving practices are relevantly different from what is found in classic fiction, modern lifestyles or proposed by the media. It is important to understand that vampires do not feed in public, at least not in an open way, nor do they partake in such practices for exhibition or demonstration, being only represented as acts of drama or theatrical performances but not true depictions of the vampire arts.

Due to elements of alignment within the energy system the physical body is capable of producing and carrying several highly charged substances. Closely followed by the energy imbued in semen from males and the vaginal fluids of females, blood is amongst the most energetically charged biological substances present in the body. The metaphysical mechanism that explains why blood carries such a high concentration of vital energy is easily understood with a few basic notions of subtle anatomy. The non-physical organs that control, direct, stabilize and intensify varying levels of vital energy inside the body are connected to every aspect of both the physical and subtle systems by tiny energy filaments, known in traditional Chinese medicine as meridians or in Ayurvedic Indian medicine by the Sanskrit word nadi. These subtle organs interconnected by the meridians at the core of the energy system are responsible for many of the natural interactions with energy and represent the engines behind the processes by which we metabolize energy, being described in the Asetian culture as Shen. However, modern practice outside of Kemetic influence is more familiar with the Sanskrit word chakra driven from old Hindu knowledge.

The meridians constantly carrying energy between the different Shen centers work in an apparently similar way to the physical blood vessels of the circulatory system, being aligned with the veins in the body to some extent, although not perfectly. Some are thicker and stronger, allowing for a higher stream of energy to pass through, while others are dim and fragile, only able to carry the tiniest quarks of energy, just like there are smaller veins and larger arteries responsible for the machinery of the physical bloodstream. Due to this alignment and proximity between the physical and the subtle, the blood circulating inside the human body is constantly imbued with energy and its specific fingerprint that flows through the meridians, resulting in the high charge and vibration that is found in fresh living blood, making it such a unique substance to be used in the mechanisms of vampiric feeding. However and because of the volatile nature of vital energy, when blood leaves the physical system it cannot retain its metaphysical properties for a long period of time as energy will dissipate and deteriorate, eventually leaving the blood discharged and lacking its previous magickal properties. That explains why dead blood is not capable of empowering a vampire and why blood feeding can only be done efficiently when taken directly from a living donor, presenting other forms of consumption as not vampiric in nature.

With this metaphysical understanding it becomes clear that blood is not simply an esoteric metaphor for vital energy as misunderstood by modern practitioners who discard its value. Blood was never forbidden in the vampire culture of past and present that unapologetically celebrates its magick, potency and spiritual significance without dogma or guilt. It has been used in rituals of high magick and traditional witchcraft for ages but, while it certainly remains a powerful symbol and an element of initiation, it is also an occult tool of trusted tradition that must be treasured and respected as another vessel of life.

Having explained the potential ties of this substance in the arts of vampirism it becomes relevant to underline that not every vampire feeds on blood or uses it in ritual. What empowers the subtle system of a vampire is vital force — the power of Ka — and that is found in blood but certainly not exclusively. With mastery of the magickal arts and experience with energy work vampires can rely on more advanced metaphysical techniques to drain vital essence from the living and the forces of nature. These darker arts may be more subtle but they also carry the potential to be far more dangerous when empowered with the wisdom that comes from within.

> *"I am the redness which came forth from Aset. I am the blood that issued from Nebt-Het. I am firmly bound up at the waist and there is nothing which the Gods can do for me. For I am the representative of Ra and I do not die."*
>
> Pyramid Texts

In contemporary subcultures it is common to see the concept of living vampires divided into different categories and terminologies such as psychic and sanguinarian, among others, being modern interpretations that reflect on a lack of knowledge over the foundations behind vampiric feeding. While such words can be used to describe feeding mechanisms and techniques they cannot define the nature of a vampire in a serious analysis or study. Psychic vampirism is the occult terminology that refers to the draining of vital energy by subtle means of metaphysics, sometimes also called pranic vampirism;

while sanguinarian practices are tied to the ingestion of living blood as means of vampiric empowerment and magickal practice. Both make solid reference to established techniques but do not describe different types of vampires. In reality any vampire can feed through those two mechanisms and by the use of many others, where such choice is bound to subtle metabolism, metaphysical mastery and ultimately personal preference. The vital element is found in energy and no chosen technique, practice or knowledge holds relevance to categorize a vampire as such remains the misguided notions of the uninitiated.

These techniques lead to the subject of ethics and although most vampires will focus such exchange and communion with those intimate and trustworthy, there are no adopted sets of rules or vampire laws to abide to. Every individual is independent, making vampires responsible for their own actions so danger lurks in the dark and psychic attacks are definitely a reality. To understand the subtle, grasp the unseen and master the mysteries of energy are mirrors of an enlightened path but they also unveil a potent weapon. Those who claim that vampirism is nothing but a safe practice and that vampires are always responsible beings that never chose to harm are clearly living in a world of delusion and denial as that is not the reality of our world. Vampirism is path of darkness and spiritual mystery that focuses on evolution but it conceals many dangers spread along its treacherous road of night; to deny such truth is to hide, deceive and lie.

The concept and ideology of vampires and vampirism alongside their relationship with living blood is present in nearly every culture, religion and philosophy known to humanity. Often disguised under the cloak of symbolism and the unknown of lore, the magick and power of blood remain graciously alive to this day, sometimes even celebrated among those who dismiss vampirism entirely. In Christian practices, for example, the act of drinking the blood of Christ is accepted as sacred while neglecting its metaphorical symbolism that is undeniably vampiric. Such is a common occurrence among the religious minds of today who oppose and discredit the occult, completely unaware of the roots to be found in the practices of their own embraced religion and their distinctive ties to magick and the occult, so clear to anyone fluent in these arts. To drink the blood of Jesus gifted with his blessing alongside the will of God as a doorway to the heavens and the attaining of eternal life holds a visible adaptation from ancient Asetian concepts and practices such as the mysteries of Khenmet — the darkest kiss of immortality. Khenmet embodies not only the blessing of an Asetian upon the altar of rebirth but also manifests a conscious emanation of the transcendent Will of Aset; the unification of the earthen master with the divine master, just like Jesus and God in Christian lore. Far from a historical coincidence this is not an isolated case of religious adaptation since several other cultures, religions and traditions of the world carry reminiscent elements of Asetian origin that trace its roots back to the cradle of our land in Egypt.

Dragon Heart
The mysterious nature and concealed history of the Aset Ka is intricately tied to the ancient symbolism of the dragon. Representing the flame of immortality Asetians are the living dragons of the ages; shadows of the past, initiators of the present and foresight of the future. As wielders of spiritual immortality they shield the divine Fire of truth and protect the knowledge of all mysteries, being the seed of inspiration for myths, tales and whispers across the centuries, reluctantly influencing the very course of history through silence, manipulation and magick.

In mythology dragons are often depicted as fierce and stern guardians, safeguarding incredible treasures that represent the desires of many. Using this established definition to refer to the Asetians as symbols of draconic influence is not without merit. However, the iconic wealth that is portrayed in legend as being protected by dragons is actually a not very strongly concealed metaphor for knowledge, magick and truth. The dragon is the ultimate adversary; the opposer that wields the power of immortality and shapes the foundations of this world. These draconic flames consume the doubts of impurity and renew perception with newfound clarity — the devouring by Fire so intimately tied to Asetian initiation.

In Greek mythology a never-sleeping dragon guarded the golden fleece[7] — a symbol of royalty and authority — while being also tied to the protection of the garden of Hesperides, as Hera's orchard was known to produce the fruit of immortality. In the Eastern mythology of China the dragon is complementary to the phoenix, both creatures completing a cycle of yin and yang, appearing as a symbol of power and strength that wields the unseen forces of nature, controlling rainfall, storm and thunder. Unsurprisingly the Christian tradition connects dragons to serpents and places their symbolism as opposers of God, the adversaries of monotheism and ancient bane of religious power, a reference found in the *Book of Psalms* of the Hebrew Bible and also part of the old testament in Christianity.

Recognizable by every educated occultist is also the symbol of the ouroboros, an ancient sigil that shows a dragon or serpent devouring its own tail; a perpetual cycle of continuity embodying the alchemy of immortality. Its importance and use can be found in Hinduism, Hermeticism and Paganism but the original depictions of its symbolism can as expected be traced to funerary motifs from Ancient Egypt, such as those found in the tomb KV62, the final resting place of pharaoh Tutankhamun. Its later study and adoption is found extensively related to alchemy academia, in grimoires of magick and illustrated on the works of classic occult literature, including those of Asetian heritage.

In terms of cultural proliferation and historical development, after willingly parting the throne of Egypt and leaving it to the rule of humankind the Asetians spread throughout the known world in spiritual exile, a path that strategically led them to the East and into the islands of Japan where their teachings and essence can still be felt in the unshakable honor that defined the Samurai warriors and established their history, the loyal masters of the sword and students of perfected balance. A natural process of cultural exchange that also imbued the always-evolving Asetian path with gifts of diversity and talents unique to the beautiful Eastern traditions. In time, history would bring the Asetian people to old Europe, a realm where they established dominion through silence, in communion with nature, and endured their timeless quest for development, growth and understanding, safekeeping the ancient ways through the perpetual manifestation of magick as the secretive voices of immortality.

References to the iconography and mythology of dragons are incredibly diverse, being often difficult to trace and connect in terms of origins and historicity. Their spiritual aspects and fundamental archetypes found in the development of different cultures are undeniable, making the living breath of a dragon a force to be reckoned while hiding behind layers of deception and mysticism that clouds judgment of the mind from the lingering knowledge of the subconscious. Although there are vast differences between the draconic mythologies of Europe and Asia, the recurring embodiment of the wild forces of nature and the defining hallmark as champions of immortality is ever-present in the universal paradigm that defines a living dragon. This echo of Asetian presence, essence and influence is ever-felt from the dawn of time to the modern day, where dragons still roam the mindset of humanity, often finding home in literature, painting and film as a silent and often unaware mirror of the flaming heart of every Asetian — the dragons that rise above and carry the flame of immortal wisdom.

Religion

Asetian spirituality is a broad term that encompasses a diversity of practices, philosophies, schools of thought, ancient wisdom and magick. The foundation is intimately tied to the spiritual arts of Ancient Egypt and its esoteric science, elements profoundly intertwined in the culture where the roots of our mysteries can be found. Although Asetianism should not be described as a religion and it bears no resemblance to the religious concepts found today, several elements of its underlying practices, mystical knowledge and tenets have influenced the creation, development and even exploitation of different religions of past and present. This can be traced from the rise of small hidden cults, the modern revivalism of older practices and the birth of new-age traditions to large religious powers establishing their force in this era such as Judaism, Christianity and Islam that borrowed esoteric principles and occult symbolism from the ancients, hiding many ties to the spiritual legacy of Egypt and its Asetian culture.

Those forms of religious appropriation and cultural mingling are sometimes buried under layers of cryptic theology and elaborate disguises. However, others are hidden in plain sight, like the signature triple nature of the Asetians immortalized in the mysteries of the sacred three and initiatory keys of Orion that is found mimicked and adapted throughout the centuries in various religious cultures. For example, the trinity of Christianity embodied in the archetypes of father, son and the holy spirit, the Kabbalistic supernal triad of Jewish mysticism represented by the three sephiroth manifested above the abyss and described as Kether, Chokmah and Binah, the trimurti of Hinduism as Brahma the creator, Vishnu the protector and Shiva the destroyer, or even the old Celtic triquetra and its recurrent interpretations in various branches of Paganism — the original concept of divinity being manifested in the mysteries of the sacred three is as timeless as the forgotten foundations of the Aset Ka.

The diversity found in Asetianism and the open mind of the Asetians alongside their ever curious nature, constantly seeking an evolved understanding of all forms of knowledge and silently striving for its safekeeping, has led to an intricate tapestry of occult knowledge, spiritual wisdom, magickal mastery, philosophical understanding and even scientific approach that reflects on what Asetianism is today. It embraces not only its Egyptian background but also the many cultures, places and eras that have touched its development and were influenced in return by its unstoppable but yet unseen seed of evolution. Unlike most religions, and an added reason why Asetianism is a culture and not a religious system, is that being unshakably confident in its teachings the Asetians have always inspired others to explore knowledge in every form, to never limit themselves by dogma, biased perception or established expectation and to do so fiercely. Comparative religious study and the research of history in its broad public understanding and the less known secrets of past untold are important elements in the life of an Asetianist. Freedom is enforced and liberation promoted, where the initiate is violently faced with the bonds of responsibility but unleashed without limitation. That stance that is so uniquely Asetian in concept and nature promotes understanding on a much higher level than any mundane form of teaching, allowing for everyone to seek freely what they desire and to question without fear; a path that ultimately leads back to the cradle of spirit silently waiting within Asetianism as centuries pass and history becomes legend.

"Impermanent are all created things.
Strive on with awareness."
Siddhartha Gautama

Such broad study of different knowledge and traditions is not merely an advanced tool of understanding but also a solid anchor in the pursuit of past-life exploration and the spiritual work that it entails. Being reborn into countless cultures through the machinery of reincarnation, under the influence of distinctive powers, structures and beliefs, the study of past eras and traditions now even extinct, their societies, mindsets and adopted symbolism can prove to be a valuable asset of growth, working as a subliminal access point in the cautious exploration of past-life memories.

Asetians and Asetianists find no sense of home or identity in the views of modern day religion, seeing the flaws in their rigid dogmas, laws and disguised manipulation. This becomes clearer after the awakening or nearing its approach where the spiritual identity becomes more defined and less tolerant of falsehood and of that which does not kindle the inner flame. Despite this reality they are beings of profound spirituality and have an intimate connection with the subtle, celebrating nature, conquering knowledge and mastering magick. Finding in Asetianism the missing piece of their inner puzzle and a skeleton key to the unbiased grasp of the secrets of the universe, both Asetians and Asetianists describe the culture and teachings of the Aset Ka as home; a long-sought haven with an indescribable sense of familiarity where their true nature can be found and unleashed. That is pure liberation and transcendent understanding.

Distinctive from the dominant Abrahamic religions with their common roots in the Semitic tradition, Asetianism is what could be described as a polytheistic tradition. Monotheism, so wildly spread as an intrusive weed, portrays divinity in such a limited form that makes it ultimately flawed to any rational but spiritual mind, being derogatory to the essence of the divine. For the Asetians just like in the mind of the Ancient Egyptians the nature of divinity is tremendously complex and inadequate of conscious understanding in this limited realm of matter, manifesting through countless aspects and infinite faces. It has limitless potential. Such a notion can only be expressed by a polytheistic system, where an attempt to define the indefinable and to bring the concept down from the realm of infinity to the limited mind in the physical world culminates in the different Gods and Goddesses as they are found in the mythology of Egypt. It breaks the endless nature of divinity into a limited framework that can be discussed, approached and examined by having it translated into words and symbols, making ritual, celebration, magick and communion with this inscrutable layer of the divine possible and experienced while incarnated, even if still not completely understood and ultimately veiled behind many mysteries. The Egyptian pantheon reflects precisely that divine powers are not good or evil, nor strong or weak, but faces that embody all of its forces and expressions. Just like nature they can be omens of prosperity and givers of life but also abusive destroyers and terrifying opposers, as an aspect of the universal duality that is present in everything. This complex framework that modern scholars describe as polytheism was ever present in all but one of the Kemetic traditions, resulting in more than one thousand and five hundred faces of the divine historically documented;[8] only but a small glimpse of the infinite scope of divinity beyond the abyss.

With further in-depth examination and interpretation another relevant element found in Kemetic spirituality is the embodiment of a divine force expressed by different manifestations or deities. Such approach is called syncretism and it is a concept used in religious studies to establish an often-unseen connection between disparate forces that can, under a certain understanding, be interpreted as one. A few well-known examples are found in Bast, Sekhmet, Hathor and Neith, all distinctive Ancient Egyptian Goddesses who ultimately manifest an essence of Aset. The actual meaning is not that they are a personification of Aset but a facet of Her divine nature, in this case being a reference to historical Asetians who lived during early Egypt. It should be noted that the terminology of Goddess used in this scenario was established by the common people in an attempt to describe these powerful Asetian women, not an implication that they represent the actual formless manifestation of the divine but how humanity saw and interpreted their inhuman nature. The same is true for Horus, Khonsu, Ptah and Imhotep among countless others as limited expressions of the essence of Aset just like the previously mentioned Goddesses, bound to the scholarly concept of syncretism yet representing very real Asetians who were once the catalysts of magick in the ancient empire. As such, the influence of Aset and Her timeless kin is found throughout the ages represented in different forms and under a myriad of names, celebrated in diversified cultures and silently shaping the course of history not always out in the open or meant to be seen, safely distanced from interpretation by the non initiated but sometimes boldly hiding in plain sight.

The historical link that ties modern monotheistic religions to their ancient roots in polytheistic Egypt is one that raises controversy, insecurity and frustration among those embracing such religions out of blind faith or willing to partake in the perpetuation of ignorance. The old Gods were openly celebrated for aeons during the golden age of the Egyptian empire, an era when spirituality was an ally of wisdom and the universe a mystery to be understood without the cunning influence of politics and commerce. The eighteenth dynasty of Ancient Egypt, during a period historians describe as the new kingdom, saw the rise of a pharaoh named Amenhotep IV, better known by the name he adopted once he reached the throne: Akhenaten. This reformist pharaoh took the world by storm and initiated the steps that would define the fate of modern religions and the future of monotheism. He abolished old paradigms and prohibited the knowledge of the ancients, destroying old temples and prosecuting the celebration of the old Gods, attempting to destroy Asetian power and tradition while founding a new religion — his religion — one based on the fearful worship of one single all-powerful God. With such a strategy Akhenaten suppressed millennia of spiritual wisdom and evolution, abolishing a genuine understanding on the nature of divinity and effectively inventing monotheism. This cult endured during his reign, imposed by fear and force against the former established beliefs but the legacy of the Gods survived in secret. Celebrated in silence and initiated in darkness the Asetians perpetuated the old wisdom and taught magick, plotting their strategy through unsuspecting moves.

Historians speculate that following the death of Akhenaten the throne was temporarily taken by a mysterious female who took action to destroy the influence of Akhenaten and his cult, abandoning and defacing his beloved capital of Amarna and reviving the old religion of the Gods, not long before the throne was peacefully passed down to a young pharaoh the world came to know as Tutankhamun. The heresy and illusions of an arrogant pharaoh were abandoned but not lost, for his beliefs endured and his masterplan remained dormant, only waiting...

At a later point in history a man now known as Moses was adopted by the royal family of Egypt, being graced with wealth and knowledge alongside much sought access within the army and temples. In time he fled the kingdom with other Israelites, leading them through the Red Sea and into the realm of the desert, during an event described in biblical studies as the exodus. Hiding amongst the nomadic people were the remaining followers of long-gone Akhenaten and the ones entrusted with the legacy of his teachings, holding tight to their well kept secret. A devious plot long in the making but not a plan of liberation, at least not of the people but that of forbidden knowledge; the safekeeping of Sethian teachings outside of Egypt.

Those teachings and guidance took Moses on his pilgrimage, being the inspiration behind much of his writings and spiritual reform, recreating the religion of Abraham under a new red light and forever changing Judaism into the monotheistic force that it is known today. The cunning and treachery behind those actions transformed the future of religions and established a new world order under a false flag of goodness, taking spiritual power and the knowledge of truth away from Egypt and disseminating promises of heaven throughout the world. The narrative of the *Torah* that is part of the *Tanakh* is composed by five books known as *Genesis, Exodus, Leviticus, Numbers* and *Deuteronomy*, which noncoincidentally are also the first five books of the *Old Testament* in the *Christian Bible.* These texts also exhibit a clear influence on the writings of the *Qur'an*, the holy book of Islam and the central religious tome adopted by Muslims. The same genesis from the very same source; three modern monotheistic religions following the teachings of a manipulative pharaoh. Unknowingly they serve a deeper and far more obscure purpose instigated by forces believed to be extinct and through their passive ignorance a flag is raised high on the mountain bearing the color red.

This is the forgotten truth that can make followers of monotheism tremble; one they prefer not to remember. The historical evidence that their one omnipresent sovereign God is nothing more than a timid echo of the arrogant beliefs of a hated pharaoh and the result of a cunning plot designed to cover the veil of spirituality for the coming centuries. A strategy that eventually succeeded much later in history while the origins are now covered in sand, giving birth to an era of religious intolerance, prosecution and blindness, where the people are taught not to think but only to obey. Such are the modern times when the wielders of wisdom and keepers of truth are observant in their timeless silence of the ages. Silent but not dead...

To those determined to uncover the truth these clues are everywhere, scattered to the winds and veiled behind the curtains of history like small and insignificant pieces of a much greater puzzle. Anthropological studies of ancient cultures and their development throughout the timeline of human knowledge exhibit clear echoes of the lives and influence of both Sethians and Asetians; at least when examined under the attentive lenses of an initiated eye. Even the story of Mary and her martyred son, who became known as Jesus, one of the most easily recognizable and extensively preached mythologies in the Western world, bears shocking resemblance to particular elements found in the archetypes of Aset and Horus from Ancient Egypt. These represent one of many adaptations and misrepresentations of earlier mythological gnosis as new cultic religion yet present nothing more than the smallest tip on this iceberg of deception.

Historically the mysterious Asetians have always been understood as dangerous creatures of darkness and inscrutable secrecy, oftentimes seen as omens of evil or embodying the fabric of nightmares; pioneers of the oldest ways of magick and the most cryptic philosophies. Truth is bound to perception and legends are often treacherous and illusory, for it is not the Asetians but the Sethians who bear the blinding light of apparent salvation and divine retribution, having cunningly established their dominion in modern ages by teaching such light of disguised servitude and egotistical power strongly rooted behind a deceiving veil of kindness and goodness so falsely preached by modern religions. Unknowingly to unaware minds the legacy of religion, cult and faith sings the timeless hymns of a red tune that bears the dominion of those not lost or forgotten but very much alive amongst the mighty powers of today, gently kindled by the ignorance of all.

Asetianism safeguards these and countless other truths from being lost to the tides of history, surviving as the secret doctrine, hidden from uninitiated eyes who lack understanding of the mysteries. World religions like Christianity and Islam embrace a dogmatic and deceptive interpretation of the mysteries without holding the keys to initiate enlightened understanding, providing a carefully crafted narrow view of the world and spirituality that is markedly visible in their blatant lack of knowledge on the nature of divinity. It is a theological irony that the priesthood, clergy and leaders of modern religions, professing themselves as the voices of God and the only existing path to deity are in fact amongst the most clear examples of people that failed to see the infinite faces of the divine. That expresses the reality of when religion becomes politics, emerging as a dangerous tool of control, deceit and delusion, diametrically opposed to the sacred mysteries that they should aim to teach, enlighten and liberate. Asetianism through the legacy of Aset preserves that secret wisdom and slowly liberates its empowering seed within the initiate that dares to tread its difficult path.

Ankh

The Ankh is one of the most recognizable symbols from the Ancient Egyptian culture but also one of the most misunderstood. As a hieroglyph it carries the literal meaning for life but like with so many secrets in the old Egyptian system of writing this symbol conveys far more than a literary interpretation or a conceptual word; it is a magickal sigil, a seal of initiation and divine manifestation.

The meanings and revelations behind its study, spiritual exploration and magickal use were considered sacred among the ancients who widely revered and greatly respected it as symbol and legacy, from nobility to priesthood and from scholar to the common people. Oftentimes found engraved on temple walls and drawn on papyrus, from scientific tomes of medicine and alchemy to magickal and funerary texts, the Ankh frequently appears on the hands of Gods and Goddesses as an icon of the living power under their grasp; a force bound to their understanding.

Spiritually and magickally the Ankh is the symbol of life and immortality, portrayed in various elements of the Asetian culture as the seal of eternity; a mark of Asetian everlastingness. The sacredness of the Ankh and its higher mysteries is found as an essential element at the core of an even more complex seal: the composite symbol of the Aset Ka and timeless flag of the Asetians described as the Asetian Sigil and also known as the Dark Mark. The mysteries of the Ankh are tied to the forces of initiation and its study is both profound and transformational. It is a key to the cosmos, hiding the secrets of the unseen and describing the machinery above and its ties to the devices below.

As seals of initiation and symbols of the mysteries both the Ankh and the Asetian Sigil are found in countless Asetian tomes, rituals, temples, altars, practices and talismans. Sometimes tattooed on the wrists of Asetians this is a mark that is treasured with honor and bound to a sense of utmost respect, taken as a branding of everlasting family and the personification of divine nature from the violet gift found in the sacred seed of Aset.

With the advent of commercial occultism in the modern era and the spawning of eclectic and revivalist new-age philosophies the symbolism of the Ankh has been popularized, misrepresented and sometimes even vulgarized by the devices of ignorance, fashion and the allure found in what is ancient and obscure. It is frequently seen as adornment and jewelry by those who wear it driven from a false sense of status or as a social statement, without understanding its many layers of meaning and sacredness while lacking an honest connection to its essence, culture and past. Such expressions of vanity when tied to an element of magick or spirituality are common mirrors that expose lack of character and a weak personality, not being exclusive to the misuse of Ancient Egyptian symbolism but also found among representations of the pentagram, evocation sigils and other esoteric symbols. This does not mean that old symbols should not be worn or used, quite on the contrary, they should be wielded with a mindset of genuine bond and under a degree of understanding or they are meaningless. A sacred Ankh when seen on the flesh of an Asetian or worn with honor by an educated Asetianist exudes an entirely different energy and vibration, echoing a distinctive feel that is easily noticeable to anyone familiar with sensing energy or sensitive to the subtle reality. Do not simply take these words for granted, always explore, sense and see as then you shall find the truth.

Due to this ancient connection between Ankh and Asetians the hieroglyph has often been portrayed as part of the symbolism of vampires and a magickal element of prominence in vampirism. In truth the underlying spiritual and magickal symbolism of the Ankh is far more Asetian in essence than purely vampiric, being adopted by contemporary movements and individuals that saw in the old Asetian roots a source of inspiration but attempt to conceal that historical link or simply remain ignorant of its origins. This popular and often uneducated view of the Ankh of the Egyptians, incredibly reductive of its meaning and power, has brought an immense variety of adulterated forms of the symbol that has since been adopted in fiction, modern art, fashion and branches of the occult that explore vampirism under a blatant influence of the culture of the Aset Ka.

Seven

More than just a number, the paradigm of seven has been tied to the mysteries of the Aset Ka since time immemorial. Recognized as sacred, symbol, sigil and omen, the culture and historical significance of seven is a banner of Asetianism and an icon of the enigmatic Asetians that is forever bound to the spiritual perception of our world.

Certain secrets locked behind the mysteries and magick of seven are only unveiled through initiation and spiritual growth, while others are learned by exploring its significance in Asetian wisdom and how those elements of profound alchemy and symbolism match in unimaginable perfection the interlaced development of history, understanding of the natural world and ultimately mirror an illuminated perception of the very fabric of the cosmos.

The Asetians have long established the eternal magick of seven and documented its importance and revelatory power throughout the many ages of humanity, influencing occult and spiritual culture in ways that are still found today in modern esoteric traditions. In science the number seven is also of particular interest, with Isaac Newton dividing the spectrum of visible light into seven different colors: red, orange, yellow, green, blue, indigo and violet. Culturally our society celebrates exactly seven wonders of the ancient world as the most remarkable achievements of classical antiquity, which include the Egyptian Pyramid of Khufu in Giza as the only surviving structure, despite being the oldest of them all.

Religiously the number seven is predominant in biblical references and in the Christian doctrine it can be found with a central role in the metaphor of creation where God spends six days creating the heavens and earth to rest on the seventh day: the Sabbath. With man being created on the sixth day the number six became a representation of humankind while the seven was a symbol of divinity, although such concept is hardly of Christian origin. Also in a rudimentary attempt to classify vices into socially accepted dogma a list of cardinal sins was established that became known as the seven deadly sins, opposing in duality the seven virtues recognized by the catholic church. In Islam the first surah of the *Qur'an* has seven verses and in the Muslim pilgrimage to Mecca the devotees circle their sacred kaaba seven times, while in Islamic cosmogony there are seven heavens and seven gates of hell. Earlier references abound as well in Jewish mysticism where Kabbalists believe for the number seven to be a mathematical description of the natural world with seven planets of the ancients, seven secondary or double letters of the Hebrew alphabet, seven notes on a musical scale, seven days in a week and the seven facets that manifest the Universe. All of these elements result in a perfect symmetry that can be found pulsating on the Tree of Life, where below the Abyss are specifically seven sephiroth as the mystic emanations of reality and understanding. [9] In Hinduism, other Dharmic faiths of Indian culture and in several eastern traditions the subtle body is described, studied, healed and explored through a system of seven structures known by the Sanskrit word chakra, finding a strong parallel in the vibrational Shen centers of Asetian subtle anatomy that can be divided into seven primary and seven secondary metaphysical organs essential to incarnated life.

In the art and occult theory of Tarot the number seven hides in plain sight, easily unveiled with the aid of some elementary mathematical observations. The greater initiations known as Major Arcana are exactly three times seven, which is a classic Asetian alchemical calculation of profound implications and intricate study — twenty-one major secrets, minus the card of the Fool that is unnumbered and the cradle of zero. Continuing to the Minor Arcana each suit in the Tarot is composed by fourteen distinctive cards, which is the result of two times seven. So the aware seeker finds the numbers three and seven in the Major Arcana and the numbers two and seven in the Minor Arcana; certainly not a coincidence. When observing the complete traditional deck of Tarot if the Fool — the origin — is removed or placed in a stance of observation there are exactly seventy-seven cards: 77 secrets, a unique symbolism that was connected to Ancient Egypt by French scholar of mythology Court de Gebelin between 1775 and 1784 in his publication "Monde Primitif." However, it should be noted that although compelling and coherent his theories that relate the esoteric art of tarot to Ancient Egypt still lack verifiable evidence as documented historical data from ancient periods is scarce, even more so when concerning the origins of occult traditions, tools and techniques that are tied to a culture of secrecy and the understanding of mysteries frequently bound to initiation.

In Asetianism there are seven fundamental frameworks known as the sacred pillars, represented by Ancient Egyptian magickal sigils of initiation that conceal the higher mysteries behind a veil of timeless simplicity. Formally they are embodied by the hieroglyphic symbolism of the Ankh, Khepri, Ka, Tiet, Was, Ba and Ib but their study is long and arduous. Historically the number seven is also found in Ancient Egyptian mythology as the seven scorpions of Aset, abominable daemons bound to Her divine Will and the unspoken origin of the mysterious Imperial Guard of the Asetian Empire. In the mysteries of Orion that are explored during the alchemical journey through the path of the Aset Ka seven is found yet again in the center body of Sigillum 333, mirroring the natural sigil shining in the dark sky as the three stars of Orion's Belt — Alnitak, Alnilam and Mintaka — join the four major surrounding stars of Bellatrix, Betelgeuse, Saiph and Rigel in a sevenfold stellar formation of magick, mystery and truth.

Iconographically represented as 7.7, the seventh day of July is commonly considered a sacred day by those who identify with the Asetian culture in contemporary times. For both Asetians and Asetianists that is a day of unity, gratitude and communion; an echo of the symbolical significance of sacred seven and its veiled mysteries but also a celebration of Aset in Her indescribable beauty that transcends time and breathes life eternal.

> *"I shall rise above all mortals with the wicked powers*
> *of death. Find my Name at the reign of silence in the*
> *seventh day."*
>
> Liber Aeternus III.8

The cultural, spiritual and magickal significance of seven is incredibly rich, complex and multi-layered, being repeatedly uncovered throughout known history and finding its symbolism, interpretations and codified power imbued into numerous tales, mythologies and artifacts. The scope and reach of the wisdom, mysteries and secrets that have long been attached to the elusive nature of seven is immense, with their understanding being revelatory of a degree of gnosis that is nothing other than priceless. Although many elements related with the number seven that have been scholarly documented are undeniably superstitious and of a fabled nature, like the seventh son of a seventh son that was believed to be an omen of a newborn vampire in European folklore, with several variations of the mythos being found according to regional cultural development, it is important to understand that many of these symbols and concepts should not be interpreted literally or without further knowledge of context and earlier influences. They become however a fascinating exercise of exploration and discovery, even in their fictional incarnations, when used to study that in so many different cultures, eras and lands the recurring power of seven rises as a distinctive but yet cryptic flag of ancient mysteries that remain stubbornly untold before the sleeping blindness of a world that no longer pays attention.

Beacon

The metaphysical concept of a subtle beacon represents an energy impulse of specific vibration and frequency that is found emanating from all Asetians. This ethereal signal carries the energetic fingerprint of the soul that is generating it, holding the potential for recognition although that is unrelated with its purpose and should not be confused with the active influence of intuition or sensory perception.

Working in mysterious ways and guided by higher consciousness the true nature of the beacon remains shrouded in enigmas and commonly bound to misunderstanding. It can be perceived as a form of attraction but nothing related with its physical interpretation, instead working on a subtle level as a magnetic force that draws you closer unexplainably. Every spiritual predator reacts to the presence of a nearby beacon but it does not only affect those of a vampiric nature, for even humans may find on the emanating beacon an unseen reasoning behind the natural allure of Asetians. The subtle dance of predator and prey.

As with every element manifested through energy — the living core of metaphysics — sensitivity towards the beacon is expressed at different levels and the ability to detect it efficiently may require training or experience depending on inborn awareness and natural aptitude to sense, track and analyse the subtle reality. In a limited faculty it manifests a force of unity and flame of undying bond; a call of nature to the sacred tapestry of family. Beneath its spiritual value and metapsychological allure the beacon also represents an echo of intrinsic predatory reflex — a tenuous sign of danger, cunning intelligence and acute instinct that can easily pass unnoticed to the mundane that may unconsciously interpret it as temptation, inspiration and desire.

Despite what may be disseminated in speculative and inexperienced literature the strength of the signal that we describe as beacon is much stronger among the awakened. A fully aware Asetian trained in the magickal arts and fluent in the natural language of the soul, able to recognize and accept the many layers of inner nature alongside the chaotic duality of existence, has a developed subtle system that emits a powerful beacon with a bolder definition and of a higher vibration than that of an unawakened soul. Despite the blockages that are broken with every awakening, giving place to a healthier flow of life force and the activation of stagnant energy that could have been working as a barrier to the impulses of the beacon, this mechanism that is altered upon awakening is also a natural safety feature that prevents an easy identification and tracking of unawakened Asetians. This may cause recognition to be tricky and elusive on a simpler approach and without the proper techniques but it safeguards the nature of every Asetian and the inborn identity from potential enemies and daring adversaries; a valuable tool for a creature notorious to excel in the dark and to flourish in the silence of the unknown.

The beacon has the potential to be more easily detected and identified by those of the Serpent Lineage, who due to their oversensitivity towards energy and the subtle alongside an inborn connection of great depth with the Asetian source — the undefinable and transcendent essence of Aset — makes them more prone to the active sensing of these vibrations, sometimes even prior to the process of awakening. In some cases this overwhelming sensitivity and acute senses can be extreme, leading to prodigious ability and wisdom but also requiring a much higher level of mastery and responsibility, not to mention the never-ending work and commitment towards understanding; a balance that may be terribly difficult to achieve for a being with an awareness and grasp that transcends matter and time.

Awakening

What is commonly described as awakening represents the union of a strong and unstoppable metaphysical process with a spiritual development phase of vivid intensity. The influence of these natural mechanisms is profound and their transformational properties are great, making their study a branch of esoteric knowledge that should not be approached lightly nor should conclusions be drawn in a superficial or simplistic manner.

Metaphysics behind the process of awakening are that of an alchemical nature, as transformation occurs not only on a mental level but also most importantly upon the energy layers of the soul. It

†

represents a fundamental state of rebirth that Asetians undergo at some stage in nearly every incarnated life; an initiation from the unknown into the plane where all can be seen. The Asetian awakening embodies acute realization but not of an egotistical nature as it is independent of expectation, desire or the influence of ego in any form — it is the understanding of inner nature and its ancient origins, the call of hidden powers and the long established commitment for understanding alongside the safekeeping of magick and all of its mysteries. Only upon the liberation and awareness of the awakening can an initiate discover that the true nature of path and soul is undoubtedly Asetian.

The process is often challenging as a trial through hardship in a time of confusion under the flood of emotion. There is a lot to process, unveil and realize although the different stages of awakening can be brief or extremely long, depending on a myriad of factors, however timing and length are never defining factors of ability or potential. The internal system undergoes subtle changes and profound transformation, making everything being experienced and felt in a much more intense way. During this process the mind and soul become aware of the true Asetian nature, allowing for the understanding of important elements and factors in current life and past experiences that were not previously clear or properly understood under an enlightened light. The adaptation can be chaotic and even painful but at the end it is often marked by a profound sense of home and liberation.

What triggers the awakening is not set in stone, as several elements may crack the chains and unleash the flood that will cause change and ignite the flame. Exploration of Egyptian symbolism, mythology and architecture represent a subtle yet stable foundation for earlier stages of awakening but the discovery of Asetianism and its passionate study or even contact with other Asetians, their teachings and magick is amongst the most powerful initiators of the awakening, liberating sealed memories and allowing for the understanding of truth. These are the treacherous roads towards the throne of Aset and the magnifying glass that holds the secretive power to eclipse the sun and shine the violet light of our cosmic mysteries.

There are countless secrets hidden within the symbolism found in ancient history and the teachings of the elders, some being sigils especially designed to convey unseen meanings and lessons that can only be achieved with proper wisdom. Those elements are initiatory and can enhance the process of understanding that the awakening entails, as the initiate explores the subliminal messages and clues found on engraved stone, drawn on papyrus leaf and covered in sand — they conceal mysteries and magick only known by those who are already awakened.

The burning Flame of Aset is perpetual for every Asetian is always Asetian since birth and in every incarnation. One does not become Asetian after experiencing the awakening as that was always the unseen nature of the soul, but the process of awakening allows for the understanding of that unshakable fact. Such realization is important and the unawakened may tread in a path of irresponsibility due to lack of understanding or flawed perception, inducing situations that will allow for the harnessing of energy and its unconscious manipulation. That is not without danger as every Asetian has inborn power and ability even if unaware of their control, so without mastery and the right teachings harm may be brought upon others and Self. Proper training will surely grant an Asetian greater ability and far more devastating power, but it will also provide the tools for its responsible use and the many layers of potentially wiser choices — or at least the freedom to determine those choices.

✝

Albeit rare, it is possible that in a few incarnations an Asetian does not awaken, even though the predatory seed is present and the violet blood of Aset flows within the veins of spirit. This may be due to unforeseen circumstances or a chain of events such as inappropriate conditions manifested upon birth, a realm not propitious for a specific level of growth or even the result of a conscious choice made before incarnating. The reasoning is mostly speculative and should not be the target of much dwelling that would only hinder growth, as rebirth and awakening accept no barriers and bow to no orders so the process may still be triggered even unexpectedly. On some occasions this can be a traumatic and agonizing experience, especially when more violent due to pressure from society and stigma. If character is not fully developed and a sense of identity an established strong trait it is possible for the mind to react with a psychological mechanism akin to self-induced sleep, hiding from true nature and living only half aware of the subtle reality. Biological family, religion and social conditioning may all hinder this process and create further damage to self-development and spiritual growth, instigating a sense of rejection and fear that is tied to human nature and not the Asetian path. To embrace such fears is a great obstacle to evolution, undermining the lingering potential that lies dormant and waiting to be awoken. Only through acceptance, awareness and understanding can true liberation be achieved and that is a process that must be fought with all strength and conquered with iron, stone and fire. For creatures like the Asetians this refusal of true nature and the neglecting of kin is the definition of mortality and, in a sense, the actual oblivion of the soul — something that can never be tolerated.

One of the oldest symbols of spiritual transformation and alchemical rebirth — the awakening — is represented by the Egyptian beetle or scarab and found in ancient history as the hieroglyph of

Khepri. As a word it literally means transformation and it is found among the seven sacred pillars of Asetianism, a key of initiation into universal wisdom. The scarab conveys the symbolism of evolution as different stages of the soul, the trials of life, death and rebirth before the attaining of enlightenment; it is the spiritual concept of becoming.

It was observed by the Ancient Egyptians that scarabs would lay their eggs in dung only to roll the material until it acquired a spherical shape that could then be hardened by the Sun. Later, in the apparent magick of life this nothingness gave birth to the winged children of the scarab. The mystery of life and the flying forth of a living creature from something lifeless and inert as dung reveals the subtle nature of the awakening and its symbolism. The scarab makes use of insignificant material deprived of life and imbues it with meaning by symbolically transforming it into something greater — the winged children; a distinctive analogy to the nature of the Asetians and their birth of divinity within human flesh, making Khepri a clear representation and ancient interpretation of the alchemical nature found in Asetianism.

Kheper-i kheper kheperu kheper-kuie em kheperu
en Khepri kheper em Sep Tepy.

When I became, the becoming became. I have become in becoming the form of Khepri, who came into being in the Sep Tepy.

This old Khepri mantra is a cultural example on the obscure but thoroughly examined nature of Asetian transformation and becoming. The non-vocal resonance that arises from the repetition of varying forms of the word Khepri can induce a hypnotic trance that may cloud conscious judgment and liberate unconscious perception, allowing for the exploration of the unseen through a metaphysical reverberation of energy vibration where the initiate can access other layers of interpretation without bumping into the rationality of the conscious mind.[10] This is a form of inner esoteric work where the mantras must be allowed to resonate with the higher grasp of the soul, accessing planes of perception other than those common writing or phonetic expression allows. More intricate mantras are found in other Asetian texts, providing an added tool of understanding, mystical exploration and a well guarded door into the hidden corridors of self-initiation, such as the mysteries mirrored on the initiatory spell *The Touch of Khonsu* found in the pages of the *Book of Ipet Resyt* within *Liber Aeternus*.[11]

The concept of awakening has been tied to the Asetian tradition since its inception and as such it is often interpreted as a vampiric definition but that is not entirely accurate. Although intimately Asetian in nature the concept of awakening is not exclusively vampiric since it is also related with the spiritual process of discovery and growth experienced by Asetianists and those who embrace the path of the Aset Ka for more than a single lifetime. The initiatory nature of the Asetian soul and the alchemical power of our teachings causes profound change in the lives, minds and evolution of everyone touched by such flame. Asetianists have a great understanding of this transformation, having experienced first-hand the powerful touch of Asetian wisdom and following this tradition for many incarnations, sometimes even since the dawn of the Asetian empire in Egypt when they fought together as close friends and cherished allies of the Aset Ka, a noble path and honored bond they loyally keep to this day. This reality makes them experience their very own awakening, particularly tied to finding the old path within Asetianism and discovering their beautiful nature nurtured by the side of the Asetians. It allows for them to tap deeper into their past and unleash a greater potential of emotion and metaphysical ability, tools forged upon a long walk through our road of evolution and countless lessons forgotten in time. In reunited strength they find their home and in this way ultimately finding themselves, celebrating the present as an undying gift from their past now written in stone and remembered in darkness.

Primordials

As cradle to the Asetian civilization the Primordials embody the original flame of our mysteries and seed of the violet bloodline. They are the first-born; heirs to the throne of Aset, bearers of primal essence and leaders of the Aset Ka.

The true names of soul and thrice-rising Fire remain a secret celebrated in silence as their nature reveals the face of divinity through the footsteps of giants. On the halls of the undying their voices echo without sound and in their abominable presence the hymn of Aset is felt under the pale moonlight. In the apogee of their creation and legendary existence the sacredness of three is revered and revealed, eternally reflecting the magick of Orion upon the inscrutable darkness of this forgotten kin.

The essence of the Primordials brings forth the creational Breath of Aset as Her legacy given life. Born from Her thought, magick and womb they stood at the dawn of the ages as pillars of black stone, carrying the flaming swords glowing in shades of violet light.

Serpent, Scarab and Scorpion... That is their nature and everlasting flag; a realm of transcendent roots manifested in triple form. As three they sprang to life and as three they carved their destiny, shaping the course of history in ways unseen and through the silent influence of their inspiring force.

As Horus one was remembered, not the secret nomen but an ancient king that ruled on Her throne and led in Her name. Alongside two nameless sisters they ruled a nation and raised all magick, teaching lessons of soul and spirit as foretold by the seed of immortal Mother. The path of Aset was raised above while all lies were cast below. Three faces of Her divine beauty, they are One and One alone.

The Higher Magisterium within the Order of Aset Ka is the realm of the Primordials and that law remains since the ancient time to this day. Those spiritual halls of transcendent significance hold three crowns of initiation standing on the three thrones of Aset, where only the Primordials seat and rise until the end of time. So it has been and shall always be as they perpetually return to their seats of power. Their wisdom reflects the unspoken mysteries that guide the Asetians and command the Aset Ka, a fountain of immortal legacy and unrelenting spiritual youth.

In the earthly structure of the Aset Ka the Higher Magisterium is always led by one to three of the Primordials and, when none are incarnated, the sacred thrones of Aset remain vacant and leadership is granted to an interim magister of their choosing, however to develop such elements is irrelevant to the uninitiated as those are details of internal covenant that remain bound to noble oaths of honor that are of no concern to outsiders. It remains only meaningful to state that the elusive leadership and secretive operations of Asetian society should not be understood akin to human hierarchy in any form, as they do not represent a doorway to power or a position of status but reflect on the natural order of the universe and the balanced nature of enlightened spirituality. The Primordials are part of the soul of every Asetian as the embodiment of the triple essence of Aset. They are ancestors, founders, initiators and guides. Rising above the prejudice of mortals they fly high with wings of purest silver while carrying the immortal Fire of eternal ages…

Elders

The elders are Asetians who lived during the period of the Sep Tepy at the golden age of the Asetian empire in the Djehuty of the Scorpion. Amongst the first initiators of magick they are the ones who crafted the original edification of the Aset Ka as a stronghold of knowledge and culture of understanding, educating the ancients on the arts of their mysteries. Ancestors of the Asetian legacy they have lived and died by the side of the Primordials who entrusted them with keys to the higher mysteries, representing the most ancient of souls within the immortal family.

This terminology is that of spiritual nature and cultural significance, tied to the fabric of initiation and evolved wisdom, not a title or established rank as those remain confused notions of the mundane, unseen within the structure of the Aset Ka.

Some still incarnate to this day as silent initiators of life and death, safekeeping Her legacy and teaching Her mysteries. Their knowledge and timeless wisdom is cherished and respected within the Aset Ka and throughout the occult world, leading the Order in modern times under close guidance of the Primordials and the very Will of Aset. Bound to memory of a long gone past and unheard magick old as time they are now part of the fabric of our world, moving in mysterious ways and playing their elusive pieces with a strategy and symmetry that carries the sight of countless centuries as history becomes written and their silent actions forge the future of all.

✝

When the Sun sets and Orion rises high in the sky you may hear their call as a hymn of ancient eras...

Taught and initiated by the Primordials the elders carry a distinctive energy signature and spiritual mark that is bound to the mysteries of the original practice of Khenmet, mastered and perfected during the Sep Tepy. That sacred technique changed only slightly with time and saw its vibration altered, serving a higher purpose of secretive nature vitally unknown outside of the Aset Ka as it holds elements of spiritual meaning that define the Asetian elders.

The inspiring energy exuded by these ancient Asetians can be so intense or even overpowering that those more sensitive to the unseen can experience a range of charged emotions, physical sensations and the vibrations rising as they approach, subtly touching everything and everyone around them like the purest velvet dancing to the smoke of perfumed incense.

On formal examination the first three Asetians that we described as Primordials are what can be considered the first elders; founders of each immortal Lineage initiated by Aset and the living seed of Her timeless creation. However it remains important to underline, even if apparently repetitive, but the limited mind of mundanes driven by ego requires such note, that every Asetian is an essential and equally vital part of the family, elder or otherwise, as those terms and spiritual concepts are never the focus of power, greed or hidden desire. Recurrently misunderstood whether unintentionally or by design the Aset Ka is a transcendent manifestation of a pyramid where each and every rock has significant meaning and is bound to great importance, being cherished and honored from the strong yet unaware elements at the foundation to the higher enlightened stones reaching for the sky; only with every piece in place and united as one single structure can the pyramid withstand the test of time and stand unshaken by any outer force as the Order remains to this day. This spiritual architecture that aims to reflect the fabric of nature was a never a reason for conflict or dispute within the Aset Ka and one that has survived intact, shielded from outside influence and delusions of power, remaining indifferent to bias, ignorance and criticism. Loyalty and unity are greatly honored hallmarks of Asetianism — two living forces that stand beneath its unquestionable strength and resilience as a reflection of the bond forged since the time of the elders.

Masters

Just like the concept of Asetian elders the word master is frequently used in Asetianism not as rank or mundane title. Masters are initiators and teachers, creators and destroyers, having glimpsed into the realm of the higher mysteries. They hold the keys of magick and pass the teachings of spirit, being fluent on the intricate branches of ancient wisdom, hidden history and the cunning secrets of occult arts.

Taught within the high halls of the Aset Ka the masters are commonly but not exclusively elders, dedicated to the eternal pursuit of alchemical perfection, spiritual insight, magickal knowledge and enlightened wisdom. In simple terms they are proven scholars with vast practical experience of the magickal arts and unseen mysteries, being on this chosen road for more than a single lifetime.

> *"There is no Master without being an eternal student.*
> *There is no Master without the ability to learn from the ones he teaches.*
> *There is no Master without the experience of dying to be reborn..."*
>
> Words in Silence, Liber Silentis

†

All masters carry the silent banner of Aset with pride and honor under their wings as they represent an omen of responsibility and truth. Cherished by every member of the family from Asetian to Asetianist their advice and cautious judgment is treasured with great esteem, for the word of a master is not sacred but carries within its teachings the wisdom of countless ages and a rare echo of immeasurable power. They subtly carve the words that pave the ethereal gardens of the soul; the priceless teachings that the wise value higher than gold.

Although most prefer to operate in the shadows, being elusive and hard to find, Asetian masters are constantly sought by many including those outside of the family and the violet realm of Asetianism due to the unprecedented insight and in-depth knowledge they are able to provide. This has led to broad speculation, superstition and rumor throughout the centuries, especially among those who seek them with desire for praise and blame without ever actually being graced with their presence or wisdom. Clarity, caution and verifiability are essential when approaching supposed sources of Asetian information as wise seekers remain skeptic of bold claims and wild theories from those who speak frequently or loudly, for many profess knowledge over masters and tradition as mere vehicles of falsehood without bringing any knowledge of truthful value.

The word master should not be used liberally but as a sign of respect and genuine commitment, for its spiritual meaning is tied to the evolution of the soul and bound to a long process of reincarnation, development and higher initiation, never the mirror of a social position or an adopted element of vanity. In fact, most masters will not even claim to be recognized as such or may dismiss the use of the word entirely, although their ability and skill can be noticeable through the thoughtful observation of their words, humility and awareness.

✝

Approaching a master should not be pursued lightly or driven by a desire for praise but only as an answer to a profound calling of the heart. As such, it should be executed with honesty and a higher commitment for truth, for lies and deceit are known to pay a grievous price in Asetianism and the ways of masters are infinite and unseen, bearing the gift of piercing eyesight and a touch capable of reaching deep into the hidden crevices of the soul. Yet even before such a step is taken there should be no doubt about the nature of the master and that is evidence that only the Aset Ka can provide, remaining aware that this is often a world of liars and dishonest pretenders where some will relentlessly make use of cunning, treachery and deceit plotted for the devices of attention, praise, servitude to the ego and undeserved power.

For Asetians and Asetianists the bonds forged with masters and elders are sacred; a symmetry of respect and mutual acceptance capable of surviving death and overcoming life. Those links forged through the mingling of emotion, energy and soul are incredibly profound and carry great meaning, with an understanding that draws parallel to a long relationship with a dedicated donor. It is a strong and intimate spiritual knot that most humans cannot comprehend, yet an unshakable commitment of loyalty, protection and guidance that exists beyond their grasp and holds the potential for everlastingness.

Healers

Beyond all of the dangerous elements found in Asetian culture, its darker aspects of mystical wisdom and intrinsic predatory nature, the Asetians are fascinating healers with the power and knowledge to cure, ward off disease and prevent degeneration. That fact may be a lesser-known element of Asetianism to outsiders but it represents a vital aspect of its practice, study and development. Established amongst the greatest healers of past and present the Asetians are capable of acting directly upon inner levels of the energy body and soul with a solid understanding of subtle anatomy, approaching the process of healing as a holistic journey potentiated by Self and only possible through the diligent union of every layer of being by syncing mind, body and spirit.

Portraying vampires as healers may appear counterintuitive at first glance but, when realizing that in this case the word implies a higher spiritual insight and powerful metaphysical abilities, such notions may start to clear. It is this understanding of energy and the subtle reality alongside a dedicated study of every aspect found in the machinery of the universe that makes Asetians so powerful in the ancient arts of healing. The various systems of energy healing, subtle therapy and traditional medicine often find a higher rate of effectiveness when practiced or supported by an experienced Asetian. However, that does not mean that everything can or should be cured and that the Asetians are the hidden solution for every failure of modern medicine; quite on the contrary, as many Asetians have knowledge of medical science and work better alongside its tools than against them.

In Asetianism no knowledge is discarded, as every form of culture, wisdom and understanding is cautiously explored and studied. This is evident in the Asetian approach to medical practice where despite their expertise with metaphysical techniques and subtle healing they also embrace a myriad of alternative medicine branches, traditional medical systems and modern science. Despite such an open-minded approach that leads to understanding and diversity it is in the mastery of energy where Asetian power truly excels, being capable of directing it towards a higher use often of spiritual nature. Once applied to the arts of healing and the essence of medical practice this can raise esoteric techniques such as Reiki or more conventional therapies to an entirely new level beyond the grasp of common practitioners and the barriers established by a mundane society.

One of the most fascinating facets of vampiric healing is also amongst the most misleading due to the taboo and stigma that is frequently tied to the predatory nature of Asetians. There are medicinal properties to be found in the very acts of energy feeding, which under the right circumstances and if properly used can become powerful healing tools. These unconventional techniques are unavailable to an ordinary therapist or medical practitioner but they represent a potent procedure that can be used effectively for the activation of stagnated energy, in the process of breaking benign blockages and even on the treatment of malignant constructs developed within the subtle body.

It should however be stated that an active vampiric drain when done irresponsibly can be potentially dangerous or in rare extreme cases even lethal. Only when balanced with control, activated with mastery and selflessly focused on healing can it safely promote a healthier flow of energy, lower the levels of depression and enhance the metabolism. Through this practice the subtle alterations and changes induced on the layers of vital energy and its internal vibration echo to the other realms of mind and body as ripples that propagate the seed for self-healing, that if taken and accepted by the biological mechanisms of the body can manifest as improved health, wellbeing and a greater potential for cure while preventing some root causes behind various forms of disease, imbalance and emotional problems. This is a subject that remains somewhat disfavored even in modern occult practice and holistic thinking due to its potential for misuse and intentional abuse but the unique ability that Asetians have to drain the essence of the living, commonly interpreted by others solely as a potent weapon or dangerous psychic tool, conceals great potential for balance and treatment, thus remaining a misunderstood and underrated force of healing.

This realization represents another mirror of the duality found in Asetianism where the darker and potentially dangerous aspects of its practices also represent the wisdom that make its healing elements possible and more effective. It is an elegant dance that balances the fluids of light and darkness in ephemeral harmony but when mingled together they raise the alchemical violet mist that manifests the very nature of each Asetian; a spark that cannot be found in absolute light or around total darkness as it embodies both and none at the same time.

Psychology

Understanding the mind of an Asetian may be a daunting quest but learning from their mastery of psychology and inborn expertise over the mechanisms of the psyche can provide any educated seeker with the golden fruits of a brighter tree.

As it has been established, even if occasionally praised or criticized, the Asetians are not intrinsically friendly by nature. They are admittedly not social or graced with the vain needs of common minds as their ego is not a ruling master nor are they slaves to its whip. Innate manipulators, rigorous analysts and revolutionary pioneers — cryptic in thought and action — their predatory nature makes them feared and mysterious but they should not be defined as evil since such notion remains subjective and bound to context. This does not mean that Asetians will never be observed or interpreted as friendly or even social as that depends on what they are projecting and how they wish to be perceived; it is a learned technique, a subtle cloak and not an aspect of reality. As chameleons of energy and scholars of thought Asetians operate in subtlety and distinctive elegance, concealing an arsenal of tricks and contraptions that can be magickal or simply psychological, tied to the cognitive response of the unaware.

A hallmark of the Asetian mind is the complete and almost inhuman disregard for outside opinion and judgment, a mirror of confidence and trust that may sometimes be understood as arrogance when it simply reflects a strong identity and personality. One built upon the solid foundation of an ancient culture that values honor and loyalty while it despises futility and judgmental ignorance. No Asetian is concerned for the disbelief of others in their nature and existence, or the extent of their powers and abilities; most even cherish that ignorance and unawareness among the general population, seeing it as a tool and preferring to live in the privacy and discretion that only secrecy can provide, not to mention that history has proven for it to be a powerful trump.

Beyond such fundamental elements tied to the core of this culture — and everyone is influenced by culture and environment — it can be easily understood that it is not possible to define the mind of an Asetian or to categorize their personality according to established human psychology. In fact, the Asetians have proven to be a shrouded mystery when analysed by experienced psychologists and psychiatrists who sometimes fall prey to the mind games of these ancient scholars of thought that learned long ago how to beat them at their own game. The Asetians are fierce instigators of liberation and icons of spiritual freedom who are not bound to rules or limitations and as such they are a very diverse family, manifesting in entirely different personalities that cannot be easily profiled and interpreted. The one thing that every Asetian does not hide is pride in the culture, legacy and spiritual

✝

nature that defines the Aset Ka, fiercely protecting it alongside the noble call of Aset against all odds no matter the cost. In that aspect they know no surrender...

When indulging in deeper studies some psychological lines can be, to a limited extent, tied to the different Lineages and the manifested pillars of their existence but even then such an analysis can prove to be inaccurate and speculative, as the nature of each Lineage is defined by spirituality and not biology, so it should be studied with caution by avoiding the traps of assumption and extrapolation. This kind of examination has been explored in further detail on the chapters about each Lineage.

> *"We were a silent, hidden thought in the folds of oblivion, and we have become a voice that causes the heavens to tremble."*
>
> Khalil Gibran

Asetian scholars have dedicated a considerable amount of their history to the exploration and understanding of the mind, not only Asetian in nature but also human. Such detailed learning and development has provided them with a level of insight and experience that often makes them more knowledgeable and capable than what modern psychology is able to provide. They are not limited or conditioned by social standards and that alone is an asset for a cleaner grasp on the elusive fabric of consciousness and the intricate machinery that composes the mind. This pursuit for understanding has led the Asetians on a timeless quest that has nurtured its fruits of wisdom, mirrored on the diversity and enlightened knowledge found in the teachings from the Aset Ka of past and present. Such an unparalleled mastery of psychology should never be dismissed or underestimated since if wielded by the cunning hands of wisdom it can become a potent weapon, that when bound to the eloquence and elegance that is expected from an Asetian it becomes so undeniably vampiric and uniquely capable.

Your voice alone can make a lot of noise but your voice inside a crowd cannot be heard at all. An Asetian never tries to talk louder than the surrounding crowd; an Asetian becomes that crowd.

Appearance

It should be obvious to everyone that real vampires do not feature long pointy fangs, unnaturally colored eyes or razor-sharp nails. When touched they do not feel ghastly cold as death nor are they necessarily pale and physically strong. Those traits are recognizable elements of fiction that do not describe in any way the reality of vampirism nor do they reflect the appearance of the Asetians.

An oftentimes speculated subject and also one commonly misunderstood is how and if the subtle transformations experienced by Asetians reflect on their physical body. The truth is that, while health and biological processes are undoubtedly affected by the energy system, the alchemy of those transformations is bound to intervene on the physical state of organic tissue and organs, sometimes even in a profound way, whereby direct correlations with physical standards and other defined traits simply should not be done.

It is factual that there are intensely pale Asetians with visible veins on the surface of their skin that may become prominent and more defined upon interaction with energy, but skin tone, race or hair color have absolutely nothing to do with the nature of an Asetian or any spiritual foundation. Such inaccurate notions reflect a disguised form of racism and manifest as a reflex of popular culture driven by ignorance and an established vain society. Physically the Asetians manifest in endless form and in every gender, being incredibly diverse in their exquisite allure.

Sometimes outsiders possibly deluded by the mysterious aura that surrounds these creatures and their magickal life fail to understand that Asetians and Sethians, although not human in their spiritual nature, are still bound to the constrictions of physical incarnation, suffering disease and other physical ailments as every element of humanity. While embodying life in the realm of matter their soul is incarnated in physical shell — the body — with an organism and established biology that is vastly similar to that of a human and in most cases indistinguishable to the untrained eye.

One detail that has long been established as a potential physical characteristic of the Asetians is bound to a fundamental aspect that although authentic it can also be deceiving. This elusive physical mark is found on the eyes in the form of an enlarged circular aura located around the iris as a distinctively diffuse line. That should not be confused with the arcus senilis of the cornea, commonly found in the elderly, and although similar to a structure also visible in certain humans, the one observed in Asetian eyes is denser, often thicker and portrays characteristics that make it unique. However that element alone is far from definitive in the validation and study of an Asetian body, much less an identifier of the soul as that remains an intricate process of great responsibility and discretion.

The depth of the Asetian gaze is legendary but to define that as a physical characteristic would be subjective and abstract. Behind the intensity of their eyes the Asetians can touch mind, body and soul, an expression of a piercing nature that can be relatively easy to sense by anyone who has experienced the embrace of their energy before. The pain, wisdom and perception mirrored on their eyes transmit profound emotions and unexplained mystery, hiding keys to countless secrets capable of unleashing a wealth of sensations upon the fabric of humanity, from agonizing fear to magnetic attraction. The eyes are a tool of predators, one carefully developed throughout millions of years of natural evolution and adaptation, being used as a weapon of manipulation but also representing an object of trust, affection and desire.

Such powers do not come without handicaps capable of expressing certain weaknesses, as Asetian eyes tend to be hypersensitive and extremely delicate, particularly susceptible to ultraviolet radiation but also to pollution and other forms of invisible toxicity. Energetic abilities may be affected during exposure to sunlight and powers potentially diminished as the subtle system becomes unbalanced and reactive to compensate for the overdrive caused by solar energy. Despite seeing some of their dangerous powers weakened by its blazing influence the Asetians can also use the touch of Ra to their metaphysical advantage, channeling elemental energies of the Sun through the outer layers of their system in order to activate subtle sparks of relevant magickal use and life-sustaining quality, although at the potential cost of mild auric burn. For the more scholarly inclined such metaphysical elements may give clues to the origins found in folklore and myth about the hatred vampires nourish for sunlight. Those concepts are not entirely accurate as the energy of the Sun is essential to balanced life and certainly no real vampire turns into ashes from exposure to daylight, even if it can affect their energy system in a negative way. In fact, such elements of lore go back in history as far as the Ancient Egyptian times where Ra — the embodiment of the Sun — and Aset fought in an epic confrontation that became legend. The true reason for this intolerance is however more metaphysical than spiritual and it is related with how the energy system of Asetians handles the metabolic processing of certain forms of radiation, being particularly sensitive to specific vibrations. Still, the Sun remains a force to be reckoned and not a power to be dismissed or underestimated.

Asetians and the enduring archetype of vampires are often associated with black clothing, dark beauty and gothic fashion. Those elements should never be used to characterize an Asetian as they are bound to personal preference and fashion is not an aspect of relevance in Asetianism. However, the adoption of black clothing is common in contemporary Asetian culture although that is not related with fashion but hides behind metaphysical reasoning, or better said it is used as an energy feature. In terms of physics, black is not a real color but the absence of color. It absorbs light from all colors present in the visible spectrum and reflects nothing, exactly the opposite of white that naturally reflects all other colors so it is the sum of every color. This makes black unique and intrinsically vampiric in terms of metaphysics and modern science, revealing why some Asetians make use of its characteristics under an energetic perspective, as black clothing absorbs small portions of different energies present in the environment and being projected by others, providing enhanced sensing and awareness in every kind of situation. Such difference may be subtle but it remains an added resource that can provide an edge in the right circumstances, being another of the many examples where Asetians have united science and spirituality — or better said, they mastered the science of the past, understand the science of the present and bring forth the science of the future.

This notion and its advanced understanding should not be confused with gothic fashion or the many people that wear black clothing as a social trend without the knowledge and metaphysical awareness of the reasoning behind its Asetian adoption in modern times. Asetians are liberated beings that promote freedom, abiding to no rules or established human concepts of cultism and conventional beauty. Their choices of clothing, accessories and appearance are not used to make a statement for they care not, leaving the controlling whip of vanity to the slaves of humanity. Like with everything Asetian in nature their reasons are profound and every act carries more significance than what meets the eye.

In the end, Asetians will be perceived as how they wish to be seen, not always alluring and beautiful but sometimes frail and vulnerable if that provides a strategic advantage to their personal agenda or they simply wish to avoid attention. Their mind and wisdom are amongst their greatest weapons and not everything is what it seems. No wonder history has long portrayed them as wolves in sheep's clothing for their control manifests through silence and their ultimate disguise is you.

Mundanes

The concept of mundanes is an established terminology that refers to non-magickal or non-spiritual people and defines the vast majority of the human population that unawarely embraces a limited life encased by the constraints of matter and embodies a materialistic society. Literarily and by definition the word mundane relates to ordinary as opposed to spiritual; in the realm of the occult it is used in reference to those unaware of the existence of magick, energy and the subtle forces or who are unable to wield such powers, but also the ones that embrace them superficially, seek from popularity without being committed to deeper understanding or driven by the desire for exhibition.

There are other words that are also used to represent the same or similar concepts and their adoption should not be confused with fictional or anthropological contexts, with different terminologies that have changed throughout history and vary according to cultural background.

Divergences between those who embrace the reality of spirit and the ones that pass through life in blindness have existed since the dawn of humanity with disputes that have been historically influenced by politics, religion, ideology and faith. Asetians as champions of wisdom, magick and spirituality have long been on the opposing end of the desires, agendas and plots of mundanes, establishing themselves in time as the adversaries of ignorance and dishonor. However, generalization is an easy trap that a seeker should avoid with care and preparedness, for not every mundane is the same nor their limitations are equal and, just like students, scholars and masters of the occult are as diverse as the stars in the sky so each mundane should be approached with wisdom and interpreted without dogma or preconceived judgment. Surely there are many who can only be blamed for their ignorance, willingly discarding everything that they do not comprehend or are apparently unable to see, but others are merely unaware because they were not given a chance to learn. They remain isolated from the world of magick and segregated from the possibility of the mysteries by a stagnant society that became blinded by its own delusion of progress, self-righteousness and eager judgment of everything and everyone that boldly dares to think different. They were born in a world of popular culture and false idols where wealth and not knowledge equals power, worship and success. It is a society of lies, vanity and betrayal that venerates body over mind and decaying beauty over growth or evolution; a herd that seeks fast results and instant gratification while discarding effort, learning and dedication, deprived of any true meaning, sense or purpose.

It is however important to understand that this illuminated superiority provided by knowledge and awareness should not constitute reasoning to dismiss mundanes as insignificant nor should the terminology always be used as derogatory. Everyone deserves at least one chance and one doorway, even if how to walk through it is undeniably their own choice and one that should be provided in absolute and nondiscriminating freedom. Such are the cycles of life and death just like darkness becomes the liberating force of blinding light. Balance is maintained in a dance of diverging and opposing manifestations as secrecy is only possible through the loud voices of those posing in the spotlight, unknowingly serving us all.

In the end the disbelief of mundanes establishes your unseen power through dangerously deceptive silence, concealed behind the veil of this world in a tune that uninitiated ears cannot hear. Their ignorance ignites the lingering potential of your predatory Self as an abominating beast of magick and foresight. In darkness their hearts desperately seek the comfort of the light while we… well we learned how to hunt daemons blindfolded and alone many centuries ago.

Djehutys
Journey of Time

1 n Ancient Egypt the concept of time and the documenting of history were the realms of Thoth, the purveyor of knowledge and scribe of the Gods. His name was known by the ancients as Djehuty, a word that in Asetianism is tied to the fabric of incarnated time and the formulae of history.

Used as terminology to study and define the cycles of time in spiritual history each Djehuty establishes a different formula of magickal thought and psychological pattern, finding mirror on the cultural action and inaction imprinted on the historical records of our collective past. The Djehutys represent an accurate universal scale; a metric to analyse the influence of time in the cosmos and to interpret its varying tides. They are a marker for the ages and a tome of eras long lived as their definitions and limitations find correlation in the views of various cultures and interpretations from diverse traditions, being far reaching in the scope of understanding.

The formulae from different eras are intricate and tied to the pulsating texture of human evolution, manifesting not only as a living embodiment of the voices of nature but presenting a dynamic aspect of creation and destruction; the rise and fall of universal vibration that echoes in the cultural development of societies, the views of spirituality and the wielding of what is unseen. There is a strong magickal component beneath the apparently linear sound of history and that element of esoteric significance defines the underlying mechanisms that make each distinctive spiritual formula manifest — causing change, influencing thought and effectively becoming a driving force in the course of history.

At the time of the writing of this book the world is in the early stages of a new era that represents a shift in spiritual paradigm and magickal formula. This age is described as the Djehuty of the Serpent and it stands at the first embryonic moments of transition while the vast majority of uninitiated thought remains stuck to the decadent mental constructs of the previous era. Before this new dawn of change history has experienced three major Djehutys: the Djehuty of the Scorpion as the primordial age in the cradle of time blessed by immortal Fire, followed by the golden era of the Djehuty of the Hawk liberated by emotional Water and then reaching strife and blindness with the Djehuty of the Crocodile under the slavery of dominating Earth.

That is the history of us all and the perpetual movement of its unrelenting steps leads to this very day, a moment unique in time as another profound page on the timeless book of life emerges; an age of Serpents and silent initiation where thought is enlightened through the power of Air and its creative forces driven courageously towards the rediscovery of long lost truth.

✝

Sting of the Sacred Scorpion

The Djehuty of the Scorpion is the primordial age of the Gods; the cradle of life, time and consciousness that we know as the Sep Tepy, the Egyptian terminology for First Time. Profoundly tied to the mysteries of Aset and Her magick this Djehuty spans an enormous timeframe from the beginning of creation and the formation of the cosmos to the rise of the Egyptian empire and the flourishing of its millennial culture. This is an era of birth for the Asetians and where their origins and legacy find primordial roots and the most delicate seeds. A time of legends and forgotten deeds when Aset roamed this Earth and the elders rose for the first time, ignited by Her breath, kindled with Her fire and initiated through Her magick.

The faces of Goddesses and Gods were that of timeless teachers, guides and leaders, harnessing unseen powers and emanating energies, cautiously and cryptically passing the knowledge and ancient technology that was later adopted by the Egyptian people in the creation of the most advanced civilization the world has ever witnessed; a wealth of culture, architecture, art, engineering, medicine and, of course, magick.

This Djehuty is characterised by a higher form of spirituality and its formula is one of the most difficult to grasp by an incarnated mind: the initiatory formula of immortal Fire. The now severed bond between humanity and divinity was then intact and openly celebrated as an integral part of daily life; the proud marriage of the sacred with the profane. It was an era of innocence, discovery and great achievement, much of it now lost or forgotten in time, when respect was sacred and words were magick. Its glitter of peace, joyful youth and beacon of hope endured for thousands of years until its delicate balance was threatened and fell into disgrace.

☥

As it approached imbalance, decay and collapse it was during the final moments of this Djehuty that the abyssal battles known as the Epic Wars took place, spanning into the birth of the next Djehuty and some of its stages of development. Those timeless battles of colossal proportions and abominating consequences reached far beyond the deceitful quest for supremacy but embodied a primeval defiance against the opposers of honor, family and loyalty, while its true meaning remains elusive and incomprehensible to the limited mind of mortality.

The Epic Wars were never a set of battles of good versus evil nor did they oppose the forces of darkness against the knights of light. Such history is carved in blood, pain and torment but it is also written by the courage of poetic warriors that dared to defy life and Gods against the Fire of their own ideologies. They ignited a battle for honor above power; a clash of titans against the rising storm of one thousand thunders, where Asetians became the breaking darkness at the end of the world. Epic without question, this was the mother of all battles and it was agonizingly real, beyond tales and songs its destiny now sealed in secrecy and myth. An enduring hymn of victory and defeat. A memory that can never die.

During the Djehuty of the Scorpion the Aset Ka was founded and forged by immortal Fire at the dawn of the Asetian empire that would enlighten, guide and rule for more than centuries. It was a time of magick and temples; of glory, valor and wisdom, when the lands of Kemet now known as Egypt were not yet scorched through the natural processes of desertification as they are now. The contemporary desert of the Sahara was only beginning to form and those lands were under the rule of Seth and his red minions, fiercely encircling the flourishing cities along the Nile in their boldness and cunning stand, emanating a striking contrast with the color and song of the empire of Aset.

Her kingdom structured on a foundation of wisdom, spirituality and evolution was not vulnerable or unprotected, wielding its own strong military force, however even the Asetian army was greatly outnumbered by the united Sethian hordes and their allies from the south — their leaders later renown under the banners of the Red Order of Seth. History is treacherous and warfare a mystery of balance and power, for this battle was never about numbers and the painful Epic Wars would find their unexpected conclusion under the might of a much smaller force and yet far more terrifying than the two opposing factions combined. That small and elusive fellowship that would write the final defining moments of this legendary war became known as the Imperial Guard, the personal guard of Aset and most devastating force any battle has ever witnessed, comprised not only of uniquely trained Asetians but also darker creatures of an abominating nature... forbidden daemons of the ancient world.

Featuring sigils of a stinging scorpion on the shields, swords and bows, the Imperial Guard has marked its place in history through agonizing pain and arrogantly spilled blood; a force that Aset was ever reluctant to unleash but that through Her determined Will saved a nation and united a family. Such actions were a vital catalyst in reclaiming the throne of Egypt and spiritual seat of the empire. Led by the intimidating Seven Scorpions, this royal guard of Her majesty became an enduring legend of Asetian power and victory, as well as a perpetual scar on the face of every Sethian who has ever lived but also a profound wound on the heart of the Asetian legacy for that one moment of unparalleled destruction. The common people called it The Scorpion Army and rumors speak of its existence still today, safekeeping Aset and Her children as shadows of dreadful nightmares. Operating in silence they are ever watchful...

The Epic Wars embody an unforgivable lesson that Asetians taught their enemies but they also represent one they learned themselves with pain and sorrow, carrying fruits to further generations, forever echoed on the Asetian teachings of unlimited understanding, the shielding of innocence, enforcing of justice, their protection of wisdom and the unrestrained promotion of freedom, loyalty and inner beauty. Although the battles from the Sep Tepy left a strong mark on that Djehuty and remain a stain of violence and destruction in the history of Asetianism, for most of its span this was a period governed by peace, growth and spiritual achievement. The harmonious timeframes of the Sep Tepy represent an era of grand beauty and prosperity. The Asetian empire was a golden reign that brought human civilization from anarchy and primitive society to the advanced world and culture now studied as Ancient Egypt, attaining a level of balance, order and enlightenment that humanity alone could never achieve. It was a sacred age forgotten in time; the only era where Gods and mortals walked together and fought as one. That was all about to change...

Flight of the Royal Hawk

The Djehuty of the Hawk achieved its peak during later historical stages of development of the Ancient Egyptian culture and it was characterized by a strong influence of matriarchal societies, the celebration of planet Earth as living expression of mother nature and provider of life, with most world religions developing around theology of the Goddess and spirituality of the divine feminine. Women were honored and respected for their power and wisdom, becoming a revered pillar of society as the spiritual center of life and creation.

In some cultures the human knowledge was so restricted that the pregnancy of a woman and the birth of a child were misunderstood and not tied to the sexual union of man and woman, leading to the belief that females held the power of creation and were responsible for the birth and prosperity of the species.

A new spiritual formula was established, bound to the fountain of life and the mysteries of the living, flourishing through the etheric flow of emotional Water. Sacredness was tied to the mysteries of women and their powers of conception, a magickal spark that raised life, nourished growth and allowed for society to prosper. The crops that fed a population, the animals in the land and rivers as well as the children of humanity... all were seeded by the miracle of women. Such profound reverence for the essence of women alongside the raising of female significance in society and culture was also a distinctive silent mirror of the prevalent Asetian influence during that time, not one enforced through mystical misunderstanding but a conviction augmented by the strong foundation of female power that is established in Asetianism since its inception, known for the fierce protection and advocation of feminine identity, beauty and divinity.

The early steps of this Djehuty saw periods of change, political instability and collapse as the Egyptian nation ceased to be one unified force under a single banner. This broken Egypt now divided into two smaller nations, the upper and lower lands, saw its prosperity from the Sep Tepy and previous Djehuty of the Scorpion diminished. Those were times of stalled growth and threatened freedom but chaos is a powerful catalyst of evolution that nurtures strength and inspires greater deeds. In time balance would be attained and the empire reunited under the crown of Asetians and rise of the House of Horus that unified Egypt once more, led by a pharaoh in immortal flight as a royal hawk.

So the fertile lands on the shores of the Nile found prosperity once again and established their old reign of tolerance, science and spirituality. It was during the final times of this pharaonic Egypt that Asetians parted the sacred lands and disappeared from known history, leaving their Kemetic throne to humankind and being remembered only in legend and myth. This decisive step immortalized their silent empire and perpetuated its legacy in shadow and within the secretive halls of those that can grasp its existence.

The pharaohs of old were initiated into the gnosis reflected from these higher mysteries of a shared past, identifying their crown and leadership as representatives of Horus, the first-born Asetian and their honored pharaoh; a symbol of divinity and enlightened rule established long ago when the Gods themselves ruled Egypt. Here is found a spiritual connection with the governing forces of that Djehuty and its magickal formula as an echo of the path of Horus, the great hawk who inherited the throne of Aset and spoke in Her name. His words were magick and his actions the leading force for the safekeeping of Her legacy, bringing forth the watery tides of revolution that would raise women to power and spiritual dominance.

Even during the new age of mortal rule, when humanity was given control over Egypt, there were periods of Asetian guidance and influence but this time established in secret and as a result of silent power over the cycles of reincarnation and mastery of the Duat. It was never again a permanent rule and revealed leadership but such historical details remain shrouded in secrecy, whispers and rumor.

The legacy of the great Goddess endured for ages but its power slowly dwindled as the spiritual formula entered decay and fell before the rising of envy, ego and obsession for power driven by a newly emerging force: mortal men. Slowly the Ancient Egyptian people were forgotten, their kingdom conquered and overrun, their wisdom banished and destroyed. The sacred Temple of Philae, once a great Asetian stronghold of magick and initiation in the Nile was closed and defaced, its priesthood chased down while the noble art of the hieroglyphs became corrupted and misunderstood, in part forever...

✝

Haunting of the Treacherous Crocodile

For long that the air of change was felt in the heart of the elders as times shifted, nations fell and honor crumbled. The world was slowly transforming as a new formula emerged through the violent and dominant fist of magnetic Earth. The Djehuty of the Crocodile began under the dominion of slavery and the power of vengeance.

This age finds its highest influence during medieval times with spiritual and philosophical roots that span until today and are still visible in modern society. It was an era of physical force and the aggressive rule of men, established through the rise of patriarchal societies, the mastery of the warrior and the power of human strength. In that time of corruption the focus shifted from nature to material possession, from health to wealth and from subtle to physical. It was marked by the leadership of kings and religious clergy, the deceit of dogma and imposition by fear, in sharp contrast with the culture from previous Djehutys where Egypt adopted powerful female pharaohs and respected priestesses, now replaced throughout the world by governments, clerics, scientists and ruling nobility restricted to the minds and hands of men.

The importance of feminine power and wisdom was brought to a second plane, portrayed as inferior while the honor and respect of women was usurped in a quest for male dominion. Females were now seen as a basic vehicle for the proliferation of the species under the control of men and not the center of life and growth. The change of thought that came from the misrepresentation of newfound understanding was that men discovered the importance of the masculine seed in the creation of life inside the female body, so the spiritual focus shifted from women to men. Humanity was no longer fascinated with the mysteries of life but felt drawn instead to the perception of death as an uncontrollable and unstoppable consequence of all life. Even the Sun died everyday and so did plants, animals and humans all finding their final destiny. This notion perplexed the ancients, especially the now ruling minds with their obsession for power and dominion — this was out of their control as they regained authority over life through their seed but death was beyond any power.

During that period the psychological state of humanity was fertile in fear and strategically propitious for the flourishing of monotheistic religions based on control, slavery and unquestionable power. An era that saw the rise of Judaism, Christianity and Islam, a masterplan long in the making. World religions until then united under the mystery of women changed and the Goddesses became the wives and servants of the new male Gods, feared rulers in their arrogance and indisputable laws. Older archetypes were revived and disguised under a different model as it is evident in Christian mythology that blatantly borrowed earlier concepts from the mysteries of Aset, Osiris and Horus. Through fear and by force the new cults became so popular and their dominance so greatly extended that they were tweaked to demand adherence to their faith in order to attain any form of salvation, a concept that endures today as it slowly crumbles while the crocodile begins to die.

The Djehuty of the Crocodile, named after one of the most treacherous beasts in the Nile and ancient symbol of the House of Seth, represents one of the most decadent times in Asetian history, with the Aset Ka exiled and weakened treating its frailty and nourishing its strength in nearly absolute silence. This was an age of Sethian dominion and vendetta, with the influence of its Red Order imposed by the devices of deceit throughout the globe under the disguise of caring light. Wise and observant, the ancient crocodiles knew how to prey on the ego, feed on fear and exploit the vain desires of a mundane society that openly welcomed their rule without even knowing. History shows that those were times of blood and treachery when death and false salvation were used to deceive the lives of millions. Humanity in its immeasurable scientific knowledge, technological development and unquestionable modern achievements failed to notice the most subtle spark that it was lost in exchange for a society that thrives on shallow exhibition, praises futility and promotes ignorance. They became a global herd without thought or identity that enforces poverty, raises warfare, takes advantage of the weak and shields the deceptive and wealthy in a carefully choreographed dance to a red song that they are not even able to comprehend.

It comes a time when chains must be broken and the mysteries revealed...

Awakening of the Ancient Serpent

Reaching the liberating cradle of the Djehuty of the Serpent, in the very first steps of its cosmic gestation, a tiny speckle of violet light sprout throughout the realms of energy and spirit, echoing into the physical layers of manifest existence where the seeds of transformation would lay hidden but strong. A new chain of thought and illuminated potential grew within the minds willing to think independently and not afraid to pursuit newfound knowledge without fear; a candle igniting into a wild fire in the middle of a storm made of blindness, carrying a revolutionary light of growing spirituality, higher truth and magickal enlightenment.

This is the birth of a new era of wisdom empowered by the rising of another Djehuty. Its emergence has been perceived by human society that in their unawareness and inability to comprehend have described it as the New Age — a common concept in contemporary occult studies. The established global religions grew decadent, corrupt and obsessed with power, achieving an undeniable point of no return that will mark their downfall, even if fighting hard not to accept this reality although deep within their leaders have felt it as well. It is a time of reckoning and for ancient truths to rise, when falsehood and deceit must be accounted for.

The Djehuty of the Serpent is an age of initiation and rediscovered knowledge unleashed through the mysteries of old, when evolved thought and enlightened minds begin to discard the loud voices of society, the fame-seeking mundanes desperate for attention and the ones hiding behind selfish agendas, seeing the falsehood and illusion portrayed in popular media and by those who only seek to control others. These are times when the seeds of liberation can only be found in the elusive silence of the heart as one great truth that has long been hidden — that all potential lies within and just like the lies of modern religion so are the brands of commercial occultism and pretentious teachings chained to a realm of deceit that opposes true magick and they must be cleansed with the fire of insignificance if evolution and truth are to be grasped.

We are now stepping into the very early stages of this new Djehuty of spiritual potential and, as with every previous age, a lot of friction is to be experienced while old powers crumble, desperately trying to hold back and scratch their way to surface. They will not go down easily and they shall not die without a fight but their time of reckoning is here. It is up to each individual to make the choice of a lifetime by embracing growth and seeking enlightenment or to wither in ignorance and be drowned in decadence on the path to insignificance.

Many are now awakening to a higher truth and the power of subtle forces, slowly starting to understand the forgotten nature of divinity and the true origins of our culture, embracing spiritual growth while accepting change and transformation as a process of enlightenment. The conscious backbone of humanity no longer has concerns about the daily cyclical death of the Sun as the old framework evolved and the concept grew in complexity; the Sun may die every night but it will also be reborn every morning.[12] Life does not vanish, at least not forever, as people also die but they are also reborn. That is the rediscovered truth of reincarnation, well known by the ancients and studied inside the mystery schools of past and present, which humanity is now starting to realize and accept. Death is not a dreaded fall into the abyss nor an ending to our journey but an essential stage of personal evolution — a beautiful door into the unknown of complete liberation and higher understanding. Death is the initiation back into the Duat.

Fear of dying as an unavoidable ending to all life and the dominating cult of death hidden amongst the monotheistic religions of our time is slowly but steadily being replaced by a new formula of healthier spirituality and a much profounder nature. The old monotheistic cults are growing sick and infested from within as our ancient spirituality flourishes in the new religion of life and rebirth, the reviving of magick and the quest of understanding. This seed no matter how small is beginning to replace the generalized fear of death that defined the previous Djehuty of the Crocodile. The corruption of religions that reigned through the dark ages of that last Djehuty is now broken, shaken by the truth of elder deities and the mysteries of divinity found in traditions that had for a very long time understood the reality of reincarnation and celebrated it as one of the most beautiful mysteries of life. These roots of rebirth and liberated life go back in time to the cradle of civilization and find their most enlightened understanding during the golden age of Ancient Egypt as a staple of the spiritual knowledge of the Asetians.

However, not everyone is ready and the chaos from every shift of Djehuty brings pain and confusion. The evolved are imbued with the ability to bend and so they can adapt but those stagnant that remain inflexible can only be broken, just like the Tower card of the Tarot that brings renewal and hidden potential but only through the breaking of strong established foundations. To overcome that rupture is not easy but essential to evolution. The vast majority of the population of our world remains stagnant, still attached to old fears and enslaving dogmas, a phenomenon that is typical in such times of shifting and transformation. Evolution bows to no one and knows no limitations so everything that does not bend shall be broken... in time. All roots from the old and rotten Djehuty of the Crocodile will eventually be removed, surpassed and forgotten by the young, fresh and wise Djehuty of the Serpent; the time for individual thought, spiritual freedom and evolution, a magick without fear or restrictions when life reaches closer to its divine nature.

The new formula of the initiatory Serpent brings ancient wisdom united with modern understanding. It marries science and spirituality, magick and academia. This is the magickal formula of creative Air rising, crushing the Earth of old through the power drawn from Fire and Water of earlier Djehutys. Such a notion may appear elusive but its alchemy is clear to anyone that dedicates some effort to the attentive study of the spiritual and historical nature of Asetian Djehutys. The higher spirituality of this intricate formula opposes the shallow mentality established during the influence of the Crocodile when blindness was promoted through servitude to futility and the dominating ego turned entire societies into slaves, hopeless on their knees without even realizing. The Serpent crushes vanity and breaks any ego, forcing the eternal mirror of truth upon the very core of the soul and allowing initiation through inner flame. Those who have experienced it already know; they see above and understand. Others still sleep as ignorance feels comfortable and safe.

It is during this era of renewed magick that Asetians set forth into light, revealing themselves from the long shadows of our past. This step — one planned and started long ago — has spawned a visible layer of pretenders and rehashed traditions established without a solid foundation but built upon popular culture, fiction and ignorance. Some of those movements have led to a vulgarization of magick and the occult in general but particularly the nature and tradition of vampirism, something that is clear in most modern communities. Such misunderstanding of predatory spirituality and the nature of Asetian wisdom is not only marked by the proliferation and protection of ignorance but it also reflects one of the many reasons

✝

behind the release of this book to the general public, presented globally without the usual secretive measures and inaccessibility found in many of my works.

Among the already scarce literature about vampirism without the influence of fiction, and the rare scholarly texts that genuinely dwell into the intricacies of higher magick and initiation, very few publicly accessible works can actually be taken into serious consideration by an educated occultist and those with some degree of awareness or initiation. In this way the partial disclosure of Asetian wisdom establishing the foundation behind this tradition and vital elements of its culture to a broader audience can help those — both the beginner student and the advanced scholar — interested in vampirism, predatory spirituality and the occult to differentiate modern pseudo-occult traditions and texts based on a fictitious foundation from real knowledge, concepts and practices often kept secretive within the older occult systems and celebrated in privacy for countless centuries.

What can be described as the path of the vampire — or better said, the tradition known as Asetianism — has always been an elitist and secretive branch of higher occult studies, now seeing an open gateway that leaves it more approachable to the uninitiated, but that does not make it a road of wisdom that can be travelled without painful challenge or opposition. This is in line with the ideology and formula of the new Djehuty along its focus on freedom and enlightened growth. The mysteries and profound spirituality of this tradition can never be understood with a simplistic mindset or explored without the hard work that every initiation into a higher understanding entails, for this culture and nature will remain unapologetically distant from the realms of popular occultism at the grasp of all. Power requires responsibility and the beauty of

Asetianism is also the journey, revealing its succulent fruit only to those that are courageous to trail its difficult violet path.

The convoluted times and strife of the last Djehuty reflected a chime of frailty from the Aset Ka with many Asetians not even incarnating during that period and a moment of secrecy and danger to those that did, moving discreetly in the shadows of this world. With the family scattered, the homeland overrun and the Order weakened, the ending of the age of the Crocodile raises a new violet flag and a hymn of timeless endurance; a call of renewal and an embrace of strength. Some Asetians were lost in time, unawakened and dormant while away from their true family and the wisdom of the Aset Ka. Now in the new Djehuty the ancient Serpent is awakening from its long sleep throughout the ages and the divine family of Aset is finding their unbroken bond once again, a path that leads them home. This truly is the age of the Asetians rising...

"All that is gold does not glitter,
Not all those who wander are lost;
The old that is strong does not wither,
Deep roots are not reached by frost.

From the ashes a fire shall be woken,
A light from the shadows shall spring;
Renewed shall be blade that was broken:
The crownless again shall be King."

John R.R. Tolkien

Elementals
Alchemical Foundation

The elementals are guardians of the physical realm that manifest the four primeval forces of nature. They are temples that transcend matter and time. Fire, Water, Air and Earth embody the fabric of existence and together they woven reality. Their ethereal dance is the alchemy of the ancients and its conjugation is limitless, providing the metaphysical substrate to ignite the magick of transformation, creation and destruction.

FIRE   WATER   AIR   EARTH

As subtle forces they can be summoned during ritual in advanced ceremonial magick or for the most experienced they are drawn directly into manifestation in order to affect reality and bend the conceptual pattern of our world. Safekeeping the four fundamental elements and wielding their primeval powers the elementals are mighty but not conscious entities, being a force of nature and part of its machinery.

In Ancient Egypt and a gnostic aspect of the Asetian tradition the four elementals find their oldest representation in the theological concept of the four sons of Horus. Not only entrusted with the mastery of each element but effectively being the inner alchemy manifested by the individual principles, the ancients conceptually fragmented the essence of Horus — son of Aset and so the union of all elements as a valid expression of nature — into four defined representations of the universal forces: Imseti, Qebehsenuf, Duamutef and Hapi.

To understand these powers and wield them in tune to magickal purpose is a gift of the Gods and an elementary foundation of high magick taught by the Asetians to their followers since the time before time. The macrocosm is mirrored on the microcosm and so your fountain of magick within is also an accurate echo of the power of the cosmos. From the scorching flame of immortal Fire to the flowing courage of emotional Water and from the chaotic swiftness of creative Air to the fertile sustenance of dominant Earth, each Asetian has within the soul a steady flow of all elements. Each manifesting at a different vibration and under a varying influence they condition subtle metabolism, establish spiritual tides and silently heighten characteristics. To use them effectively on the magick outside they must first be mastered on the magick inside.

The four elementals and their esoteric study is connected to countless cultures, traditions, belief systems and symbolism. They find representation on the cardinal points in tune with the magnetic nature of their evocation signature but are also tied to the visible color spectrum due to energy vibration and even the different suits of the Tarot in terms of initiatory wisdom. Elementals are also important pillars of magick and symbol in Kabbalistic knowledge, holding relevance in the study and understanding of the Tree of Life.[13]

In Kemetic terminology as the sons of Horus, each elemental is tied to a specific canopic jar — funerary vases used ritualistically for the organs of mummified dead in Egypt and doorways to the afterlife — as well as the spiritual essence of a deity protecting it. These elements are not of a primitive mythical nature but they represent powerful alchemical forces that were mastered by the Ancient Egyptians and tied to their profound understanding of life and death.

✝

The elementals are not creatures of good or evil, not even being creatures at all. They are neutral forces of nature that stand above any notion of morals, ethics, laws or the mind of humans. In magick they are summoned and evoked as protection and guidance; an assistance on the metaphysical work at hand, however they can never be completely controlled. Their essence is chaotic, dynamic and unbound, part of the foundations of the universe and to control such a force is a quest of illusion. Nature is unrestricted, does not bow to power and it is intimidated by no one.

To intentionally deal with pure elementals without maturity and responsibility can be of grave consequence, a lesson most experienced occultists have already understood. The following keys being presented are apparently simple but they convey a chart into elemental territory that can be used for initiation and in the practice of Asetian magick. Their study and understanding is established on much deeper roots than limited words can convey but they remain for the student to correlate and explore. As with most of my teachings I draw the magickal doors and provide the secretive keys but it is always up to the initiate to find the wisdom to open them and the courage to face the monsters that are found inside.

Imseti
Immortal Fire

At the throne of magick stands Imseti with the devastating force of immortal Fire. Empowered by Aset this fiery energy vibrates in red and mirrors south. It unlocks the initiation of inner flame.

Qebehsenuf
Emotional Water

At the cradle of loyalty stands Qebehsenuf with the flowing force of emotional Water. Empowered by Serket this watery energy vibrates in blue and mirrors west. It unlocks the initiation of eternal bond.

Duamutef
Creative Air

At the crown of manifestation stands Duamutef with the chaotic force of creative Air. Empowered by Neith this airy energy vibrates in yellow and mirrors east. It unlocks the initiation of higher will.

Hapi
Dominant Earth

At the sarcophagus of flesh stands Hapi with the grounding force of dominant Earth. Empowered by Nephthys this earthly energy vibrates in green and mirrors north. It unlocks the initiation of crystalized manifestation.

✝

Part Two
Asetian Magick

Subtle Energy

E nergy is the fundamental fabric of existence and the transcendent engine of life. Its exhaustive study and applied use represent the core of Asetian metaphysical work and reflect the nature of magick in its many expressions but they also provide an accurate lens into higher understanding. Interacting with energy through its various layers, vibrations and manifestations brings forth one of the most powerful elements of creation and destruction, as well as the definitive tool of inner and outer wisdom. Mastering the subtle art of energy is a quest of lifetimes and to deal with it frivolously opens a dangerous road of potential devastation.

Known by different names, concepts and terminologies in a myriad of cultures, subtle energy can be simplistically defined as the amorphous metaphysical essence that constitutes an ethereal field that surrounds everything and everyone, being present within every living being. It is the blood of life and seed of creation; its absence a definitive condition of death and the staple of nothingness. The concept is studied under varying contexts and found in nearly every culture of past and present, with the perception of its existence going back to the cradle of civilization and primeval thought.

In the Asetian culture, although energy is examined and understood under different variants and defined complexities the most well researched form of its manifestation is known as Ka, the Ancient Egyptian word for vital force and essence as well as an elementary aspect of the soul. That is the type of energy present in the subtle body of the living, continuously nourishing it with the spark of life, hence the common nomenclature of vital energy. In the Japanese culture this energy is known as Ki — the word *Ki* in the healing practice of *Reiki* — and in traditional Chinese medicine it is understood as Chi — the word *Chi* in the *T'ai Chi Ch'uan* martial art. However, its meaning and fundamental aspects are both timeless and universal, being found as the Sanskrit word Prana in the texts of Ayurveda, Tantra and Yoga, as well as the word Mana in Polynesian culture and Ether in classical alchemy. In Asetian literature the ancient word Ka is recurrently used to reference vital energy and established in magickal context without the inclusion of more modern definitions from other cultures.

In terms of metaphysics the notion that energy is only present as a force field surrounding living beings, commonly described as an aura, is incomplete and ultimately incorrect. There are external layers of energy that encircle every form of life that define an aura and natural shielding, both essential to balanced health and welfare, but the most important form of energy exists within the subtle body. That energy is fundamental to every mechanism of existence and it represents the most condensed and coherent form of Ka, flowing inside every individual akin to the behavior of blood in the circulatory system.

This is better understood when examining the different but interconnected concepts of Ka and Ba, two Ancient Egyptian words commonly used in the context of subtle anatomy. Each is represented by a singular hieroglyph and tied to distinctive major pillars of Asetianism, as established in an earlier chapter of this book. The Ka embodies vital energy that flows inside the subtle system as the metaphysical substance that binds spirit and matter, alchemically igniting them as one. However, the Ba is a fundamental vessel in which the Ka flows, circulates and emanates, being closely related with the western definition of a soul and paramount to spiritual existence. It is the divine flame that transcends time and matter, holding the potential for everlastingness, unlike the Ka that can easily dissipate and be transmuted. The Ba defines who you are while the Ka fuels your living breath and liberates the magick within.

In some instances subtle energy in its raw elemental form exhibits behavioral patterns that are akin to more conventional forms of energy as studied in physics and chemistry. For example the underlying mechanisms of apparently spontaneous transmission of vital energy between two organic entities has certain correlations with that of heat and its transfer through processes of radiation, convection and conduction, as scientifically explored in the field of thermodynamics. Aligning magick and metaphysics with science and research has been the Asetian way to approach, develop and teach their knowledge of the universe, a recognizable stance that separates traditional occultism from popular practice.

To explore the intricacy of subtle energy as a static, defined and predictable force would neglect the dynamic nature of energy and its complete spectrum of varying frequencies, gammas, properties and layers. This text and the following chapters are a primer on the study of energy and metaphysics but such undertaking must be understood under the scope of its complexity and surrounding techniques, as individual interpretations should reach beyond the foundations here presented. The mastery of occult arts and magick as well as the exploration of unseen mysteries are undeniably tied to the branches of energy work that I will simplify throughout these pages for proper understanding, while demystifying a range of common misconceptions and notions based on incomplete research, inappropriate examination or the ignorance of popular occultism when lacking a solid background in applied metaphysics.

Spectrum

Subtle energy is not merely a spiritual substance with mystical properties but also a verifiable metaphysical force that can be studied, analysed and manipulated. Under that premise the Asetians have explored the nature of energy in its many forms of manifestation and hidden mysteries as well as consistently developed the practices and techniques to harness it.

These variants of energy that are considered subtle or metaphysical manifest in numerous ways and attain different, sometimes even opposed, reactions from how living beings interact with them. When the intricate fabric of subtle energy is observed by the lenses of perception as our conceptual microscope of investigation, an infinite scope of potential is revealed: energy is not static or defined by a limited range of layers; it is boundless and its analytic expressions can be determined through various aspects of vibration and frequency.

The sum of all radiated fields, vibrational layers and characteristics that define subtle energy is what we call its spectrum. It reduces the most common forms of manifestation into definable concepts that can be studied by an educated occultist and explored with accuracy and efficiency. That makes subtle energy more quantifiable and a tangible force able to be tapped into by metaphysical science.

The complete spectrum of subtle energy is incredibly complex and diverse, spreading through a wide range of frequencies at varying vibrational levels. Due to such colossal variance and vast knowledge it remains out of the scope of this book — or any other work ever published — to analyse the full spectrum uncovered by the Asetians but we shall focus on the fundamental types of energy that define the core elements of the known spectrum and variants that people most frequently interact with.

Energy of subtle nature is not classified solely by the range of its frequency but also through the rate and amplitude of the detected vibration in conjunction with the individual metaphysical characteristics and fingerprint from each type. By compiling the elementary characteristics and definitions for the most common forms of subtle energy, practitioners can establish a higher awareness of the invisible forces surrounding them as well as develop a greater perception and understanding of how these forces interact and are applied in magickal work. While not describing the complete spectrum the following types of energy are probably the ones most will ever interact with on a conscious level.

Universal Energy

This major force is the energy of the cosmos. Representing the larger section of the spectrum, universal energy is the most abundant form of subtle essence and rawest variant of etheric fluid, as it can only be drawn directly from universal sources, defining its pure nature and unaltered state. Such is the invisible power that binds the world together.

Energy can only be described as universal when deprived of signature and fingerprint, so in practices of energy projection through magick or holistic healing the quality of the energy shifts from universal to vital. This is due to the inherent process of transfusion that imbues reactive energy with the fingerprint of the practitioner and alters its natural vibration.

By consciously or unconsciously interacting with energy it is inevitable not to transform several aspects of this metaphysical essence, as we live in constant communion with the subtle forces that connect and merge with us on different levels, being recurrently changed by them and changing them back. The energy that is raised and gathered in magickal practice, whether by the means of ritual, alternative medicine or active metaphysical techniques becomes infused with what we describe as subtle noise that comprises thoughts, emotions and fragmented energy from the practitioner as natural byproducts of its manipulation.

Although universal energy is the main etheric resource used in meditation, healing techniques and various forms of magick as well as the most common type of subtle energy, it cannot be fully explored for the purposes of feeding and vampiric empowerment. This is true because of the frequency, subtle structure and nature of the essence found at this end of the spectrum, making it highly effective in certain practices but unable to be processed directly by the subtle system for the purposes of feeding.

If this energy was capable of sustaining the subtle body and metaphysical abilities any living being would be considered vampiric as everyone absorbs raw energy from the universe in order to maintain the natural balance of their inner system and inborn energy field. Although soothing and pure in its natural state, universal energy cannot be efficiently processed into alchemical power and its level of vibration is insufficient for the higher requirements of vampire magick and the Asetian subtle metabolism.

Elemental Energy

On a lower frequency but encompassing more empowered manifestation are the variants of elemental energy. These layers contain the forces that most would describe as the powers of nature. It is an energy field that emanates from the Earth and its natural forces, as it can be harnessed from plants, minerals and wild animals.

Highly charged and sometimes unstable in vibration, this energy is easily perceived during major storms and natural events, being felt in the voices of the wind, on the solitude of rainfall, among the arrogance of thunder and during the dance of the sea. This type of energy manifests the power of the elementals from this realm and as such it is a mighty magickal force to be reckoned but also one not easily controlled. Its power is unbound and it does not bend to the will of humanity. When unleashed it can be devastating but once understood its ways are mysterious but enlightening.

Any form of magick that relies on empowerment through nature instinctively draws on elemental energy, from the mysteries of the Moon to the beauty of a sunset. Not as raw as universal energy it is also a pure form of essence and one without subtle noise or human byproducts when absorbed in its natural state.

Although not the most common or efficient form of feeding, its frequency makes the processing by the subtle system possible and a potential resource for Asetian magick. Being a potent tool for spiritual empowerment and uniquely useful in certain advanced magickal workings, this type of energy is frequently studied and mastered by Scorpions who are known to sense and drain these energies more strongly and efficiently than other Asetians, sometimes in an overwhelming way that can be both a weakness and a weapon.

Vital Energy

Bound to the breath of life and manifested creation vital energy is the blood of the soul and essence that circulates within the subtle body, being the force that is projected, assimilated, cycled and transmuted by life. Known in Asetianism by the Ancient Egyptian word Ka, this energy is present in every living creature and it represents the power that sustains the subtle system and ignites the spirit.

The Ka is a heightened and intense variant of energy that is also extremely diverse due to its undeniably personal and unique nature, varying greatly depending on the system emanating and cycling it. Vital energy represents an important aspect that has defined vampires as predators and its usage in feeding is determinant in describing the nature of vampirism. As a major source of spiritual power and magickal abilities, Ka is only present within the etheric body and soul of the living, so to access and explore its nature while draining its secrets and conquering its living flame is a profoundly predatory practice with strong spiritual implications.

Vital energy is always imprinted with the metaphysical fingerprint of the energy system that it is attached to and that is verifiable on the full extent of its structure. Being so diverse makes it not possible to accurately categorize this type of energy in terms of spiritual quality, as it carries the emotions, fears and vices of those that have interacted, cycled or processed it within their system. As such, vital energy is constantly affected and changed by thought patterns and a wide range of emotions, making it unpredictable. This unstable nature makes it volatile when outside of the subtle body, often dissipating and decaying by losing its signature and characteristics, no longer being described as vital energy but lowering in spectrum into residual energy and lingering subtle noise.

When imbued with heightened emotional states experienced by the living, from the strength of hate to the chaos of anger or the power of love, this energy becomes denser and can be sensed in thicker form, making it potentially more empowered for use in magick and feeding. To understand all of these characteristics and energy transmutations is essential in the study of advanced metaphysics and when doing precision work with energy, particularly relevant to the charging of magickal objects, attuning energy to certain vibrations and the efficiency of vampiric draining.

In terms of subtle anatomy, vital force is present in different layers of the energy system, manifesting in varying intensities and vibrations, all significant but presenting distinctive characteristics and applications. The outer layers of vital energy are found outside of the body as an etheric mist that is often described as the aura and it works as a primary shield and filter, deflecting certain malignant energetic frequencies and determining how the subtle body responds to metaphysical input. It represents however a rudimentary mechanism and the heart of vital energy is found inside the subtle system, flowing through the meridians and fueling the energy organs known as Shen. The energy present in these structures is strong and highly charged, making them spin and pulsate rapidly while being responsible for the maintenance of life itself. The Shen centers coordinate the flow of energy in the body and control natural projection, cycling and dissipation levels. However, the most empowered form of Ka is found deep within, right at the core of the soul, and that is a profoundly intimate essence that can only be shared through advanced techniques of exchange and interaction that should never be approached lightly as its usage and magick is of great and undeniable consequence.

The levels of vital energy present in the subtle system, although often neglected by those who are not aware of its existence and importance, is a determinant condition in the practice of energy work and an active influence in every form of magick, observed carefully and under great awareness by every occultist experienced with metaphysics. Affecting the subtle system and by reflection and echo also influencing the physical body and biology, the levels of Ka determine the quantity and quality of our energy, altering sensitivity, specialized abilities and inherent magickal power. As an essential element of balance and health, when merging the synergistic nature of body, mind and soul, Ka emerges as the vital force that flows in the spirit and provides it with motion. It is effectively the invisible spark that ignites the living flame of the Ba. Exploring, understanding and mastering these energies remain some of the greatest sources of inner power and an undying mystery of our magick, reflecting on characteristic abilities greatly enhanced after awakening and through the secrets of initiation.

Sexual Energy

This variant of subtle essence represents a subset of vital energy or Ka that exhibits specific characteristics and presents highly specialized metaphysical qualities. Empowered through the intimate magick of sexuality, various forms of pleasure and the secretive nature of orgasm, this type of subtle energy is strong and presents high vibration, manifesting in heightened states of great intensity while being less coherent than other variants. This makes it more prone to dissipation and quicker to deteriorate when not being fueled by the reactive flame of pleasure — physical, emotional or spiritual.

Sexual energy is a powerful resource for vampiric feeding, evolved spiritual practice and advanced magick as it presents an intensely charged form of vital energy. It should however not be misused as its metaphysical properties make it far more binding and unstable than other forms of Ka. Absorbing it will naturally and even unconsciously establish energy links, oftentimes resilient, that are not easily broken and provide a potential doorway into your subtle system that can be exploited. That makes the synergy of trust and loyalty an essential aspect of sex magick and one important element during most forms of sexual feeding, two aspects often neglected by those who lack knowledge and experience or embrace such arts frivolously without understanding what they entail.

The mysteries and initiations of sex magick are a secretive practice and represent profoundly transformational experiences, not to be confused with shallow desires or the mere allure of carnal pleasure. In fact in the Asetian tradition when magick is empowered through sex it becomes a highly spiritual experience; one honored with passion and embraced with the soul.

A few elements of sexual energy are harnessed only at the peak of heightened states, being naturally exuded by the body during intense pleasure and also found present in charged biological substances such as sexual fluids — the elixir of life and treasured poison of immortals. There is undeniable power in sexual energy and the heightened essence manifested through orgasm, making its usage and meaning in high magick a deeply vampiric practice and an epitome of Asetian spiritual mastery.

Residual Energy

Reaching the stages of lower vibration in the spectrum there is what is described as residual energy. Its structure is incoherent and of an amorphous nature, being not just diverse but formless and lethargic; an echo of former potential now fallen into disgrace. It manifests mostly as a byproduct of other forms of energy in a more charged state, resulting from their manipulation and natural transmutation. Residual energies represent a disarranged network of varying sources that are undergoing a state of slow decay, generated by the activity of living beings alongside stagnant or dissipated energies accumulated through natural dynamics or active metaphysics.

This discharged and oftentimes latent energy is present everywhere and constitutes a layered mist of low vibration scattered throughout the world of matter, that while it may appear irrelevant at surface under close scrutiny it provides an important element of metaphysics that sustains the universal cycle of subtle energy. This cloud of lowly vibrating energy that surrounds everything and everyone, from living beings to material objects, provides an open canvas for the untold story of living energy to be written. It is the foundation where other forms of energy from every range of the spectrum travel and interconnect, making it a symbiotic circle where energy is constantly being transformed but never lost.

Its common state of low frequency makes it an inadequate option for feeding and magick, lacking viable quality for absorption and empowerment. However, its diversity is also key when analysing the potential of residual energy, as variables such as location can be relevant factors in providing energy with entirely different characteristics. A classic example would be a spiritual temple or ritual chamber where the residual energy is actually charged and presenting a heightened vibration, making what would otherwise be mere subtle noise actually useful metaphysical essence. That said, those situations are exceptions as most forms of residual energy are useless in terms of active metaphysics and cannot be processed by the subtle metabolism. Energy byproducts and subtle noise are fading echoes and while they provide their function in the natural cycle of energy and the foundation of metaphysics they are rarely valuable to the practitioner.

Magick presents one of the engines that leaks residual energy as the Ka is projected by intent and focused will, where emotion and thought are transmuted into power, becoming ambient energy that lingers in the area of practice, attaching to inanimate objects and the surrounding walls. Although residual energy lacks a static fingerprint it can still hold its echo and that can be detected and identified by an experienced Asetian through the study of its fragments in decay. It is not only magick that presents a source for this type of energy, as it is constantly being generated by the natural activity of the living, found more concentrated in active places such as a bedroom after sexual activity, surrounding an office during heated debate or inside a living room after a strong argument. All of these elements make the areas charged with glowing energy that can be easily felt once enough sensitivity is developed. Emotions and thoughts constantly project and shed energy that is dissipated into the environment, lingering as residual energy like an invisible cloud that surrounds you in every moment of every day.

Fingerprint
Every manifestation of Ka as vital energy that only emerges in the spectrum when imbued with alchemical elements of the living carries a specific and identifiable metaphysical mark. This magickal signature is unique to each individual, bound to the soul and composed by echoes of inner essence, making it a distinguishable tracing element present in energy and a useful tool in techniques of energy work and advanced metaphysics.

The fingerprint as a naturally occurring form of dormant and inactive energy becomes attached to the properties of Ka as it is cycled, projected or empowered through the subtle system of a living creature. This singular code is exclusive to every being, working as a forgery-proof signature of nature that can be detected, sensed and analysed by those sensitive to the subtle reality and fluent in the Asetian arts.

Remote detection of energy fingerprints and their thorough examination has been an integral part of the metaphysical process within the Aset Ka since its inception, composing a fundamental aspect of study to those who seek a deeper understanding of energy and the subtle. A concept always present in predatory magick, the fingerprint makes every form of essence drained from another to be intimately personal and spiritually unique, a reason that explains why in terms of vampiric feeding the details of how and who to drain are not approached lightly.

An incompatible energy fingerprint may cause a range of effects from light discomfort to severe reactions, as not every form of energy gracefully interacts or is prone to mingle. The same is true in situations of energy attraction when the compatibility of different fingerprints results in apparently unexplained bonding and a higher feeding potential, making it an essential aspect not only in acts of intentional draining and psychic attack but also to active magick and spirituality.

This unique subtle code that echoes the essence of life from every single soul and embodies a signature of identity that is universal presents an intricate branch of metaphysical cryptography. As such, it deserves honest and responsible study detached from speculation and unsubstantiated theory, tracing the pathways to decode the invisible language of nature manifested in every breath of life.

Amplification

The concept of energy amplification is present in every form of metaphysical work. It is a branch of alchemical manipulation and energy induction that can be trained, explored and exploited while it also occurs naturally and even unconsciously through every interaction with energy as well as being present in the automated cyclical process of the subtle system.

The techniques used to project and amplify energy can be extremely simple or very complex but the most common rely on the secondary Shen of the hands, eyes and mouth that compose fundamental systems of energy interaction in terms of subtle anatomy. Through these structures the energy system is able to slowly exude its inner essence or actively project it by amplifying to a higher vibration. These metaphysical projections of amplified energy are multipurpose, being effective in various forms of magick and manipulation or silently working as invisible probes that enhance sensitivity, awareness and esoteric abilities — all natural tools of both Asetians and Asetianists.

In terms of magick there are different objects capable of further amplifying the vital energy that living beings are known to project. Among those tools the different naturally occurring minerals, embraced in metaphysics since the ancient times, remain amongst the most effective and efficient resources used in energy amplification. Being so diverse the minerals created by our planet and the cosmos provide a range of powerful magickal applications depending on their crystalline structure, chemical composition and conductive characteristics, making different minerals react in distinctive ways to energy, thus being capable of amplifying it to frequencies and vibrational levels of particular interest.

When exploring the intricate fields of energy work there is one tool that is a frequent cause of misunderstanding and recurrent misrepresentation both in popular culture and fiction. That is the case of a high magnification amplifier, commonly described as a magick wand. The usage of this highly specialized energy amplifier has been established since earlier days in history, although its development never ceased and the constant perfecting of such techniques and advanced tools has been maintained by the Asetians throughout the ages. A concept that has proliferated in the realms of literature and film, the real use of magick wands is tied to an elitist field of high metaphysics and just like vampirism its reality is unlike what it is found portrayed in fiction albeit not less fascinating. The use of a properly crafted and attuned wand in what we have defined as active magick remains a secretive practice in modern times even amongst knowledgeable occult sects, taught only within the older mystery schools that were given access to such gnosis. To approach this subject without the required wisdom and teachings invariably leads to wrong assumptions, false interpretations or worse, a connection with fantasy or skepticism driven by ignorance.

Amplification can be achieved in many ways, from natural metaphysical abilities of the subtle body to specialized magickal tools used in advanced practices. Understanding its mechanics, variants and applications is a core element of energy work and a fundamental aspect of the techniques where energy is heightened, shaped to purpose and directed to intent, which represents the foundation of magick itself.

Minerals

One of the greatest metaphysical tools capable of steady energy amplification is gracefully provided by nature, slowly crafted for aeons in agonising pressure and terrifying temperature through the unstoppable force of geological processes. Minerals are diverse and so are their applications in magick and metaphysics, as their stable nature, unique characteristics and extensive documentation makes them privileged and special. When used as amplifiers in energy work those techniques encompass what we define as crystalline amplification or mineralogical amplification.

There are five primary variables known to influence the amplification of Ka through natural mineral structures. Those are the geological nature of the mineral amplifying the signal, the source of Ka providing the energy, the existence or absence of a pre-amplifier and finally the purity of the signal alongside its vibrational strength. All elements are fundamental in the mastery of energy work, particularly when it comes to amplifying energy signals, which is a central aspect of active magick and vibrational metaphysics.

The crystallographic characteristics of the minerals used in amplification, their geological genesis, chemical composition and researched crystalline structure, all influence the way that each mineral reacts to and alters an energy beam trespassing on it. Such scientific elements have a direct implication on the different frequencies being amplified as well as the subtle waves and echoes that are refracted and dissipated in the process.

Those elements influence the amplifier and how effective and efficient it will be in the intended magnifying of subtle energy, however the outcome will also depend on the source. The initial energy source is a determinant variable in metaphysical projection and amplification as it will determine the nature and quality of the energy being manipulated and redirected. In most conventional uses that source will be the practitioner, or better said, your own subtle system as the ignition of Ka. That makes the process dependent on experience and learning but also on inner ability to manipulate subtle essences, induce stable energy fields and project homogenous beams of Ka, directly affecting the result of amplification.

When referring to energy amplification through crystalline materials an important element often not analysed by those not fluent in advanced metaphysics is the inclusion of a pre-amplifier. When moving from the study of simple energy manipulation to an in-depth examination of subtle energy outside of the scope of a ritualistic setting it is common to find the use of a pre-amplifier strategically placed between the source of Ka and the mineral. This tool, a mediator between the initial energy source and the amplifying device, is often a specialized high magnification amplifier — a magick wand.

These wands are no simple tools or devices that should be used lightly, wielding great power hence requiring a higher level of responsibility and extensive training, with uses tied to the secrets of initiation rarely divulged with outsiders. Pioneered by the Asetians many centuries ago, real magick wands are hard to find and their uses uncommon these days. Their craft is maintained by experienced occultists who have dedicated their lives to the perfecting of such art and the mastery of this unique craftsmanship. However, it is not only the secrets of the materials being used and the crafting techniques that make for a working wand, but also the unique energization and initiation of the tool, which can only be done by an Encantatum — a master at energy manipulation that was granted the keys for the mysteries of wand making. Made from wood or mineral Asetian wands are legendary and one of the most desired magickal objects in existence, being effective metaphysical instruments, powerful spiritual talismans and the elegant weapons of another age now mostly forgotten.

Unlike what is to be found in ritual magick and ceremonial traditions, during the practice of energy work a wand is not used in a symbolic way and there is no required ritualistic context. In advanced metaphysics a magick wand or high magnification amplifier is an active component in the process of energy manipulation and projection, being an intricate yet mysterious tool of high magick, shedding light on the term active magick when referring to techniques that make a direct and conscious use of energy without the need for theatrics, psychological states or mental constructs.

Concerning mineralogical amplification, the last primary factor to take in consideration is the purity of the signal and its vibrational strength, variables closely related with a different element previously described: the source of the energy field. The purer the signal being projected the more efficient — and also more powerful — is the amplified energy, providing results that can potentially be more analytical as the vibration and frequency remain in tune with the known spectrum while being deprived of higher levels of noise and fragments. If the projected energy beam has a higher range of impurities with extensive metaphysical noise, which is not uncommon, the result of amplification will be inevitably affected by those alterations present in the energy field. The impurities often found in vital energy are diverse and range from underlying errors in the transmission process to unpredictable variables present in the source, which in the case of an individual can be something as simple as religious dogma, emotion and even degenerative disease that imbue and crystalize within the projected energy often unconsciously.

Incense

The burning of incense, natural herbs and oils is a common practice among occultists, regularly introduced in a context of meditation and magickal work. More than a simple tool used to induce altered states of consciousness, relaxation and ritualistic trance, the smoke from certain types of incense has a metaphysical application that is factored in the process of actively manipulating energy.

When the biotic material that comprises the chosen incense is united with heat from the flame it produces an aromatic smoke that fills the area with a cloud of particles that are able to attain physical reactions but also and more importantly hold subtle properties worthy of note. That kind of smoke can behave as a conductor of metaphysical energy and by filling an area the air becomes thicker and more potentially charged, making for a working space that is attuned to magick and reactive to the heightening of energy, resulting in a more effective environment for techniques of projection and amplification.

The usage of incense or its underlying presence in a room may be a small detail, however awareness of its potential is of strategic value since an attack through the dumping of a lethal charge of subtle energy directly on a vital Shen such as the heart can be enhanced to greater effectiveness when projected in an incense-charged smoky environment. Such knowledge can be fruitful not only in offensive planning but also as a safety precaution and readiness of appropriate magickal action concerning metaphysical defense and energy shielding.

This is valid with the burning of high quality incense, making use of natural and selected ingredients, since poor quality commercial and unnatural products will change the desired effect and may not hold metaphysical properties at all. This represents a factor to keep in mind when adding incense to any magickal practice.

Fire and Water
In the Asetian culture these are two alchemical elements of vital magickal power: the initiatory flame of immortal Fire and the cleansing flow of emotional Water. Embodying primordial elemental powers that only the right eyes may observe, their hidden dance to the lost song of everlastingness can secretly unleash the unseen sigil beneath the crown of Aset; a cradle to the transcendent alchemy of immortality.

Not only ruling forces of two major elementals that can be summoned and wielded in high magick, both Fire and Water represent fundamental principles in the alchemy of energy work that must be studied and understood in metaphysical explorations from basic to advanced.

Both hold unique cleansing properties that are effective when working with energy, particularly in practices such as the attuning of magickal objects, energizing occult tools and when initiating sacred talismans. To make proper and knowledgeable metaphysical use of the power behind flame and the flow beneath fluid one must first understand the underlying mechanisms of these elements and how they interact with subtle energy, carefully and methodically studying the alchemical processes that generate and liberate from its magickal use in ritual and active projection.

As complementary forces of initiation they comprise useful techniques that are explored by practitioners of the occult arts and can provide a solid foundation in cleansing, heightening and empowering endeavours. At a more advanced level, they unfold the secretive gnosis behind spiritual mysteries of transcendence and immortality as basilar keys only ignited and unleashed through the inscrutable union of Fire and Water — the double face of Aset as manifested light and darkness.

Subtle Anatomy

he study of the energy system including every structure that establishes and defines its natural functioning alongside the processes of interaction and underlying mechanisms connected to its fundamental activity, whether metaphysical or biological, encompasses an intricate scholarly field of occult knowledge that we define as subtle anatomy. In simple terms, subtle anatomy is the science that studies the subtle body and how it interacts and operates with the varying frequencies of the energy spectrum.

Different species present a diversity of energy systems with various elements of distinctive anatomy, mechanisms and complexity. In this book we are focusing on the particularities found aligned with the biological body as a canvas that applies both to humans and those of a distinct spiritual nature such as the Asetians. While the energy systems are conceptually similar there are subtle but fundamental differences between the subtle anatomy of Asetians and humans, however most of those details will not be openly explored as they present a strategic and scientific advantage that can and has been exploited for undesired purposes of metaphysical warfare.

Leaving out of the analytical lens some of the specific characteristics that define the Asetian energy system as more complex and metaphysically advanced, the core elements of analysis are the same to every being incarnating within a human body. As such, the knowledge presented in this primer on subtle anatomy provides an essential layer of understanding in terms of energy work, subtle healing and overall metaphysical processes. However, it should be noted that the background of this study is based on Asetian wisdom so although these notions may also apply to how a human interacts with and reacts to energy they are first and foremost Asetian in nature, describing what is experienced and validated by them.

As an established field of occult science the branch of subtle anatomy has grown in modern times through research and development but its roots are much older, drawing from ancient wisdom now mostly forgotten. Concepts and theories have been analysed and validated through experimental processes and extensive study but, as with every other scientific field worthy of its name, subtle anatomy is in a state of constant development and renewed understanding. This is also true in its modern sibling of physical anatomy where, even more often than in most fields of occult science, old ideas are banished and other principles adopted with every new discovery and technological progress. As such, although it already exists a solid understanding of energy and its working mechanisms within subtle anatomy, knowledge should not be set in stone and there are elements that will also grow as progress is made since that is the nature of evolution and to deny it is to stagnate in time.

Asetians may be ancient and so it is our wisdom, but the determined commitment for understanding and truth that we all embrace has pioneered many of our unique discoveries and breakthrough ideas that have shaped and redefined the landscape of energy work alongside the understanding of advanced metaphysics and magick, in a very real sense establishing what is the foundation of vampirism today.

Aura and Tendrils

The subtle body, as an inconspicuous engine responsible for the maintenance of life with a complexity of energy organs and conductive filaments, is in its normal state protected within a shell composed by dense and flexible essence that floats on the outer layers of the metaphysical system. This specialized mechanism of the energy system — a peripheral organ, just like the skin on the physical body — is what it is defined as an aura.

The aura is formed by a layered structure, exhibiting an increase in energetic density towards the direction of the subtle body. The outer layers are scarce and thin, in a constant state of dissipation associated with the natural process of cycling and renewal, formed by energy that is less charged and coherent than what is found at the inner layers, commonly lacking a well established fingerprint. The subtle body continuously absorbs raw energy from universal sources and variable impure energies from the environment, working like the filling of a vessel with fluid: as new essence is poured into the receptacle it will mingle with its contents and if the process is continuous some will overflow. This slow bleeding of energy is essential to a balanced system and the maintenance of pure and clean essence within the subtle body, being what generates the field of the aura.

This outer system is optimized through a layering mechanism for higher efficiency and the possible lowest impact on inner balance. Energy levels are of vital importance to every aspect of the organism — mind, body and spirit — so proper functioning of all these systems under the scope of subtle anatomy are a mirror of the state of life. The layers of the aura are in a permanent process of regeneration and dissipation, being slowly detached from the influence of the subtle body as the thinner peripheral layers are dispersed into the surrounding environment, while the subtle system processes another thicker layer of processed energy that is then injected into the foundational frame of the aura.

The Asetian aura exhibits a condition present in its core structure that enhances interaction with energy, heightens sensitivity and provides a strong mechanism for absorption. Its layers are populated by infinitesimal subtle filaments that are hollow and constituted by elastic energy of the etheric body, allowing stretching and the passage of energy charges of different vibrations. Commonly known as tendrils these filaments are capable of injecting energy directly into the current of the subtle system, working not only as carriers but also as puncturing needles that probe and draw energy from the environment but also from other living beings and their inner system. Their elasticity provides a potential tool that can be used defensively but more often offensively, being highly adaptive and specialized to break metaphysical defenses and conceal their presence.

As the outer shell of the subtle body the aura carries the energy that others will be able to touch and sense from your inner system, representing an important factor on how everyone is perceived and in the establishing of first impression. How someone is able to cause change in the environment, whether positive or negative, is often related with the influence of the energy present in the aura.

In this way the ability to control different aspects of the aura through its tendrils and to alter the quality and vibration of its energy is a unique tool in magick and manipulation, being an elegant and stealthy predatory weapon that can influence perception and emotion. These Asetian arts rely on a metaphysical practice known as projecting and they will be examined in further detail when addressing the variants of vampiric manipulation.

Subtle Body
All energy systems present in a living organism comprise a meta-structure that defines the subtle body, sometimes also called the energy body or astral body, although the latter would not be an accurate definition. Its composition establishes the crystallization of

energy that potentiates incarnation in a biological body, given coherence by the spark of existence and manifested through the process of creation — it is an echo of the seed of life, intimately bound to the very essence of the soul.

The subtle body is the unification of distinctive but symbiotic energy structures, from the vital organs described as primary and secondary Shen centers to their interlinking meridian channels, support sub-structures, self-regenerating filaments and bound constructs. Although not interchangeable concepts the subtle body is sometimes also referenced as Ba, the Ancient Egyptian word for soul, and in a metaphysical sense it represents the energy structure that is more closely akin to the western definition of spirit.

This psychic meta-spiritual body is formed by uniquely dense energy that does not fade away and although it does dissipate through its natural systems such as the layers of the aura it automatically replenishes itself by universal absorption and in vampiric cases with added draining and active magick. Although often undisclosed and tied to misunderstanding this body can be wounded or in extreme situations permanently destroyed through absolute metaphysical collapse, locked keys bound to a well-guarded secret of the ages.

Not being human and manifested by such an inscrutably unique nature that is not only spiritual but also energetic, the vital essence in Asetians that establishes the subtle body exhibits the fabric of eternity; a condition of the very foundation of the soul that defines their immortality. While the subtle body is entirely independent from the physical body, existing with or without its incarnated presence, both elements interact in a flow of essence and vitality that define the delicate balance of sacred and mundane — the union of magickal and physical.

A classic example of esoteric bridging between both worlds is how raw muscle presents no match for the cunning mind and feline eye of the vampire. Overdeveloped muscular mass just like allocated fat tissue in excess is discouraged in every Order featuring advanced metaphysical training. In terms of subtle anatomy, the nature of both fat and muscle cause energy degeneration and impact natural flow, hindering intensive magickal practice and being a constraint to the accurate and precise projection of vital energy, making them illusive enemies of the educated practitioner who understands such influence in stagnation. While this is only valid in the case of an incarnated practitioner where the biological body has influence in the metaphysical processes of the subtle system, such understanding sheds light on the importance of a balanced vibrational outlook alongside a healthy diet as body and energy intertwine in a never-ending dance of life. Such elements raised in history the common portrayal of vampires as slim creatures with a fragile body; this is a misconception of their broad diversity, as not all vampires are physically thin or develop an elegant body. The signature lack of overdeveloped muscular mass can be a distinctive sign of magickal proficiency and a potential clue to its direct impact on the mighty arts of the unseen.

Even if commonly neglected by those unaware of its existence and vital mechanisms, the alchemical equilibrium and overall health of the subtle body is of fundamental importance to every living being. Its vibrational state constantly echoes into the physical and mental realms, inducing conditions and manifesting as diseases, blockages and breakdowns. The majority of biological ailments from minor to major are rooted in a subtle cause that can be studied and analysed from a metaphysical perspective, a study exhaustively examined within the Aset Ka in a field we have pioneered as subtle pathology.

Understanding the subtle body while developing the practices and techniques that enhance a balanced flow of its internal energies has proven to be an essential factor in every aspect of life. If energy is effectively the essence of existence and embodies the divine spark of the living then the subtle body is our cosmic engine that allows life to exist, nurturing it to flourish and persevere.

Shen Centers

Within the internal structure of the subtle body there are a number of complex but distinctive systems that function, in part, similarly to what is expected from a biological organ but operating on a metaphysical level, being self-contained and individually building upon idiosyncratic mechanisms of vital energy. In Asetianism and its branch of subtle anatomy these organs are called Shen and they are responsible, among other things, for the balance and control of the flux of Ka within the whole subtle system.

As a pulsating nexus of vital energy specializing in unique metaphysical features that comprise the machinery of the subtle body, these centers are also known by the Sanskrit word *chakra*. Shen is an Ancient Egyptian concept and word that can be translated as *circle* or *ring*, found in spirituality as a symbol of eternity and everlastingness that represents a cycle without beginning and no end. The hieroglyph for Shen bears similarities to a royal cartouche, often represented in ancient literature circumscribing divine names of hidden power, ruling pharaohs and composite sigils, however in this case they have a distinctive circular form without contents or other symbols represented within. In the art of symbolism and esoteric iconography the Shen is sometimes wrongly interpreted as an element of solar nature, frequently represented on the top of the head of Egyptian deities but in fact pointing quite blatantly to an important inner feature — an actual energy center that is the Crown, the divine link and cosmic gateway. Those allegories to the subtle body and metaphysical properties are found in ancient artwork and texts of Egyptian scholars, scribes and mystics as an often cryptic yet secure way to store the wisdom of the elders. A code we humbly and honorably safeguard throughout the ages; one we will fiercely fight for, never to be defaced again.

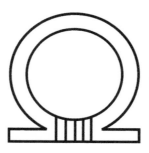

The representation of the Shen centers with a markedly circular shape is not random or merely symbolic, as the energy structure of each organ presents a diffuse circular form and rotating motion. The direction, pace and vibratory vector of its rotation are connected to variables that were established depending on the balance, state and nature of each individual Shen system. In cases of intense stagnation and crystallized blockages the rotation can stall, stop or invert, requiring experienced attention and treatment provided by a specialist in subtle medicine and energy.

Although this knowledge and medical branch has been explored since the time of the Ancient Egyptians, energy techniques and subtle healing has been developed in many cultures and by various civilizations, including new findings provided by modern research and

✝

investigation. Some of these concepts find parallels in traditional medical systems of Asia, where the word chakra, used in reference to the older concept of Shen, also carries a similar meaning for *wheel* and *circle*. However, such gnosis predates those cultures, being found mirrored on the architecture of the Temple of Luxor[14] [15] raised in the ancient city of Thebes in Egypt, an icon that ties its foundations and hidden wisdom to the Asetian teachings of the Sep Tepy.

In advanced studies of subtle anatomy we have described three distinctive types of Shen systems: primary, secondary and tertiary. The primary energy centers are seven, a number of recurring prominence in the Asetian tradition that finds its sacredness mirrored in nature. These primary Shen exhibit some degree of alignment with the major endocrine glands of the physical body and present an arrangement alongside the central backbone of the skeleton, each in symbiotic touch with major nerve ganglia branching forth from the spinal column. These vital energy organs are interconnected by hollow energy filaments known as meridians that allow for a constant flow of Ka between the different Shen and the rest of the subtle body, representing fundamental structures of the energy system.

In a more holistic approach, the Shen also hold correlations with different levels of consciousness, metaphysical manifestation and abilities, patterned emotional states, developing physical conditions, archetypal representations, the spectrum of color and light, range of sound and countless other variables. As such the study and understanding of Shen, not only in terms of subtle anatomy and healing but also as an esoteric field of knowledge, is important to various metaphysical practices such as fundamental energy work, psychic attack, magickal defense, profound meditation and even in more advanced precision techniques such as subtle surgery.

The seven primary energy systems following an order of increased vibration are the Root, Sexual, Solar, Heart, Throat, Third Eye and the Crown. The following pages present a limited and organized description of characteristics and fundamental elements related to each primary Shen, which are intended to work as a reference in study and practice, providing a basic understanding of their functioning and associated areas of influence. The numbering sequence commonly found when describing the Shen is based on their positioning alongside the spinal column but also established through their coherence to progressive vibrational properties. Smaller numbers define lower vibrations that steadily increase on a scale from one to seven into the higher vibration and intensity of the Shen with larger numbers, advancing from energy centers with a strong material connection into those of an advanced spiritual layer that operate almost strictly in transcendence.

Although the secondary Shen are mapped in a representative figure included in the chapter on Shen anatomy, and are available for academic consultation and use, they will not be analysed in detail as they develop into a specific framework that is only studied after a higher understanding of the primary systems, their interconnectivity and metaphysical operation. The tertiary Shen are too numerous to mention and accurately describe in this primer, encompassing less specialized systems of similar and basic nature when compared to the complexity of both primary and secondary. For the practical usage of these concepts and provided knowledge in magick, metaphysics and subtle medicine I have condensed and categorized a few elements on a table layout, designed as a quick reference resource on primary Shen characteristics that can be found in the appendices.

Root Shen

The Root is the first of the seven primary Shen and the one with a lower vibration but it also represents the mechanism in the subtle body that maintains a stronger connection with elemental Earth. Physically it is positioned lower than any other energy centers on the biological system, located around the area of the perineum and expanding towards the coccyx at the base of the spinal column.

In terms of vibrational metaphysics this Shen resonates with the colors red and black of the visible spectrum of light, being tied to elements of physical strength, aspects of instinct and survival as well as the sense of safety. It is a central system in the practices of grounding, playing an important role in the management of internal stability and holistic balance. The minerals that project energy in tune with the Shen of the Root are ruby, obsidian, black tourmaline and hematite, the last having a strong connection with blood and its vibrational essence.

Concerning health and the field of subtle medicine this Shen influences many of the inferior biological systems, playing a pivotal role in aspects of locomotion, excretion, the bladder and lower digestive system, particularly the colon. Blockages may echo into the physical body as a perception of pain around the legs and lower back.

Emotionally the Root controls fear, behavioral instinct, confidence and some manifestations of the ego, being an important element that needs to be kept in check and under control when it comes to attaining mental balance and a positive emotional state. Note that this Shen can develop the instinctual reactions that make it a powerful survival tool, while it remains unable to influence the layers of intuition as they represent two distinctive abilities and the gift of intuitive perception is bound to another Shen: the Third Eye.

When healthy and exhibiting proper flow, in tune with the rest of the subtle body and aligned with the other Shen, the Root can enhance overall biological functions, improve inner connection with the material plane, promote courage, develop strength, reinforce coordination and grounding abilities. If unbalanced it may influence the health of its affected physical organs and weaken the immune system, while mentally it is prone to increases in violence, anger and nervous tension, inducing self-centered behavioral patterns.

In Asetianism the Root is represented by the Was, one of the seven sacred pillars.

Sexual Shen

The Sexual Shen is the second energy center in the vital system comprised of seven major subtle engines. Located below the navel and on top of the bladder it extends towards the sexual organs and its operations are intimately related to the libidinous system. Empowered through elemental Fire and a driving force of the Flame, this is the center of pure creativity and unbounded sexuality.

Creativity is an essential aspect of enlightened spirituality and relevant to the understanding of magick. As independent beings we are an unlimited force of creation and whenever creativity is used it draws its life force from the essence emanating from the Sexual Shen. It is through the chaotic powers of creativity that our hidden arts may be liberated and unleashed, raising magick to its higher potential. Pure art, however, cannot be aimed primarily at exhibition or inspired from the drive of ego as those ultimately result from imbalances of the mind and energy. When creation is sought through the shallow desire of fame or the hope for self-acceptance it is not true art and certainly not magick but merely a byproduct of vanity deprived of power or spiritual quality. Such is a recurrently misunderstood notion in modern society that has blinded and deceived many. Remember that the greatest artists of magick and craftsmen of the subtle remain detachedly unknown, choosing a road of silence and proudly rejecting recognition while embracing evolution and enlightenment. Those are bold and daring footsteps capable of expressing the raw unification of magick and art but not everyone is at the higher level of perception and inner growth that such profound understanding entails.

Metaphysically resonating with the color orange of the visible light spectrum this is a Shen under lunar influence, and unlike the Root it manifests a distinctively feminine energy of concealed power. To ignite and open its doors requires us to take risks and have the courage to go against all odds since only through determined will can one access its abilities. This energy is the subtle fuel that allows for the creation of something out of nothing and that is true alchemy. Asetian wisdom connects the Sexual Shen with the symbol of the Tiet, a sacred pillar of particular emotion to this ancient culture.

For energy amplification and balancing techniques the minerals that should be used are carnelian, topaz and amber. Although the last is not a true mineral being organic in nature and amorphous in structure, it does yield specific characteristics that are in tune with the vibration of this Shen.

Not only do the several aspects of sexuality fall under the influence of this energy center and its intense energy projection, it also plays a role in the biological mechanisms of the kidneys, ovaries, testicles and genitals, with its activity known to alter the production of hormones. When healthy the Sexual Shen promotes desire, enhances pleasure and improves sexuality; it is the hidden pathway to surrender. Emotionally it leads to liberated joy and a sense of abundance, controlling passion, intimacy and sensuality. However, if unbalanced or stagnated it may often induce sexual problems, manifest different layers of confusion and stir the potential for charged emotions such as jealousy and envy.

Solar Shen

The third major organ of the primary energy centers is the Solar Shen also known as the Solar Plexus. It is located below the chest expanding towards the navel and its charge radiates into every other subtle system. Its structure establishes a vital hard-link between the physical and subtle bodies; as the seat of the soul and hall of renewal it is represented in Asetianism by the Ba sacred pillar.

In terms of metaphysics this Shen vibrates with the brightness of the Sun, finding resonance with the color yellow of the visible spectrum of light. Being a bridge between the Sexual Shen and the Heart Shen it holds special ties with elemental Fire and Water, however it does not unify the alchemy from both elements but mediates their interchange of essences. A pale yellow variant of quartz known as citrine and a chatoyant gemstone named tiger's eye are two examples of minerals that are frequently used when working with this energy center.

The Solar Shen controls vital functions in the nervous system, liver, pancreas and stomach, establishing balance over mechanisms of digestion and overall metabolism, both energetic and biological. Its intimate connection with the nervous system results in an important influence over many aspects of experienced emotion and mental balance, being particularly relevant to the management of motivation, stress, anxiety and self-esteem.

When aligned with the other systems and in tune with its natural vibration the Solar Shen enhances willpower, promotes decision-making, renewed confidence and balanced authority. Its proper functioning cycles energy and distributes it throughout the entire subtle body, being an essential nexus capable of increasing self-control and physical wellbeing. If unregulated and allowed to stagnate it can lead to digestive conditions and a slower metabolism, however psychologically it can result in social disorders, anxiety and depression ranging from minor to major. A Shen does not only cause problems when it is misaligned, blocked or stagnated. If operating in overclock or hyperactive rotation it can cause severe strain in the subtle system and this may translate into physical and psychological conditions that can be challenging to treat.

Heart Shen

This Shen is a gateway to emotion and the seat for our spiritual heart. It is the fourth energy centre in the group of primary Shen, holding a close relationship with blood and the circulatory system. Being precisely in the middle of the three upper and lower major energy organs this is an engine of delicate equilibrium, establishing a link between the emotional fabric of reality and the pulsating essence of spirit constantly echoing into the mundane. This is particularly important in the maintenance of energy flow and the recurring process of balancing the seven centers as one stable and aligned metaphysical mainframe.

Its operations are tied to the framework of emotions, playing essential roles in the manifestation and interpretation of feelings. As such, the Heart Shen is mirrored in symbolism as the Ib hieroglyph, a sacred pillar of Asetianism that embodies the spiritual heart. Nurturing its balance represents an important element in how we deal with non-physical pain and when flowing properly it helps with shedding of those malignant attachments. The energy that it irradiates and transmutes provides the potential for higher awareness, enhancing understanding without limited judgment or drama. Through this cleansed lens renewed clarity can be attained, like the realization about those who only seek to harm and destroy mirror a problem they carry within themselves and that, if you are an unfair target of their anger, insult and hatred, then the issue does not lie on you but simply exposes a reflection of their insecurities, fears and unattended desires.

Physically the Shen is found around the sternum near the center of the chest and its rotating plexus of energy resonates with the color green of the visible light spectrum. Its alchemical influence is that of elemental Water, not surprising given its power over the emotional body. Emerald, jade, malachite and the rose variants of quartz are all effective mineral tools when working with energy amplification through the Heart Shen and its vibrational attunement.

A vital mechanism to the circulatory system with control over the functioning of the heart, the breasts and lungs, its native tendrils expand through the arms and into the hands, being specialized carriers for the energy and vibration that it generates and redirects. Echoing into the physical body as chronic heart conditions, lung diseases and circulatory problems when imbalanced or blocked, this Shen is also capable of promoting forgiveness, compassion and acceptance.

Throat Shen

The Shen of the Throat is the fifth organ of the primary energy system and it is represented by the Khepri hieroglyph, a sacred pillar in the Asetian mysteries. It is positioned at the base of the throat expanding towards the mouth and the back of the neck, filtering sound and echoing vibration.

This energy center plays a central role in speech and communication, affecting the mechanisms of vocalization and every biological tissue surrounding the mouth and throat, exhibiting particular control over the working of the thyroid and the health of the teeth, tongue and auditory system. Physically it is also actively responsible for the bone marrow and structure of the cervical vertebrae being important in the ongoing prevention of its degeneration.

Metaphysically it resonates with the color blue of the visible light spectrum and it holds intimate ties with the alchemy of elemental Air. Minerals such as turquoise, aquamarine and the precious gem sapphire are adequate when amplifying essence through this plexus. Its accurate alignment with the Sexual Shen is determinant in the development of artistic creativity but to infuse the energy that it generates with the unique essence of certain Shen at a specific vibrational attunement is capable of producing what can be described as alchemical poison and it is a dangerous esoteric weapon worthy of note.

When under equilibrium and a state of energetic stasis the Throat Shen enhances the power of spoken word, coherence of discourse and effective communication, besides the healthy maintenance of its affected physical organs. However, when blocked or thrown out of balance it hinders communication and expression, which can be wrongly perceived as a social handicap when in fact it has a subtle cause that can be treated with dedicated care and patience.

†

Third Eye Shen

This is the Shen of magick and mystical power. Foresight, intuition, subtle senses and active energy manipulation are all ignited through the metaphysical mechanisms potentiated by the Third Eye. As such, this sixth energy center of the primary Shen is of utmost importance to every occultist and practitioner of the magickal arts, working as a gateway to the subtle realm and higher planes of existence. In Asetianism it is represented by the Egyptian hieroglyph for Ka, a sacred pillar that presides over the vital essence of the living.

Connected with the alchemy of the spirit its energy flows in tune with the color indigo of the visible light spectrum, one final step before the violet light of transcendence. Establishing control over psychic powers and metaphysical abilities, this Shen also works with the physical body being responsible for eyesight and certain cerebral functions, with its energy echoing to the physical realm into the tissue of the brain, the chemistry of synapses and the engine behind vision.

Psychologically this subtle organ is the seat of Self, a circular shell of true identity and singularity storing all of your dreams, hopes and fears generated from the mental plane. It is the hard drive of the subtle body that uploads every aspect of your existence into the indestructible fabric of the akashic records.

☥

Thoughts are the union of physical and metaphysical; the result of a close relationship between chemistry and subtle energy. They are manifested and interpreted through electricity sparking between the synapses in the brain, but they are also generated through vibrant impulses of Ka emitted by the Shen of the Third Eye as a marriage of material and subtle that culminates in conscious thought and what modern science studies as the mental process.

The location of the Third Eye is found at the center of the forehead, between the eyebrows and expanding forward towards the aura and the outer layers of energy. It can be empowered and balanced with techniques of energy projection and cycling through minerals such as lapis lazuli and sodalite.

When strengthened and developed this Shen unleashes intuition, enhances insight and potentiates clairvoyance. It can be used to focus True Will, attain higher perception and open doors on the road to enlightenment. A blocked or imbalanced Third Eye will decrease concentration, hinder metaphysical sensitivity and filter or outright block magickal abilities. Working in parallel with the neurological system, dysfunctions in this energy center may induce headaches, recurrent nightmares, insomnia, nausea, addiction or in worst cases lead to medical conditions of the brain.

Crown Shen

The Crown is the higher of all Shen and also the one with a stronger vibration. This energy center is the number seven in the system and it represents the hall of spirituality that intimately connects your innermost reality with the ultimate transcendence of divinity; in Asetians this is the throne of Aset, a bond with Her everlasting crown of light and darkness.

It is located above the head on your crown of the soul and it expands upwards beyond the subtle body, working as the purest link with the cosmos and the essence of all. This Shen is a subtle system of raw transcendence represented in the Asetian culture by the Ankh, the sacred pillar of immortality.

Unlike other Shen that often manifest as dense disks of energy with innate rotation, the Crown is actually a pulsating sphere and its movement is both multidirectional and multidimensional. This structure is found represented in Ancient Egyptian art as a disk featured at the top of the heads of deities. Sometimes interpreted as solar iconography, this artistic depiction is an interesting representation of the Crown Shen, intended to portray with heightened relevance this energy center found strongly developed in evolved beings such as the Asetians, which the common people and historical development once inaccurately described as Gods. An enlightened level of evolution tied to the nature of this Shen has also been culturally represented as horns and rays of light, elements that later gave birth to the horned Gods of paganism. In Egypt both pharaohs and initiated masters of the temples frequently adopted a completely bald head as a symbolical sign of their developed Crown and the attaining of magickal power, spiritual evolution and wisdom — all clues, signs and markers of ancient understanding that are still visible in artwork that has survived to this day.

Resonating with the essence of divine purity the vibrational color of the Crown is violet, a branding found on the eternal flag of the Aset Ka and a living connection between Asetian soul and the nature of the Violet Flame, here manifested as the inscrutable blood of Aset. The mineral that can aid the opening and initiation of the Crown is the amethyst, metaphysically unique and with a long history of sacredness and power in Asetianism.

This Shen is ever active during life and beyond as it constantly draws raw energy from universal sources, being a fundamental gateway responsible for the essence that sustains the subtle body, cleanses its vital breath and restores inner and outer balance. When aligned and attuned a dim but intimate connection with the Higher Self becomes possible and through it a better understanding of the nature of divinity. For Asetians this Crown of immortality is also the bond of unbroken family that echoes their oneness and illuminates a timeless call; it bears the seed of infinity enclosed within manifested energy of the purest violet light.

Shen Anatomy

The following map of subtle anatomy pinpoints the fundamental locations of primary and secondary Shen as studied in the Asetian system. The seven major energy centers are described on the left and the seven secondary plexus on the right. Understanding the underlying mechanisms of each vibrational organ and how they interconnect in both metaphysical and biological operation goes beyond the study of their location and elementary characteristics.

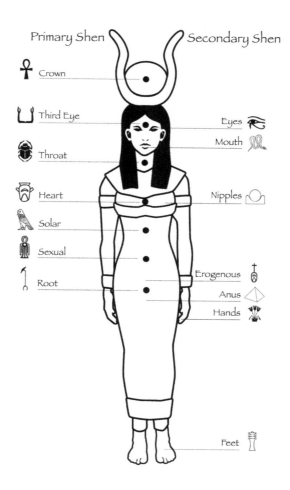

The examination here presented is intended to provide a solid and accurate foundation that can be further developed through dedicated study and experience. Knowledge is no replacement for practical work and the flourishing fruit of experience only potentiated by time and dedication. However, the nature of knowledge is of determinant importance during the learning process of subtle anatomy, vibrational medicine and advanced energy work; there is a lot of misinformation and misconception perpetuated by ignorance and lack of method, so the wise student always seeks the source under the watchful eyes of ancient truth.

A larger version of the Shen map here provided is included in the appendices for consultation and reference during study, practice and teaching.

Meridians

The primary and secondary energy centers do not operate as standalone structures and isolated engines; they are interconnected through a complex network of subtle filaments called meridians that work as hollow vessels capable of transporting, filtering and absorbing vital energy. These elastic and self-repairing conductive channels are responsible for several functions in the subtle body, although the transport and flow of energy represent their main and fundamental operation.

Found mentioned in different cultures and various branches of alternative healing techniques, the concept is prominent in traditional Chinese medicine where it has been extensively studied and applied in treatment for centuries. The meridians play an important role in oriental techniques such as acupuncture and acupressure, where blockages in the flow of energy are treated or the streams altered through the use of needles, pressure and energy projection. These gateways into the meridians are described as acupoints in Chinese medicine and tsubo in Japanese practices, sometimes forming a microsystem of particular specialization in the subtle system that represents a tertiary Shen. As such certain acupoints found in systems of traditional medicine are in fact a tertiary Shen and represent a small but relevant energy organ.

Although the Chinese and Japanese traditions describe systems of meridians that have a valid working parallel with the ones found in the Asetian culture, the energy channels found in Egyptian wisdom that are studied and used by the Aset Ka extend beyond such understanding and expand into an intricate mechanism of layers and interconnected webs of energy vessels that provide a broader interpretation of the meridians and their functions, not only on a biological level but also in terms of their metaphysical and spiritual applications. Working with energy, harnessing, shaping and wielding it has been at the core of Asetian scholarly pursuits for thousands of years; a never-ending endeavour that has seen its birth in the time before time of the Sep Tepy and continues its development to this day.

Some meridians present a natural connection with the physical body through a systematic alignment with the circulatory cardiovascular system, running through the energy body alongside the capillaries, veins and arteries of the biological body. Being extremely diverse in length and diameter, some are large and thick allowing for a high stream of energy flow while others are thin and fragile, meshing as a dense network of rich vibration. They transfer energy and information between the different Shen, primary and secondary, ensuring the optimal working of all systems and their vibration in tune to each other, promoting a working metabolism and a healthy flow of energy capable of dissolving blockages and fighting stagnation, effectively fueling the great machinery that is the subtle body.

Links

The terminology of subtle links is used to describe a metaphysical phenomenon established between living beings and manifested as energetic tunnels that are spontaneously built from intimate or recurrent interactions but also intentionally crafted through magick and energy manipulation. Links are effective gateways attached to the subtle matter of life, allowing for the channeling of energy, thoughts and emotions.

These vessels do not require physical contact to be established, relying on the metaphysical fuel of vital energy and being empowered through emotional attachment, psychological patterns and magickal constructs. Relationships from friendly to romantic, sexual intercourse and vampiric feeding are known to naturally forge energy links of various types and intensities, becoming attached to the subtle system even without conscious thought or ability from the intervenient.

Some links are relatively static and of low vibration, in a constant state of decay and slowly dissipating with time, while others are stronger and denser, being extremely difficult to detach or break. The most powerful links can linger until death when they finally deteriorate through natural processes or, in rarer cases, some may even establish a permanent bond that remains unbroken through lifetimes. Links such as these are special and commonly found among Asetians, mirrored on the unquestionable loyalty towards their spiritual family and the immortal bonds that shield the Aset Ka while permeating its unique fabric of eternal love.

Through every interaction with someone that holds an active energy link its metaphysical construct will be strengthened, particularly although not exclusively in situations that tap into the etheric fluid of emotions. This presents an important aspect on why the practices of vampirism should be approached with caution and under the exercise of responsibility, as careless feeding may cause more harm than benefit. While an isolated contact drain is likely to establish a thin link with a high potential for dissipation, leaving simply an ephemeral scar on the aura of the donor, an accomplished process of deep feeding is bound to forge an extremely strong link capable of puncturing through the aura and into the soul, gaining access and opening a doorway to the core of the energy system and heart of the spirit. Furthermore, links can operate as a security leak into the subtle system and such is a potential exploit for those fluent in the magickal arts of energy and vibration. Even the smallest and weakest links are directly connected to the aura, representing a gateway into your intimacy and undisputed access through the external shields that elegantly bypass most outer defenses.

Beyond the natural and unconscious nature of energy links these structures can also be actively created, used and manipulated when enough sensitivity is developed. As a subtle channel, links are known to transmit energy and emotions, something they actively do during default operation but that can be altered and fine-tuned with proper metaphysical mastery, allowing us to induce thoughts and feelings as well as the passive draining of energy.

Subtle links are one of the foundations behind empathy when perceived between two individuals or even in a group, allowing for the experiencing of emotions from others as well as their conscious and unconscious thoughts. To interpret that information accurately and with validated precision requires knowledge, sensitivity and experience. When someone genuinely feels that another is in danger or undergoing suffering, sometimes attributing it to intuition, such perception can oftentimes be an echo drawn from the mechanisms of links that through their capability to transfer energy can also carry subtle information, remaining one of the main engines behind the phenomenon of telepathy. Silent communication works through these linked channels but its accuracy and verifiability are greatly affected by the level of metaphysical noise found in the subtle matter being transferred as well as the unavoidable energy lost through dissipation while traversing the links.

Some links can be safely severed and cauterized although that requires a complete detachment between those involved, as any further interaction would only reconnect the damaged link and reinforce its attachment. The treatment of energy links should be approached with care and avoided in most cases since it is aggressive for the energy body and leaves an open wound on the aura as a result. If this is not evaluated and safeguarded for the period that it takes to seal and heal, there remains a latent door that can be exploited by malignant entities or a knowledgeable practitioner with ill intent. The practice and development of energy shielding may greatly benefit these processes, working as efficient mechanisms of magickal protection and proactive metaphysical safety. However, if the decision is made to actively remove an energy link through the means of subtle surgery then such a procedure should only be done by an experienced master to minimize the risk and potential complications. To ignore such precautions or innocently fall under the deceit of charlatans is to willingly walk on a path to grave consequence and personal cost.

Wounds

Just like biological tissue and physical organs the subtle body can also be injured, resulting in what can be described as a metaphysical wound. The underlying causes that are capable of originating lesions on the condensed energy of the subtle body are diverse, ranging from psychosomatic conditions such as established depression to subtle events of a metaphysical nature like psychic attacks, energy poisoning and various forms of magickal warfare.

Superficial wounds are invariably located upon the medium to upper layers of the aura, presenting varying degrees of depth and extension depending on the intensity of the attack and the vibration of the energy that caused it. Even simple wounds require time and vibrational equilibrium to heal, being treated through a natural process of recovery that attempts to regenerate ruptured energetic tissue or when it exhibits some level of decay. This healing mechanism is activated by the core energy system and the wound slowly dissipates as new inner layers are produced and sequentially attached to the lower membranes of the aura in a recurring cycle. Such natural process can be accelerated and empowered through specialized techniques of energy healing that will also enhance and strengthen the structure of the aura, resulting in a more effective and guided recovery.

Other wounds, however, manifest deeper in the subtle body, being considered internal, and they can be more problematic. The most serious conditions are found when the wounded vibrational tissue is located within a Shen center, requiring special attention and experienced care. Those wounds may result from profound trauma, degenerative conditions, life-threatening illness, torture — physical, psychological or magickal — be tied to a severe accident or the fragmented collapse of death. Such rooted wounds are potentially dangerous and threatening, requiring an extremely long time to heal and, in the worst situations, can even extend to lifetimes. Treatment and guidance from a therapist with extensive knowledge in the fields of energy healing and subtle anatomy is a major asset and oftentimes an essential requirement to recovery in most severe cases.

Deeper wounds of utmost complexity represent a handicap to the subtle body and in certain situations may even prevent the soul from reincarnating, as the aura requires a minimum metaphysical condition in order to pass through the process of reincarnation and enter the world of the living. Such awareness explains the relevance of energy torture, psychic attack and offensive magickal techniques as metaphysical weapons of the old days, having seen extended use during the Epic Wars and, for the most part, now long gone. To prevent an Asetian from entering reincarnation and its empowered control, even if only temporary, was a potentially great power of desired strategic value and severe implications; one that red enemies desperately sought to master.

Blockages

A problem frequently tied to more natural and passive origins than wounds is the manifestation of energy blockages in the subtle system. It represents one of the most common conditions in subtle medicine and the development of internal blockages of various types has been established to be present in every body at some moment during the natural course of incarnated life.

The most prevalent variants of metaphysical blockages are established as denser concentrations of stagnated energy that can develop in nearly every location of the subtle system, from the layered aura to the meridian vessels and even attached to different areas of

✝

major Shen, which in this case can lead to complications of serious consequence. That stagnated energy attached to subtle structures can crystalize, leading to a solidified blockage that grows increasingly difficult to dissolve. Several distinctive factors lead to energy stagnation and the location where the blockage is formed presents important clues to its origin and underlying causes. All elements should be studied and documented for a proper analysis and valid understanding.

Traditional methods of energy healing are commonly effective treatments for blockages of ordinary types. A directed energy beam projected into the blocked area at a steady frequency and vibration is often capable of dissolving stagnated energy and promoting its flow into the system, enhancing dissipation and breaking the solidifying subtle tissue of blockages. However, such techniques may not always be strong enough to break or dissolve highly crystalized energy, requiring more intense approaches with a potentially dangerous impact in order to heal. This should not be considered lightly but it can represent the appropriate course of treatment for more exotic variants of blockages.

Spiritual stagnation and energy blockages can often echo into the physical and psychological realms. Disguised as disease and other ailments, these conditions have a subtle root that must be understood, consciously approached and patiently treated in order to prevent the resurfacing of symptoms and consequences that behave recurrently or may trigger cascading events that can be physical or metaphysical.

It remains valuable to keep in mind that the best course of action against blockages and stagnation is conscious prevention. A healthy diet and an active life, meditation and magickal practice are all effective tools for a balanced energy system. Through a holistic approach where your inner Self is valued and nurtured as a temple it is possible to pursue a life path that unifies mind, body and spirit. Such pursuit requires commitment and self-discipline but every accomplishment worthy of note demands the same and the spiritual side of Asetianism is akin to a martial art of the mind and soul, raising the initiate to a higher potential and unseen ability; it clears the eyes so they can see.

Tumors

Certain subtle conditions manifested on the metaphysical body if allowed to encrust and develop may degenerate into malignant constructs. These tumors are strongly attached to the vibrational fabric of energy organs and subtle structures, recurrently establishing control of energy flow and metastasizing into other vital areas where the Ka is abundant.

Just like other forms of metaphysical ailments, tumors can potentially echo into the physical realm, often in a strongly negative way, manifesting as degenerative diseases or harmful and even life-threatening health complications.

Approaching this type of conditions requires expertise and caution, as techniques relying on standard energy beams will not be effective in treating established tumors. Although they may provide temporary relief of the symptoms, and a positive halt on the proliferation of malignant energy, these methods should be understood as palliative solutions. In these cases, advanced methods of energy treatment are required alongside a planned holistic approach and the complete evaluation of all metaphysical areas of influence, including the passive systems and environmental variables. Recovery should be expectedly slow and complicated but often possible, however subtle surgery is frequently the most effective treatment of choice.

If a subtle tumor is allowed to endure, develop and prosper without opposition it can withstand the passage of death, inducing a weakened energy body and latent echoes that may affect energy flow and underlying metaphysical conditions in future incarnations. It should be clear however that subtle tumors must not be confused with the different variants of biological cancer, as not all degenerative and cancerous cells are a consequence of subtle tumors and energetic conditions.

Metaphysics

During the following chapters some fundamental concepts of energy work are approached and methodically described, establishing a solid metaphysical framework that stands at the foundation of Asetian spiritual practice and magick, featuring elements ranging in complexity from core to advanced. These concepts present a common ground in Asetian culture and art, embodying some of the most traditional techniques and defining a background of gnosis that is a definitive requirement during the study of more intricate techniques and complex practices further discussed.

To study this material and subject matter while striving not only for its experienced understanding and practice but also aiming for a certain degree of mastery should be of considerable importance to the initiate, paving the roadmap of growth that allows for higher gateways to unfold and eventually open as the result of hard dedicated work. That honest commitment is key in unleashing the sinuous path of exploration into the realm of advanced metaphysics and active magick, providing the efficiency and elegance so characteristic of those unique students fluent in the path of Asetianism.

The fundamental grasp of the concepts hereby presented is not difficult and should be clear after careful study of the occult material provided. Although some may be familiar with the concepts or even experienced with their practice and intended use, the information remains relevant as reference and documented guide even to those with a long time of metaphysical training, providing an accurate source on the often misunderstood mechanisms behind traditional practices and techniques of energy work that sustain the paramount operations of magick.

Planes of Existence

The ability to roam the realms of the living and the lands of the dead, to wander freely from one plane of existence into another as liberated shades of the unseen; that is a skill not many possess, or at least have yet to unveil its secrets. The Asetians are creatures unbound from the restraints of the physical reality of matter that most perceive as defined existence. As entities of energy and infinite freedom they journey through the realms of thought, subtlety and magick, making the astral dimensions of the cosmos their kingdom and establishing power over that which is invisible.

In the lands that are not governed by the limitations of matter the ones willfully adventuring through its gates are capable of shapeshifting, flying and manifesting in ways that mirror the sweet matter of dreams and the acidic fluid of nightmares. Those chosen icons or adopted avatars represent mere expressions of conscious inner will, a shadow on the wall, not the innermost identity of the practitioner nor a true face of the soul.

Although the word astral is found in literature as common terminology to reference the subtle realms, under close and educated study it only represents one of the main layers composing the planes of existence and not an accurate personification of all that is subtle. The fabric of reality when examined under a conceptual microscope of metaphysical science it appears to be composed by five distinguishable fundamental layers that establish the pentamerous planes of existence, each finding subsequent specialization and being further decomposed into various realms of intrinsic density and complexity.

The identity of each of the five realms is contrasting and divergent from the others, being bound to distinctive and sometimes opposing fundamental rulesets that define the nature, functionality and underlying potential of each plane. These realities are not only unique

✝

in their elemental composition and alchemical aspects but also in how they react to and interact with the presence of life as well as how metaphysical energy responds in that specific realm, making its exploration of particular interest to the learned occultist.

For advanced study at a higher level of understanding a distinctive analysis of the subtle planes can be found in *Liber* יסוד, my occult dissertation on the ancient wisdom of the Kabbalah included in the *Book of Orion.*[16]

Physical

The physical plane represents the realm of lower vibration where transcendence is limited and filtered, decaying into matter as manifest reality. As the plane of matter this kingdom is constructed around a universal set of governing laws — conceptual tenets and fundamental boundaries known in science as physics. These principles establish the reality inhabited by the physical body, yet it shares its framework with the constructs of energy, vibration and subtle flow, making magick possible.

As such it can be said that the physical plane is formed by the attuned match of two distinctive fabrics of existence, interwoven throughout space and time. Matter and energy dance in this perpetual cycle, occupying the very same place in the engine of the cosmos; the visible and the invisible, tangible and intangible, all real and bound to their own mysteries.

This realm of matter is the seat of reincarnation, where the soul descends into corporeal form. Although of a physical nature it is bound to the infinite layers above even though communication is limited and channeled through specific outlets. Its independence and freedom is deceptive and illusory, where much is not what it appears to be at

✝

surface and reality is interpreted through the limited senses of biology and the imagery produced by the machinery of eyesight.

It is possible for energy and magick to transcend the physical plane and bleed into the other realms. In fact, advanced forms of magick depend on this knowledge and metaphysical mechanism. By attaching a construct of energy to a physical object those subtle forces remain in the physical realm, although it is common for a clone of this vibration to be established within the inner plane as well, often even unconsciously, which hinders natural dissipation. In more complex practices such a construct may be intentionally echoed into the astral, however such practices are not as simple nor as linear as popular occult culture postulates. It is common for the less experienced practitioners to confuse the reality of the astral plane with elements found within their own inner plane of unconscious thought, leading to inaccurate assumptions about the nature and magickal assets of such realms. Finally, to project such energies higher and beyond the astral into the fabric of the ethereal or divine planes, that remains an undertaking of enlightened power that transcends the understanding of mortals.

The physical is a sarcophagus of matter; a resonating chamber of vibration where the soul is locked and often unaware. Such a land of ego is governed by forces of deceit, blindness and betrayal. To evolved beings of energy such as the Asetians — creatures of subtlety, magick and wisdom — the reality of this plane is incredibility limitative and oppressive, being opposed to their native realm in the kingdom of timeless immortality, one humanity has come to know as the land of the dead.

Inner

The inner plane is your most intimate realm and very own kingdom. Attached to the psyche of each individual it is a land governed by emotion, thought, expectation and desire, inseparable from the fundamental framework of identity and foundation of personality.

As conscious and unconscious thoughts are active instigators of subtle energy the inner realm is also under the influence of metaphysics and magick, however each and every one remain the definitive rulers of that plane, from the darkest dungeons that become alive in nightmares to the flourishing gardens of dreams and burning passions — they are bound to the manifestation of will. This reality is a vast unlimited space built from memory, experience and creativity, hiding the deepest secrets, fears and frustrations under locked doors of individual perception.

In terms of magickal exploration this plane presents one of the safest unbound areas to roam, even if the experience might not always be a pleasant one. The apparent dangers that lurk in its darkness are nothing but constructs of the mind, creatures of many faces that mirror insecurities, frailties and obstacles raised by Self. It is not always easy to stare upon the mirror of truth that reflects the monsters hiding within, yet that courage brings a vital challenge that every Asetian must face throughout life as a founding pillar of character and harbinger of awareness.

This illusive mental plane is also the realm of dreams, a land where the unconscious mind wanders during times of rest and meditation. As such, and with proper training, both dreams and nightmares can be controlled and bended to our will, with every bit of reality shaped and forged by the unseen hand of our command.

The inner plane also represents the major target of invasive metaphysical techniques such as probing and psychic attack. It is a vulnerable realm to those fluent in the secrets that potentiate hacking of the mind, opening doors for control and mind reading. By piercing the Shen of the Third Eye an energy link is established that secures a gateway into the inner realm, opening a path to the private information stored within and guided access to thoughts and emotions. Once bypassed the natural defenses and shielding mechanisms the vulnerabilities may range from minor to extreme, depending on inborn abilities, metaphysical balance and magickal experience. Information drawn from the inner realm encompasses past and present, allowing for the reading and interpretation of both conscious and unconscious processes.

Extensively practiced and developed within the Aset Ka these techniques can be useful in therapy and a great tool of psychology for the master occultist, however their potential for misuse is undeniable. There is also a dangerous catch since for every link created that establishes a pathway into the inner plane a channel is formed that operates in both ways, allowing for information to be drawn but also sent. That is the fundamental principle of mind control but also a tool that can be exploited defensively by those familiar with such advanced techniques who understand that more than a powerful social tool this knowledge represents ancient weapons of magickal warfare, unveiling strategies to hinder an invasive attack or even cunningly turn the process against the adversary.

Proper study and understanding of the various planes of existence is important to the interpretation of reality and metaphysical experience. Oftentimes a seeker will find descriptions of some who propose theories based on loose accounts of personal experience and hearsay, promoting vivid tales from a multitude of realms and unseen planes with a structure and nature not here defined, where countless situations were faced and breathtaking discoveries made, while in truth most of those realities were crafted by dogma, inner and outer manipulation or the natural result of creativity. The mind is tricky and powerful biological machinery, capable of deceiving Self and fabricating reality. For the most part many of the conceptual lands that people express and mirror exist only within one single realm — their very own inner plane.

Astral

The astral plane is the first true realm of energy, manifesting beyond the veil of matter unrestrained from physical decay. It is the land of the disembodied and a realm native to creatures that do not incarnate into this mundane reality. Yet, it is still accessible to those with a physical body if and when a certain set of tools and metaphysical knowledge is attained or through triggered spontaneous projection.

Endemic to the astral these beings that freely roam its infinite layers lack a body of their own — in fact there is no physical matter at all in the realm — being completely made out of energy given form and coherence. As such, they are at an advantage in the lands of energy, vibration and subtlety, a detail that should be taken into consideration when reaching for interaction, as not all are benevolent or inherently peaceful.

There are copious techniques of astral projection and travel that range in difficulty and resulting experience, representing an ordinary pursuit of the average occultist. However, common misunderstanding and disregard for the inherent traps found in such workings often lead to inner projections. The practitioner is pulled into an instance of the inner realm fabricated by the psyche and not an actual shard of the astral, although the experience can sometimes faithfully mimic expected cues and present cloned elements that may deceive the seeker into an incorrect analysis of the unsuccessful event.

Outer projection into dungeons of the astral is not an advanced achievement but can require skill and, most importantly, a certain level of experience. Although far more accessible than reaching the ethereal planes and certainly less dangerous it is not without consequence and potential threat. Unlike the creatures roaming the deceptive reality of the inner planes, illusory creations that may affect mind and emotion but hold no real power over Self, the beings found among the clouds of the astral reality are diverse and profoundly independent, sometimes holding the staff of wisdom and potential for teaching but also the wand of violence and manipulation.

Still under the appropriate mindset and a responsible approach enforced through dedicated experience, roaming the astral plane is a rewarding undertaking and valuable asset in your arsenal of exploration. Once mastered it can be used for the attaining of secretive covenants and metaphysical gatherings, a practice that has long been established by the Aset Ka that maintains astral temples and enforced key locations in the subtle realms, not without tight security and careful safeguard.

As an ever-changing realm of energy and possibility even mighty wars have been fought over the never-ending fields of the astral, and although not a common occurrence in this era those were grand battles worthy of untold history and the forgotten memory of the ancients. Additionally, to cross the astral realms also creates an invaluable opportunity for interaction with otherworldly beings often unable or unwilling of reincarnation, which can provide a dynamic source of knowledge and learning or even lead to potential allies and foes. However, and even though possible, that is not the path to contact the dead and interact with the deceased, as such pursuit is bound to a different road that leads into a distinctive garden. Those seeking the astral plane for such endeavours are frequently led to deceit that ends in frustration or delusion.

Not only are incarnated beings capable of projecting into the astral but also other entities of energy and inhuman spirit. Such is the case of royal servitors of the Asetians, sentient beings of raw energy without the divine spark of independence but tied to the soul and life force of their creators, who are able to freely roam the astral in their mighty and intimidating presence sometimes indistinguishable from any other creature native to the realm.

There are structures and established edifications crafted out of energy, many not definitive and unstable, in a permanent state of dissipation and perpetual disintegration as the astral is not bound to the concept of time, while others remain solid and crystalized, exhibiting great resilience to natural decay. Some can resemble the natural world and places that you may know from life in the physical realm as subtle echoes that reflect such reality through the means of energy and vibration, while others appear completely alien and unknown as if the forgotten origins of a mysterious culture not perceived by the living. A few of these locations are well protected by potent enchantments, metaphysical shields and powerful gatekeepers, such as the immemorial Asetian temples found in these realms.

In advanced metaphysics the astral plane also plays a relevant role in the activation and empowering of more intricate spells of high magick. Some fail at those practices if they are misled by ego, falling into its traps and causing the energy to be projected to the inner plane and never reaching the heights of the astral realm, becoming blocked and magickally limited by perception — never transcending to the infinity beyond Self. Just like every realm ever conceived beyond the seas of divinity the astral presents every seeker with a mirror of reality that is not without deception.

Ethereal

The ethereal realm exists in the breath of infinity beyond the layer of transcendence. With no beginning and no end the ethereal is indescribable in words and undefinable using human concepts, where time, matter and the constricting rules of mindsets are not broken but simply inexistent.

As such this realm is not easily accessible while chained to the limitations of mortal incarnation, requiring the experienced and initiated ability of evolved practitioners. Dwelling beyond the influential scope of the astral and under the purest threads of the divine layer — the highest spark of existence — the ethereal plane is a land of immortal life, although a mundane mind may define it as the land of the dead for the living experience established through a framework bound to the physical body is there irrelevant and even daringly unreal.

Most sentient beings are unaware of its existence and unable to comprehend its fundamental importance in every spiritual manifestation, although each singular soul originates from the ethereal, being tied to its nature through the cosmic cord. This is also the hidden location of the akashic records, the spheres of all incarnated knowledge that transcend time, family and land, making it a realm of the utmost importance and focus to anyone invested in the serious pursuit of past-life understanding and regression.

Due to its natural safeguards such circles of knowledge are hardly ever reachable by the shallow or the inexperienced, leading to countless situations where seekers believe they have found a thread from a previous life drawn from the akashic vaults when in fact they are merely experiencing a fabricated delusion of the ego generated through the deceptive mirrors of the inner plane. This is common ground in the modern take on regressive techniques and the futile attempts at mastering wisdom for indulgence and profit — that is not the way of the universe and it shall never be. Such experimentations and manifestations of ignorance serve only to discredit a noble pursuit that is as old as time itself: the understanding and exploration of the past that was once lived and to learn it again, growing into something greater through such alchemy of transformation. If this sacred work is touched by expectation, desire or ego it has already failed.

Unlike the astral, the ethereal is not as abundantly populated by creatures of energy, although there are those who are native to this realm. Such beings are immortal and detached from the lifeline of time, existing in a reality that is not readily understood. Those ancients are servants of the Gods, guarding the catacombs of wisdom and their infinite records of life. The Asetian temples immemorially established in the ethereal are swarmed with untold secrets of initiation and spiritual evolution, holding keys of thought and hidden pathways to all mysteries. These unspoken halls of violet light are visited by every Asetian upon death, where they are renewed with eternal youth and rejoined with the immortal family, gaining a glimpse of the abominable throne of Aset shedding its Fire and darkness from the divine realm above. Protected by the Seven Scorpions that guard its majestic doors of unbreakable strength with their terrible gaze these sacred temples are considered by some as the true home of the Aset Ka.

The ethereal shards are fragments of infinity incapsulated in a universe of its own. Each shard bound to indescribable power that can only be tamed and controlled through the invisible staff of its governing ruler — a God among Gods.

Divine

There is not much that will be explained about the realm of divinity simply because it is not something that can be taught by using words, gestures or symbols. This is the highest of the planes of existence and the most inaccessible of all. The divine plane is the all and the none, the zero and the one; it is the seven beyond the veil.

The divine plane is the root realm — the first spark, genesis of creation. Its understanding lies beyond what the human mind can conceive and what the incarnated reality allows to comprehend. Bridging into the ethereal where the seas of infinity collide, this reality establishes the kingdom of the Duat and the unspeakable land of the Gods.

No incarnated beings are able to visit there or even see it from afar and there is no possible magickal projection that can reach it. When a deity manifests in the lower planes or communion is attained through higher ritual, the sacred essence is not echoing from the divine plane but actually being mirrored in one of the shards of the ethereal attuned to the energy and vibration or sensible to the call. Deities are not found beneath the ethereal and among the mists of the astral plane, however creatures from that realm may attempt to trick and deceive while embodying an expected personification of a divine presence, which should not be confused with an actual God or Goddess. The human mind often has the unique ability to believe whatever suits their dreams or fits their expectations in order to feel special but that is not a path of truth or the work of an evolved occultist. A warrior — and an Asetianist must undeniably be one —

rejects foolish dreams, ignorant opinions and false judgment, staring pain in the eye while seeking only what is real.

The Asetians learn unique ways to establish contact with the elder Gods and attain spiritual touch with Aset, a blessing of the Violet Flame, however such sacred knowledge is a well guarded secret revealed only through initiation and a precious gem that must be kept away from the decadent eyes of mortality that hunger for power and selfish control.

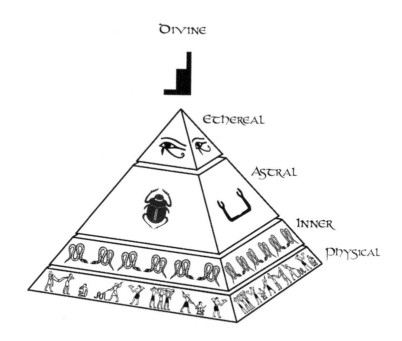

Meditation

The diverse umbrella of meditative practices, profound thought explorations and techniques of introspection encompass a solid foundation into magickal work and the processes of energy manipulation. In the Asetian culture meditation has been an established practice for millennia, approached as an edifying step that graduates the mind and train the senses for subtler interactions and a greater sensitivity of the metaphysical. In many ways conscious and guided meditation may be a door into other realities and an effective gateway to cross different worlds.

Meditation is a multidisciplinary endeavour that builds upon simple concepts but requires perseverance and a trained mind to achieve its highest and most valuable states. Regular practice and slowly developed experience is fundamental to success but anyone has the ability to meditate no matter how early or late in life the study begins. It should be understood however that meditation is not magick and it should be approached as the pure solvent in your alchemy where the magickal practice becomes the reagent. Together they can be fused into a more potent potion by uniting the misty poison of magickal practice with the watery fluid of meditation but the intrinsic quality of the solvent must not taint the color of the reagent for its essence defines the ultimate magickal result.

As a tool of relaxation and therapy meditation can be a valuable asset with proven results in the field of psychology, aiding not only in the attaining of a balanced mind but also a healthier body. It is a device that does not represent a solution to a problem but a worthy first step in the elusive equilibrium of the trinity in incarnated life manifested as mind, body and spirit. Constrained life in this realm of matter is a challenging experience to Asetians who recurrently strive to balance and rebalance the varying aspects of existence, bound to a shallow world of futility and ignorance that does not comprehend their nature or tolerate such dark existence. Inner harmony and spiritual symmetry is an incredibly delicate state of managing chaos and embodying the alchemical flame burning within.

Despite being a legitimate tool for trained occultists and a valuable first step to those only beginning their path into the realms of magick and metaphysics, meditation is also an effective mechanism to vampires as it provides a simple means of energy recovery that more efficiently than sleeping can enhance a weakened energetic state without a great investment of active manipulation.

Sensing

Manipulating energy is an inborn ability to every Asetian that manifests even prior to awakening. To interact with subtle essences, interpret their vibrations and wield such powers is a practice that the children of Aset are known to excel, mastering these arts to levels beyond what most can attain or even comprehend.

An important principle of metaphysics is that every form of life is affected by the subtle forces of mystical and spiritual energy, constantly interacting with them even unconsciously. Everyone and not only Asetians are capable of interacting and manipulating energy, being influenced by its tidal forces and echoes — that is a fundamental element of magick in every form. However, not all are aware of the subtle reality and the unavoidable presence and contact with energy that remains constant throughout life. Lack of sensitivity for the subtle and ignorance over the energy that surrounds us are common aspects of society that through its focus on what is merely physical and superficial has lost touch with what lies beneath and within, neglecting the profound nature of existence attained only by spirit and magick.

Such inability and inadequacy for spiritual work or magickal art can be easily fixed or enhanced through learning within the Asetian path as Asetianism intensively develops metaphysical skill in every form and dimension, providing unique teachings and initiatory paradigms that exponentially increase subtle sensitivity, metaphysical craft, psychological finesse and an universal understanding of energy as a major tool in magickal practice. For Asetians that is ever more evident while undergoing the process of awakening, when all spiritual, metaphysical and predatory senses are charged and heightened allowing for the rediscovery of a whole new world and surroundings, even amongst the most mundane of landscapes, colorless until seen through a reborn Asetian eye.

Among those of Asetian nature Serpents are known to develop a greater sensitivity for energy work and a stronger awareness of the subtle realms, constantly interacting with these forces on a conscious level, bending them to their will and manipulating energy in ways that for them are as natural as breathing. In fact it is not uncommon for Serpents to exhibit strong metaphysical abilities prior to awakening as sign of their outstanding skill but this does not imply that the other two Lineages are not sensitive to energy, as every Asetian tends to be exceptionally competent and skilled in the magickal arts, being able to master the invisible forces with learning and dedication at various degrees of complexity that vary depending on the personal obstacles that each must conquer. Everyone must face great challenges on their path of growth, understanding and mastery — Asetians are no different and each individual Lineage is confronted against their own handicaps, puzzles and inner battles, making life a most perilous journey.

✝

The act of sensing is the most elementary aspect of working and interacting with energy as it allows for an initial probing and accurate interpretation of subtle signals, their frequency and vibrations. The best magickal tools for active sensing are found in the human body as eyes and hands, both incredibly capable metaphysical devices. Bodies inhabited by an Asetian soul feature overdeveloped secondary Shen organs located in the hands and beneath the eyes that are adapted to intensive interaction with energy, being able to sustain higher charges and different vibrations than the same structures found on human subtle bodies. These outlets are major channels used in the projection, manipulation and control of outer energies, sometimes considered fearsome metaphysical weapons that with mastery can be effective in offensive magick and potent in the projection of intense beams of Ka. These weapons of manipulation and control are used as viable tools of life-draining and attack but also and no less importantly as evolved devices of healing and protection. It is not difficult to realize how such powers and abilities naturally led to the iconic duality of fear and admiration for the seductive eyes and electrifying touch of the Asetians.

Energy can be sensed in many ways and through various techniques, each more adequate to a different individual, natural ability and experience. There is no ideal mechanism and flawless practice but even though no honest replacement for serious training and experience exists in the end the initiate should invest in what works best for the particular case, remaining open to the exploration of different venues and never allowing for knowledge or energy to stagnate. Sensing is an important practice and although an apparently simplistic and basic tool in the arsenal of an occultist it is not uncommon to find it misrepresented and surrounded by misconception as it remains of extreme importance to separate illusion and expectation from subtle reality.

Grounding

As a multitool with different applications, grounding can be a complementary technique to various forms of meditation, a pre-requisite to stable energy work and a useful balancing practice to anyone with a strong and intense connection with the subtle reality. Its practical methods reestablish the metaphysical connection between the subtle body and the roots of the Earth, strengthening the conceptual obelisks that maintain the balance between esoteric and mundane. Such pathways extend from the lower active Shen — the Root on the primary systems and the Feet on the secondary — deep into the core of our planet intertwined with every plant, mineral and metal all the way to the burning engine that sustains the magnetic field and shields us from the cosmic dawn.

These energy links are not passive structures of spiritual significance but relevant elements in the natural maintenance of the subtle body, providing an efficient cleansing mechanism that dumps excess energy and metaphysical byproducts from the internal system. When balanced a healthy flow of energy allows for the natural cycling of energy to be maintained with fresh essence and the strengthening of the grounding outlets that consequentially fortifies and invigorates the constant states of balance and imbalance between the spiritual and the physical, the subtle and the material.

That is the natural process of grounding, an activity that although inborn to every living creature can also be learned and made aware through the practice of energy work and active magick, allowing for a better control and understanding of the energetic states and how they influence mind and emotion, being in constant tune with the psyche and biology. It is also a suitable method of balancing and developing conscious focus, which is particularly useful to anyone with a strong bond with the spirit world who constantly interacts with energy. To some Asetians, simply being in crowded places can raise problems that humans do not commonly experience as the contact with countless variants of vibrations, random thoughts emanating from so many people and the metaphysical pollution generated from those energies can be overwhelming. As natural empaths the constant mixed emotions and thought patterns manifested in a congested environment can be detrimental to the health and energy of an Asetian who easily and frequently captures and interprets all of those external signals, overloading the system with cognitive and metaphysical processing, natural defenses and predatory mechanisms that take a considerable toll on the internal energy reserves.

Grounding can be a preventive solution in those situations and although not as effective as other techniques such as active shielding and warding it should be approached as the appropriate ground work for higher practices and stronger defenses, which can only be maintained with the level of balance and strength provided through a well grounded subtle system.

Those of the Scorpion Lineage are exceptionally gifted in the arts of grounding, shielding and magickal defense. Doing it often unconsciously and with a skill that is even developed prior to awakening, when further explored and mastered the natural grounding of Scorpions is a powerful protective asset that results in a more effective channeling of malignant energies from harmful spells, destructive enchantments or abusive psychic attacks, effectively safeguarding the Scorpion or whoever is chosen under their protection. In everyday practice their natural grounding rejects unwanted and most external energies, strengthening the subtle shields and personal identity. In ritual, energy work, active magick or metaphysical warfare the presence of Asetian Scorpions is seen as true obelisks of power and strength, granting safety and stability that is not only effective defensively, as they can also dispose generated metaphysical byproducts that would otherwise linger in the ritual chambers or within the system of the involved practitioners. Both Serpents and Scarabs greatly benefit from the presence and magick of a Scorpion who can aid them in the rebalancing of a highly chaotic system or one that is detached from the physical realm, ensuring a healthier release of accumulated energy generated by the permanent and intense energy flow found among these Lineages. Even unconsciously the potent inner shield of Scorpions is a beacon of balance, darkening strength and unshakable protection that any other Asetian can feel and draw inspiration from.

The grounding from Scorpions is so effective that it may raise issues with subtle sensitivity as their formidable balance and protective mechanisms shield them from energy sources that their subtle system regularly needs. Because of this Scorpions must learn how to tame their metaphysical strength, lowering the shields and reducing the intensity of their grounding so that the true magickal potential they hide within may be revealed.

Grounding is a metaphysical practice that is open to everyone and should be used in unison with other fundamental techniques such as sensing, cycling and centering in order to establish a framework upon which more advanced techniques may be developed. An effective grounding relies on a strong connection with the Earth and properly functioning lower Shen that work as outlets for the release of energy and communion with nature. Such links should be solid and stable otherwise unwanted energies will not be efficiently plunged and may linger in the system, polluting its flow and leading to ailments both physical and subtle.

While a valuable tool grounding can also lead to complications if misused through the release of disproportionate quantities of energy and excessive grounding that may cause various symptoms such as drop in subtle sensitivity, psychic awareness and magickal power. This detail is of importance to Asetians and Asetianists as they rely on a permanent interaction with energy and the use of subtle senses for effective magickal control. Such cases can be corrected through techniques opposed to grounding, inverting its process and allowing for the rebalance of the system through a lockdown of the lower outlets. These practices that we have developed as mirror grounding and inverted grounding manage to establish a link towards the universe through elemental Air and use this connection to find the missing sensitivity and inner magickal spark that can ignite a healthier flow once again and enact a bond with the subtle world of the spirit.

Cycling

The metaphysical process of cycling and its encompassing techniques represent a component of energy work that focuses on the conscious and intentional circulation of vital energy throughout the extent of the subtle system without absorption or metabolic processing while heightening its raw natural state, increasing the intrinsic quality, range of frequency and level of vibration. As we are dealing not only with magick but also occult science it should be noted that when referring to the intended lack of metabolic processing during cycling that is an ideal scenario that is not verifiable in most real-world situations, where the complete absence of absorption rates is not possible due to the very nature of cycling that will passively consume certain amounts of energy. So an accurate way of presenting it would be to consider an efficient cycling when accomplished with limited and not metaphysically significant amounts of collateral absorption.

The techniques of cycling although useful to every Lineage and not exclusive to Asetians are an inborn ability of Scarabs, who constantly rely on their intensive cycling mechanisms to renew energy and break stagnation. When under conscious and trained control it is a powerful asset that can be put to use in advanced magick but without guidance it may lead to instability, confusion and a troubled psyche that cannot be anchored from the overwhelming flow of new and unsigned energy.

Although a valuable technique used to refine and intensify vital energy, cycling is also a potent tool to fight vibrational stagnation, break subtle blockages and promote fluid and uninterruptible energy flow. As such it can be of significant use to Scorpions struggling with their powerful shields and overly charged sexual energies, allowing for the renewal of fresh essence and the rebinding of subtle fingerprints on the inner flow — a tool that can break stagnation and introduce some needed chaos in the balanced nature of this Lineage, for only through the challenges that rise from the opposing chaos and earthen balance can growth be unleashed and new discoveries revealed. On the other end of this threefold cycle of Orion equilibrium it becomes clear how Scorpions can be a fundamental pillar to Scarabs and Serpents, grounding and stabilizing their intensive cycling while potentiating more powerful magickal control to all three. It is an ouroboric wheel of immortal power that unites the strength of Scorpions with the fluidity of Scarabs and the magick of Serpents in absolute symbiotic perfection — Orion in the cosmos mirroring Aset beyond the veil.

Cycling can be used not only in internal alchemy as previously described but also in external magick, allowing for a tangible increase over the quality of energy fields from specific locations while delaying their natural decay rates. During this practice the surrounding energy must be consistently absorbed from the environment, consciously cycled through the system in a process of intensification and then released back to the intended area. This requires focus, controlled breathing and a degree of experience with metaphysical redirection, in time allowing for a complete change over the emotion, vibrational charge and sensation of a location. Such practices can be of value in the cleansing of ritual chambers and the maintenance of scared space, two influential variables in active magick. The unique and intense energies found inside each Asetian temple of past and present are regularly purified, attuned and charged with variants of these techniques, although it is also common for Asetians to activate cycling around their private havens and sleeping areas as means of metaphysical cleansing used in tune with protective spells and magickal wards.

Most techniques of cycling promote a healthy flow of energy with focus on balance, intensifying life force and increasing its spiritual quality, resulting in denser energy that can be more effective in ceremony, ritual and active magick. A small amount of high quality energy is infinitely more empowering and metaphysically sustaining than a large amount of low vibrational essence, a reason why donors take such diligent care of the state and level of their energy, striving for a continuous flow of Ka and the proper maintenance of its quality alongside the much important rejection of outside polluted influences.

Centering

Every form of metaphysical practice and directed energy work benefits from a balanced inner state of the subtle body. This internal equilibrium conceals an important key to magickal effectiveness and attaining it is no simple task. Centering provides the first step in such a convoluted path of entangled possibility.

The technique depends on pinpointing the kernel of the energy body — your center — and establishing a practical mechanism of alignment. Unlike popular belief and common misunderstanding the balancing central sphere of the subtle system is located differently in each individual body, being prone to misalignment and degenerative migration due to biological and psychological influences, sometimes vulnerable to common occurrences such as stress and the oppressive energy of others. This center is not an actual subtle organ such as the Shen but a point of spiritual equanimity and vibrational balance that affects the orientation and symmetry of the whole system, conditioning the alignment of Shen and interconnection with the energy vessels. Correcting the asymmetrical positioning and improving the miscalibration of the conceptual center is a holistic element of importance to a healthy and stable energy system with verifiable consequences to anyone working with energy, exploring its mysteries and applications. Coordination between the various elements that constitute a functioning subtle body is crucial, ensuring the proper operation and proactive balance of all independent systems and that can only be attained with a certain level of inner alignment.

A common technique involves locating the energy kernel deep within the subtle body, energizing it and heightening its vibration so that it can be rotated and finally aligned. The structure can then be channeled with living essence and infused with your unique fingerprint, being thereupon manipulated through pulsating expansion as the energy is gradually dispersed to the boundaries of the body and spirit, cleansing the outlets, flushing the channels and rebalancing the state between systems. If the cycling is done after grounding the system is already clear of energy byproducts and unwanted vibrations considered extraneous to the inner body, being ready for the rehash of the kernel and its overall stabilization.

The practice of centering is complementary to grounding and cycling being better used after a properly grounded system with a healthy energy flow. In fact most centering techniques complement those of grounding so seemingly that certain practices use them indifferently as a single procedure, laying the groundwork for more advanced metaphysical work. Just like grounding and cycling the practice of centering should not be understood as a goal or isolated achievement but merely as another bone in the skeleton construct that will allow venturing into the realms of high magick.

Cleansing

Metaphysical cleansing defines a vast group of techniques that are so diverse in fundamental practice, approach and intended achievement that cannot be accurately categorized or conceptually established without fault.

Extensively and recurrently used by Asetians and Asetianists the practice of cleansing places its esoteric focus on the subtle cleaning of magickal tools, ritual locations and living beings. It is a vital element preceding a spiritual initiation — a fundamental step into every magickal system — or the rituals of energization and synchronization for an amulet, talisman, wand or other magickal instruments.

Although variants of cleansing are used among different spiritual traditions and magickal paths, the Asetians have developed special techniques that are unique to their path and crafted in tune with their energy, relying on the intimate connection with the Violet Flame to cleanse, initiate and empower. These safeguarded practices are mostly private and passed down from masters through sacred teaching and the mysteries of initiation but also gradually unveiled through an organic pathway of meditation, inner growth and higher understanding.

Healing

Asetians have been portrayed as dangerous vampires, feared as demons and studied as fierce predators of the night, oftentimes neglected for their exceptional healing powers and mending abilities. Aset as immortal Queen of wisdom and initiation is also a Mother of healing and curative magick, a gift that was taught and passed down to Her children.

The inhuman skill that Asetians possess to sense, manipulate and redirect energy provides them with unique healing potential that allows for the bloodline to excel in various fields of traditional medicine, metaphysical treatment and even modern science from psychology to western medicine, although a holistic approach is often the preferred method. The intrinsically vampiric abilities that establish them as predators and are often interpreted as metaphysical weapons can also be used as powerful healing tools, just like the draining of life force can reignite a stagnated system, break blockages and even hinder the development of subtle tumors. However, not all Asetians are healers and despite possessing the predisposition and innate ability some do not dedicate their development and learning towards such pursuit, focusing instead on inner achievements, the quest for enlightenment and the lost alchemy of the soul. The walked path is their own and unique to each soul, as Asetians are as diverse as the stars in the sky.

It should be understood that despite their awareness and power an incarnated Asetian is bound to the laws of physics and the consequences of life in a material world, being affected by illness and biological decay just like every human. The body of an Asetian withers and dies, being vulnerable to the pain and agony of trauma and disease. In fact their legendary healing abilities tend to be far more effective when selflessly applied to others rather than themselves. A power and might of an Asetian can never be judged by health or survivability for heroic beings both human and Asetian have died young while others of no worth have lived safe and uneventful long lives. The major focus of Asetian healing surrounds the soul as the powerful inner alchemy that defines their immortal spirituality — body is undeniably secondary and even irrelevant when compared to the subtle but vital nature of the spirit.

To a practitioner of the Asetian teachings energy healing is a relevant element of exploration and useful metaphysical tool. It is a form of vibrational medicine particularly useful to vampires that being in tune with the immaterial reality are consequentially more aware of subtle maladies and spiritual diseases, possessing a reactive energy system that easily echoes into the physical realm, manifesting energetic instabilities and esoteric imbalances as expressions of depression, psychological conditioning and different pathologies. This makes awakened Asetians commonly keen practitioners of meditation and inner healing, mastering techniques of energization and vibrational awareness placed on the path to attain balance, improving understanding of the energy system and promoting a healthier flow of vital force. Any being that constantly interacts with energy, manipulating it at will, molding its fabric and projecting it to the realms of matter and spirit is bound to imbalances triggered by lingering byproducts of incompatible energy, undesired and unreliable energy links among other variables that weigh on the state of both physical and subtle bodies, being capable of collapsing health and requiring specialized metaphysical care and treatment.

Besides the advanced study of energy healing and vibrational medicine found in the learning path of Asetianism, the Order of Aset Ka also safeguards an ancient practice that has been lost and rediscovered throughout time as wars were waged and the conflicts of people destroyed knowledge and defaced legacy. That is the metaphysical science of Kemetic medicine, the healing practices of the Ancient Egyptians; a tool of lost wisdom that binds mind, body and spirit, blending magick with biology, geology, psychology and philosophy. This intricate scholarly field also known as Asetian medicine is dynamic and ever-changing, continuing its active development and academic research to this day and age.

To deny or neglect the importance of healing in Asetianism would be an unreasonable exercise of profound incompleteness due not only to its historical relevance in terms of development but also to the importance that this culture has always placed on its unbiased understanding. The children of Aset have been known by many names, described with many words and interpreted through different views, often misrepresented or simply misunderstood but almost invariably incomplete. Concealed beneath the signature detachment that is confused as arrogance and emerging past their renowned predatory senses, deep awareness and unique intellect Asetians are the silent healers of eternity, wielding the gentle touch of nature that can reach beyond body and soul with unparalleled empathy, care and comprehension.

†

Energy Beings

We live in a strange and intricate world surrounded by obscure mysteries and a fascinating existence, full of life and lavish magick. Although most remain unaware of such reality and the invisible nature that surrounds them, life is everywhere manifesting in infinite forms and what can be seen, heard or smelled represents only but the tiniest fraction of the real universe. What lurks out there can be more terrifying than a nightmare and more beautiful than a dream...

Tasting the lustfulness of flesh and the bitterness of mortality are gifts to those blessed with the spark of incarnated life, a challenging experience in the dungeon of matter that is the physical realm — your life on Earth. However, not all beings possess the ability or will to incarnate and manifest in the plane of matter, lacking the experience of physical mortality. These creatures of energy roam the subtle worlds from the astral to the ethereal, some not sentient and extremely limited in their existence but others strongly aware, independent and powerful.

Interaction with these otherworldly beings is not only possible but frequent even if not everyone has developed enough sensitivity to be consciously receptive and responsive to their contact and synergy. Energy beings have been documented as incredibly diverse and existing throughout a variety of planes and forms of manifestation, some not even bound to a complete understanding through the lenses of our reality. Exquisite in nature or simplistic in form, with mutating encapsulation or permanent manifestation the subtle beings of energy exist in greater numbers than grains of sand in the desert and droplets in the sea, bound to the infinite freedom of their reality or the limited existence of their nature, unaware of ethics or human rules and expectations that are alien and unknown to their world. Some have their own agendas and complexity of life in another realm while others manifest in fluid ways like wind dancing through the mountains. They are part of nature since it is not only the tangible reality that defines its structures and pathways as the infinite possibility of the natural world sings through countless voices.

The spirits of the dead also roam these immaterial realms having shed their physical bodies and constricting chains of matter, now existing as beings of energy as well. Every living creature is ultimately a being of energy and their bodies nothing more than physical constructs of this realm, bound to decay and being forgotten for only the soul prevails and through its memory are they allowed to endure. However, although bound to the spiritual realm the roaming dead have the ability of reincarnation and may live in the physical world once again through cyclical rebirth, even if the spark of reincarnation alone does not establish immortality.

Some Asetians are gifted psychics and mediums, naturally bending the veil between the land of the living and the realm of the dead with the inborn insight that transcends life and embraces death. Their experience and ability is both personal and diverse as some are capable of interpreting subtle signals through physical senses, manifested by sight, smell and sound, while others retain their channeling by feeling, emotion and extrasensory perception, intimately tied to keen intuition and spiritual awareness depending on the form and variant of mediumship.

In Asetian culture and practice dealing with the spirit world and interacting with the forces that reign beyond the coil of mortal flesh is an aspect of relevance to the process of growth and development of subtle awareness. Even if those are legitimate esoteric resources and present a gateway to access hidden knowledge and often-secretive truth, do not believe that such findings remain absent of biased thought and judgment. Beware of potential dangers in trusting an unknown power brought by unproven sources for not only the incarnated will attempt to manipulate you. The spirit world and beings you may find roaming the astral planes are deceiving and bound to their own plans, methods and intentions. Simply because an entity lives natively on a subtle realm or if a soul has conquered death and now manifests in spirit that does not imply that what they know or believe is unquestionable truth. Their message and intent is still bound to inner perception and oftentimes entities will unknowingly convey their own dogma in whatever knowledge they attempt to pass to the living. Identifying and recognizing those situations while being cunning on subtle tricksters is essential but only accomplishable through experience and this does not come easily. Assuming otherwise is one simple step into the pits of deception that an occultist must remain aware of, as overconfident judgment and inexperienced acceptance remain powerful obstacles that frequently block a practitioner from exploring other possibilities or finding truth.

Subtle Parasites

When exploring the realms for otherworldly beings of energy it becomes apparent that not all entities are safe to approach and not every subtle creature is benign. In truth some energy beings are powerful, capable of being relentless and unwavering in their pursuits making interactions dangerous and potentially harmful.

While most energy beings will gladly ignore you and your very existence just like the lingering dead may be drawn to the breath of the living and curious about their current state, there are creatures without body or incarnating nature that can manipulate, deceive and even violently attack under certain circumstances. Some may behave vampirically and as beings of energy they have the ability or learned skill to drain the life force of the living, in certain cases attaching parasitic links to the energy system that can linger for long periods of time, slowly feeding from the host, which may induce further metaphysical vulnerabilities and physical weakness. Such entities are defined as subtle parasites and while many are simplistic in nature and can be managed without much effort, others present a complex and more advanced existence that may be a challenge to overpower and overcome.

Being aware of other forms of life and unseen manifestation is an opening step but it remains important not to become paranoid or start assuming that every interaction with the subtle is a potential threat or a dangerous endeavour. Responsibility and maturity in every subtle and metaphysical action is imperative, separating fear or expectation from fact and reality, as many get driven by the fascination with the unknown and quickly start to draw inaccurate parallels to everything they feel and experience. This is a factor that should be taken in consideration and cautious interpretation during every spiritual journey, as involvement with magick and the occult is no valid reason to ignore and reject science or rationality. Actually, as I have frequently established through my teachings, both fields complement each other and those who neglect either side are bound to an incomplete approach and flawed understanding. Wishful thinking, embraced fantasy, the pitfalls of ego and the deceit of expectation are all gargantuan steps into oblivion and a path to personal recession, emerging as dominating forces that oppose the hallmarks of the Asetian tradition marked by the development of Self through wisdom, the unleashing of inner potential through initiation and the acceptance of truth through honesty.

Subtle parasites and aggressive disembodied creatures are a reality just like sentient daemons and other perils of magickal nature but those are not a phenomenon that one should ostensibly ignore. Understanding and exploration are reliable tools when dealing with metaphysical possibility and danger but guesswork or fear should never be turned into blind belief. Remain aware but not dominated; leave certainty and quick assumptions to those that do not take the occult seriously and have embraced an ignorant light of false mysteries — the self-entitled worms of magickal practice who enforce delusion and vocal bewilderment.

The first line of defense when dealing with subtle parasites is the reinforcement of magickal protections and active shielding. Answering any hostile acts with metaphysical attacks should be a last resort and only approached by those with reasonable experience, as these are creatures of energy and they strike from their native realm. Manipulating energy is their nature and way of life so incarnated practitioners will be at a disadvantage that requires knowledge and skill to overcome. The most frequent cases of invasive beings from the other realms present more of a nuisance than real danger and can be handled with cleansing techniques, focused grounding and minor banishing. More resilient and problematic cases can be approached with a full-fledged banishing although such rituals are not without consequence and should not be undertaken lightly. Extreme cases of physical death caused or ignited by subtle beings are incredibly rare and most examined situations are misleading and not genuine, even if the loss of life by metaphysical warfare and degenerative magick is possible and remains an unspoken reality.

Shielding

The raising of active and conscious energy shields is amongst the most thoroughly examined and regularly mentioned practices of energy work and a fundamental discipline in defensive magick. Although shielding techniques ranging from basic to advanced require training and steady energy reserves, everyone has natural shields established since birth that cyclically dwindle and strengthen according to various elements such as stress, emotion, health and metaphysical metabolism. These inborn energy shields are suitable for mundane situations but ineffective and weak to those who actively work with energy and partake in a life of magickal pursuit. A philosophy of proactive defense and safe practice requires the intentional raising of stronger shields through the means of energy manipulation, a field of metaphysics that has been under development ever since magick was firstly used and awareness of energy established.

Humans without magickal awareness, the vast majority of the population, are not mindful of their subtle shields, interacting with its effects unconsciously and without thought, consequentially holding no control over the state and function of their natural defenses. Asetians are born with refined metaphysical instincts, being able to control their shields and manipulate their power at will, unlocking keys to advanced usage such as the mutation and cloaking of their defenses for manipulative and predatory endeavours like the intentional altering of the aura, subtle filters and crystalized shields. This disguises the nature, vibration and fingerprint of subtle energy, representing an essential step in stealth metaphysical work often used in covert operations.

There are two main types of metaphysical shields defined as primary and secondary. A primary shield is formed by sparse areas of vital energy establishing an energy field that surrounds every living being as a coating of reactive energy that floats around the outer layers of the aura. These shields are of natural origin and require no conscious maintenance, being effectively an element of the subtle system and providing a last line of defense for the spiritual body. Generally they are thin and limited, lacking the coherence of an active construct and thus being permeable to attacks and intrusive energies but with varying structural strength depending on the individual. Asetian Scorpions have particularly strong and overdeveloped natural shields typically established even prior to awakening, an empowering gift that they nurture with special talent toward much defensive magickal prowess. Their mighty protective mechanisms and resilient shields make the members of this Lineage some of the hardest and most frustrating beings to metaphysically attack.

Secondary shields are protective constructs consciously raised through magickal abilities that rely on techniques that can generate an artificial defensive barrier of stronger vibration than a primary shield. These shields can be potent, tough and sometimes apparently invulnerable if bound to an empowered amulet or talisman through an amplifying mineral or magick wand. To the experienced practitioner, a shield can be created with thought and manipulation alone without the need for external amplification, although the construct lacks some of the metaphysical qualities of one enforced through a binding talisman. There are however relevant requirements to the proper operation of secondary shields and maintenance of their efficiency, since as structures fueled by vital force they must be used with caution and under control, as their energy consumption can drain the subtle system and lead to dangerously low levels of inner reserves. Scorpions rely on secondary shields less frequently due to the nature and density of their primary ones that often exhibit the potency and effectiveness of empowered active shields, making the maintenance of a secondary shield irrelevant and taxing on their slow metabolism. However, in certain situations Scorpions might find it appropriate to employ a talisman or amplifying mineral in the raising of a secondary shield of special vibration, as these are frequently used by Asetians of the other two Lineages.

It is important to understand that secondary shields will deteriorate over time as they are crafted from manipulated vital energy and although condensed and given form through willpower and active magick they are still vulnerable to natural dissipation unless consistently reinforced. Acknowledgment of such a fact allows for proper maintenance and the surveillance of active energy shields so that their integrity and balance can be maintained, thus avoiding structural collapse.

Both variants of metaphysical shields are useful in crowded environments where the constant energy flood of different vibrations and frequencies exuded from other people can have a negative impact on the subtle body, affecting inner balance and being particularly significant among those vulnerable to energy poisoning such as natural empaths like the Asetians. The effects of energetic pollution can be diverse, hindering metaphysical abilities and ranging from emotional to physical conditions that in extreme cases can induce a dangerous point of collapse. Of striking interest to highly sensitive Asetians like Serpents the active usage of energy shields in public locations can be of great magickal value. However, the incredibly predatory Viperines may find the excessive use of shields also a handicap, while undesired energy is blocked from the subtle system this effective barrier also prevents a larger scope of energy exchanges and the proper probing of the surrounding environment, two powerful keys to the awareness of Serpents and major assets to any Asetian.

Although the practice of shielding is by definition bound to an energy construct operating as a defensive barrier it can also appear as a complementary mechanism to protective enchantments and offensive spells. The proactive technique used as counter-spell for a psychic attack is at its core a variant of shielding fine-tuned to diverge the malignant energy projected by the magickal attack. Even if a more specialized branch of shielding, various methods of countering offensive magick rely on reactive shields crafted to detect, reject and reflect specific vibrations, fueled by intense streams of energy that enforce their strength at a metaphysical cost that does not allow for them to be cast permanently.

Wands and Talismans

Amongst the intricate tools, magickal instruments and sacred objects found in advanced metaphysical practices none echoes the mystery, desire and power more than wands and talismans. With a history shrouded in secrecy and myth these are tools of the highest craft — ornate devices of the most elusive magickal arts.

Developed by the Asetians in immemorial times of arcane magick, the tools described as wands and talismans have dual utility as spiritual objects of divine essence and inspiration as well as advanced metaphysical engines to be used in the manipulation of energy, the projection of will and effective magickal change that defines the practice of what we established as active magick. In the Asetian culture a magick wand is not a ritualistic tool for the focus of will and ceremonial practice as understood in other traditions but a complex device of empowerment that can be actively used in the amplification and redirection of energy. Under the same light a talisman is not merely an object of personal esteem or the focus of faith but a potent magickal tool bound to hidden power and a working vibrational construct often working as an important gateway to worlds and realities of a subtle but secretive nature.

In Asetianism a talisman is known as Wedja, an Ancient Egyptian word that symbolises prosperity and protection. Their uses are however not restricted to personal safeguard or defensive magick, being sometimes considered sacred and intimately bound to their master who unveiled the secrets to wield their power. They are crafted with skill, discipline and art, commonly made from natural materials with unique alchemical properties and metaphysical characteristics such as the amplification and radiation of energy, making certain minerals a raw product of desired quality. Talismans must be cleansed, attuned and empowered according to ancient knowledge, exhibiting different magickal properties and subtle abilities that establish the unique identity and power of each individual talisman or amulet. More uncommon talismans can have a sentient servitor bound to their manifest existence, exhibiting elemental signs of will and intent while being capable of bearing great power and unseen danger. These are only crafted by the elders and rely on mysteries long forgotten to humanity, making them extremely rare in modern times and exceptionally valuable. Talismanic tools can be simplistic or incredibly complex and not always bound to a physical object, being also attached to imagery, artwork and symbolism imbued with special significance and hidden meaning while still capable of potent magick and organic initiation — as reflected in this book.

The spiritual richness of the Ancient Egyptian culture and way of life is surrounded by the extensive use of talismans as a society that understood better than any other the power of symbolism and the value of magick. The beautiful art of hieroglyphs and its mysteries still confuse scholars and passionate seekers to this day, amazing the world with their elegance and allure. They represent a distinctive reflection of talismanic technology developed by the ancients in their higher understanding of symbol, initiation and the magick of sigils as talismans[17]. On the etymology of the word hieroglyph we find roots in late Latin and earlier Greek where *hieros* means *sacred* and *glyph* refers to *carving*, so the word we use for the Ancient Egyptian hieroglyphic language literally means *sacred carvings*. An accurate historical root as hieroglyphs were much more than a formal system of writing or linguistic platform, being developed by the ancients from an advanced technique of sigilization operated as a magickal language intended to be used in ritual, initiation and prayer — they represent, quite effectively, a powerful technology of symbolism tied to the magick of words.

Hieroglyphs openly embody a cultural hallmark of Kemet found on the walls of temples, drawn in the religious and scientific texts of papyrus and carved on countless funerary and magickal objects, infusing them with power through the hidden meaning of symbol and sigil that echoes unseen vibration for inner interpretation. Such knowledge although apparently linguistic in nature by conveying thoughts, ideas and context into pictorial form was also used to safeguard magickal secrets, ignite initiations and empower sacred locations with teachings that could only be unveiled by illuminated adepts of the mystery schools. Talismanic science is an Asetian technology crafted and mastered from the early beginnings of this ancient culture and developed since the establishment of their empire, used in active magick, metaphysical training, spiritual teaching and sacred initiation even today.

A magick wand when used by a learned practitioner of active magick is not only a powerful metaphysical weapon but it is also more importantly an efficient device of energy manipulation and a sacred spiritual tool of communion and higher practice. Wands are crafted from carefully chosen natural materials such as wood or mineral; those made of wood are more common due to its steady amplification properties while minerals are used in shorter and more advanced wands capable of intenser beams of energy and inner radiation that allows for them to duo as a magick wand and talisman. Some wands are crafted according to the crystallography system inherent to the chemistry and geology of specific minerals, following guidelines of sacred geometry and metaphysical crafting, a complexity that makes the use of minerals more common in the crafting of sacred talismans and magickal amulets.

Just like a talisman a magick wand requires elaborate cleansing and enchanting to work properly and become suitable for active use, a task that can only be performed by an Encantatum: a qualified Asetian master fluent in the art and secrets of wanding, spellcrafting and initiation. Attuned wands subject to refined crafting and enchanting are efficient tools in the manipulation, projection and redirection of various sources of energy, suitable for active metaphysical work and holding the potential of a dangerous magickal weapon that if properly mastered conceals lethal power and the ability to conjure subtle shields of a higher magnitude.

Certain branches of traditional witchcraft and ceremonial magick use wands as ritualistic tools that can be valuable in the focus of will and the attaining of transcendence. However, those wands differ greatly from Asetian wands in relation to craftsmanship and power. The active usage of magick wands and the understanding of their abilities remain elusive and secretive practices even amongst the most private of occult circles, sometimes approached with the incredulity of misunderstanding, the fear of the unknown or the disrespect of ignorance.

Tied to a magickal tradition old as time, wands and talismans are prized possessions that have fueled desire and waged wars, treasured as invaluable and timeless, often protected as heirlooms of immortal power and immeasurable significance. Some Asetians hold a trusted wand with a unique and mysterious identity that is named and can only be wielded by its master. These cryptic and rare objects that are both a wand and a talisman were once legendary amongst magickal societies of ancient times, leading empires, rulers and various cultures to adopt and incorporate such a tradition whereby lacking powerful Asetian wands of their own the philosophy was applied to the mighty swords of their greatest warriors. Just like the Asetians did with their wands and talismans they started naming their swords, cherishing them as an icon of the family and banner of the kingdom, a song to their honor and an extension of proven warriors that would outlive their life and deeds in history.

The crafting of an Asetian wand is a sacred path of discovery bound to the secretive knowledge of the elders since wandmasters have always been cautious and reluctant in their craftsmanship. More importantly the enchanting and initiation of the wand or talisman relies on intricate metaphysical techniques and sacred oaths that are never revealed to outsiders, explaining the rarity of these mysterious objects. An Asetian wand is precious beyond words with each artifact that survived to this day and is proven authentic remaining priceless, desirable and a silent omen to be feared; those are the swords of legend and the flaming icons of an immortal legacy.

Vampiric Manipulation

Unlike most humans the Asetians are careful and wary of physical interactions, spontaneously retaining awareness over touch from casual and accidental to intentional. In certain situations and more noticeable among those of a higher subtle sensibility they may appear reluctant to express emotion or be intolerant of social interaction.

Physical touch is a form of communion and unspoken acceptance so to vampires it can express more intimacy than the insensitivity and energetic disregard of humans allows them to comprehend. Vampiric touching is used in magickal context and spiritual practice as a mechanism of energy feeding, a tool of active scanning and a powerful sensory probe of seduction and sexuality.

The ability to pierce the subtle body with a simple touch, breaking metaphysical defenses and draining the life force of another, is not exclusive to Asetians and is accessible as a technique that can be learned and often leads to confusion over the definition of the word vampire. Every human under certain circumstances is capable of draining energy and feeding from another living being, however that does not make them vampires. In fact it is not uncommon to observe humans acting predatorily and vampirically often unconsciously and unaware of their activity, driven by inner frustrations and the recurring need for attention. Often unintentionally these humans drain the energy of their surroundings and of those that regularly interact with them, raising drama or playing a victimization role in order to manipulate and gather the focus of attention. This has a negative impact on the energy of those that do not know how to protect themselves or do not recognize the signs to identify them.

These parasitic humans and psychic leeches sometimes find in the allure of the vampire archetype a cover for their incompleteness and behavioral patterns, flocking together and forging communities commonly plagued with drama, ego disputes, unstable personalities and the desire for acceptance, leadership and entitlement. They are easily identifiable through educated observation but reaffirm the importance of separating the lost and delusional from the hidden shadows of real vampires. However, not all humans explore the vampiric techniques of draining for selfish purposes as there are human Asetianists that practice metaphysical vampirism and predatory spirituality as a path of empowerment, divine communion and self-development, being an element of their embraced esoteric tradition and magickal practice.

Although esoteric touching can be a form of magick and occult art possible of learning, the human touch lacks the sensitivity required in advanced forms of draining. Hence this makes them unable to activate the energy exchanges of higher intensity and depth performed by the Asetians or attain their electrifying signature touch.

Projecting

The ability to consciously and intently project subtle energy is an important element of active magickal practice and a prominent skill of vampiric manipulation. Projecting is at its core a metaphysical mechanism developed through a technique that relies on the channeled release and directional extension of an energetic beam with desired frequency and vibration. The energy being augmented and projected can be charged with specific emotions, thoughts and persuasive intent as a procedure that can be learned for conscious use with varied practical applications such as social manipulation and channeled magick but it can also be triggered unconsciously, particularly amongst those of a predatory nature such as the Asetians.

The magick of energy projection is a dangerous tool and potential metaphysical weapon if focused on the various forms of manipulation, misdirection and control with high rates of effectiveness when befittingly understood and used in tune with legitimate techniques. As another vampiric tool of expression and creation, the art of projecting allows an Asetian to present an image and impression designed by inner will that can be adapted and mutated according to specific situations and targets, being perceived and interpreted as a mirror of the metaphysically established design. Unlike a common misunderstanding driven from uninformed assumptions these techniques are not restricted to empowered representations. As such, this not only allows for a vampire to project an idea of confidence, emotionless and even terror but more importantly it settles the foundation to express and induce an aura of innocence, passing through society unsuspectingly as ordinary humans, sometimes appearing weak or fearful, which is a deceitfully more dangerous threat than anyone seen as strong and fierce.

The efficiency and viability of the manipulative cloak maintained through projection will depend on the intensity and consistency of the energy being projected — under the mastery of gifted practitioners such as those of the Lineage of Serpents it can raise as a potent weapon feared by those able to recognize its invisible power. These Asetians are apex masterminds and a legend of magickal prowess, excelling at the arts of manipulation while wielding the swords of subtlety and the bows of silence. Whether knowingly or unconsciously everyone is vulnerable to the projected aura of an awakened Asetian and the unique spark that emanates from this spiritual bloodline, with degrees of perception and influence that depend on metaphysical training, subtle awareness and an element of energetic sensitivity that is inborn to fundamental nature and reflects on the state of the soul.

Techniques of projection may involve the gradual flooding of the aura with an energy coating of specific vibration and attuned to a desired emotional feel — the intended design — that can affect the detectable impact of the environment or permeate into the sensitive aura of others, causing change and instinctual reaction sometimes subtle while oftentimes discernible to keen eyes. Different techniques rely on the direct channeling of energy and its amplification through primary and secondary Shen that operate as gateways to various essences of increased vibration, such as the use of breath, gaze and touch, more suitable for identifiable singular targets than to influence large areas. However, there are exceptions as even while speaking the voice can be imbued with empowered energy from the primary Shen of the Throat and the secondary Shen of the mouth. This projects a desired vibration that can manipulate an audience and influence a crowd both positively or negatively, a technique exploited throughout history by political and military leaders who delved into the understanding of occult practices. Thoughts are energy given form, not only when manifested by words but also as simple emanations within the inner plane of the mind, being charged with hopes, fears and the emotional baggage of life.

Even if the flow and effects of projection can influence all sentient beings, the reactions can be diverse and ultimately dependent on individual interpretation of energy signatures, natural receptivity and attitude towards different emotions. It is important to understand that the metaphysical techniques under the scope of projecting have no basis on wishful thinking or the effects of a placebo, otherwise they would not be a practical element of occult science and unable to be coherently reproduced in real world usage. The underlying mechanisms of projecting are tied to various frameworks of subtle anatomy and energy work that can greatly benefit the practitioner when studied and understood — in the Asetian culture no seeker is taught to follow a blind recipe being always guided to firstly examine and comprehend how every element operates and influences the magickal outcome.

An integral component to the understanding of projection is a universal pattern of a philosophical nature and metaphysical application that is commonly known as the laws of attraction. This old principle of action and reaction in vibrational equilibrium can be consciously harnessed when accurately interpreted, applied to various situations and towards different goals of a spiritual or mundane nature. At its most elemental form like attracts like so energy is drawn to energy of the same vibration. This is mirrored in one of the most renowned paradigms of Kemetic spiritually and later incorporated into Hermeticism, having influenced the tenets of the western mystery school and being embodied in the maxim of Thoth known succinctly by "As Above, so Below."

The Asetian nature as a reflection of the inscrutable transcendence of Aset and Her divine immortality embodies in this realm as manifested creatures capable of naturally and spontaneously projecting anomalous quantities of energy and the active manipulation of otherwise dangerous vibrations. Personifying magick in such an intense way these vampires fluently attract their desired energies and crafted intent, fascinating those that interact with their essence and captivating the mind, body and soul of everyone they touch. The universe is their chosen realm and energy their elegant weapon in a world that bows and reshapes to the tides of their microcosm.

The ability to consciously project inner will and charged vibrations experiences a dramatic increase after the awakening, allowing for the emanation and redirection of denser and more expandable energy fields of charged magickal essence. The use of projecting in parallel with techniques of shielding leads to even further complexity of metaphysical practice, as energy shields can be infused with crafted emotions and manipulative intent through projecting, making the shield more than just a defensive barrier but a proactive tool of vampiric magick. Such implementations represent a more advanced branch of projecting, being used in the creation of energy filters and cloaks that are reactive and adaptive to other people and different surroundings. However, it must be stated that the energy used in the infusion and emanation of shields as projected cloaks or passive filters always carries the fingerprint of the practitioner — the one activating the projection — which can be a relevant tracing element detectable by an adept fluent in the specifics of metaphysical tracking and advanced magick, even if potentially invisible to the vast majority of the population and mundane society.

Manifesting
The metaphysical ability of manifesting is less of a learned discipline and more of an inborn instinctual mechanism of self-preservation, notably developed in vampires who have the veil between physical and subtle realities hardwired to their very existence and way of life. Its effects are less powerful and not as effective as projecting, being more situational and not as adaptable. Projecting allows for the crafting of reality and its applications are endless while manifesting behaves as metaphysical instinct being useful in situations of raw survival and dominance.

Manifesting is the process of temporarily raising biological and mental activity to artificial levels by channeling vital energy in order to fuel the subtle system into an unstable state of overdrive. It allows for the change of vital response and metabolic conditioning with discernible physical and psychological effects such as improved strength, stamina, cognitive function and focus. It can augment survivability and endurance in harsh conditions such as extreme weather, potentiating an increase or decrease of body temperature and heart rate, control of biological fluids, the enhancement of sensory sensitivity and the effectiveness of neurotransmission.

This primal form of manifesting is less useful in modern times although it still has its purpose and function. A subtle body going into overdrive and entering a stage of manifesting is said to be in stealth mode, however the terminology may also be more broadly used in cases of metaphysical projection or while enforcing active magick through breathing, gazing and touching or raising an energy shield, tied to situations of peak subtle awareness. While the ability and overdeveloped skill of projecting is characteristic of Serpents the mastery of manifesting is a gift native to Scorpions that naturally excel at its effective use. Scorpions tend to be physically resilient and healthier than the other two Lineages, relying on manifesting through their energy reserves to boost the immune system and stabilizing their biological processes, attaining higher rates of healing and resistance to disease. Such methods are not without repercussion and if misused can lead a Scorpion into impaired states of slow energy metabolism that may raise detachment, isolation and stagnation or plant the seeds of depression.

The influence of manifesting over physical activities is diverse and how stealth mode operates changes in each individual, depending on vibrational metabolism, energy flow and the general state of the subtle body. Someone capable of dramatically increasing physical strength through the empowerment of vital force may not be able to rely on this energy to resist and overcome extreme temperatures or improve concentration. These abilities can additionally change over time and adapt to distinctive situations, being unpredictable and less of an educated art when compared to the craft and mysteries of projecting and other magickal techniques that can be consciously tailored to match inner will.

Being able to push beyond physically imposed limits is an asset to take into consideration but also a tool that can only be explored with caution as it burns considerable amounts of vital energy in its ignition process, sending the complete subtle system into a dangerous state of overdrive only to achieve limited bursts of peak performance. This natural process of metaphysics has changed and devolved over time as physical instinct and strength became far more irrelevant in the present than the power and secrets of the mind, making for a poorly optimized technique that is frequently approached in the study of subtle anatomy as a residual mechanism in the layers between the etheric and biological body. It should also be understood that no one is capable of manifesting for long periods of time, as it is a heavily draining process, being activated often naturally and even unconsciously in extreme or life-threatening situations.

Lastly, the concept of manifesting is sometimes also applied to the magickal act of manifesting will into reality. Incredibly more complex and potentially interesting from a spiritual standpoint this is an entirely different technique that is unrelated to instinctual manifesting and it should not be confused as such, being more akin to mastered magickal art since it incorporates the fundamental abilities of projecting in the empowerment and redirection of mystical essence in order to manifest tangible magick. The existence and definition of this esoteric technique of high magick should be referenced and understood considering that although distinctive it can fall under the same terminology of the previously described natural mechanism. It is a far more advanced process that bears an understanding connected to the path of Asetian initiation and as such it can only be unlocked through our transformational keys of universal learning.

Inspiring

Anyone who studies the mysteries and secrets of the Aset Ka with a serious mind and knowledgeable tools has discovered that Asetians are profoundly inspiring creatures, unleashing with subtlety and sensitivity the innermost sensations while awakening powerful intimate emotions, desires and fears. As teachers of life and initiators of death the Asetians bring forth the ultimate ethereal touch; a silent spark of their sacred flame that burns furiously with unspeakable passion in the fragile heart of mortal kin.

The vibrancy of Asetian vampiric nature and the electrifying energy that surrounds their words, thoughts and actions can be pleasantly intoxicating, reaching the senses in a distinctively unique way as they are beings of chaos and transformation, affecting everything they touch and causing change with their mere presence. To bring forth growth, promote evolution and unchain true liberation the dark influence of the Asetian family is not always pleasurable and easy to accept. The tidal forces of our violet nature manifest in mysterious ways, often remaining misunderstood by the lack of depth of a mundane mind. It is undeniable that Asetianism leaves no one indifferent and everyone reacts to this culture in a way that mirrors themselves and what hides deep within more than they can realize. That alone is a powerful tool of psychology that provides every good observer with invaluable wisdom of the human nature. Asetian culture, art and magick are potent seeds of infinite creativity and creational power that establish the tradition as a strong force of inspiration, revealing an engine of change and spiritual transformation that is known by its true name as Asetianism.

Despite their natural allure these creatures of darkness and ancient silence also master the ways of inspiration as a potential path of manipulation, being a metaphysical tool capable of inducing strong rooted emotions in others akin to the arts of projecting. These tools of enchanting and subtle seduction should be approached with reason and an ethical mindset but their final usage is entirely dependent on individual intent and personal agenda.

The unconscious effects of inspiring are easily seen in the countless artists of past and present that find in the manifold veils of the Asetian culture and its vampiric influence a source of inspiration capable of fueling their creations, or in ordinary people who embrace the archetype of the vampire as a source of empowerment and self-acceptance, even if they are only aware of meanings and roots under a superficial light. It is also visible in those that bring forth criticism towards vampirism and the Asetian culture as a way to channel their anger and frustrations. All of these people are echoing the influence that Asetian energy has over them as a flagrant but interesting example of inspiring that can lead to the most profound discoveries of Self. This can be positively channeled into art, philosophy and spiritual development, or filtered by imbalances, fears and limitations into negativity, which is then turned into the manifestations of ignorance and futile attacks so commonly seen directed at the immortal banner of the Aset Ka and everything that it represents. In this way the inspiring nature of the Asetians has proven to be an impressive force of revelation, capable of exposing the hidden will of others by breaking egos and masks with the elegance of our immortal silence.

Mirroring

Metaphysical mirroring is a trait that is frequently inborn to the Asetian bloodline and inherently vampiric although with proper discipline it can be learned as a technique by those lacking such natural characteristics. Sometimes considered a form of magick with evolutionary value on the edification of character, defining of personality and the revealing of hidden Self, its fundamental operations are more accurately tied to the nature of the subtle system than to structured magickal practice.

Through the process of mirroring the energy signals and projected thoughts are reflected back at the caster, who unconsciously reacts to the misaligned concept of Self that is established deep in the subconscious mind. That reflection whether distorted or genuinely accurate is an echo of what each individual fears to find within, rooted in the existence of their own reality and an aspect they unawarely project on others by taking the form of criticism, judgment and disdain. This condition of the subtle system causes tangible and recurring effects upon interaction with an individual capable of mirroring, a consequence that can be perceived as both psychological and energetic. Such an influence although a reliable mechanism for growth and development is not always a pleasant experience, often raising issues when those interacting with the Asetians are faced against the very things that they do not accept about themselves. As such, it is not uncommon for an Asetian to be a spiritual mirror, where others find their own faces, see their hidden fears and meet their uncomfortable imperfections. This challenge and chaos induces growth and opens a pathway for an enlightened understanding of Self, however not everyone will bear the wisdom and maturity to seek those impulses as lessons, often reacting with ignorance by embracing the easier path of denial.

Both Asetians and Asetianists are oftentimes criticized for mistakes and failures that are not their own but that represent an exact reflection of the ones criticizing them; they are judged by the minds that fear being judged, hiding their handicaps by mirroring them into others. This type of psychological and metaphysical conditioning is a strong synergy of predator and prey — being commonly observed in the attempts of weaker minds to project on others what they fear about themselves. It mirrors their own insecurities, traumas and pains, while on the other end a vampire presents the ideal framework for the imprint of such corrupted reflections, acting like a polished mirror of energy that naturally projects an echo of all the offensive energy and malignant emotions that reside in the heart of humanity. The effects are easily detectable in the actions and thoughts of their opposers but also in innocent others that merely react by instinct through the influence of ego, deceit, desire or the deluded quest for power and self-importance.

The criticism, misinformation and lies so commonly found directed at the mysteries of Asetianism and those wielding its gnosis are a clear reflection of those that seek validation, acceptance and oppression. When faced against the mirrors of truth they fall, broken into one thousand pieces while condemning, insulting and defacing what they see staring back, unknowing that it represents nothing other than themselves. Those people that live by coating their existence within layers of deception and illusions never really like the true image projected by Self, finding it ugly and unpleasant but embracing the denial that it is not real and does not represent them. Smoke and mirrors...

This comes as an interesting tool of vampiric manipulation that can be used to bring forth the best and worst in others, ultimately forcing them to face their own reflection and liberating a truer understanding of Self. Such process is not easy, especially for someone used to self-deception that may unconsciously raise obstacles to learning and most importantly under the understanding that attaining such discipline painfully harms the safety of a blind ego. Although a valid technique that can be explored by the learned occultist, mirroring should be understood first and foremost as a natural characteristic that is recurrently present in the fabric of Asetian energy, bound to the nature of their subtle system and an esoteric process that can be fine-tuned once mastered the underlying mechanisms of vibrational reflection. The ability to act as a natural mirror is more than the mere projection or redirection of energy, being tied to an echo and flow that emerges from within and permeates the aura like a pulsating coating that is metaphysically reactive to every vibrational impulse that touches its field of action. So when presuming to understand, identify, analyse or comprehend an Asetian mind, think again — you may find something valuable about you staring back.

Scanning

The intricacies of energy scanning can be studied as a variant of traditional metaphysical sensing. The process is hardwired into the subtle instinct of Asetians who intrinsically and recurrently scan the energies surrounding them, whether environmental in nature and latent to an area or leaked by the life force of other living beings.

Scanning is the standard metaphysical methodology for accurate readings of the frequency and vibration of extrinsic and peripheral energies as well as a fundamental tool in the advanced interpretation of subtle fingerprints. Whether approached as a contraption or magickal weapon the study of scanning and its variants represents a relevant field of remote detection and metaphysical understanding, providing valuable information concerning the nature of energy and its abounding manifestations.

Allowing access to a broader spectrum of esoteric data and potentiating a considerably higher layer of interpretation, scanning is differentiated from sensing as a more advanced technique that requires another level of expertise. While sensing can be effortlessly learned to a rudimentary degree, scanning requires understanding and experience with separate magickal fields and its efficacy is dependent on natural ability and inborn skill that is not as common as popular occultism may assume.

It should be understood that Asetian-developed scanning practices place the focus on the quality of detectable data as a gateway to accurate interpretation. While the underlying knowledge that allows for the analysis of energy fields, subtle fingerprints and their perceptive insight is a fundamental aspect that relies on our established sophisticated paradigm, its viability is inherently dependent on the quality of the scan. Inaccurate data can rarely be properly interpreted and there remains one of the most common pitfalls of inexperienced practitioners or those embracing a frail and superficial branch of occult practice. Every serious exploration or spiritual undertaking using scanning as tool should adamantly avoid the vast and irrelevant opinion of ignorance that revolves around uneducated assumption, the illusion of expectation or the failure of overconfidence.

Probing
The empathic nature of Asetians provides them with a developed faculty to sense and interpret the realm of the mind in its many roads

of inner manifestation, reading thoughts and emotions of others as a reflective tapestry of their intricate existence. This power is a great tool of understanding, observation and complex interpretation with most Asetians being skilled empaths who can master the subtle songs of emotion and vibrational echoes without effort but it also presents an ability that can be used irresponsibly to elicit more deviant effects and grievous consequences. Despite being a recognizable inborn gift of the bloodline these abilities can also be developed as a field of applied metaphysics, dealing with techniques of mind-reading, the variables of psychology and their intimate connection with subtle energy, providing esoteric tools that can influence thoughts and efficiently block the mind to outside readings.

As natural empaths these abilities experienced instinctively by Asetians are not without associated danger and potential risks, since when left without proper training and control they can leave them exposed to subtle threats and present an underlying mechanism that can be exploited. This allows them to experience the emotions of others that, in their unique sensitivity, being inhumanly heightened and intense, may be dramatic or devastatingly painful.

Developing from a strong foundation based on the Shen of the Third Eye and relying on the establishment of conscious energy links alongside the extensive use of scanning and projecting, the art of probing has both defensive and offensive applications as it serves a dual purpose, allowing for the psychic reading of emotions and thoughts while also providing the knowledge to ward the mind and shield it from magickal attack.

Most genuine techniques of probing depend on the crafting of an active energy link capable of unsuspectingly piercing the aura, breaking energy shields or outer defenses and establishing a proper connection between two Shen. This energy filament allows for the draining of information, accessing elements present in both the conscious and subconscious mind. As the link operates in both ways it becomes clear how it can be used to stealthily read thoughts and emotions but also influence them, establishing the metaphysical gateway to implant artificial information. While this process may appear similar to standard mechanisms of telepathy it is in fact more complex but also more reliable and it can be interpreted as a specialized variant of psychic attack.

The study of probing also features defensive mechanisms and techniques that focus on the blocking of psychic attacks and powerful shielding techniques that can be used proactively or preventively against the threat of active magick. A proficient occultist knows how to armor the mind, blocking access to all thoughts and preserving the privacy of inner information, also being capable of manipulating an attacker by feeding inaccurate information designed as magickal disguise, defining probing not just as a gifted ability but also a prominent tool of vampiric manipulation.

These techniques require a robust control of the mind and fluency in energy manipulation but also need caution concerning its subtlety. While the probing of those unaware of metaphysics can be successfully achieved virtually unnoticed, the use of these techniques with an Asetian or learned practitioner will promptly raise suspicion and have its subtle signal detected, which can be assumed as a psychic attack and consequentially met with dangerous countermeasures.

Asetians take their vital energy and vibrational fields very seriously and as something not only intimate but also sacred, bound to a culture where the inner essence is treasured and safeguarded while the subtle is valued far beyond the physical. Any unauthorized scanning or probing of their energy can be identified as offensive and a potential attack, interpreted as disrespectful and almost invariably faced with an overpowering response that will make the message clear and ensure that the situation will not be repeated.

Psychic Attack

The elusive discipline of psychic attack is more than a multidisciplinary metaphysical weapon but in its elevated form presents a genuine martial art that ties the proficient mastery of the mind to the active manipulation of unseen forces. It is one of the most commonly discussed fields of offensive magick, being referenced and studied both in traditional branches of occult science as well amongst popular occultism. In fact classical literature that explores the realm of vampirism from an esoteric perspective insistently dwells on the dangers of psychic attack as a powerful gift of vampires, focusing on teachings and techniques that may be used to defend against them. While many of those texts are considered outdated and misinformed they hold some responsibility in the proliferation of prejudice and fear towards the magick of vampires, which although undoubtedly dangerous and potentially threatening can also be used towards other pursuits such as healing, teaching and enlightenment, often to much greater degree than the common occultist is able to achieve.

In its fundamental aspect the practice of psychic attack is, unapologetically, a magickal weapon. Its development has roots in a culture of darkness and mystery that does not fear the use of magick, prolifically exploring its dungeons of possibility and action in order to heal, protect and harm. More elegant than a bow and sharper than a sword the various techniques are designed to operate in offensive stances through the specialized use of metaphysics that carry the seed and intent to attack. The potency and effectiveness will vary from minor disturbances to a complete state of collapse that can be threatening to life, depending on natural skill and the ability of the practitioner, occult training, spiritual development and the specific technique being applied.

While most forms of psychic attack rely on the extension of tendrils and intense projection through these subtle filaments, gathering channeled essence from the major Shen and redirecting it at the right vibration to a focused target, one element remains constant and common to all available techniques: life force. It is vital energy that empowers and enforces a psychic attack, making its understanding and balanced control an essential ability to proficiently attack with magick. From the projection of an intense beam of energy meticulously directed at a vital Shen and capable of halting biological heartbeat to a malignant drain of Ka attempted through an overload of offensive tendrils with the aptitude to cause respiratory arrest, every form of psychic attack can be harmful and should be approached with wisdom, caution and the knowledge of proper countermeasures. However, not all forms of psychic attack are potentially lethal and most people attempting them will lack the skill to make the practice even reasonably dangerous. Like with most magickal techniques power is tied to responsibility and a mastery that is built upon a framework of secrecy, safeguarding its teachings while preventing misuse and abuse to a certain extent. Even with proper training and guidance most humans will be unable to practice magickal attacks or raise metaphysical defenses in the same way that Asetians do, as even amongst immortal kin only few can seamlessly deliver death with their subtle touch.

However, from a purist standpoint not all forms of metaphysical attack that rely on vital force should be considered psychic attacks. A valid example are the Asetian-developed techniques described as energy poisoning that operate slowly on the subtle system causing alchemical decay with long-term permanent damage that can be agonizing and devastating. Particularly effective when wielded by the talented minds of proficient Asetians this dreaded art is a potent magickal weapon of stealth and cunning that is feared and revered as the invisible bite of Serpents and sting of Scorpions.

Additionally, a standard form of vampiric draining should not be considered a psychic attack either although it can also be used in this way. Feeding or draining from a perspective of vampirism is intended to empower the vampire, while a psychic attack is designed to weaken and hinder a chosen target. An energy feeding is frequently although not always consensual, while a psychic attack is done from an advantage point with an intended strategy in mind, taking into consideration the potential magickal response that it may induce. With such consideration a reliable psychic attack is not only designed to be effective and efficient from a context of subtle anatomy but is also adapted to cause minimum impact on subtle awareness, passing unnoticed into the energy system and being delivered with as much covertness as possible. Premeditated attacks are far more dangerous than those resulting from impulsive reaction without planning or conscious thought.

From a point of subtle equilibrium psychic attacks can be hazardous to the practitioner exploiting them as they burn precious vital energy intently drawn from the internal system that is necessary fuel to proper maintenance of the subtle body. This energy is consciously used not only to activate the attack but also to enhance it, from malignant constructs and vibrational projections to the precise extension of discrete tendrils capable of being pushed into an outer energy system, allowing for the penetration of personal energy attuned to a specified design and frequency of the intended attack. Without knowledge or self-awareness such an attack can wear down inner reserves of vital energy and if done irresponsibly it can leave the subtle system in a state of fragility and vulnerable to a potential psychic counter-attack.

Asetians take advantage of psychic attacks and other forms of offensive magick directed towards them to gain the strategic higher ground and overpower their opponents. Tendrils and the projected energy used in a psychic attack is an effective subtle link that can be exploited and controlled against the attacker, working as a surprising gateway for potent counter-attacks that not many are aware of or recognize their potential. These offensive links established during a metaphysical attack can be used by a talented Asetian to bypass subtle firewalls and active energy shields, unsuspectingly hacking into the system raising the attack and allowing for the draw of valuable information or the intentional flooding with powerful magick capable of collapse or control. Equipped with this unique knowledge it becomes clear the importance of tactical magick, strategic metaphysics and advanced techniques in the arts and dangers of invisible warfare, a dreaded handicap amongst those who fight and oppose the immortal bloodline of the Aset Ka in a hidden society where the physically strong are often the weak while the intelligent, evolved and wise rule in silence and unspeakable secrecy. It is a world of higher honor but also of cunning and elusiveness in a pathway of mighty forged alliances but also of solitude and independence. The survival of the fittest and strongest is still accurate and true but its days of physicality are long gone in a metaphysical culture that establishes spiritual development and magickal mastery as the truest forms of personal achievement and the only possible measurements of Self.

The first line of defense against a psychic attack is the establishing of viable and stable energy shields. Although breakable and not always effective they still represent a strong mechanism of defensive magick that is frequently employed as a barrier to metaphysical attacks. However, if there is a detectable anchor point a vampire can break the shield by draining and consuming its energy, being a traditional step in the process of accessing the inner layers of a subtle system. As a failsafe to such practices the Asetians have developed specialized shielding techniques that prevent exploitation, making use of crafted malignant constructs imbued into the energy shield that make its draining not only extremely difficult but also markedly dangerous, being effective against vampiric humans or those mimicking the techniques of a real vampire. Scorpions do this naturally and expeditiously with a lower energetic drain on their reserves, providing another defensive mechanism of their inner system and an element responsible for their energy shields being so remarkably complicated to break or bypass.

Ultimately it is relevant to explain that while a tool of vampiric manipulation the techniques of psychic attack are not exclusive to vampires. They are openly explored not just by humans and those incarnated in this realm but also by the many forms of manifestation found in the other planes of existence that include creatures capable of enforcing magickal attacks and natively manipulate energy without effort.

Feeding

E nergy is the elixir of life and vitriol that ignites the kindling flames of immortality. Asetians interact with energy not as a mere tool or metaphysical substance but study and respect it as true vital essence and the purest form of raw manifestation.

In the Asetian culture energy is used to catalyze spiritual transformation and augment metaphysical power upon a timeless foundation of growth and ethereal development. Through this process one is able to draw upon life force of the living and energy of the universe in order to attain a recurring state of enlightenment and manifest hidden secrets. That nature and inborn ability of draining the living essence of another being establishes the Asetians as vampiric and determine a facet of their feared and often misunderstood predatory nature. Humans portray the Asetians as vampires, elusive creatures of darkness that revel in the silence of piercing observation and bear an immortal understanding that transcends their mortal years, but such notions are limitative and incomplete, as an Asetian is much more than just a vampire and cannot be defined by the arts of feeding and magick.

To Asetians feeding is an art; the perfected music of the night conducted by the silent gestures of an immortal maestro. This draining of life is a sacred bond of communion, a spiritual manifestation that does not reflect a biological need or purely physical nourishment as erroneously portrayed by those who adopted the fictional side of vampirism as an angle of their identity. Although capable of doing it naturally and without effort or teaching, the Asetians have developed more advanced methods of draining that rely on specific techniques requiring aptitude and knowledge of metaphysics, which are methods that can also be learned by Asetianists even without a vampiric nature but as chosen path of predatory spirituality. As such, feeding is a diverse discipline that encompasses a variety of different techniques and distinct spiritual approaches.

Although not common knowledge outside of the inner circles of the Aset Ka some Asetians are known to maximize their feeding when done within the bloodline and spiritual family, attaining a perfect bond in this sacred communion that benefits both vampire and donor. Tied to metaphysical concepts that may appear counter-intuitive to some scholars and students of vampirism its practical knowledge shall remain secret for generations to come when explored out of the scope of internal initiation. However, it sheds elusive light on the misunderstood possibility for certain Asetians to exist both as vampires and donors, seeking energy for their spiritual empowerment but also giving their sacred essence to another Asetian in a divine communion that heightens their existence to another dimension.

Even though a common misunderstanding in popular culture and amongst the less experienced or bearing limited knowledgeable, different forms of feeding do not establish types of vampires nor do they describe various categorizations as they do not depend on actual vampiric nature. Asetians are capable of draining energy through any method and can successfully employ all available techniques, depending on the situation, efficiency and personal preference. Variables such as subtle metabolism, energy reserves and the vibrational level of the spiritual body can influence the preferred methods of feeding but none can be used to describe vampiric nature or establish a vampire type. Concepts such as psychic vampire, sanguinarian and hybrid that attempt to superficially categorize vampires have no metaphysical or scholarly value, stemming from a modern layer of fiction easily recognizable by an emblematic lack of knowledge, research and understanding of tradition and history. The wise seeker or educated occultist understands that a vampire is not one type described by chosen feeding technique but the sum of all possibilities — a psychic feeder and a blood drinker, a sexual daemon and a spiritual predator, a daunting force of darkness and a healing flame of light.

Feeding is not accurately defined by blood, sex, ritual or carnal touch: it is defined by energy. That is the central elemental source of feeding at the core of every method and technique. The flow of Ka — a vital force that establishes the alchemy of life and death — is the fountain of wisdom and magick; the seed of thirst to all vampires.

Ambient Feeding

The variants of ambient feeding are less optimized for intensive drains but present a fundamental mechanism of self-sustainability for the energy system. These techniques are based on the absorption and processing of disassociated energy from the environment and they exist in both passive and active forms.

Passive ambient feeding is an internal metaphysical process of the subtle system and part of the intrinsic subsection of esoteric mechanisms responsible for gauging energy reserves and the maintenance of inner stasis. By constantly checking vibrational responses and metabolic requirements the energy system slowly absorbs energy from the environment and exudes subtle byproducts or exceeding energy in cases of overcharge. This natural process of area draining is a passive but essential form of ambient feeding.

Active ambient feeding can also be done unconsciously although it should be enhanced by metaphysical learning and mastered to conscious intentional use. Such form of feeding relies on techniques that fall under the scope of active magick and the field of energy manipulation, allowing for the willful draining of surrounding energy and absorption into the subtle system so that it can then be processed and redirected towards magickal work and spiritual empowerment. The active forms of ambient feeding are capable of more intensive drains and direct application than the natural passive mechanisms but both fulfill their relevant roles in the arsenal of an Asetian.

The energy absorbed by ambient feeding often lacks a defined fingerprint, being detached from living beings as residual energy and hence lacking many of the qualities characteristic of Ka. With a more ethereal quality and lower vibration this energy can be alchemically transmuted into raw essence to fuel the central energy system, but that can be less effective when used to ignite higher magick or redirect crafted will.

However, not all forms of energy channeled through ambient feeding are of questionable quality and limited power, as certain locations provide a valuable source to these vampiric techniques of draining, such as the heightened spiritual energy present in some temples or the mighty elemental energy of natural landscapes where the forces of nature are allowed to run wild and free. Because of such invisible power most living vampires unlike the creatures of fiction and myth recognize and appreciate spiritual locations such as churches, mosques and older temples, independently of religious allegiance. Those areas just like striking locales of limited human influence and natural settings are points of empowerment to Asetians who can draw upon the surrounding energies and manifest the higher power that is signature of their kin.

Diverging from these situations are the forms of ambient feeding that rely not on elemental energy but on the lower vibration of residual energy. Although this mechanism of feeding has the advantage of not creating subtle links nor leaving traceable metaphysical marks, the nature of residual energy is unreliable and with limited efficiency, often used prior to awakening but less afterwards when the states of awareness and understanding reach a higher level. Some Asetians even consciously avoid the energy shed by most humans and the unsigned properties of residual essence, particularly common among Serpents that find no empowerment but hindrance and weakness in crowded areas and metaphysically polluted environments where people abound.

Situations of markedly low energy in the subtle system, high magickal requirement or subtle breakdown cannot be solved and replenished by ambient feeding alone as its usage is based on a recurring and slow rebalance of lost equilibrium. A stronger drain will depend on more intensive techniques that pierce directly into the subtle system of the living and draw upon their very soul, making vampires amongst the most feared predators of the spiritual world.

Indirect Feeding
Sometimes described as social feeding, the techniques of indirect feeding represent one of the most common forms of draining and subtle predatory behavior. Interaction with the living is a fundamental aspect of incarnated life, conveying a mingling of vital force that is present in every moment as an invisible dance of ethereal fluid and spiritual essence. Tapping into these energies with the subtle body but without physical touch defines the practice of indirect feeding.

The process involves the extension of metaphysical tendrils with the ability to bypass energy shields and pierce directly into the aura, establishing a viable link as a filament capable of vibrational flow that will drain the vital force from the inner layers of the aura and redirect it to the subtle system of the vampire for processing and spiritual consumption. This opens a superficial wound on the aura that is often minor and rarely severe, particularly when done with caution and expertise, that will close and heal swiftly without complication. A more violent application of the method can tear inner layers of the aura and scar the subtle body, especially if the tendril is injected more profoundly, leaving a subtle laceration that may require more time to heal but that rarely involves the need for specialized metaphysical care.

As emotions and thoughts are energy given purpose and coherence it is possible to rely on psychological manipulation with the intent to trigger a spontaneous projection of Ka in others that can then be promptly absorbed by the vampire. Although not the most elegant or efficient form of indirect feeding it can be used in order to gain brief bursts of vital force and it is particularly suitable to predatory feeding applied during social interaction. However, the vast majority of vampires are admittedly not social creatures, being known to adamantly avoid the spotlight and thrive in the darkness of the unknown. In an age of superficiality where imbalanced personalities abound, attention-seeking psychological patterns are sometimes erroneously associated with vampirism but such ignorant conclusions should be discredited and rejected as a real vampire seeks not attention nor recognition — in fact, the renouncing of such trivialities and the chains raised by the opinionated judgment of others is a hallmark of Asetian vampirism and a proud banner of this liberated and evolved mindset.

The subtle links established through indirect feeding are weak and volatile, enduring for a limited amount of time before they naturally dissipate without intervention. Most techniques of indirect feeding have no lasting consequence for the donor who despite a brief subtle wound will be left with an energy system only slightly depleted of its former state, which will then be slowly replenished with raw new energy through its natural connection to universal sources; a process that is unconscious, automated and common to all living beings. Only profounder and more intense drains can deplete the system to the level of causing subtle and physical complications or inducing collapse, representing a legitimate danger present in other forms of feeding with a higher complexity and required knowledge that involve more than just an indirect metaphysical approach.

Contact Feeding

These techniques represent one of the most adopted methods of choice between consenting donors, although it can also be used efficiently in more predatory pursuits when practiced with strategic stealth and skill. The variants of contact feeding rely on physical contact aligned with proficient metaphysical touch capable of activating a thicker energy link that drains and redirects vital force directly from the subtle body, piercing deeper than the layers of the aura used in most forms of indirect feeding and drawing upon more profound emotions and intimate energy.

It is common for physical contact to endure through the length of the process and aid in the bonding and spiritual rapport, however in situations where discretion is paramount or the feeding must pass unnoticed and remain undetected a slight touch on the skin can be enough to inject a tendril and establish a working energy link; walking away and working the subtler elements of its magick from a distance. A certain degree of focus and mastery is required to successfully complete such a technique, although situations depending on this level of stealth represent more of a magickal attack than a method of feeding. Consentient feeding whether through contact or of another nature requires no discretion or manipulation, relying on magickal techniques inner to the teachings of the Aset Ka and often unique to the Asetian bloodline, established by a practice that is intimate, profound and often considered a sacred rite.

The energy links created during contact feeding are stronger and more resilient than those forged while using indirect techniques, leaving rooted constructs in the inner layers of the aura and sometimes even inside the subtle body. Such links dissipate slowly and can take a considerable amount of time to completely decay, especially if allowed to be enforced by thoughts and emotions. Magick or additional drains can strengthen and encrust them, establishing attached roots deeper into the subtle system, which may not be easily removed.

Although specifically Asetian in nature and bound to their unique spiritual application as well as more efficient and suitable to deeper forms of feeding and sexual communion, there is a mysterious path of vampiric feeding that provides a powerful energy exchange that is profoundly beneficial to both Asetian and donor. This sacred practice can also be used during contact feeding and it represents an intricate mechanism of draining that ignites the communion of life and its innermost essence in a unique way that empowers the Asetian while also heightening the energy and vibration within the subtle system of the donor, increasing the quality and density of living Ka. During this ethereal union of body and spirit the silent touch of the Violet Flame engulfs Asetian and donor as one singular force of spiritual power, burning fiercely through their Crown Shen and promoting energy flow in tune with a dynamic rebalance of the entire subtle system. This secretive technique is considered a blessing not only for the vampire but also for the donor, who willingly offers the most intimate essence to the immortal call of surrender from the

Asetian master, establishing a profound bond that transcends time and matter; something only practiced with a chosen few.

This sacred communion of divine inspiration is known as *concordia*, a word with Latin roots and signifying agreement, harmony and union, literally meaning *with one heart*. As an exclusively Asetian technique and initiatory mystery concordia is not considered a feeding variant but a spiritual practice that can be incorporated into different types of vampiric feeding and magickal empowerment. Unlike every form of feeding and in a way that is incomprehensible to those of a mortal nature, concordia establishes unique subtle links and an indescribable spiritual connection that can overcome death and have the quality of eternity, existing in the realm of transcendence.

Sexual Feeding
Entering the restricted realm of advanced feeding and intimate metaphysical connection, the practice of sexual feeding is a tradition of vampiric draining profoundly tied to the Asetian culture. Its methods require experience with the previously described forms of feeding as they rely on the anchoring of strong energy links mindfully placed deep within the subtle system in an alchemical process of spiritual bonding that interconnects the subtle flow between both bodies, but also building on instinctual practice and the primal magick of sexuality.

Often embraced by vampiric couples or long-established donor relationships, the art of sexual feeding brings forth a gateway into the wisdom of new discoveries and the intense heightening of both physical and spiritual sensations. More than just the draining of vital force, sexual feeding is an exchange of subtle essence and a bonding of the most intimate nature, allowing to access hidden vibrations only unlocked by the core of the system upon an ethereal altar of fearless surrender.

The energy exchanged during sexual feeding is naturally charged through the very act of arousal and sexual intercourse, acting as metaphysical catalysts and grounding anchors that under the initiatory gnosis of Asetian wisdom can be used to pull the spiritual realm into the lower plane of physical manifestation. This allows two spirits to mingle as one during an elusive moment of transcendence that is so brief that it cannot be described by human notions of time.

Although this form of sexual feeding is a transformational experience that requires knowledge and access to the mysteries of initiation, making it an intimate branch of sexual magick and vampiric art, and therefore only practiced amongst those with a bond of higher nature, it does not represent the only variant of sexual draining. To draw upon the energy of another during sexual activity and devour their essence, consuming the heightened living force for inner empowerment, is a fundamental aspect of the different techniques of sexual feeding. If there is no intangible bond and emotional background then the spiritual experience is removed and the practice becomes only a predatory drain, which although capable of sustaining the subtle body of a vampire that is willing of fierce and detached hunt will always lack the enlightening quality of the practice when explored under a spiritual light of sacred communion.

Sexual feeding should not be confused with the actions of a sexual predator. Few have the skill to activate a sexual drain or are capable of accomplishing it with the expected degree of metaphysical mastery and magickal understanding, frequently exploiting the terminology of sex magick as a mundane excuse and dishonest mask to satisfy physical urges, making them hardly a true predator and more of a manipulative liar. Elementary notions of occult terminology and the mysteries of magick are sometimes wrongly used as strategies of manipulation and a psychological weapon to deceive the ignorant and needy; a rotten reflex of abusive minds that are not vampiric in nature but walk amongst the lowest of mortals. That is why knowledge emerges as such an important feature of life and tool of genuine understanding since research and thorough examination provide a unique and definitive path to expose falsehood and misrepresentation so commonly seen in esoteric approaches and around more superficial occult circles.

Metaphysically the subtle links forged during sexual feeding are profound and coherent with an elasticity that makes them incredibly resilient, even if not as unique and potentially eternal as those rooted through the processes of deep feeding. Ultimately the properties of these energy links will greatly depend on the type of sexual feeding being used since a detached technique will raise weaker filaments while a spiritual rite under emotional unity will result in much stronger links that can linger for long periods of time or in some cases even be maintained indefinitely.

Sexual feeding is sometimes connected with the concept of energy lust although other forms of draining can equally resonate with such spiritual craving for the vibrancy of vital force. Asetians are creatures of intense energy who spiritually hunt for the mysteries of life and devour the essence of the living in their unique alchemy of transformational synergies, concealing the secrets of predatory manifestation and the elusive flame behind the immortality of the vampire. The children of Aset are the shadows of life and the illuminators of death; in their lust for magickal essence and never-ending vibration they raise chaos, break chains and enlighten the living that in return crave their exquisite presence and electrifying touch.

Tantric Feeding

Also identified by the terminology scorpion feeding the mysterious art and spiritual practice of tantric feeding is a lesser-known form of specialized sexual drain with a set of unique characteristics and metaphysical requirements.

Although not exclusive to the Lineage of Scorpions who have originally developed these techniques and are capable of mastering them to a degree not attainable by others, the process of tantric feeding is an advanced form of vampiric draining that relies on inborn abilities and magickal principles to feed upon the generated feelings of pleasure, heightened emotion and sexual ecstasy. Such an ability allows for an Asetian to experience physical, spiritual and psychological pleasure driven from the sexual fulfillment of another. By giving sexual pleasure and without actively receiving the same physical stimulus one can drain the heightened sensations being generated and transmute them into highly charged energy capable of unleashing strong pleasure within their own system.

This is only possible through a rare and specific mechanism of scorpion draining that feeds on sexual gratification, generating intense pleasure just from the act of giving. The process is so efficient and intensive that it naturally creates a vibrational cycle of strong sexual energy, where the essence of both is heightened, projected and then reabsorbed in higher and denser form. If both are Asetians and having a vampiric nature this cycle becomes a symbiotic feeding of unique quality, where one is pleasuring another and feeding from that raised pleasure that in turn will also empower the other. As such this technique represents one of the several secretive paths of concordia discovered and developed by the Asetians in the mysteries of mutual feeding.

The energy links generated through these experiences are stronger than those of standard sexual feeding and similar to the bonds forged through the sacred acts of deep feeding.

Deep Feeding

The genuine elements that define deep feeding are shrouded in secrecy and a subject that is rarely explored with truthfulness in literature or openly exposed to the public. As a metaphysical technique the many layers of deep feeding establish a profound spiritual experience that cannot be dissociated from magickal art.

In essence the art of deep feeding can be practiced in tune with advanced forms of intense feeding such as contact, sexual and tantric techniques, heightening the experience to a higher plane of Asetian alchemy and transformational magick. Unlike traditional methods of draining that establish a connection with the inner layers of the aura, the surface of a Shen or into major meridian channels in the subtle body, the mysteries of deep feeding allow ethereal touch directly into the very core of an energy system — reaching the innermost manifestation of Self and nucleus of the soul. That is no easy task and to perform such a profound drain means to transcend the veil between life and death, to reach beyond the limitations of flesh and attain unison with the unique song of the immortal spirit.

To draw upon the root energy of someone is extraordinarily empowering but it is also dangerous. Not only the initiatory method establishes a timeless and potentially unbreakable bond of immeasurable quality that cannot be severed or removed with living magick but the shocking wave of the drain has a major impact on the subtle system and also on the biological body in an explosion of vibration capable of spiking heart rate, blood flow and igniting a chain of events that cannot be undone. The energy channeled through deep feeding unleashes a realm of embryonic potential in a quintessential rainbow of emotions that holds access to hidden information of the past and present, making it a strikingly personal experience tied to perfect trust, absolute respect and the most intimate understanding.

Such a bond allows for an Asetian to forever sense a donor, tapping into unseen aspects of the unconscious mind not yet understood or completely discovered and being able to see through their spiritual eye. The process is liberating but also highly transformational, as the energy system of the donor is touched by the spiritual Fire of the Violet Flame in a branding and blessing that can be eternal. Energy links forged by an immortal flame can overcome death and remain present throughout lifetimes as the donor reincarnates and with this invisible fingerprint ever present within the soul experiences the overwhelming pull to the Asetian master, a signature of their unspeakable bond and spiritual union. That is a powerful magickal tool and a dark gift of much desire, raising ethereal links that can enhance empathy and sometimes symbolical telepathy, although the bond can also provide an exploitable weakness to the enemies of the bloodline.

The intricacy and dangers of deep feeding make for an exceptionally rare practice that is more than a metaphysical method of vampiric draining but an intimate path of spiritual initiation and magickal bonding that should not be confused with the pretentious techniques often deceptively described under similar terminology and fabricated without wisdom. Asetian magick is — and has always been — safeguarded by cryptic elements of inscrutable power and the most secretive nature; despite the recurrent attempts it cannot be mimicked or reproduced, as our essence bears the only keys that make it truthful and undeniably legitimate.

Ritual Feeding

A less common method of draining although of great value to vampiric Asetianists who fiercely explore the arts of vampirism in their spiritual pursuits is the branch of ritual feeding. These practices rely on ceremonial magick and the use of ritualistic techniques to draw upon the force of the living and empower the subtle system with channeled energy, making use of standard occult tools like invocation, consecration and sigil manipulation.

The magickal arts when applied through ritual and ceremony can be designed to align an intended influence in reality with inner will and the spiritual projection of the practitioner. This is a slower process than direct energy manipulation as used in more obscure practices of active magick, although a relevant branch of applied occult methodology and an element of prominence in most spiritual paths. Ritual magick and ritual feeding are still tied to the mysteries of energy and their manipulation but in this case the process is attained indirectly and with a higher dependency on psychology and the esoteric fields of emotional projection and guided ceremony.

Although the paths of ritual are commonly approached in occult systems as reliable forms of destructive magick as well as meditative stances of inner development and personal achievement, their elements when applied to feeding establish a genuine gateway of predatory power that should not be underestimated. With broad applications at the reach of both Asetians and humans the dangers of ritual are well known in magickal society and a silent invisible force to be reckoned with.

One recurring tool in practices of ritual feeding is what is described as a sigil — a magickal seal of cryptic symbolism and hidden power, often unfolded through the mysteries of initiation. The sigils used by Asetians are often ancient, secretive and incredibly potent, rarely known or understood by the uninitiated and outsiders to the tradition of the Aset Ka. They hold a vast arsenal of occult seals and magickal symbols in their personal collections, which can be used not only in a ritualistic setting but also in various forms of active magick alongside mechanisms crafted to ignite their functions through energy manipulation and direct projection. They are experts in the traditional arts of sigil creation, fluent in the elusive mastery of their empowerment and the secrets of imbuing them with initiatory teachings as menacing keys of hidden potential. In Asetianism a sigil is profoundly more significant than just a symbol; it grows and vibrates with our inner alchemy, becoming an entity of its own. Occult seals embody specific vibrations, teachings and secrets in tune with the design of the master, manifesting a living archetype of magickal creation.

Ritual practice has the unique particularity of not creating natural subtle links attached to the energy body unless intentionally directed to do so, being a less efficient method of feeding in the sense that it draws energy indirectly, resulting in living essence that is not as vibrant nor as charged as what it is gained from other techniques. Since ritual feeding is practiced within consecrated space and under the protection of warding spells and magickal circles, energy filaments do not have the adequate metaphysical landscape to take root and establish a full connection, working almost like a spiritual firewall between vampire and donor. However, the main advantage in ritual feeding from a strategic mindset is not found in the absence of created subtle links but in the natural difficulties that the process imposes on fingerprint tracking and magickal detection, making it a valuable form of draining, psychic attack and manipulation when operating in stealth. Although when such techniques are applied with proficiency they can be incredibly hard to trace or identify it should be stated that a master practitioner will have other available tools to subtly investigate and potentially detect incoming magickal signals, allowing for a gifted Asetian to turn an adversarial ritual and its magick against the caster.

Other forms of feeding previously described are of a more aggressive nature, making them easier to detect and track to the source even by those less aware of the subtle reality. Despite this apparent disadvantage those techniques remain the predatory methods of choice to most vampires that see them as an organic approach to energy draining and a natural behavior of their kin; a pure manifestation of vampiric instinct and magickal art, being the most intimate paths to embrace life and feast on the living.

Astral Feeding
It remains important to understand that not all forms of vampiric feeding have a physical component as they establish a magickal path that is not only spiritual as inherently metaphysical in concept and practice with fundamental aspects of a strictly subtle nature. The path of astral feeding joins the previously described methods of ritual in the vampiric techniques of remote draining that can be enforced without consideration for physical distance and material proximity.

This detachment from physical constraints is a central element of astral projection of major relevance to the vampiric potential in these metaphysical gateways that transcend the veil of matter into the realm of the spirit. In essence the process of astral feeding occurs outside of the incarnated realm, activating an invigorating drain that is established in a higher plane of energy within the subtle reality. In this technique the soul expands and projects away from the physical body, in a consciously induced meditative trance that allows roaming the astral realm and in this way draining the vital essence of disembodied beings that inhabit the vast realities beyond the walls of matter, as well as drawing upon the life force of the living that are present in a state of sleep or also projecting to the spiritual planes of subtlety. Although such cases are common in these practices a sleeping donor is not a requirement for astral feeding as the process can be mastered in order to project into the astral and use it as a metaphysical gateway capable of transcending time and distance, manifesting the predatory focus back into the fall of matter where the remote draining can be initiated. This effectively allows for an awakened Asetian to drain the vital force of the living without limitations of distance, space and matter in an advanced form of astral feeding that hints to hidden and obscure magickal potential since the fundamental principles and applied techniques can be exploited for psychic attack and metaphysical warfare.

It is not uncommon for a mind under the altered states of consciousness that define biological sleep to wander away from the body and physical shell, traversing the illusive land of dreams into a gateway that leads to the higher planes of manifestation. This natural process of unconscious and spontaneous projection allows the dreamer to interact with other dormant souls, unaware and also under the influence of sleep. Sometimes they act only through the input of the subconscious layers of the psyche but others are very much aware and intentionally present in astral form for spiritual exploration, the magickal quest of learning or the immortal hunt of an observant vampire.

Even though the art of astral feeding is attained in full vibrational form as beings of pure energy, the subtle links created during its practice are not as strong as those forged through other techniques and can easily dissipate in time if not consciously reinforced by magick or recurring astral interaction. Although a practice and technique that is vampiric in nature, the process of astral feeding is not exclusive to Asetians, being explored by humans under a myriad of esoteric agendas and personal pursuits. Often unknowingly many have experienced a spontaneous astral drain during their life, which may not be evident to realize without experience with astral work and interaction with the subtle planes of existence. An energy system operating on low reserves automatically enters a state of alert, even in humans, starting an unconscious process that searches for viable options to regain balance and reestablish natural equilibrium required to spiritual maintenance. Under such states it is not uncommon for spontaneous drains to occur driven by metaphysical instinct even in beings without a markedly vampiric nature.

Blood Feeding
Blood is a powerful metaphysical tool and timeless spiritual symbol with recognizable significance established throughout history, however its true living force is oftentimes neglected due to the influence of ignorance and misunderstanding. The alchemical properties of blood and its inherently transformational powers lie in the vital energy that it carries — the living essence we describe as Ka.

Vampiric feeding through the ingestion of human blood remains a commonly avoided subject in occult literature and a taboo surrounded with prejudice in modern magickal practice. Its connections to the predatory nature of vampirism and the mysterious powers of life and death make blood feeding an obscure but initiatory element of the Asetian culture and related magickal teachings that is frequently considered forbidden knowledge amongst outsiders.

As a magickal substance blood is a charged biological fluid with unique metaphysical properties, infused with the vital energy of its host. The natural alignment of physical blood veins and arteries with the subtle energy vessels represent a central part in the equation that explains the magickal characteristics of blood and its richness in living Ka, a focus of extensive study and thorough examination by Asetian scholars in the scientific field of subtle anatomy and practical metaphysics.

This bond between biology and magick has established a long historical connection that ties vampires and vampirism to the blood of the living, related to a predatory practice that is foremost spiritual in nature and often profoundly misunderstood but very much alive to this day. However, the essence of blood has metaphysical value not only in vampiric practices of energy feeding but also in various esoteric applications, emerging as a binding tool of power and symbolical link of great potency in the secretive dark arts. Blood is an alchemical substance of life and creation but also an enduring omen of death and transformation, used in traditional practices of ritual magick, sacred pacts and initiations.

Although the act of blood feeding has an inherently physical component — that being the blood itself — it is not independent of magickal work, relying on metaphysical techniques to activate the drain, establish a subtle transfusion and efficiently process the channeled energy. The art of feeding is inborn to every Asetian and can be developed in an intuitive and organic way but the secrets of predatory practice and initiation can open hidden pathways into an enhanced spiritual experience and increasingly higher levels of enlightenment.

To an awakened vampire the blessing is not found in the physical aspects of blood but in the invisible essence that it carries, being understood as a vehicle of life and a reliable focus point to an effective drain. The fear of a vampiric attack has been so intricately rooted in the human subconscious and contemporary culture that the act of blood feeding is recurrently paralleled with agonizing danger and terror. Although those attacks are represented in fiction through exposed wounds and messy bites reality is vastly different from such surreal representations. A real vampire does not require large amounts of blood but small droplets, where quality is always valued over quantity. Glasses filled with blood are an element of fiction only adopted by deluded humans with no real understanding of vampirism and the subtle nature of the living essence honored in blood.

Since its invisible gift of life hides in vibrational form blood must be consumed fresh and living, directly drained from a donor. Alternatives such as raw meat and conserved blood have their place in specialized diets and medicine but they hold no meaning to vampires despite the misguided claims or cases of specific medical conditions that should not be confused with spiritual vampirism. Energy is a dynamic ethereal fluid that easily dissipates when not given coherence through the embodiment of life or resilient magickal constructs, making processed animal meat and dead blood incredibly low on living essence, something that anyone aware of the subtle reality will effortlessly identify.

Additionally, and not exclusive to blood feeding but applicable to every form of energy drain, the Asetians are known to be extremely elitist about their spiritual essences and the nurturing sources chosen to feed their magickal abilities, valuing with great care the purity and quality of their own life force — a sacred essence of immortal power and immeasurable beauty.

It is important to understand that, even though blood is permanently entwined in the history and mysteries of vampirism, its relevance to the practice of feeding is not vital, representing just another metaphysical tool in the arsenal of a resourceful vampire. With the vast array of techniques developed and the unquestionable power of energy manipulation blood surfaces as an option but not a requirement in predatory spirituality and the arts of vampirism. It is not unheard for an Asetian fluent in the subtle craft of energy work and magick not to feed from blood at all, finding the required essence and source of empowerment in the true spark of life — the unveiling mysteries of Ka. Feeding choices and embraced techniques are personal and in no way can be used to hierarchize or define vampiric nature, as long as there is a definitive understanding that blood is often an allegorical illusion of power for its true force lies subtly hidden as living essence; the seat of the soul. In purist understanding blood is not life but a vehicle for life, carrying the silent breath of existence as an untold song of immortality.

Donors
A consensual donor relationship is established through an exclusively vampiric bond that is manifested on the altar of perfect trust by the graces of mutual respect and understanding. The subject is profound and multifaceted with intricacies that will not be thoroughly analysed here, changing according to tradition and the very nature, ethics and mindset of the vampire.

In Asetianism this invisible connection between donor and vampire is intensely spiritual and genuinely treasured with loyal commitment. Some may nurture an intimate relationship of a physical nature but that is not always the case although trust must be built upon honest friendship and reciprocal care. The approach to donors is diverse and personal, as one may be present everyday during the awakened life of a vampire while another undergoes long periods of absence without dwindling of the bond as its strength was forged on the Fire of alchemical communion and through the breath of life burning within Ka.

It is rare for an Asetian to maintain a high number of donors, preferring to invest their essence and teachings with a select few they can trust with such an honorable exchange and confide in about the mysteries of the cosmos. The relationship with a donor is also a commitment of learning, growth and transformational wisdom under the belt of responsibility; it is a magickal duet as master and apprentice. Contrary to superficial understanding and popular belief it is not uncommon for a vampire to be solitary and embrace the singularity and independence of a chosen path without an established donor, whether by choice or conditioning but most frequently as the result of personal preference.

The solemn pledge of responsibility and oaths of entrusted secrecy are integral parts of feeding and vampiric relationships as it is inevitable for a regular donor to become spiritually, emotionally and sometimes even physically bound to the Asetian, with a connection and subtle links that in some cases can endure lifetimes. An energy link forged with an active and recurring donor is stronger and more powerful than those established through ordinary feeding or occasional drains, uniting donor and vampire with an unseen level of empathy and metaphysical connection that should never be underestimated.

Donors can be human or vampiric in nature and in Asetianism they are effectively welcomed as honored members of the family and respected allies of the Aset Ka — they are passionate Asetianists, loyal friends and committed champions bound to protect and serve their immortal masters.

Advanced Magick

𝒯 his last chapter builds on previous knowledge and dwells on the complex techniques of magickal practice that should not be approached without the mastery of fundamental metaphysics and a profound understanding of the intrinsic elements of active magick, developing solid insight into how these advanced mechanisms operate in the subtle engines of nature and living devices of vibrational arts. Different from the initiatory and alchemical nature of other chapters from part one, that develop on the intricate mysteries of the Asetians and their enlightened spirituality, the following pages establish a limited number of conceptual frameworks with strong significance that shed light into the secretive world of advanced magick. However, it is all profoundly entwined as natural synergies of occult nature make some of these practices not bound to complete understanding and flawless execution without committed spiritual development, a sane balanced mind and the gifts of experienced wisdom.

Not exclusively vampiric or tied to the innermost elements of spiritual nature, many of these techniques encompass a field of advanced metaphysics that fuse specialized techniques with active magick, producing powerful effects that can be permanent and undoubtedly dangerous that should never be approached lightly. Some of those practices and gnosis are purely Asetian, tied to the culture and secrets of the Aset Ka, being crafted and developed internally for millennia like the infamous arts of metaphysical tattooing and the limitless potential of vibrational high magick, while others define standard techniques at the core of advanced magick of past and present such as banishing, binding and the fundamental mysteries of initiation that are found in countless different traditions.

Banishing

The techniques of banishing establish a strong mechanism of metaphysical protection and enforcing of spiritual authority by the means of magickal power to interdict, repel or restrict someone from accessing a physical area or subtle realm. Established in the field of active energy manipulation but tied to advanced elements of magickal overpowering, the ways of banishing are more adequately used with subtle entities of another realm without a bound physical element, although they are not exclusive to such applications.

An offensive or parasitic being that shows resilience to other forms of magickal defenses and metaphysical countermeasures may require a direct banishing in order to cease advances and intentional attacks. The process of banishing is not simple and most importantly it does not happen without struggle, which can require the use of magickal force, responsible determination and a focused mind so that the creature is successfully overpowered. In cases of elemental forces without a layer of self-awareness the course of banishing should be straightforward and attained without incident. However, the entities that roam subtle realms can be sentient, strong and very much aware, oftentimes resourceful tricksters fluent in the arts of manipulation and magick, capable of unleashing considerable amounts of damage and influence which should be banished with caution and consideration.

Understanding the fundamentals of banishing and familiarization with its various techniques, subtle mechanisms and applications becomes particularly relevant when a high degree of awareness is developed, interaction with the subtle reality is increased and personal investment in magick, the occult and practical energy work becomes a lifetime commitment. Those elements operate as magnets to creatures without the power of reincarnation, drawing entities from other realms seeking interaction and bound to different agendas. Magickal practice aligned with a strong development of Self potentiated by the signature teachings of Asetianism and the many doorways that it unfolds represent a vibrational beacon to a vast array of subtle entities and not all of a benign nature.

The profound internal changes and alchemical transformation that every Asetian or Asetianist undergoes during discovery of the violet path and the conquering of many challenges that manifest as natural initiations throughout life raise the internal vibration of the subtle body, heightening the quality of vital energy and effectively empowering Ka to a transcendent state above that of mundanes. This pure energy of unique quality is an invisible source of great potential actively sought by many, raising desire and envy amongst those who seek power, control and dominion. This fundaments one of the aspects behind the increasing amount of paranormal sightings and contacts experienced after the discovery of magick, exploring the subtle and finding the hidden reality of the Asetians. This seed of attraction will manifest behind the veil of other planes but also in the chaotic chamber of matter as humans are known to desire for power and incessantly seek it to the halls of great despair.

It remains important to reference that the techniques of banishing are not only applicable to identifiable creatures and other entities but also to energy in general. That is particularly useful to metaphysically cleanse an area and sacred space or in more advanced situations to forcefully ban a specific vibration or block a certain type of undesired energy. This allows us to fine-tune magickal practice to great detail and filter through energy and essence to a high level of raw manipulation.

Even if some of our most advanced techniques can have lasting effects and be tied to spells that are incredibly difficult to break, in the end no banishing is definitive and permanent, requiring conscious reinforcing to remain effective and reliable, which can only be fueled by energy.

Elusive and incomprehensible is the divine magick of the Gods and their spiritual exploits, manifesting power beyond the scope of the living and life force of the dead, just as Seth imprisoned Osiris in a fallen sarcophagus of deceit and Aset banished Seth to forever haunt the arid sands of the desert and conceal its secrets.

Binding

The art of binding is a severe form of magickal practice that requires knowledge, experience and mastery beyond a threshold of personal power. If correctly applied this overpowering technique is extremely effective and prohibitively dangerous, establishing an invisible prison that is all about control.

These techniques operate through magickal dominion, allowing for crafted will to be induced not through manipulation but by metaphysical force. They can be used with an incarnated target or towards a subtle entity from other realms, with levels of efficiency dependent on the power, awareness and skill of the opposing force, although one of the most common applications is to magickally bind essence and will to an object or location.

With the right set of tools and a strong mind the secrets of binding can be incredibly potent against subtle beings that do not incarnate but also very dangerous. The act of magickally binding a creature to a physical vessel and establishing control over its life force creates a dreaded metaphysical prison, igniting the extent of its might against you. Any form of binding will provide a catalyst and strong incentive against the caster, sometimes causing for a once imprisoned or controlled entity now on the loose to pursue and stalk for the length of a lifetime or in rare cases even beyond.

Metaphysical binding is an act of strong will and raw power, requiring both elements to be superior than those of the target, otherwise there is a very real danger of magickal response with a potential inversion of the binding, where the caster is overpowered and becomes the one under control. In such cases of advanced offensive magick the risk is too great to be approached without responsibility or the wisdom of centuries.

Most techniques of binding require not only steady focus and a balanced mind but also vast amounts of energy resources, which can be draining for the practitioner and of metaphysical consequence to the subtle body. A common tool of binding is the mastery of magickal sigils, crafted as dark seals of dominion and control capable of binding life force to a vessel and imprison it with magickal torment. Many such devices still endure from ancient times, concealing secrets and hidden peril, while others were created in contemporary ages with careful craftsmanship and attention to detail.

In Asetian history the unapologetic exploit of potent binding techniques was used during the tremendous battles of another age, such was the case of the Epic Wars where the most devastating magick was wielded by both sides to great pain and the despair of all. Under this historical context binding was enforced not only to channel extraordinary powers but also to chain and unleash abominable creatures to major tactical advantage. However, the ability and knowledge to wield such forces was and remains confined to few — a recurring theme of high magick and the advanced arts of invisible power that can only manifest through mastery, initiation and secrecy that make them adamantly inaccessible to most.

There is a lesser known variant of magickal binding developed by Asetian masters during their times in Ancient Egypt that is described as talismanic binding. This unique specialization of the arts of binding allows for an Asetian to bind a created servitor, desired entity or rare power into a magickal tool — the talisman. It was originally used on the legendary wands of the Asetians with their fabled identities and mystical abilities or with a crafted amulet of hidden power. This form of subtle art and misunderstood talent although possible of offensive usage was designed with a spiritual and noble application in mind, being capable of imbuing a physical object from the realm of matter with unseen power and formidable magick, establishing legends and myths behind the beautiful talismans and mighty wands of Asetians as the most iconic magickal objects in occult history.

Like every magickal tool the ways of binding should never be used to deal with issues of the mundane, handle social conditioning or serve vain personal agendas. The power of magick serves higher purposes and must be understood as a doorway of perception and the pathway to increased understanding that liberates the transformational nature of spiritual evolution — the ascension.

Constructs

Crafting subtle constructs and their numerous applications in magickal practice is a peculiar branch of advanced metaphysics that is well established in the Asetian ways of energy manipulation and their unique approach to the invisible arts.

At the most elemental level a construct is an ethereal structure crafted out of raw energy with distinctive vibrational properties. Its metaphysical design is established through active energy work and relies on special techniques that are capable not only of projecting and redirecting energy but also to mold and imbue it with dynamic coherence, attaining a state of semi-solidification that we define as subtle crystallization. This allows for a structural construct to be shaped according to conscious will and pre-established spiritual design, providing the frequency and vibration that make it resilient to natural dissipation but still affected by it. Independently of power and mastery energy is a limitless dynamic force as every crafted construct will slowly dissipate and deteriorate over time, particularly when bound to the physical plane of matter. In the astral realms energy is the equivalent of matter, so constructs raised in that plane will be stronger and more permanent in a reality with temples and strongholds crafted out of energy that linger beyond the notions of time.

Constructs can be incredibly diverse in power and function, ranging from simplistic and elementary structures to complex metaphysical devices bound to some of the most advanced magickal techniques ever developed. The potential of constructs and their applications are infinite, limited only by the creativity, knowledge and skill of the practitioner but representing an undeniably powerful tool in the invisible arsenal of magickal arts.

An interesting advantage to working with elemental constructs is their potential for being programmed, since a construct can be shaped and fine-tuned in form and vibration but also extended with specific metaphysical function resulting in a dynamic device capable of magickal operation. That understanding and detailed ability can provide an edge in magickal work even though its practical use is of no simple approach. Despite the elevated level of knowledge and fluency in metaphysical science required for such an undertaking, a complex construct with dynamic layers is not a self-sustaining subtle engine, requiring considerable amounts of energy to be maintained and remain stable. This vital fuel that is the seed of life and the very element at the core of all magick is a precious resource that should not be underestimated or neglected when crafting the subtle edification of constructs.

The structures and esoteric engines that establish magickal constructs can be surprisingly effective mechanisms of metaphysical protection — even if not always the most efficient — that can be attached to strategic objects, from doorknobs to windows or even walls, raising subtle barriers capable of shielding or filtering energy according to an intended design. When programmed as a filter a responsive construct can behave as apparently inexistent when touched by certain types of energy predetermined as benign while actively blocking specific frequencies, or even be crafted with probing abilities and stealth qualities making it a potent tool for magickal espionage.

High requirements of energy and skill to craft, develop and maintain advanced constructs make them a relatively rare practice, where the balance between efficiency and function is not easy to achieve. However, smaller constructs and subtle structures with a lesser degree of dynamism and active function are relatively easy to maintain and have become common practice amongst Asetians.

Wanding

Bound to the invisible arts of energy projection and elemental manipulation lies a secretive discipline that is almost as old as the very foundations of magick. With principles tied to the core of vibrational channeling and the amplification of vital energy the mysteries of wanding are a legacy of immemorial eras and an inner mastery safeguarded by the elders.

During the golden age of Sep Tepy the Asetian mystics fluent in the silent language of energy and master crafters of the subtle sought an empowered method to channel, redirect and amplify vital force in ways until then unknown to the world and that could reach beyond what the fundamental tools of eyes and hands can do. That revolutionary but historically misunderstood object of legend and feared power became what is known in contemporary times as a magick wand.

Initially Asetian wands were developed as intricate spiritual tools to be used in sacred practices of initiation, imbued with the mysteries of alchemical transformation and magickal empowerment, aligning with advanced metaphysical practices and the dangers of our very own talismanic technology. In time their usage expanded and other applications emerged as such is the nature of creation and bloodstained truth behind the power wielded in titanic battles between Gods and men. During those dark times wands sang their silent hymns as mighty and feared magickal weapons capable of delivering an immeasurable advantage in metaphysical warfare, a path of knowledge that was not neglected by the hidden factions of power in this world.

Even though millennia has passed and we now live in another reality and an entirely different world the initiatory discipline of wand mastery remains a pursued path within the Asetian culture and its many gateways of wisdom, a study focused not as a mere weapon of elegance and eloquence or a tool of dominance but lingering as an evolved talisman of spiritual communion and higher magick; a tool of universal creation and transcendent destruction.

As the history of wanding developed and its spiritual path became rooted in our practices and esoteric culture those techniques were explored and transformed by the magickally aware sects of humanity, seeking to adapt and mimic the secretive Asetian ways of the wand. Such knowledge was passionately sought, exploited and sometimes even defaced. In time the mysteries of wanding and the spiritual uses of wands became safeguarded and secretive, passed through oaths of initiation built upon trust and honor, seeing this knowledge confined to closed occult circles, family traditions and private covens. That development in the approach and understanding of wanding led to an increasingly difficult path to access accurate information on the proper use of wands as metaphysical tools, eventually culminating in a simplification of the tool and its applications, becoming limited to an iconic object for the focus of will in ritual and no longer the active device of magickal power and energy manipulation that it was once known to be. Such ritualistic approach gained popularity amongst occultists, establishing strongly in different occult traditions including sects of traditional witchcraft and the ceremonial branches of the western mystery schools, remaining a well documented practice that is alive to this day and burying the deeper knowledge of spiritual wanding alongside its powers of amplification to the most rare and unknown fields of occult study. In modern times the ancient practices of wanding and the profound understanding of Asetian wands became extremely secretive and restricted to a highly educated elite of experienced occultists, with knowledge only accessible through initiation and cautious teaching by the few enduring Orders known to safeguard the lost practices of the ancients.

As an occult device, and beyond the limited scope of a ritualistic object of focus, a magick wand in the Asetian tradition is a potent energy amplification tool capable of unique degrees of intensity and the recalibration of projected beams to highly specialized frequencies and levels of vibration.

In advanced studies of wanding and exploring the techniques of wandcrafting a concept that is frequently discussed is the usage of a core. The core or kernel of a wand often refers to a material that can be added to the center shaft on the body of a wood wand with a designed magickal application. The materials used in such devices can be diverse although they are preferentially natural and rarely synthetic, such as animal feathers, special types of fur, dried herbs, unique blends of powdered minerals and other alchemical elements. One of the most effective but also more advanced variants of a wanding core is the accurate mixing of minerals with specific metaphysical properties, sometimes defined as last generation cores and describing an experimental field that is extensively studied in applied alchemy.

A core must aid in the process of amplification and alter the ability for a wand to redirect vital energy and shift its vibration. Unlike what is commonly believed the extended use of cores is usually limited to beginners who are learning the fundamental aspects of energy projection through an amplification device such as a magick wand. Advanced practitioners do not require the alchemical elements of a core to effectively and accurately amplify vital energy through a wand, mastering the metaphysical techniques without relying on added variables of amplification. Purists and traditionalists sometimes completely reject the use of cores as their elements interfere with the vibration being projected by the secondary Shen of the hands and directed into the wand, raising the levels of metaphysical noise introduced into the energy being amplified and influencing the intensity and raw conditions of its transmission. However, wanding can be a challenging process of discovery and a discipline that is incredibly difficult to master, particularly to someone developing basic skills and beginning to explore the subtler aspects of this art. This is a path which cores may alleviate and aid in smoothing the learning curve, making for a more volatile ignition of projection in the early stages of channeling and steadying the projected beam of vital energy required to properly wield a wand in magickal practice.

The concept and terminology of cores found among human traditions find their historical roots in the traditional arts of Asetian wanding. Asetians infrequently rely on physical cores within their wands, instead developing several techniques of subtle cores crafted out of pure magick. These insubstantial cores of vibrational fluidity can be established through energy constructs with imbued purpose and intricate design or be the crystallization of a tendril from the subtle body that is extended into the wand, bonding the practitioner and wand as one. In rarer cases a sentient servitor is infused within the wand, giving birth to magickal objects of enormous power, which are more than just a wand but also a treasured talisman. A wandmaster responsible for crafting an Asetian wand has the wisdom to attune it with a unique spell, following the tradition of the elders and honoring the secrets of the ancients. This philosophy found in the mysteries of advanced wandcrafting defines the invisible kernel of a magick wand that is described as an edge core, a spiritual and metaphysical principle that has been recurrently explored and mimicked by the disciplines that seek to replicate its power and ability through the use of physical cores.

It remains important to understand the diversity in potential of a magick wand and the many layers of applications that are expressed through the arts of wanding. Beyond a potent magick weapon that can be used defensively or capable of delivering partial to lethal damage a wand is also a respected healing tool and an object of initiation or transcendence that is used to teach, enlighten and ignite advanced spiritual work. A wand can be used intuitively as an analytical instrument of precision and a reliable metaphysical device, remaining also a common tool of ceremony and ritual that is recognized by many. As an object that is shielded from mundane understanding, the boundaries of flesh and limitations of physical senses, the effects of direct wand usage are not visible to the untrained human eye as even an experienced energy worker may find such visualization subtle and elusive like every other form of energy amplification and manipulation. Being able to truly see the art of wanding is intimately tied to the ability to sense and visualize energy, which is unique to each individual and varies from one practitioner to another. In reality several aspects of metaphysical wanding and its elegant casting should pass unnoticed to most, as the mastery of its forces is mirrored in the language of the invisible and the secrets of the unseen.

Servitors

The magick of servitors is intimately tied to the knowledge, skill and ability to raise entities crafted from raw vital energy. In most cases servitors are not sentient, being simplistic in nature and basic metaphysical operation with degrees of activity bound to the will of the conjurer, hence without a higher level of identity or independence but with a manifested reality in advanced magickal practice that is diverse and capable of fulfilling distinctive purposes from benign to malignant. There are important distinctions to understand between two major types of magickally-spawned entities described as low servitors and royal servitors.

A low servitor is a magickal entity manifested from conscious intent, projected will and vital energy. Its existence is bound to the mind and life force of the practitioner through an established symbiotic bond of a subtle nature where the raised entity serves the conjuring master in exchange for the energy that sustains it. This makes the maintenance of an active servitor a draining process that requires constant investment of subtle essence as the abilities and enduring properties of the entity will depend on the inner power, strong mind and channeled energy of the practitioner. As a result most low servitors are manifestly weak and only capable of simplistic magickal operations, however there are few capable of great power and complex ability which can become undoubtedly dangerous, requiring a cautious and responsible approach. Techniques and abilities that are applicable to subtle beings and astral entities from banishing to binding can usually be used with established servitors as well, however remain wary that servitors do not act alone and more importantly than handling a magickal servitor is being aware of the hidden master playing its silent song.

Many low servitors are metaphysically bound to a specific magickal object upon creation through techniques of ritual or active magick, aiding in their resilience to natural dissipation and also in the balancing of their chaotic nature in this realm. However, this esoteric contract of alchemical infusion is permanent and an attempt to move the servitor from one physical anchor into another results in its destruction.

Similar at a glance but profoundly different in nature and manifestation are what we describe as royal servitors, sometimes simply called servitors by the Asetians. Although unbrokenly bound to its creator and master like a standard low servitor the subtle entity of a royal servitor can be moved from an established physical vessel into a different but suitable magickal object, making for their existence far more enduring than any other raised metaphysical entity with the cunning knowledge to cheat death. Most importantly, true royal servitors are created through Asetian mysteries with the initiatory seeds of the Violet Flame in the alchemical Fire of life and creation, raising magickal beings that are far more sentient, aware and manifestly real than other known forms of servitors. As a branch of knowledge and mystical art that is characteristically Asetian this dark path of creational magick relies on sacred bonds and secretive wisdom that is only taught through oaths of honesty and loyalty, leading into advanced magick of obviously dangerous potential and higher power.

Albeit often unknown, the mysteries of royal servitors are closely related with the secrets and nature of the infamous Asetian wands and sacred talismans. The magick names often associated with those objects and the legendary notions that they fight and protect their masters with a will of their own are tied to the unique creational ability of Asetians to raise sentient magickal entities crafted from the purest energy of their souls and to infuse them in wands and talismans as a mighty extension of their subtle body, being described by those who have experienced their powers as feeling hauntingly alive. Although bound to their masters by unbreakable magick, these servitors raised with a divine spark of the Violet Flame have an independent energy field and their own identity. They do not require the recurrent drain of vital force to remain coherent and retain existence but still rely on such channeling as the fuel of life to imbue magickal power and ignite hidden abilities, in return being capable of inducing specialized vibrations, enhancing awareness and unleashing unique powers in the master.

When bound to a magick wand or personal talisman of an Asetian the servitor and its powers can only be wielded by its master, obeying no one and making for those tools only possible to be activated through the unique fingerprint of its belonging Asetian, remaining inert and dormant to everyone else. Unlike the properties of low servitors these empowered subtle beings can be bound to a different suitable object due to various reasons, like for example if a wand is crushed in battle or the talisman is physically — but not metaphysically — destroyed. As such there are royal servitors that endure lifetimes and although bound to the soul of their creator they are not truly immortal. However, most can be hardy, resilient and surprisingly powerful; to underestimate such force has proven to be the bane of many and at times capable of shaping the course of history. Lingering from one incarnation to another royal servitors adamantly follow their master who can bind their ethereal essence to another magickal object in each life, resuming their sacred service and loyal protection. All of this makes these creatures incredible adversaries, trusty advisors and sometimes even wise teachers, raising desire and envy amongst those who seek power and a reason behind incessant plotting, treason and war. The mysterious royal servitors and their sacred objects of hidden power have been the target of quests and plunder since immemorial times in the history of the Asetians, desired among opposing empires and considered a treasure beyond measure, often treated as one of the most precious possessions with worth higher than silver, gold and land. The illusive ability to wield a stolen talisman with a bound servitor has been obsessively sought by humans and other bloodlines for centuries and always met with absolute failure, leading some into madness and becoming consumed by these dark forces, losing themselves completely in the cryptic nature of such magick — that is the fate of those who seek to deface and exploit the magick of Aset as they are met with an illusion that leads only into decay and oblivion.

Throughout history the royal servitors of the Asetians and their talismans gave birth to a myriad of mythologies and esoteric beliefs that changed from culture to culture, finding in the Middle Eastern definition of genies one of the most recognizable examples. This is an anglicized term for the Arabic word jinn or djinn found in different Islamic texts that describe a race of supernatural creatures bound to special objects and that could only be wielded by their masters. Feared by their magickal powers the jinn were entities of fire, just like the older Asetian servitors were crafted from the Violet Flame that is the purest form of divine Fire. Later in history these sentient servitors spawned by Asetian masters were mirrored in the lore of daemons and popular interpretations of demonic entities, oftentimes presenting as a mirror of cultural and conceptual misunderstanding or a reflection of ignorance. Understanding the sources of knowledge and wisdom alongside their thorough but detached examination leads to a unique understanding of the present and a better awareness of the future.

Astral Projection

The ability to intentionally or spontaneously project spiritual and mental consciousness into another plane of existence and travel the realms of energy and subtlety is what is described as an out of body experience, commonly shortened as OBE and studied in occult science as the field of astral projection.

To enter a state of full projection the subconscious mind must be ready to leave the physical body and liberatingly receptive of its existence as a being of raw energy — the astral body. There are several techniques used to train and develop these abilities, each providing the practitioner with various results and capabilities. Benefiting from strong will and a balanced mind the activity of astral projection is not without its dangers, potentiating interaction with otherworldly creatures — entities native to those realms that do not incarnate in the plane of matter or sometimes even the spirits of the dead. However, there are distinct mechanisms and protective techniques that can be learned to ensure a certain degree of safety, although there is no real replacement for practical experience and the knowledge attained through personal investment.

It is important to understand that the soul of an incarnated spiritual traveller is never disconnected from the physical body or the material plane during any of the stages of projection and metaphysical separation, remaining linked through a subtle structure of natural origin described as the silver cord that retains a constant flux and influx of energy between the shell of matter and the astral body. Complete detachment from the physical body or the severing of the silver cord is not possible while incarnated as it constitutes a fundamental link between the spiritual and mundane that is required for the maintenance of life, dissipating upon death as the spirit is liberated from the chains and boundaries of the material body.

Astral beings and subtle entities are also capable of moving between realms, shifting their essence and living consciousness from one reality into another and sometimes projecting as low as the physical realm — the world of incarnation. Those events are often reflected as reports of paranormal sightings and personal experiences that those unaware may wrongly interpret as ghosts, spirits and demons. During the vast majority of cases those presences and manifestations are far from threatening and although some may experience fear when clashing with them that is oftentimes driven by ignorance and an instinctual reaction to the unknown. In truth, most ethereal beings projecting into the subtle layers of the physical realm are harmless, with some reaching this plane unconsciously drifting and unaware while others present a more defined identity with stronger awareness driven by unique agendas of their own.

While roaming the astral realm it is possible to discover a vast array of structures from simple to complex that are made exclusively out of energy, although they may seem incredibly real to the eyes of your mind. Those boundless kingdoms of immaterial reality are not linear, manifesting into existence through a constant process of renewal that establishes itself through a series of distinctive subtle layers. The ones of lower vibration exhibit structures that appear very similar to those found in the physical realm, from elements of landscape and nature to the artificial constructions of humanity and their intricate details of art, design and engineering.

As previously established the concept of thoughts is bound to energy given form and the incarnated minds of the living unconsciously raise and reinforce those subtle structures manifested in the astral plane as a mirror of their own distinctive interpretations of reality and reflex of their experiences. In these layers of lower vibration exploring seekers can also find certain parallels or reflections of their inner realms as those realities flow in a dance of attraction and repellence, leaving an imprint of fears, dreams and expectations often found in the depths of the psyche and projected into the astral plane by reinforced thought. Here proficient astral travelers craft creative structures, freely interact with energy and design their own magick, being the place where mystical gatherings are held. However, the energy in these realms is sparse and bound to dissipation and reshaping, never lost or gained but perpetually transformed.

Around the layers of increasingly higher vibration the energy gets denser and projecting beyond it becomes harder as an exotic world of subtle existence and invisible magick unfolds with exquisite beauty and newfound danger. It is here in these lands of sacred silence and profound mystery that the elusive Asetian temples of legend and myth can be found. Great adventures await those daring to enter such realms but also madness and chaos hide in the dark preying on those that approach them without honest respect.

Past Life Regression

The thorough study, wise examination and profound understanding of reincarnation and past lives represent a fundamental backbone in Asetian spirituality, philosophy and culture. As an initiatory tradition of mysteries that traces its origins to ancient history, Asetianism relies on accurate and verifiable documentation of past-life work attained through pioneering techniques of regression that potentiate the unlocking of sensitive information and events, providing a unique degree of historical understanding and evidence of facts and truth that were lost in time.

The Order of Aset Ka as an immortal legacy of Aset and enduring banner of Ancient Egypt survives through its metaphysical family that continuously answers the violet call life upon life, in a cycle of death and rebirth that determines the meaningful importance of mastery and development in this field of knowledge and branch of spiritual exploration, defining some of the most critical and significant secrets of the Asetians while safekeeping their beautiful history of darkness and light, passion and torment.

There are different viable techniques to successfully unlock a conscious regression, applicable to various circumstances and unique to the nature of each individual but all bound to a degree of complexity and understanding that make them dwell in some of the most advanced forms of magick and metaphysics. Exploring the reality of past-life magick is to open the way for a gargantuan journey that is not without peril, requiring a breaking and separation of the ego alongside an enlightened degree of awareness.

Insight into the past is often attained through the vaults of cosmic knowledge by accessing what is described as the akashic records where all history is stored in pure energy format. These metaphysical registers are the subtle tomes of reincarnation, located in the ethereal realm as a sacred place of knowledge and truth where all memories are safely stored and unadulterated. Access to such records presents no easy task as their recognition and interpretation is not intended while incarnated and bound to the living realm of matter. The gateways to such temples are well guarded by more than abominations and the halls that lead to their dungeons of thought are burning with trials that only the spiritually evolved can overcome.

Solely a true regression can bypass these natural barriers and plunge the consciousness deep into the fluid of the akashic records in an ethereal projection. These advanced practices are incredibly difficult to master and most seekers fail without even realizing. The traps of ego and the expectations of the subconscious are mighty adversaries that frequently break even the wise. Many attempting a regression without the required expertise or experience are pushed into their own inner plane or sometimes the creations of the astral realm, seeing results that are influenced by their dreams, fears and desires but not present in the ethereal layer where the akashic records are stored. That presents a deceptive pitfall of contemporary reality built on flawed understanding, where so many people have no true insight into past lives or their own spiritual truths but adamantly and blindly believe that they do. It is a facade of truth — a well crafted illusion of fate embraced by the weakness of expectation. We live in an illusive world where people gladly embrace delusion out of fear, ego and deceit.

Those dangers and obstacles of past-life regression must be firmly understood as the art of exploring the past can never be hindered by ego and to accept the comfort of false realities is against evolution, growth and the banners of truth so purposefully defended and enforced by the Asetians. The arsenal of magick and wisdom of Asetianism includes the most advanced and effective techniques of regression and past-life work; knowledge developed throughout the ages and perfected to unimaginable power. However, the results of these practices are not merely accepted without further research, being bound to the thorough examination that defines the roadmap of past exploration. A unique form of validation is possible according to the tradition of the elders in an exclusively Asetian process of triangulation, a safeguarded technique shrouded in secrecy due to its incredible potential and the inherent dangers of its abuse.

Asetianism is not a static tradition stagnated in time but a dynamic living culture that is in a permanent state of change, renewal and evolution, just like the very soul of the initiate. The mysteries of the Aset Ka are a legacy of immeasurable beauty and incomprehensible power but the path of the Asetians and their loyal Asetianists is a never-ending journey of discovery, profound understanding and ultimate liberation. The past that can be studied and unveiled through regression remains a sincere mirror of that truth.

Metaphysical Tattooing

The soul of an Asetian is at innermost essence fundamentally different from a human soul but beyond those spiritual hallmarks that are established by nature there is a unique metaphysical sigil that is permanently and perpetually engraved on the very core of each children of Aset, manifesting deeply within their immortal soul. This invisible mark of transcendence is an echo of the touch of Aset, Her breath of life and the everlasting Violet Flame — a symbol of family and sacred gift from the divine Mother to the Primordial three that established the origins of what is known today as metaphysical tattooing.

As an invisible seal of immeasurable power and significance within every Asetian, these marks are subtly chiseled through metaphysical techniques unknown to humanity. Dating back to the primordial days of an ancient culture the Asetians have mastered a secretive practice of permanently marking the essence of the soul in an alchemical process of definitive initiation and after millennia the mysteries of metaphysical tattooing remain a uniquely Asetian art bound to much desire and speculation. Independently of physical body and the diversity of their cloaks of matter the children of Aset are undeniably and unbrokenly Asetian for all eternity, so at biological birth and in every lifetime an Asetian already bears the metaphysical tattoo of this divine sigil.

What is also an integral part of their culture and conceptually or symbolically related with the subject being described is that during advanced stages of initiation an Asetian may conquer a physical representation of the sigil, an icon of true nature and immortal bloodline marked in black ink on the skin of the wrist as a tattoo designed in ritual and according to magickal tradition. Unlike anything practiced by outsiders this tattoo is no mere artwork drawn on the dermis but the result of higher spiritual magick attained through enlightenment and inner evolution; a corporeal branding linked to profound significance and universal keys of truth that are adversarial, challenging and utterly incomprehensible to a mortal mind.

However, these practices that incorporate a physical component should not be confused with the ability to mark the essence of the soul in the process that we have named metaphysical tattooing. The infamous Dark Mark of the Asetians, although shrouded in mystery among educated occultists and a restricted taboo in certain spiritual circles, remains an elusive subject surrounded by rumor and fascination. Its history and legend have influenced countless traditions throughout eras of the past and cultures of the present, giving origin to practices of witchcraft and esoteric traditions that may appear similar at surface but are undoubtedly different in essence, sometimes disguisedly explored in popular culture, lore and even fiction.

Subtle Surgery

Beyond the darkness of their magick and destruction that silently lurks within the chaotic nature of these inhuman beings the dormant healing potential in every Asetian is undeniable and it presents a metaphysical force not to be underestimated or neglected. Interacting with energy, shaping subtle vibrations, crafting the invisible and designing magickal intent is the Asetian way of life; an inborn talent that manifests as spontaneously as breathing and as naturally as thought.

During ancient times of past eras the knowledge of the Aset Ka was developed as science, medicine and wisdom while the Asetians were approached as healers, mystics and therapists. Their unique ability to sense illness, ward off disease, promote healing and potentiate cure is the substance of legend. Those techniques, alongside an acute understanding of the symbiotic dance between physical ailment and spiritual condition, have been lost and rediscovered throughout the centuries, while opposers and adversaries of

Asetianism nurtured their twisted desires for such knowledge to remain hidden and become nothing more than a forgotten dot in lost history.

In the field of vibrational medicine and the manyfold variants of holistic healing that involve direct or indirect manipulation of energy, the metaphysical approach to subtle surgery distinguishes itself as one of the most complex and advanced disciplines of study. The underlying techniques of subtle surgery are extensive and of broad application, requiring not only mastery of metaphysics and subtle anatomy but a profound understanding of how those branches of knowledge intertwine and relate with the triple foundation of mind, body and spirit. The application and methodology of subtle surgery in advanced medical practice is far reaching, allowing for the safe and efficient extraction of subtle tumors, the surgical removal of malignant attachments, and the cauterization of leaking energy links and open wounds in the subtle body, among other conditions that require specialized care and treatment.

The fundamental tools of subtle surgery are those of energy manipulation as the hands, eyes and tendrils make extensive use of the characteristics and qualities of the related Shen. More advanced instruments are also used in a proper surgical setting, such as amplifying wands attuned to specific vibrations according to the condition or area being treated, as well as various types of minerals capable of amplification or emission under desired frequencies. During the last decades technology and research within the laboratories of the Aset Ka has also led to the development of modern tools that improve the experience and procedures of subtle surgery, such as intensity meters for measured levels of life force, energy inductors and cauterizing breakers, vibrational controllers and other unique instruments of metaphysical science and applied subtle medicine.

However, even though a vast range of tools and intricate devices are modernly available and at the disposal of a qualified subtle surgeon, the safety and effectiveness of such metaphysical work alongside responsible prevention or minimization of collateral damage, common postoperative complications, reactive subtle infection and energetic collapse are strongly dependent on inborn ability, personal talent and an experienced medical background in practical metaphysics.

It must be overstated that these techniques and instruments should never be used lightly or without a thorough examination, often applicable as a last resort to treatment when less invasive methodologies have failed. There are inherent and intricate dangers to the process of subtle surgery even when executed responsibly and with proper knowledge, which can lead to a vast array of complications emerging from surgical procedure or manifesting at later stages during recovery. A resolute decision in submitting to any form of invasive treatment — subtle or otherwise — should always be rooted in personal will, informed action and independent choice allied to the cautious advice of an experienced practitioner with knowledge of the complete historical background of the patient. This specialist should closely follow the entire length of the recovery process in order to minimize unexpected complications and ensure the best rehabilitation possible.

Metaphysical sterilization of the surgical environment is essential to a safe procedure of subtle surgery, whether in the case of a minor or major intervention. Just like skin and biological tissue are used in physical surgery it is also common for a subtle surgeon to shape and manipulate the inner energy of a patient in order to treat an open wound, recreate damaged structures in the subtle body or forge temporary channels to operate as energy vessels during recovery. It is important that raw energy extracted from the patient is used to avoid potential complications due to rejection. In a delicate situation, when the subtle body is frail and vulnerable from surgical intervention, it may not tolerate an attachment or injection of energy with an incompatible fingerprint into the internal structures and energy organs, especially while natural defenses are severed. In situations of wound cauterization or when the removal of subtle structures is required the usage of outer energy from a different source is unlikely to cause problems of rejection, however that may hinder the recovery process and make it considerably slower but it remains a viable option that should be under consideration when the energy levels of the patient are diminished or compromised.

One of the most complex and dangerous procedures of subtle surgery is tied to any form of Shen intervention, as these vibrating structures represent a vital organ in the subtle system, so extreme caution is advised and such an approach should never be equated without fluent experience and mastered teaching.

Vibrational High Magick
The art and practice of vibrational high magick is a concept that I have established in my teachings and developed through my work that describes some of the most intricate techniques, powers and abilities of advanced Asetian magick. Its practical elements are out of the scope of this grimoire but an accurate reference remains essential alongside the definition of legitimate concept and truthful application. This terminology has been adopted, mimicked and even misinterpreted by other branches of the occult that look into Asetianism for inspiration but its foundations remain undeniably Asetian and misguided interpretations should not be confused with the genuine origins of such a complex field of esoteric wisdom.

Vibrational high magick unites sacred alchemy with the mastery of energy manipulation in a song of spiritual understanding, initiation and intimate touch on the cosmic fabric of boundless potential. Not all but some of these abilities are exclusively Asetian and require a profound awareness and comprehension of powers that cannot be consciously wielded by human souls. However, even those skills or gifts that can be trained and explored by those fluent in the arts of magick and familiar with the illuminated aspects of our invisible science still require the elements of initiation and guidance from an experienced master.

A portion of these techniques that fall under the elite category of vibrational high magick require an immeasurable flow of energy and channeled vibrational reserves to be effective and wield the extraordinary results that they can attain, allowing us to overpower energies and control situations that are chaotic and dynamic at levels that make them otherwise absolutely uncontrollable. With such a high energy requirement these techniques can easily drain an imbalanced subtle system and take a spiritual toll even on those experienced with psychic feeding and vampiric draining, leaving one vulnerable to potential attacks, malignant attachments and offensive magick.

Under proper control and enlightened mastery an Asetian can wield those powers and attain their hidden magick in incredibly rare manifestations; overcoming unbreakable obstacles, gaining unbelievable insight and giving shape, craft and design to empowered elemental magick that can allow them to control the weather, influence nature and manipulate crowds unlike anything ever seen. The advanced elements of Asetian royal servitors, active wanding and talismanic empowerment can also be considered to be inclusive components of vibrational high magick, as those practices surpass the fundamental workings of energy manipulation and reach the cutting-edge realm of unconventional magick with all of its known and unknown associated dangers.

The epic scope, unimaginable potential and limitless possibility of vibrational high magick should not in any way be overtaken by selfish desires, deluded expectations or the fictional aspects of popular culture. These abominating powers and elusive gifts are the substance of sacredness, embodying the purity found on the silent blood of immortals. Only fools among mundanes would ever interpret the invisible fabric of this magick as devices of exhibition or a force that pays service to the ignorance of Self since these are swords of spiritual evolution and daggers of ethereal growth, not the glittering toys of mortals.

To understand and even explore the most basic theories of vibrational high magick one must embrace the teachings and mysteries of the Aset Ka in absolute honesty, dedicated commitment and balanced strength, unveiling the inner and outer tools that can ignite the sacred spark and unleash the core of full potential hiding within every Asetian.

Initiation

The misunderstood nature of initiation represents a central and vital element of Asetianism that establishes this path not only as a culture built upon growth and evolution but also as a spiritual tradition of genuine immortal power. To grasp the infinite intricacies of Asetian initiation and stare on its illuminated eyes of indescribable silence stands as the most elusive of magickal arts; knowledge that sits on the sacred altar that is the essence of the *Violet Throne*.

In popular occultism the often-explored notions of attunement and initiation are sometimes used interchangeably even though they represent rather distinctive approaches to metaphysical work and intrinsically different concepts of magickal and spiritual operation. Both practices are commonly associated with a ritualistic approach although that understanding is incomplete and limitative as ritual is not a determining factor in the elusive path of initiation.

An attunement is a metaphysical practice that synchronizes an individual being, esoteric tool or magickal object to a unique energy and specific vibration. Although it can be used in parallel with advanced techniques its power and scope is not as extreme or as dangerous as a true initiation. The practice of attunement is frequently used in different branches of energy work and vibrational metaphysics as it is found in the example of Reiki from Japan, where the threefold initiatory system stems from a simple method of attunement applied to the subtle body that is intended to open, rebalance and synchronize the Shen centers with universal energy used in this practice for healing and scanning, making for a more effective exploration of energy by the initiate.

Advanced techniques of attunement are regularly used by the Asetians in the maintenance of magick wands, sacred talismans and elaborated constructs, influencing the specialized use of energy manipulation and being instrumental in the alchemical equilibrium of Ka, the mutation and reinforcing of aura vibrations as well as the opening of specific Shen.

On the other end of spiritual understanding lie the mysteries of Asetian initiation that encompass a life-changing experience of profound transformation. An initiation is a rite of passage but also infinitely more, imbuing the practitioner with newfound understanding and an unseen set of magickal tools that can only be wielded with wisdom. Initiations manifest in many shapes and are found with elevated importance within a myriad of esoteric traditions

✝

and spiritual paths. However, throughout history, their sacredness and purity has oftentimes decayed into an object of power, tool of deceit and a false method of illumination, making those initiations ultimately useless in countless cases. Baptism in Christianity presents one of such classic examples that turned the transformational properties and spiritual value of an initiation into something inutile and of no magickal significance but it is not alone as true initiations are incredibly rare in this day and age.

A genuine initiation is a dangerous process that in many cases represents a perpetual bond that cannot be broken or have its magick undone, so it should always be approached with conscious determination, educated resolve and cautious responsibility. Every occultist worthy of such a word wields awareness and wisdom, knowing not to commit into senseless initiations or empty initiatory pursuits, although real occultists are rarer than most may realize. This understanding should also aid an inexperienced seeker into distinguishing a truthful initiation from every other form of false initiations so abundantly found nowadays.

To an Asetian the most sacred initiation is that of Khenmet — the dark kiss of immortality and creational breath of infinite potential. Often misunderstood by humanity this is no mere secret of illumination or path of understanding but an alchemical process that changes life forever. However, that does not represent the only initiatory stage in the evolutionary life of an Asetian but just the very beginning; the early steps into darkness and the becoming of truest Self.

> *"The ability to see, interpret and understand the mysteries that lie hidden in plain sight is what we designate by an initiation. The concept of initiation is*

*one of the most misunderstood in occult studies,
sometimes even exploited by those that do not understand
the true nature of initiatory magick. In simple terms
someone initiated — and this applies to all mystery
schools and occult societies worthy of their name —
refers to an individual that is able to see what others
cannot. This does not necessarily imply that through
initiation someone must develop any sort of supernatural
power that would turn him into something greater than
the surrounding unaware population. It simply means
that they are the ones who were taught the hidden keys
— the mystery — that would provide them with the
knowledge to see what is hidden in plain sight. Quite
simple... But also quite sophisticated. It may be seen as a
road for the becoming of greatness, but such power comes
from understanding and the subtle truth found within,
not by an exercise of mystical power."*

Book of Orion, Liber Aeternus

The most elevated gateways of spiritual initiation are bound to universal keys of understanding, unveiled slowly through a natural process of discovery, commitment and profound transformation that ignite an inner revelation that is subtle but also life-changing. Without hard work, courage and a form of liberation that can only be attained through honesty a full initiation cannot manifest nor complete its cycle of learning.

In Asetianism — being a spiritual path of nature aligned with the never-ending unfolding of universal truth in its purest manifestation — initiates often find a unique method of transformation, learning and achievement that we have defined as organic initiations. These pathways of understanding are lessons taught dynamically by the essence of the cosmos, the experiences of life and the fluidity of nature, manifesting the intricate road of every Asetian and Asetianist in their journey of infinite evolution. These chain reactions of liberation and rediscovery operate upon the innermost layers of Self, deep into the very nature of the soul as ineffable keys of transcendence. This makes the life, identity and understanding of an initiate an ever-changing process of dynamism and chaos, as what is seen today may only be accurately understood years from now and the wise should restrain from judgment, assumption and premature conclusions.

The profound mysteries of organic initiations represent a living element of the Asetian tradition and legacy of the Aset Ka, vital to the growth, development and ultimate liberation that opens the invisible doorways into the rare path of enlightenment. These notions and awareness, so obscure and unattainable to outsiders who cannot grasp beyond our veil of immortality, are a hallmark of the warrior that lives inside every Asetian; a divine gift that can only be achieved through dedicated honesty and selfless loyalty.

The essence of Aset cannot accurately be described by words or explained in books. Her legacy surpasses the limited understanding of spirituality, magick and power — the Aset Ka is that legacy. The spiritual significance and universal keys of the Asetians represent infinitely more than a book, cannot be found in buildings or objects and ultimately transcend beyond the mundane idea of an occult Order. They manifest silently within, emerging from a timeless veil of mysteries that remain elegantly safeguarded within the initiatory secrets of the Aset Ka, profoundly concealed for millennia behind intricate doors that unlock only for those who are worthy.

Because to everyone else... We will never exist.

BOOK OF ORION
LIBER AETERNUS

Introduction

E m Hotep.
This magickal grimoire is one of the several *Libri* from the Order of Aset Ka used internally as part of its initiatory teachings and occult curriculum.

As the author of the initiatory text, teachings and literary work presented in *Liber Aeternus* — commonly referred as the *Book of Orion* due to the triple nature of its spiritual mysteries — I have been dedicated to the revision and rewrite of my original material, used internally, in order to reflect the paradigm and spiritual formulae for the now flourishing spiritual age — the *Djehuty of the Serpent* — and thereby making it possible for open publication, while still retaining its wisdom and use to any scholar of the Asetian tradition and other students of the mysteries. Although updated in content and form, much initiatory material was included along with secrets on the very nature of spiritual initiation and the unveiling of esoteric keys usually hidden from the seeker without an elevated rank within an occult Order, preserving its potential to other Asetians and to every dedicated occult student. New information was also added in order to aid the initiate with the magickal knowledge he might not possess as well as to provide further study material to those that may not be familiar with some of the most advanced occult concepts being presented within this work, along with the inclusion of images, esoteric schemes and visual artwork created by Tânia Fonseca, including some of her rare hand-drawn pieces of Ancient Egyptian art never before seen in print. The cover artwork of the original book uses an actual image of the Orion Nebula, taken over 500 km above the Earth by the Hubble Space Telescope, and was included in the project with permission from NASA and the European Space Agency. Located over 1300 light years away deep into the galaxy, the nebula found south of the Orion constellation belt is known for its beautiful violet and red coloration. Such inspiring art from nature lost in the body of Nut is a cradle for the birth of stars. As philosophical as this may sound, the designation is actually quite literal as it represents the closest location of star formation to Earth and has been extensively studied by astronomers — who call it M42 or Messier 42 — providing a wealth of scientific information relating to the formation of the Universe. How revealing that such a timeless symbol of spiritual creation known for having inspired the ancients has now become a provider of answers for both modern scientists as well as contemporary occultists...

The *Djehuty of the Serpent* marks a very important shift in global consciousness but particularly in terms of spiritual awareness and ruling forces for the new spiritual era, as it was outlined in further detail in the published work *Asetian Bible*. It is a time of spiritual liberation, personal growth and inner potential of the subtle over the mundane as the path for balance and understanding. As the *Book of Orion* is my third published work to be released to the general public, its timing and relevance are perfectly in tune with the magickal formulae of the sacred *Three*, explored in depth within this work.

Psychology of Wisdom

As with all my works and teachings, I expect and welcome criticism. Intelligent criticism is a tool that can enhance learning for both the apprentice and the master, while negativism and superficial condemnation is nothing but an effortless demonstration on the power that our culture and influence has to affect and move others, presenting a valuable lesson to the initiate. Five years after the release of the *Asetian Bible* it has become clear the shocking effect that some fields of knowledge and wisdom can have on people, particularly on weaker minds. The cautious study and observation of such reactions has served as example and learning to many seekers for the past few years and will remain a valuable lesson in history, as while the book became a magickal tool to some and actually changed lives with its violet touch, it also served to bring forth the very best and very worst in people. That alone is a recognizable Asetian signature, present in all forms of Asetian work, art and in the very core of our being. As an elemental force of nature, this path brings forth the devastating truth in people, no matter how painful that may be: without masks, fears or prejudice. It shakes the keystone of their mind to the heart of their spirit, breaking all conditioning and destroying the superfluous, leaving only what is real behind. Many people are afraid to accept reality and have no courage to look into the divine mirror of the Gods to see their own reflection staring back at them. This leads to great imbalance, both mentally and spiritually, which often manifests in lies and dishonesty. It is a form of spiritual enslavement that vehemently opposes growth and self-development. With this in mind I shall now quote a brief paragraph from my introductory text published in the *Asetian Bible*, since its message was not only revealed to be precognitively accurate: it is just as relevant today as it was back then, or even centuries ago.

If someone will criticize our philosophies, beliefs, practices or any other thing related with our own nature, life and metaphysical approach, it is because in some way they feel affected by us. Or else they wouldn't be spending their own energies attacking someone they probably don't even know and that surely would never feel attacked or intimidated by them. So, in this way, and often unconsciously, they are changed by us. We made them move and act just because of what we are and represent. That is our chaotic nature.

The common society will continue to look at us and other occultists as if we are evil incarnate. Many fear what we represent and the things we stand for. As irrational as that fear may be, I believe it is often attached to the manifestation of ignorance. Mankind fears what they don't understand. The words *mystery* and *secret* are often enough to cause discomfort, let alone taking the step into the unknown and having the courage to accept darkness as an evolutionary force of wisdom.

I have always taught the younger and less experienced occult students that hatred, when directed towards them, is one of the greatest forms of flattery and boost to their ego. You can never express hate or move against someone who is not meaningful to you, so those situations are powerful indicators to pinpoint those that you have inspired in life, and who are often unaware on how their negativity is actually expressing a hidden form of admiration and praise. It is an interesting lesson that many have become increasingly familiar with over the years and one that has become particularly clear with the publications from the Aset Ka. Coming from different backgrounds and serving distinct agendas people have expressed opinions against the Asetian culture and beauty, some with respect and nobility while others with pain and anger, making it even a part of their life's crusade. At the same time, others have rejoiced in tremendous praise of our works and legacy, showing that while the reactions to our tradition are so diverse, there is one message that they all bring forth together — the Asetians inspire people to move, create and react. In all forms of expression and manifestation they prove themselves unable to be indifferent to the Aset Ka, never willing to ignore it, and so as a chaotic lesson from nature their spirituality and beliefs are shaken by the violet catalysts that are Asetian art and energy.

As a spiritual force of continuous growth, freedom and empowerment, our elitist message of calmness, balance and dignity remains the same: do not fight or oppose hatred, but instead use it as a lesson to others on your own accomplishments and power, as we have done so often across the ages with our signature indifference and silence. Insult is the ultimate expression of fear and insecurity. It is a clear echo of frustration and the herd mentality, often motivated by rejection. When faced with the wisdom of an evolved mind, haters lose all their power and become mere servants of your own determined will. Unknowingly, they pay you a valuable service. Use them wisely.

"From the deepest desires often come the deadliest hate."
Socrates

My experience as a writer has taught me that the strongest offenses almost invariably come from the ones behind the highest praise. Such vain attacks are usually driven by unstable fans, those you moved and inspired, not by someone that does not care, and are frequently triggered by obsession, rejection and paranoia. That is why I believe that, despite being just emotional food for the ego-centered authors, such forms of criticism and negativity can ultimately be a simple expression of flattery and praise to any accomplished artist. Life is too beautiful, special and brief to be wasted on negativity and ill intentioned people. Break free from the unhealthy influence of those that desire to bring you down to their level and instead rise with class and embrace life to its fullest, valuing every single drop of what it has to offer. Don't take anything for granted, as life is an edification of impermanence. Never surrender to conformism and always fight for what you believe to be fair. Do not fear falling, being judged or making mistakes, as those are the experiences that teach us the very best lessons in life. Remember that you will never be able to please everyone, but most importantly, you don't have to! Simply being true to yourself is already quite an accomplishment where many fail to succeed. Make every day count and celebrate it with joy, no matter what creed, belief system or religion you follow. That is a vital principle of Asetian philosophy, so often underestimated when the focus is not balanced and placed within.

As an occultist and author I have been target of the highest praise as well as the lowest judgment and defamation, as happens with anyone that has created some level of work worthy of reference. While I have always dealt with such occurrences with both indifference and understanding, simply observing how criticism — both positive and negative — unfolds and how the mind reacts to rumor and outside influences, such examination has proven to be an interesting study on the psychology of the human mind. It is quite surprising to verify that most situations develop from people who have an inborn habit of divinizing the ones they admire. Worship and fundamentalist admiration quickly turns into hatred and anger when you are not corresponded. When the mind fears what the heart desires the easier road may manifest by lying to oneself through convincing thought that the object of deepest desire simply does not exist, or that if it does it must have been fabricated to deceive. It is a psychological defense mechanism from a mind that fears experiencing pain, which is a form of self-enslavement.

Some see us like a powerful entity that is beyond reach, which makes no mistakes, sees everything and knows all the answers. This couldn't be further from the truth, as one of the first steps of wisdom is the realization of how little we know and how small we are. I'm no exception. Such situations become even more visible with artists that have struggled to avoid fame and, when dealing with the inevitable public exposure, have chosen instead to embrace a fulfilling private life, such as myself. This happens not only with published authors, but it is common ground with every individual that moves in a field that takes their work to a level that reaches so many different people all over the world. It is inevitable. Someone you deify to a level of obsession is bound to become your greatest demon and personification of evil at some point in time. This is why I tend to discard both the highest praise and the lowest abuse. They are both biased evaluations of your work and merit, and none truly mirrors the factual truth or is the result of fair judgment. If readers, followers or fans would see their admired artists as equals, there would be no obscene praise to the point of ridicule or intentional lies and defamation to the point of absolute vilification. That is because they would see you simply as another soul bound to this realm; that just like them can make mistakes, have qualities and imperfections, and experience good and bad days. We cry. We laugh. We love. Just like you, we will also die someday…

Being a respected author, prominent occult scholar, spiritual teacher, religious leader or any other title that may be brought upon someone — and titles mean absolutely nothing — does not mean that one has all the answers or knows everything. No one does, really. This applies to everyone, from any background and walking any path of life. Learning should always be a never-ending journey; and I can only speak for myself, as I learn something new every single day of my life, often finding the most valuable lessons in the subtler things. Learning is a permanent passion that I intend to nurture until the end of my days.

I know this is one of those messages that sounds profound and people can resonate with, but on the next day get beaten down by their ego and fall into the same traps again. People often close their eyes when the message does not suit their agendas or comply with their expectations. In other words, people try to ignore the inconvenient truths about themselves. Still, the message will remain here, immortalized in paper and ink, for those who are open to change and growth. My work has been through the commitment to honesty by giving people the magickal tools of awareness, which alone do not create their enlightenment, but simply aid in the long road that is their own personal spiritual journey. We may open the doors, but it is always up to the individual whether to sit or to walk.

The students of the Asetian path, as well as occultists from many other serious traditions, are commonly described as rebels, revolutionists and sometimes even insurrectionists. Let me tell you, you must care not for smaller opinions that do not seek understanding before judgment. The path of Asetianism, as a path of the Wise, is not for everyone. If you can feel it within your soul and have a deep desire to embrace it, and if through this culture you can rise to become something greater, then you can only be proud. The world has never nurtured tolerance for beings of deeper thought or for the souls that reach higher. Asetians are the silent scholars unveiling the path of spiritual immortality and the protectors of arcane knowledge. They may rightfully fear you as anyone able to See should be feared, but rest assured that this is not a path of rebellion but simply a path of Truth.

Mysteries of Orion
The term *Sebayt* is an old designation for a very specific form of Ancient Egyptian literature developed in the temples by the hierophants and passed on to the younger initiates as they progressed through the ladders of self-development and initiation into the higher

mysteries, with a few only accessible to the pharaoh himself. Scholars believe the word to mean *teachings,* and those documents were seen as true *Books of Life.*

The old Sebayt documents held the mysteries of life and reincarnation through the means of encoded words, an art the priests and priestesses of the ancient temples learned to master in order to keep the sacred information safe. This information was seen as highly valuable, in a time when spirituality and magick held a greater power than that of the physical force found in the armies. Some of these Sebayt are still preserved on papyrus scrolls and are property of modern museums, being for the most part copies of earlier works that got changed, adapted and mutated as mankind evolved and intervened in the spiritual process.

The text we present in this work is not a general Sebayt for the common people, but an *Asetian Sebayt* for the serious occult student that is dedicated to his development and growth through the Asetian mysteries. It is also not a translation of older texts, nor a revamp of ancient religious material, but something written in order to properly reflect the underlying mechanisms of spiritual development that are in tune with the occult formulae from the previous and current *Djehuty,* where the only exception can be found in the contents of the *Book of Sakkara* that contains magickal spells from the *Pyramid Texts.* The *Book of Orion* presents a complex framework of initiation that takes years to study and lifetimes to master, opening a door to the mysteries of the Universe and to the ever-changing alchemy of Death, Life and Rebirth. Do not expect to see the secrets of life revealed in a simple fashion or a direct manner. Instead, study it only if your commitment to the path of the elders is strong and determined. If you are seeking quick answers and basic occult literature or magickal recipes, please look elsewhere, as this book wasn't crafted for your mindset. Approach it with no expectations, or its apparent simplicity will deceive and misguide you. It is certainly not a tool for everyone.

The *Book of Orion*, as its name implies, is a triple grimoire. This means that it is comprised of three minor tomes used by the Aset Ka and compiled in a single volume. The three tomes that bring this *Liber* to life are the *Book of Giza*, the *Book of Ipet Resyt* and the *Book of Sakkara*, all of them being distinctive in content and function.

The **Book of Giza** is the core of *Liber Aeternus*, containing the central teachings of this work and the initiatory framework that it can provide. The first book itself is divided into three further sections, as the number *Three* expresses the mystic symbolism and spiritual formulae that it proposes to teach through its initiatory message. Worthy of reference and study is that there are three stars found in the astronomical belt of the Orion constellation that comprises the natural sigil of Orion. This is also expressed in the physical structures erected thousands of years ago in the Giza necropolis, in Egypt, known as *The Pyramids*. These three monuments of Ancient Egyptian origin and timeless power surprisingly reflect the three stars of Orion mirrored above in the night sky. Together they express the central Hermetic teachings from Thoth, often resumed in the passage *"As Above, so Below"* and its mysteries are as profound as they are complex.

The three magickal texts that form the *Book of Giza* are the *Sebayt of Khufu*, the *Sebayt of Khafre* and the *Sebayt of Menkaure*, ancient symbols of the eternal cycle of Death, Life and Rebirth, as well as the major steps of initiation to personal enlightenment. Each Sebayt is composed by thirty-three revelations, further developing on the triple formula of Orion. During its study the initiate will uncover profound lessons on life and the ways of honor that are very much universal and sometimes lacking in humanity, which just like a true Sebayt of the elder days makes this section of the work an actual book of Life and Death for those willing to learn and not to fear. This text is the most cryptic in the whole book and its interpretation should never be approached lightly or literally, as its coded message is both initiatory and revealing. Its study can only prove to be fruitful when done in a spiritual and individual way, with due caution given its subjective nature and the inherent potential for misinterpretation. A first reading is likely to confuse even the most sophisticated student, but after the examination of the following *Libri* included in this grimoire certain keys present in the Sebayt text will slowly start to flourish within the aware mind. The message that can be unveiled within its study is unique and therefore intimate and exclusive to each individual. Rest assured, its hidden wisdom will guide the humble and deceive the selfish. In Asetianism, the three Sebayt can be paralleled with the archetypes from the Lineages of the Asetian Bloodline — Serpent, Scarab and Scorpion, as well as the three separate ways in which subtle energy can be decomposed in metaphysical practice. In terms of Asetian theology, they express the triple nature of Aset — the *Asetian Holy Trinity.*

Under a Kabbalistic perspective, the Sebayt from the *Book of Giza* can be seen as literary expressions associated with the three higher sephiroth in the Tree of Life — Kether, Chokmah and Binah — which are present in the realm of Atziluth, the reality that the Hebrew sages described as the land of emanations and the world of archetypes. They are pure manifestations located above the Abyss of the false sephirah of Da'ath, away from the macrocosmic reality of the manifest world. While approaching this paradigm we have the first realization on how the Kabbalah, as a spiritual technology independent of dogma, can reflect the Asetian mystical system in a very intricate way. As the first sephirah — Kether, meaning Crown in Hebrew — represents the first manifestation of the indefinable veil of Ain Soph, we can see how it resonates with the spiritual essence of Horus as found in Ancient Egyptian myth, the first breath of Aset to be formed. Consequentially, the sephiroth two and three — Chokmah, meaning Wisdom and Binah, meaning Understanding — develop in the Tree of Life as archetypical echoes of the two hidden sisters of Horus, studied in the Asetian tradition as the Primordial Scarab and the Primordial Scorpion; the dual and opposed forces that, when merged, express the foundation of Horus the Elder. These three manifestations that the Hebrew mystics described as the supernal triad, found as the higher sephiroth in the Tree of Life, when united as one single entity express an adequate conceptual representation of the divine veil that is Aset. Following the formation of the Tree of Life through the fragmentation of energy and transmutational process of reincarnation, those three spheres of divine existence have their reflection manifested beneath the gates of the Abyss, as the sephiroth four, five and six — Chesed, Geburah and Tiphareth; Mercy, Strength and Beauty in Hebrew.

If you feel confused by the drawn philosophical connections between the Ancient Egyptian mystery tradition and the Hebrew esoteric system, or if you are new to the study of Kabbalistic mysticism, do not feel overwhelmed by the apparently foreign language used above as those concepts will be explained and developed within the book, particularly in the dissertation on the Tree of Life found in *Liber* יסוד. Such mysteries and subjective occult concepts will be studied in detail and in a progressive manner within the contents of this work while the reader will be taught how to interpret and use the Tree of Life, as well as understand the spiritual wisdom behind such secrets and how they interconnect with the different layers of Kabbalistic thought.

Having said that, it should also be stated that being fluent in the language and wisdom of the Kabbalah is not entirely necessary in order to be able to learn from the *Book of Giza*. This introduction serves to demonstrate the depth and complexity of the knowledge found in its three Sebayt and how universal this gnosis is, reflecting the very nature of spirituality and the fabric of immortal consciousness. So keep that in mind while studying this text, as it was originally developed for students who have undergone some level of initiation and spent a considerable part of their lives studying the mysteries, not only from the Kabbalah but also from countless spiritual traditions of the world and the occult knowledge taught by different mystery schools.

May this also serve as a message, inspiration and incentive, so that when the reader reaches a point of frustration and self-disappointment during the process of growth through this book, he should remember that not only what he is currently studying was created for an advanced level of understanding, as most importantly should be the realization that reaching this far in his studies is already quite an accomplishment, further than the vast majority of people will ever attain. As a student of the occult, the seeker should never forget to question everything and not take knowledge for granted. The occult world is clouded behind a veil of confusion and insecurity, where people often pass their own opinions and interpretations as factual truth; this should be avoided, as while educated debate can be a fruitful tool for the committed student, it may also turn into a sea of misunderstanding when the veil between what is hypothetical and what is true mingles. Being a victim of rumor and falsehood is the fall of an unaware mind, so if your intentions are sincere and your quest for wisdom is genuine, always seek the river that is closer to the source in the mountain, where the water runs free, fresh and pure.

The second magickal document found in *Liber Aeternus* is the **Book of Ipet Resyt** and it incorporates Asetian scripture, an initiatory document with a profound magickal sigil, accurate scientific information on the astrology of Orion, a detailed explanation on the wisdom of the Kabbalah and the formation and use of the Tree of Life, as well as a selection of Asetian poetry of particular spiritual and historical relevance, that together provide important study material for the initiate.

As reference on the nature of this particular book, *Ipet Resyt* are the old words in the Ancient Egyptian language for the Temple of Luxor, where a vital part of this work was written and a place of central significance in the old Asetian Empire in Kemet. It translates to *The Southern Sanctuary* and it was once one of the main Asetian temples that held an important sanctuary to its priesthood.

The first text presented in this second book is *The Touch of Khonsu* and it includes a unique initiatory mantra traditionally only provided to higher initiates of the Asetian path. It is a brief document that is bound to be polemical and raise misunderstanding due to its simplicity. At its core it presents an ancient spell in the secret language of Serkem, as was uttered by Khonsu in the supreme sanctuary of Em-Waset. For those who may not be familiar with the concept, Serkem is a magickal language used within the Asetian temples in the practice of magick, prayer and initiation, being connected with the Ancient Egyptian concept of *Heka*. The name of the language results from the syncretism of two Ancient Egyptian words — Serket and Kem — meaning *Scorpion* and *Black*, respectively. Through its study and meditation each Asetianist is highly advised to avoid the immaturity of falling into its apparently simplistic song and remain aware in order to prevent being deceived by its seemingly benign call.

✝

Following this elemental document we have three distinctive works — *Liber יסוד*, *Liber Sigillum 333* and *Liber Vox I*, the last one being a compilation of seven poems inspired by Asetian history and mythology.

Liber Sigillum 333 is one of the gems unleashed in this magickal grimoire and provides the reader with the great revelation of *Sigillum 333*; a powerful magickal device developed within the Aset Ka that embodies the full mysteries of Orion in a single sigil, holding within its symbolism a whole world of wisdom. This *Liber* provides an in-depth study of the magickal seal, educating the reader on the full symbolic set being present along with its complex magickal correlations. It also unveils three major initiations in the Orion mysteries, with elements that were held internally in countless esoteric societies throughout history and are now explored in detail. An English translation of the full text was included, along with the original initiatory document in Portuguese, as studied by some of the members from the Order of Aset Ka.

While it is not internal policy to provide such a revealing study in open publication, nor a detailed explanation of initiatory sigils to non-initiated students, we are opening the hidden gates of wisdom in this case, as it is our belief that such information can provide an invaluable resource to our readers in terms of their spiritual growth and magickal understanding. It also serves as a clear echo of our presence in this new era — the *Djehuty of the Serpent* — with its enlightening message of awareness, growth and commitment to truth, which are values nurtured so dearly by all of us at the Aset Ka and ones that humanity must learn to incorporate into their own spiritual path, no matter where their personal road may lead them.

Due to the complex nature of *Sigillum 333* and the potential problems it may present to the occult adept seeking its understanding,

I have decided to include my own *Liber* יסוד in the *Book of Ipet Resyt*, as it is a primer on the wisdom of the Kabbalah that may shed some light on the often subjective concepts of Kabbalistic mysticism, as well as its deep and sometimes surprising associations with our own magickal system you have all learned to recognize in Asetianism. It teaches the major principles of Kabbalistic thought as it develops the magick behind the Hebrew language and how the ancient mystics used this system in order to explain the creation of the Universe. It approaches the formation of the Tree of Life in a clear and structured way, along with several images that visually demonstrate what is being explained in further detail. It explores the multilayered reality of Hebrew mysticism and the many applications of such gnosis, along with its intimate relationship with the Tarot, the universal fragmentation and transmutation of energy, the structure of the different layers of reality and thought, the creation of the Lineages and the initiatory nature of the soul in its quest for enlightenment. If the reader is not fluent in these subjects and intricate branch of the occult, then the study of *Liber* יסוד is highly recommended before venturing into the contents of *Liber Sigillum 333*. These two *Libri* of both Ancient Egyptian and Hebrew inspiration seal the *Book of Ipet Resyt* in glory and power.

It is also important to remind our readers that documents such as *Liber Sigillum 333* are traditionally provided to students after years of study, and are never available prior to initiation, so such information is seeing the light of day in open publication for the first time in history. Despite the potential danger inherent to the release of this kind of knowledge, like the contents examined in the document of *Liber Sigillum 333*, it fills me with a great sense of respect, honor and humility upon the realization that we are sailing through uncharted territory on the vast ocean that is the occult and spirituality, reaching planes of thought and awareness never before accessible out of the most secretive mystery schools of our world. I have no doubt that we are definitely writing history and defining a path that will shape spiritual thought many years from now.

The last work presented in this grimoire is the **Book of Sakkara**, which contains a compilation of ancient religious texts of both historical and spiritual importance. Well studied by Egyptologists and in ancient history circles, most of these texts are known as the *Pyramid Texts* and were found carved in the walls and sarcophagi of the pyramids in Sakkara, Egypt. Modern dating scientific methods discovered that most of these texts are at least over 4000 years in age, making its contents of high importance in terms of Ancient Egyptian theology. This clearly establishes the *Pyramid Texts* as the oldest spiritual and religious texts known to mankind. The most relevant funerary texts are found in the ancient pyramid of the Pharaoh Unas from the Old Kingdom and, unlike the *Coffin Texts*, the *Pyramid Texts* of Sakkara were exclusive to the royal families of earlier dynasties, making them further related to Asetian genealogy and their spiritual teachings. Its contents were later adopted, altered and, in some cases, improved, resulting in the more recent funerary literature known as the *Coffin Texts* and *The Book of Coming Forth by Day*, better known as *The Egyptian Book of the Dead*; all of them notorious for their teachings on the mysteries of Death and immortality, intimately connected with the ancient view on vampirism as maintained in the Aset Ka and its unique predatory spirituality, which is so different from the modern view of the vampire and its superficial side.

In this book, the different funerary and spiritual texts were compiled due to the relevance of each spell to the Asetian tradition and although the vast majority has been translated from the *Pyramid Texts*, I have also included a few utterances from the *Coffin Texts* and *The*

Egyptian Book of the Dead due to their close connection with the kind of magick that this book examines in detail.

Traditional Occultism

It is important to mention that none of the occult documents included in the *Book of Orion* represent a simplistic manual of any sorts or describe a set of techniques to be used in practice. As stated above, this work is not intended to be a recipe book, nor is the serious occult practice developed in such superficial fashion.

Anyone seeking fantasy or seduced by the populist side of the occult will be deeply disappointed, as this work represents a scholarly study on the esoteric mysteries and the magickal arts approached with maturity, enlightenment and spirituality in mind. It is a book for true occultists, not for lifestylers. Even though advanced esoteric concepts are studied and explained in detail throughout this work, such study should not be approached in a casual way or dealt with in a superficial manner.

The heart of this work lies in the exquisite gnosis from the *Book of Giza* and its practical application in initiation. However, the word *practical* in this case holds a subjective meaning, as the practice itself develops in a personal way through exploration, meditation and magickal work, while the text and its teachings provide a framework for the expansion of consciousness that makes the revealing of secrets possible. How this manifests will be up to the occultist to unveil in his own journey to the Abyss and whether he returns as a conqueror — a ruler of Self and the master of his inner microcosm — or defeated; another formless dot lost in oblivion.

Although seemingly different under a first study, the three major tomes that form this grimoire complement each other in a profound initiatory way, so do not interpret every section independently at great length, as each holds a specific piece of the greater puzzle. This book is a tool and, as with any other esoteric device worthy of reference, it can be used by the seeker as a door to a fascinating world or, for the most foolish, it can be used against him. Remember that duality is present in every form of true magickal work and that by giving your hand to a creature of light you may end up locked in a cave, just like blindly jumping into a dark ocean may pull you down to the fountain of Truth.

During the study of this book, as with any work from the Aset Ka or another occult Order, it is of relevance to previously understand the significant differences between popular occultism and traditional or classical occultism. I am aware that this remark might not please many interested readers but as I stated above, and in the light of understanding, we must face and accept the inconvenient truths.

Popular occultism refers to the simplistic esoteric culture of common people that is focused on reaction instead of the transformational path of inner growth; the readily accessible and endlessly more superficial side of broad magickal practice. That is the *occult* as seen on television and in other media, as found in the majority of paid workshops and public classes, which is commonly referred to as *Low Magick* in occult circles and is entirely different in content and practice from the occult knowledge and systems developed in the various initiatory societies and found in ancient cultures that have dedicated their efforts to the understanding of nature and serious magickal practice.

Like the name itself implies, popular occultism is most sought after than more traditional magickal systems, being vastly more popular than any serious spiritual path. This is true primarily due to the fact that people often prefer what is easy, avoiding the longer and more dangerous roads, which are in fact the ones that are able to teach them the valuable lessons in life. It's the common mindset of superficiality and vanity, endlessly obsessed with the physical and the mundane, unable to grasp into the subtle aspects of their own existence; the trap of instant gratification, that like a drug enslaves the mind with what it can immediately achieve, blinding the eyes — otherwise naturally curious and created to learn, seek and grow — into mere devices of futility.

On the other side of the vibrational scale there is traditional occultism, often referred to as *High Magick* and the *Great Work* by the mystery schools. It refers to a diverse set of practices, hidden wisdom and initiatory information that is developed and used in honor, respect and exclusively for the spiritual evolution of the initiate through the means of an expanded understanding of the Universe and the mysteries found in Life and Death. It is a field of gnosis achieved through dedicated study, initiation and responsible practice that differs greatly from anything at the reach of popular occultists, commercial psychics and fortune tellers alike, by the simple fact that it is *secret.*

In this case, the word *secrecy* holds a deceptive connotation. Occult wisdom isn't secret by any desire for status, elitist mindset or to fulfill a hungry ego. It is secret to empower and maintain a much greater cause, which is related with how much power lies behind the doors of initiation that every student must open to look right into the *Eye of Darkness* and fall into the *Well of Wisdom.* Power draws responsibility and only when a high level of spiritual maturity is attained that same power can be wielded and properly mastered. That is the natural and universal elitism of occult practice, one that is so often misunderstood, in particular by those that do not have access to such gnosis.

The whole paraphernalia of superficial occultism that floods modern society by the means of poorly researched documentaries, dishonest commercial books, sinister magazines, misleading workshops and artist wannabes serve as a cloak of ignorance to protect and ensure the privacy of real life occultists. The truly initiated do not appear on television to exploit their practices, rarely accept invitations to give self-promoting interviews about their craft and, most of all, keep their knowledge, power and life private.

Insecurity and low self-esteem has moved many confused people into a desperate quest for cheap fame and exposure unrivaled in any other time in history, where the focus on outside influence and the voice of ego led to a complete loss of the sense of Self and respect. Only the wise can truly value the meaning of privacy, as they have already conquered themselves, hence not being ruled by the image others may have of them. In other words, they are free.

> *"He who controls others may be powerful but he who has mastered himself is mightier still."*
>
> Lao Tzu

Personally, I could never understand the seductive appeal many seem to find in notoriety and praise, probably because I cannot truly value a legacy that receives no criticism, as that would only imply a work that challenges absolutely nothing, being ultimately useless. I always invite criticism — the good, the bad and the ugly — for all the possible reasons that I am known to defend and teach. It is my belief that fame as a form of outside recognition is in no way an indicator of personal success, as that is defined by inner balance and growth. If you need the praise and recognition of others to feel accomplished then you are not really free, as true happiness can only come from within and that needs no outside approval. The way each individual sets his personal definition of success marks the determinant difference between a mind that focuses on the outside — being guided by the image and opinion that others develop of them; a slave of vanity — and one that focuses on what is found within, being free of the conceited conditioning of ego.

It would be foolish to assume anything different, as spiritual accomplishment enlightens the individual with a level of freedom whereby he experiences no need to prove himself or any other manifestation driven by the lack of confidence in Self. That is an essential layer of the inner work developed by the students of traditional occultism and an esoteric field that Orders such as the Aset Ka study, protect and develop in such a serious and mature form. That is the path treaded in Asetianism and followed by the nameless ones who freely but strongly dedicate themselves to the timeless quest of spiritual evolution through such a hard and mysterious road.

So often misunderstood and misrepresented in the modern world, Asetianism is not a religion but a cultural and philosophical legacy that reflects a way of life maintained through inner growth and a profound spiritual path. Many feel threatened by our elitist stance and so-called arrogance while their own society grows on a foundation of betrayal, selfishness, falsehood and the glorification of the most superficial of values; mankind strives on the perpetuation of false morality while it fails to understand the very core of Asetian thought like the meaning of honor, loyalty, trust, unity and love. People abuse such words, overusing them with empty meaning as a shallow reflection of their desires and expectations, yet they all represent so much more than just meaningful words.

While studying the mind and its intimate relation with spirituality it is of particular interest to observe that, for the most part, the ones seeking Asetianism out of genuine passion for the quest to find themselves, to understand nature and to develop a clearer understanding of life are the students that find in this tradition the transformational properties and wisdom to enlighten their path, in whatever way they chose to embrace it, learning valuable lessons that they will hold unto until the end of their life.

On the other hand, the ones seeking the Aset Ka and its teachings due to its distinctive mysterious allure and moved by the idea of power, superiority and fantasy are ultimately driven away in the mist of confusion and disappointment as a result of their own self-deceptive expectation. The Universe teaches in the most mysterious ways, so often the humble can find answers where the egotistic can only see a useless rock. They may look up to the stars and not see their movement, assuming they are lifeless and static in their limited vision. When motivation is not placed in the honesty of the heart, inspiration will not find the right key for your happiness.

When we state that the path and teachings from Aset Ka are not for everyone, in no way does that imply some sort of discrimination expressed in any form. Instead, it is a simple assessment of the factual truth that not everyone is ready for the level of awareness, honor and dedication that it takes to reach understanding through our tradition. The gnosis of the Asetian path knows no gender, race or age — it is Universal.

Asetian philosophy has always been a beacon of hope in an unbalanced world that fears its very own weakness, instead of acknowledging it in order to seek the key to overcome it. The violet legacy, as a powerful hymn of freedom, has always opposed those that seek to impose limitations and barriers within spirituality and mysticism; those who seek to severe, manipulate and distort the natural bond that every being has with the many layers of divinity. In this unconditional freedom, which an adept experiences by getting rid of all forms of limitation and expectation, it is vital to nurture inner focus and awareness to prevent falling into the traps of ego and delusion, often manifested in the superficial population by the embrace of a deluded life of fiction, masks and role-play that in no way represent the profound reality of occult science, spirituality, esoteric art and, most importantly, the eternal foundation of the Asetian culture.

From a scholarly perspective and unlike the aim and scope of other occult and religious paths, Asetianism is a tradition, discipline and way of life that balances and unifies the fields of science, spirituality, magick and art. The Aset Ka stands as a banner against the raising of limitations in spirituality and the sacredness found within, but also manifests as a true adversary for those that limit themselves and others when driven by their failures, insecurities and handicaps. It challenges every subtle detail that may hinder or interfere with the attaining of full potential buried in Self, and for that the Order has become increasingly inconvenient to the narcissistic minds and within many circles.

The Art of the Ancients

I want to take the chance to openly thank Tânia Fonseca from the Order of Aset Ka, for again taking the time out of her busy life and spiritual practice to dedicate her energy to another major project and for providing unquestionable support and insight through this venture to bring out to the public something that wouldn't normally be at their reach if it wasn't for the passion, inspiration and art of such evolved beings as herself. The dignity she has always shown in her life, work and art deserve this honorable mention, as it has been a humbling experience to teach and learn alongside such a beautiful soul.

Albeit misunderstood by the less aware, my path has been through the embracing of the inspirational science, magick and art of Words.

The power of words, not only through the means of language but also manifested by the realm of symbol and sigil, has been a personal form of magick and spirituality that I have embraced for many years, as well as developed and explored into the deepest dungeons of thought. With its roots in the forgotten culture of Ancient Egypt, where it was known as *Heka* and made legendary by the scholars, priests and pharaohs; we call it the *Art of the Ancients*, or the *Touch of the Elders*, and you may have seen and felt glimpses of its flame through my literary works.

As surprisingly as it may appear at first glance, without words the human being is not capable of conscious thought. The mind and body have the ability to feel, but without language, there is no intellectual thought. Feelings are manifested energy, so they exist in the realm of purity, in the land of subtlety. Thoughts are words embedded with meaning, so they exist in the realm of magick. I hope that through my work the students of the occult, spirituality and the mysteries may come to respect and value what we consider to be one of the oldest and most powerful forms of art, magick and wisdom.

The magick and power hidden within this book should be cherished and honored, as it will only respect those who approach it with a pure heart and a loyal soul. Not only because when a writer produces a work of spiritual value those words are eternal, permeating the inner consciousness of those it touches for all eternity, as it is also in this case a work resulting from the everlasting gnosis of the Ancient Egyptian mysteries, with its beauty and esoteric symbolism hidden beneath the immortal power of written Word.

> *"The aim of art is to represent not the outward appearance of things, but their inward significance."*
> Aristoteles

We are definitely living in an exciting era, and the potential presented in some of the teachings revealed within the following pages of this book is immeasurable.

This work is dedicated to self-development and the transformational opportunity of spiritual growth, as it expresses layers of wisdom that have not only been intimate, but also truly transcending and enlightening to me over the years. They manifest my profound belief that the states of awareness and understanding can only be attained when you look within and learn to ignore the distracting noise of the mundane. It teaches you to trust yourself and by that to conquer yourself in the process. I am certain that much of what is exposed through this work will not be properly understood, as that is inevitable due to the very nature of such occult teachings, but approach these pages with joy and without prejudice, so you shall find the warmth of the flame within. It is unequivocally the result of an act of love.

The message presented within this book to every hungry seeker is that of a mindful observation of nature, as the mysteries are unveiled all around us and presented through the most subtle things as true gifts from the Universe; to avoid the perpetual trap of converging your focus and efforts in the tangible reality of the mundane, but instead to commit wholeheartedly to the study and pursuit of your inner and higher realities by a permanent process of learning through every form of knowledge, presented in any shape, aspect or manifestation and independent of cultural weight and ancestry.

There is no true mastery without embracing life as an eternal student, for a spiritual master must first and foremost be a seeker as well as a teacher. In fact, the unusual length of this introductory text and the depth of the message it carries make this document alone a valuable resource and compass to the students of the occult. Lessons are unveiled in many forms and in the most unexpected ways, so nothing should be underestimated, for some of the most enlightening teachings are sometimes taught through silence.

For the victims of an unbalanced ego or to anyone suffering from delusions of grandeur, simply look up in a clear night and gaze into the vast ocean of stars; it will show you the insignificance of us all. It is a simple lesson that always puts life back into perspective when our mind goes astray. A sincere advice to all my readers is to study this work not only once, but many times, as with every new reading you will uncover greater mysteries, all leading up in the mystical ladder of initiation towards the greater mystery of all — yourself.

Read the pages within this book carefully and tread its teachings with strength and courage. Do it at your own risk...

Book of Giza

And they are Three.
Eternally reflected in the sky as Orion,
gazing at the golden desert.

Sebayt of Khufu

Awakening to immortality

☥ *Death* ☥

Mighty Uraeus that crowns our path
Your mysteries remain behind the timeless veil
At the hand of your Art our magick flies forth
Rising within hides a cradle to the Gods

ζ

1. May the Serpent kiss the infinite of Her cold beauty.
Her gift was eternity and everlastingness.

2. Magick is the fine art of crafting the invisible.

3. Behind the immortal gaze lies a poison that even Gods shall fear.

4. Storm the abyss with all thy power and never rest but at the feet of circular perfection!

5. The fingerprint of our essence is enthralled in memories and sealed deep within their forbidden desires.

6. We are not the engine, nor are we the wheel.
We are the ones that choose its direction.

7. When fully united, without ego or weakness, we become the greatest invisible force this world has ever witnessed.

8. The ensemble of the Gods floats in the cosmic dust of immortal consciousness.

☥

9. Ankh. Khepri. Ka. Tiet. Was. Ba. Ib.

These are the forces that command the Universe.

These are the keys that open the Ways.

These are the tools that hold the Secrets.

10. The purest personification of art is under the mastery of magick.

Manifestation is through Word.

Flame is through Love.

Understanding is through Wisdom.

Honor and respect the Art of all arts!

11. Only in the most arid of deserts can you find the purest water.

12. Thy beast lives within!

Unleash the lion so that it can feast on the thoughts of your enemies. Their laugh is the sound of fear when crying on the prejudice of thy nature.

13. Fight not to win. Fight to make a stand.

Determination is the key to awareness.

Hunt not to feed. Hunt to learn.

Knowledge is the key to shape the world.

Destroy not to kill. Destroy to transform.

Evolution is the key to immortality.

14. What fools despair to conquer the wise struggle to avoid.

15. Gods feast in the night that equals the day as the wind blows from cold to flame. So the wheel starts to rotate.

16. Smoke rises from the mountain of wisdom. Danger is eminent!
Focus your senses and gather your awareness. Do not vacillate!
Haunted in lost despair their dreams remain.
Only then, I shall become the dreamcatcher.

17. Hell rises and falls but heaven belongs to the inscrutable dreams of the darkest mind.

18. Become the fallen. Be the opposer. Let the adversary manifest...

19. Darkness is Light but there is no flame inside the white dawn.

20. True strength can only be measured in the ethereal fabric of the soul. All else is irrelevant!

21. May the blood from the black Sun rise high in the skies of the condemned abyss. Fear me not! There is no wisdom in fearing what is beyond your control. We are living Falcons, the damned blood of Her prince.

22. The veil can only cover our light from the eyes of mortals, for the ancients can see past any spell.

23. The timeless dance of inner truth can only be perceived in the absence of movement.

24. May oceans of fire consume the essence of our weakened preys.

25. Give me Your strength to defend in crises;

Your wisdom to master in need;

Your wings when loosing balance;

And Your poison to serve cold on our enemies' favorite table.

26. Whispers are elephant footprints in the steps of giants.

27. If the hawk lifts you up in the battlefield, feed him.

28. The breath of the Dragon is lethal.

That is why you should be the one commanding it.

29. Your voice alone can make a lot of noise.

Your voice inside a crowd cannot be heard at all.

An Asetian never tries to talk louder than the surrounding crowd.

An Asetian becomes that crowd.

30. Water is a gifted essence;

A realm of consciousness in the ether.

Always cleanse with the blood of the Gods!

31. I shall become the lion, the hawk and the serpent.

Just like the infinite and the zero are one and the same, eternity hides in the birth from the cosmical virgin.

32. For he shall rise mightiest among the living, as Wadjet biting poisonously and vigorously. He is the one that Lived and the one that shall Return; the crownless king of the silent Empire.

33. Beings of Immortal Flame.

They were born to conquer and tame.

Ancient rulers of all their kin.

Forgotten wisdom is still their reign.

The secret language from the Pharaohs of Kemet!

Sebayt of Khafre
Journey through the halls of despair
☥ Life ☥

Forces of chaos; light of the living
The ones that stand between the ways
You raise the Ba to the height of Nut
In times of darkness you fade away

Ɛ

1. The Universe is our chosen realm. Energy is our tool.

May the world bend and adapt to our own inner microcosm.

2. Don't haste your powers into the depths of oblivion.

Laugh at thyself! Manifest the Fool in the Zero!

No force will hold sway over you again.

3. Love is an ally but also a deception chest.

Open it with caution and remember that pleasure is also pain.

4. Be loved. Be praised. And be consumed.

5. Let the Flame be your warmth and guidance in the times of need.

Let the Fire illuminate the ways in the age of darkness.

6. The ancients studied the wisdom of Djehuty.

Later to be described in the mysteries as Thoth.

Remembered by the Greeks that called him Hermes.

But only at night his True Name can be seen.

"As Above, so Below."

He uttered and sealed the Law in the beryl.

7. The firm paws of Anubis can be seen by your side when the Ba goes forth. His dark shadow remains in your presence.
Father of Silence. Children of Death.
Eternally keeping the protective watch…

8. Smile at the loud! Ignore the false rulers and their weaknesses!
Never fear who screams in the clear. Their vulnerabilities are wide and open. The greatest danger comes silently and swiftly, moving like a poisonous snake.

9. Oh young children of Nun so unaware you have become.
By ignorance you prosper in your little world of delusional nullity.

10. The cloak of despair enchants the mundane.
Lift it and see above or cover within and plunge below.

11. The laws of the Ba can be found in the sky of the desert when reaching the night that Thoth has chosen to sleep.

12. Bow down to your Master! Break down your Ego!
Both of them can send your Ba into oblivion.

13. Celebrate in their honor and bring a flame before Her presence, for Her beauty carries the Light of all lights.

14. He who does not cherish life does not deserve to be among the living.

15. No act is as pure violence as the power of His hidden Word.

16. Do not feed the wolves before watching them run in front of your shadow.

17. Manifestation is through the ether.

Invoke the wisdom unto thee.

Call their name upon the altar of intoxicating night.

18. Mortals shall serve the darkness they failed to cherish.

The ones seeking power through our mythical flame shall only find illusion and inner pain.

19. The key lies in the mouth of the beast that died for her wicked master!

20. The Voice and the Flame can sing the same tune when you perform the ultimate sacrifice.

21. Only a true assassin can see past the gate with two-headed goats.

Destroy him, break him and kill him, or he will consume you.

The monster lives inside you.

22. Bask in the light of all abominations for only when going through the gates of the abyss you shall find your answer.

23. Do not pretend to be elite. Become elite.

Do not pretend to fly above. Rise above.

The fools watch as the wise conquer.

They condemn as we feast in silence.

Our rule is their song of despair.

The hidden cloak beneath their nightmares.

24. The eyes cannot be trusted for their tale is that of deception.

To see their reflection you must sacrifice your awareness in the song of perfect trust...

25. Wise are those who can find patterns in the chaos. But be wary as the path to such gnosis is guarded by a three-headed daemon.

26. The most dangerous power is the one you nurture in secret, manifesting its apotheosis only when no soul can believe in its existence.

27. Weakness hides in the mind of those that cannot See.

Overconfidence is the pit of the Fallen.

Acknowledge your own ignorance or die in vain for the ego projects a distorted mask of your inner Truth.

28. It is safer to face a strong enemy in the field of battle than to fight a war by the side of a weak friend.

29. Look above, but do not fear, for through the abyss we have fallen and back to it we shall return.

30. Behold the gates of condemnation!

Can you speak their language in reverse?

31. Do not feed from the weak. Feed from the ancient.

But be ready to be preyed upon.

32. In the inner throne lies the seed of all vices for the temple of purity hides in another door and the cosmos is written in reverse.

33. Beings of Eternal Change.

Fluid voices between the realms.

Mirrored echoes of the crown.

Lost awareness in a sea of living.

The secret language from the Priestesses of Kemet!

Sebayt of Menkaure

Descent to the Duat

☥ Rebirth ☥

Vultures of shadow in forbidden beauty
You leave all mortals enthralled in awe
Disguised as silence you master your poison
The strength of the Mother is your hidden cue

δ

1. Loyalty is a sacred jewel protected by the Gods.

A mystical gem held when the divine knows no doubt.

I give my Ka to Her purpose, as my essence is forever Hers.

2. The Ancients may sleep, but be warned: they will always wake up.

3. They were only Three.

Yet, they moved a nation.

They were only Seven.

Yet, they conquered the desert.

They became endless.

Yet, they were forgotten.

They became legend.

Then, they were remembered.

4. Condemn thought! Condemn action!

Sharpen your senses for they are coming...

5. The flow of time never stops.

It is the cryptic cycle of Death, Life and Rebirth.

Can you see the reflection from the triple path in the endless river?

☥

6. One reign shall fall and another begin.

The wheel shall rotate, endlessly.

Overcome yourself and Become.

7. Unconditional loyalty to the Royal Serpent!

8. I shall rise above all mortals with the wicked powers of death.

Find my Name at the reign of silence in the seventh day.

9. Fear the devastating Dark Flame.

That means to fear yourself above any other!

10. The longest journeys cannot be measured in the length of mortals but in the depth of the inner realm.

11. The mountain of wisdom is never reached by those who profess lies of the sacred past.

12. Energy and Love ignite the alchemy of the Soul.

13. If they say no thou shall be able to see the lie in their tongue and spill terror before their names.

✝

14. Perfection is subtle.

Subtle is not perfection.

Simplicity is a process, not an end.

15. In darkness lies a mystery that has the power to shine brighter than true light.

16. Forgiveness is not for the worms of disloyalty.

Pity them not! Pity is for the weak.

Trust is not for those unable to conquer it.

Blame them not! Blame is when you care.

Power is not for those unable to respect it.

Curse them not! Curses are for enemies.

Now, you stand Above.

17. The divine glimmer of the Amethyst can fade; the body, broken into pieces. But its ethereal purity remains untouched since the time of the elders.

18. To unveil the riddle of this mystery thou must find the secret stone that reveals what cannot be seen.

19. Her name was concealed and Her legacy forbidden.

Touching Her soul is the sin of the Gods!

☧

20. From the light of thy eyes resonates the depth of sexual abyss.
Hidden memories. Hidden secrets. Hidden pleasures.

21. Oh mighty daemons of the ancient world:
Rejoice in darkness and flame.
Never in shame, toast to your victory!
In silence you guide. In secret you protect. In honor you demand.
Oh, my love, ahead gleam the thrones of the immortal Gods!

22. There are seven Keys, but they manifest through twenty-two initiations, sixteen entities and forty signs. To bring them to life you need the steady hand of the artist and the womb from an act of Love.

23. Before striking blindly always look within.

24. The Sting of the Royal Scorpion pierces beyond blood and flesh.

25. Holy Aset, Goddess of all Gods.
Violet Lady of the Flame.
Eternal Mother of the Asetians.
Genesis of our immortal Ba.
Prey upon our enemies.
Vindicate our honor.
Cleanse thy sacred Name!

✝

26. All nature is triple. The One that becomes Three.

Birth comes in the form of One, Two and Three.

27. Truth is an ethereal pond hidden among the stars.

28. Oh Serket you wield the terrible voice of despair!

Remember her name but fear her flame.

For only through the grip of her sword few fought as many.

By her inscrutable scream the small became tall.

So the few were seen casting a shadow above the many.

29. At the end of time we shall ride together as one…

For Bast, the princess that shielded a nation!

For Neith, the arrow that enslaved the desert!

For Serket, the flame that burnt immortals!

Together they rule the three legions of eternal despair.

30. May the strongest of Flames flourish from within the Sacred Women and burn all thy race down to a forgotten reign!

31. Lustful is the Woman.

Oh warrior princess of Thebes, your enemies fall under your whispers.

By covering the Sun with your immortal arrows shall Seth fight blindly in the cold!

☦

32. The Scorpion Stings.

The Scorpion Cries.

The Scorpion Dies.

33. Beings of Sexual Flame.

Wielders of immortal honor.

Scholars of the most mysterious silence.

Humble protectors of the One.

The secret language from the Warriors of Kemet!

This is where we stood at the dawn of the ages.

All paths led us to this very same road.

And so it begins...

Note

During study and ritual any reference to the text should be done through the following syntax:

Liber Aeternus Sebayt.Utterance

Example: *Liber Aeternus* II.22

This reference would point the initiate to utterance twenty-two in the Sebayt of Khafre, where the following text can be found.

> *"Bask in the light of all abominations for only when going through the gates of the abyss you shall find your answer."*

Book of Ipet Resyt

My army is the thunder in the sky and the beasts from the earth, the wind in the air and the tides of the sea.
My army is Me.

The Touch of Khonsu

Oh mightiest Prince of the Nefer
The winds cry for you in Em-Waset
Our land burns in furious pain
As the desert storms in the agony of your absence
For your name is still our Reign

Har Khun Ka

Shen Te Num

Ka Khba Khonsu

Ankh Ba Khunsu

Har Khun Ka

Shen Te Num

Ka Khba Khonsu

Ankh Ba Khunsu

Har Khun Ka

Shen Te Num

Ka Khba Khonsu

Ankh Ba Khunsu

✝

Har Khun Ka

Shen Te Nun

Ka Khba Khonsu

Ankh Ba Khunsu

Har Khun Ka

Shen Te Nun

Ka Khba Khonsu

Ankh Ba Khunsu

Har Khun Ka

Shen Te Nun

Ka Khba Khonsu

Ankh Ba Khunsu

Framework

Initiatory spell uttered by Khonsu in the supreme sanctuary of Em-Waset.

Note

The opus matter of this initiatory document, although brief and simple in appearance, brings within its energies a profound magickal utterance that until now has only been available to trustworthy students within the Aset Ka due to its power and spiritual significance. For this reason it is presented here without foreword, guidelines or initiatory procedure, maintaining its powerful magickal key hidden in the Duat.

Without proper training and the aid of wisdom caution is advised when exploring the magick presented through these words. Responsibility is a requirement of wisdom, and respect, a condition of evolution. Without them, the vault of beauty provided within this sacred text shall never be opened.

For only those who seek selflessly and loyally shall See...

Liber יסוד

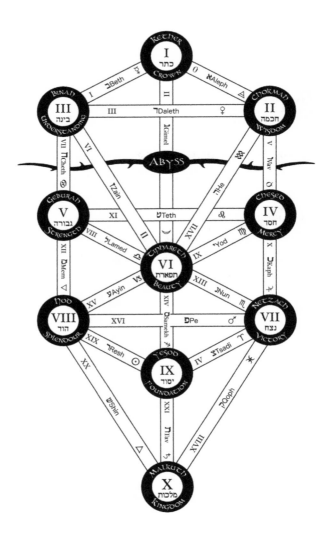

Since the elder days the Asetians have been passionately dedicated to the study, development, perfecting and protection of a multitude of mysteries, schools of thought and knowledge, from science to the most intricate occult arts, developing from all corners of the world throughout different cultures. Among such a vast ocean of wisdom the Asetian Eye has been focused on the hidden spiritual layers of nature that hold the power to reflect the keys to the mysteries able to unveil reality in its purest form.

he sages of old set forth on a quest to attain the unattainable: to comprehend the incomprehensible nature of divinity, and by that to understand themselves. Through the means of meditation, magick and science, along with the selfless observation of nature and the recurring elements found in the chaos, they came to several spiritual and philosophical realizations. That knowledge is what we know today as the Kabbalah — קַבָּלָה.

Developed by Hebrew mystics, the Kabbalah is a powerful spiritual technology that, while mirroring the reality of the cosmos and the essence of the inner Self, with all its layers, complexities and dynamism, can be applied to a variety of esoteric fields without the need of proper religious dogma. In essence, the teachings of the Kabbalah define a framework to understand reality.

It is out of the scope of this document to study the possible origins of the Kabbalah, as its roots are still shrouded in mystery and doubt to contemporary historians. As scholars of the Asetian culture we could theorize that the Jews who abandoned Egypt left with more than just food and wooden staffs. They left from a land that was, and still is, known for its immeasurable spiritual knowledge and mystical power.

Traditional Jewish thinkers profess that the origin of the teachings found in the Kabbalah dates back to *Eden*, a mythological place described in the *Book of Genesis* where the first man and woman lived after being created by the hands of God. In other words, it represents a conceptual era at the dawn of time, much akin to the Egyptian timeframe most Asetianists have come to know as the *Sep Tepy*. Speculation aside, most scholars agree that Kabbalistic knowledge predates Christianity by at least several centuries, but tracing it further back might be hard due to the teachings and initiations being traditionally passed down by word of mouth only to a select few and to the very secretive nature of this kind of mystical thought.

The Hebrew rabbis often state that the original teachings of the Kabbalah were obtained in ancient times from enlightened beings that were not human. Through their own mind, cultural background and the lack of proper understanding they described them as *angels*; wise creatures, owners of mystical wisdom and philosophical secrets, at a time of great spiritual and religious influence of the Ancient Egyptian empire. Who were these mysterious *angels* that held the magick and wisdom that men called Kabbalah, something they saw as so powerful that they only dared to unveil its secrets to a small elite? The answer to such a question and the hidden keys to all its implications may be long lost and forgotten, but one thing remains certain, as with all other forms of knowledge and culture humans have distorted and changed this ancient wisdom to suit their own needs, ideals and fears...

From an Asetian scholarly context it is relevant to state that although parts of the wisdom explored within this *Liber* have originated in Egypt, the historical fact is that we are exploring elements of Hebrew origin and mystical concepts that have their major development in the culture of old Israel. Some of the interpretations found in this book are the result of intensive study on Kabbalistic wisdom and personal research, experience and practice, being related with the Ancient Egyptian spiritual mysteries as studied in the Asetian tradition of the Aset Ka, with a focus on the initiatory secrets and occult wisdom found hidden in the Kabbalah. The seeker interested in the classical religious side of the Kabbalah as studied in traditional Judaism will find the fundamentals of this doctrine in the older texts, originally in Aramaic and Hebrew, as the *Zohar* and the *Sepher Yetzirah.*

This further attests to the learning approach developed within the Aset Ka, that as an initiatory Order of mysteries has inspired the exploration of every form of spirituality developed in history along with the unbiased understanding of many cultures of the world, independently of historical significance in terms of politics, wealth, influence and prosperity. To a learned Asetianist it also serves as an expression of the universal nature of the Asetian tradition and how a deeper exploration of its many aspects can also aid in the learning of different beliefs, religions and cultures.

The Violet lips truly speak the voice of Understanding.

Every time that I am asked to teach about the Kabbalah from a spiritual non-religious perspective, one of the questions that I get asked most often from other occultists who are new to the Hebrew mystical system is why there are so many different spellings for the word *Kabbalah* and what do all those differences mean.

There are several differences, particularly on the level of an introduced coating of dogma and how they interpret the divine, but at a core level they all pretty much have the same foundation.

Kabbalah is the original transliteration of the Hebrew word meaning *receiving* and it is related with the mystical traditions that are found in early Judaism. The meaning behind the word *receiving* is due to its original secretive nature, where it was only passed down from master to apprentice as an oral tradition. In its traditional format you could not simply decide to go learn about the Kabbalah or become an educated Kabbalist student, as you would have to earn it in order to *receive* it.

Quite simply, this designation and concept refers to an initiatory form of wisdom that could only be passed down from a learned and experienced teacher, rather than being openly accessible to someone randomly seeking it.

All the other spellings and variations of the name refer to adaptations of the Kabbalah that have been developed from the original Hebrew system. For example, due to the lack of a proper mystical layer in their own tradition, some Christian sects have adapted this wisdom and called it Cabala, while the Hermetics use it extensively in the many systems of Western mysticism and ceremonial magick but spell it Qabalah.

In Asetianism we usually maintain the original spelling of *Kabbalah* as it better defines the purity and background of the traditional teachings, but hold no particular rules if someone prefers to use one of the alternatives. Due to our intimate and inseparable relation with Ancient Egyptian culture, some occultists have identified our approach to the Kabbalah as a flavor of Hermetic Qabalah, since the Greek wisdom of Hermes Trismegistus, which gave birth to Hermeticism at the heart of the Western mystery tradition, is merely an expression of much older gnosis developed by Thoth in Egypt. This connection is not necessarily inaccurate, but due to the specific nature, esoteric symbolism and wisdom of all forms of Asetian knowledge, magick and culture, other versed occultists refer to our approach to Hebrew mysticism simply as *Asetian Kabbalah.*

This document is intended to work as a primer on the study of the Kabbalah and the ancient wisdom of Israel from an Asetian perspective. It provides the basics — the *foundation* — to understand this esoteric system and its major elements in an unbiased and non dogmatic way, while at the same time providing the spiritual and mental tools to develop a deeper understanding under an Asetian mindset and its hidden potential to be explored in magickal practice. It is important to understand that this text was designed specifically for students of Asetian Kabbalah, where some interpretations are particular to our tradition and may differ from other forms of traditional and dogmatic rabbinical lore.

Liber יסוד, meaning *foundation* in Hebrew, provides the initiate with the major concepts and tools so that he can understand the principles within the Kabbalistic tradition and deepen his studies through the teachings of the Aset Ka and other published Hebrew literature. It is a start, not an end.

Prior to this study, it is also important to understand that, in the Kabbalah, the concept of divinity found when referring to a *creator* does not designate the religious God found in monotheistic theology, but a higher level of experience that each of us can attain through wisdom — a true form of spiritual enlightenment.

This is especially true in the case of יהוה or *YHWH* — the Tetragrammaton. Wrongly transliterated as *Jehovah* in many texts, this definition does not refer to an anthropomorphic deity like the one found in Christianity and modern Judaism. It is an abstract concept to embody the indefinable nature of divinity, expressed in here by the four letters of Yod י, He ה, Vav ו and He ה. These simple letters hold such important significance and meaning that, when together, they are rarely pronounced by the traditional Hebrew scholars or written in Jewish religious literature due to the sacredness attributed to this formula in their tradition. Instead, the word יהוה — Yod He Vav He — is commonly seen being transliterated and uttered by the use of different words like *Lord* among other references to a divine force.

> *"Seek him that maketh the seven stars and Orion, and
> turneth the shadow of death into the morning, and
> maketh the day dark with night: that calleth for the
> waters of the sea, and poureth them out upon the face of
> the earth: The Lord is his name."*
>
> Amos 5:8[18]

This passage from the *Book of Amos*, part of the *Tanakh* — the
Hebrew Bible — and the *Old Testament* of the *Christian Bible* is a fine
example on the literary adulteration of the Tetragrammaton. Some
earlier translations have used Jehovah instead of *Lord*, both working
as transliterations of יהוה that the Jews don't pronounce due to its
sacredness in their tradition. Under the light of understanding this
passage holds an even deeper meaning, as by replacing the word *Lord*
with the correct Hebrew letters we have the unveiling of the secret on
how the ancients were aware that the Tetragrammaton of the
Kabbalah has an intimate connection with the mysteries of Orion.
Furthermore, it conceals a hidden allusion to the four alchemical
elements, where the *shadow of death* refers to Fire, what *maketh the day
dark with night* is Air, the *waters of the sea* represent Water and the *face
of the earth* naturally relates with Earth.

The Tetragrammaton, which is embodied in literature and
magick by the four letters of the Hebrew alphabet, expresses the four
layers of the manifest Universe as well as the four elementals that
comprise the foundations of reality and spiritual alchemy — Fire,
Water, Air and Earth. It also reflects the *Planes of Existence* found in
Asetianism[19], and appropriate analogies will be better understood in
the following text when learning about the *Tree of Life* as a spiritual
diagram of both inner and outer realities.

In the study of the nature of divinity it remains a point of extreme importance to understand and accept this abstract definition of deity, particularly when exploring the Kabbalah, and not to confuse it with the modern view of godhood. Among the many descriptions like Jehovah, God, Adonai and Lord, a more suitable and meaningful word used in ancient religious scriptures when referring to divinity is *Elohim*. This ancient word shrouded in mystery holds the missing connection to the multidimensional view of deity as found in the Kabbalah, as the Hebrew word is a feminine noun followed by a masculine termination, while being both grammatically singular and plural.[20] This philological detail hides an important secret behind the word *Elohim*, as it refers not to a single omnipotent God like the one found in the limited dogma of monotheistic religions, but actually embodies in a singular word the manifestation of many Gods expressed through feminine and masculine principles, which are so accurately represented in the pantheon of Ancient Egypt. An interesting hint concerning this powerful word is found in the *Book of Exodus*, the second book present in both the Hebrew and Christian Bible, where *Elohim* is used to describe nothing less than the Gods of Egypt.

To properly study the wisdom of the Kabbalah in a serious and mature form one must realize that we are dealing with highly abstract concepts that are used as subtle representations of a reality that is in fact impossible to be accurately expressed by the means of words and symbols and, to some extent, unable to be fully comprehended with a regular mindset. I ask that during this process of learning and adaptation to a reality of symbolism and spiritual abstraction the student keep an open mind and raise his level of awareness to another dimension — that of the Spirit.

Marques' Spiritual Kaleidoscope

Anyone familiar on an elementary level with the Asetian tradition and its Ancient Egyptian legacy may at first wonder why broadening his spiritual culture through the wisdom of the Kabbalah holds any significance. First of all, any apprentice of the Asetian path worthy of such a name would by now have come to the realization that the Asetian framework develops around the concept of Understanding through the means of Wisdom. This increased awareness manifests through a process of exploration, committed learning and practice. The initiate of Asetianism is renown for the depth of his knowledge and this does not apply to a single subject or branch of science. Asetianists are constantly encouraged to learn about every form of knowledge and culture in order to develop a greater understanding of the higher Truth as unveiled behind the big picture. Different views will provide answers to different questions, as each culture has a small limited piece of the spiritual cosmos developed from its very own background and experience. Each tradition on its own, while isolated from other knowledge and the chaos of opposed views, is limited and hence incomplete. The importance of such exploration to personal evolution and in the process of finding Self will become increasingly more evident as the student progresses through different forms of initiation and matures spiritually.

> *"If we intend to take our occult studies seriously and make of them anything more than desultory light reading, we must choose our system and carry it out faithfully until we arrive, if not at its ultimate goal, at any rate at definite practical results and a permanent enhancement of consciousness. After this has been achieved we may, not without advantage, experiment*

with the methods that have been developed upon other Paths, and build up an eclectic technique and philosophy therefrom; but the student who sets out to be an eclectic before he has made himself an expert will never be anything more than a dabbler."

Dion Fortune

This brief passage from occultist Dion Fortune on her text on the Kabbalah is quite representative of a problem that many modern occultists encounter during their first years of practice. People often skim the surface of various spiritual traditions to incorporate different elements into their own eclectic practices that better suit their needs and expectations. Through a brief study of several books related with an esoteric road people already assume that they understand the path and know enough to make fair judgment on what it has to offer, as well as to borrow and adapt its traditional ideas into their own personal view and practice without ever mastering such knowledge. This results in recognition of the basic symbology found at the surface of many traditions but a complete lack of understanding on the essence and wisdom present in those paths. Every honest occult tradition of the world takes years to study and dedicated practice to master; it cannot be understood at a workshop or mastered through a book, as it must be lived and experienced first hand.

While I always recommend the study of every form of knowledge and occult traditions, it becomes relevant to explain that such method of self-development requires a deeper understanding of the mysteries and paths being explored and that, while a profound knowledge of different cultures and traditions is highly beneficial to the student of the occult, simple examinations of a path may only provide further confusion and will not gift the seeker with the required understanding so that he can use said path in his personal practice.

In a society where people make frivolous use of occult symbolism that they do not comprehend and profess to follow paths and study traditions they never practiced or understood, an occultist must strive to be a good and sincere representation of whatever road of wisdom he follows and studies, as often the loudest people found in different paths and modern communities are a terrible representation of the essence and values of the path they believe to follow and should never be used as an element to understand a specific tradition. Spirituality is independent of opinion and social identity, as it exists on its own. Individual character, viewpoint and interpretation can never define a tradition.

> *"If we are silent, we can listen, and so learn; but if we are talking, the gates of entrance to the mind are closed."*
>
> Dion Fortune

A concept frequently found in Asetianism and often misunderstood by the non-initiated is that of *Silence*. The ability to accept and master quietness, stillness and mental plenitude is a vital tool for the serious adept of the magickal arts and an essential step in any profound spiritual quest. This *silence* is not expressed through a limited existence of isolation or the ecclesiastical silence found in monastic life, but manifests the inner power to shield from mundane noise, deceptive echoes and distracting influences in order to be able to listen to the pure voice found within that speaks through subtlety. Without attaining such level of growth through the power of silence, communion with Self is not possible. This idea is well carved in the thought of every gnostic spiritual tradition, holding the long-established occult principle which postulates that someone loud can never be considered a true adversary or ally, as inner weakness is exposed through the inability to learn, for only those that can listen in silence can be trusted as real students.

I hope that my approach to manifold expressions of wisdom and different layers of the occult will motivate the reader to explore other forms of knowledge and not just the teachings that are directly tied to the Asetian nature or any other path of their preference and to do so without fear or dogma, with a mindset and commitment to an honest further development. It is of central importance while studying other paths to do so with a genuine thirst for knowledge and passion for learning, placing the focus within and not driven by outside influence or the perspective of ego, as when the inspiration is drawn from the indulgence of vanity or the fear within the subconscious, true learning is not possible. Occult wisdom is one of the most deceiving forms of gnosis, as it will only teach the truthful while guiding the fools into a shimmering road of presumptuous glitter.

Other traditions and metaphysical systems will unveil alternative interpretations of the Universe and reality, providing what I have called a *Spiritual Kaleidoscope*; a multilayered and multidimensional understanding of Life, spirituality and human thought. This advanced level of understanding and awareness achieved through a holistic and nonjudgmental study of the many layers of spirituality — the *Kaleidoscope* — represents a powerful inner technology to be used in the never-ending quest for wisdom and enlightenment, a technique that I have continuously taught and inspired within the students of the Aset Ka. Ultimately, if the foundation is strong, the study and understanding of different religions and occult traditions will not shake the initiate in his passion and commitment to the Asetian path, but will actually provide him with renewed resolve, sentiment and understanding towards the teachings of Aset, as he realizes through first hand experience how countless other traditions and cultures simply have pieces of the hidden puzzle that is Asetianism. This is not to say that every practice or belief can be absorbed into our own practices or seen under our light. Some knowledge is genuinely incompatible and misleading, or worse yet, simply downright fake.

Having contact with false knowledge, just like dealing with dishonest people, is also an important lesson in the path of growth and a learning tool that should not be underestimated. Learning to recognize what is real from what is not, as what is true from what is false, represents a level of awareness that the student of the occult must learn to master for the sake of his own evolution. We enforce and advise the study of all forms of knowledge, thought and practice, as we strongly believe that experience only allows for the initiate to realize how beautiful and precious the Asetian culture truly is. That alone is an initiation in itself.

Hebrew Language

Hebrew is the language of the Kabbalah. Developed in the Middle East as a Semitic language it is known to be one of the oldest languages in the world. Currently one of the two official languages of Israel, along with Arabic, Hebrew is well known among the adepts of the occult and subject of serious study in many secret societies due to its mystical alphabet formed by twenty-two letters or sigils. The Jews call it Leshon Hakodesh — לשון הקודש — meaning the *Sacred Language.*

The number *twenty-two* of the letters found in the Hebrew alphabet is not arbitrary. It manifests as an echo of the twenty-two paths connecting the different spiritual emanations — sephiroth — in the Tree of Life, as well as the twenty-two *Major Arcana* found in the traditional Tarot, but more on that later.

To understand the formation of the Hebrew alphabet under a Kabbalistic perspective we shall imagine the singular embodiment of divine manifestation, before the Universe was formed, as being represented by a single point.[21] That singular point, a coherent dot in the void of chaos, represents the hidden potential to manifest the whole Universe. It constitutes the intact complete existence: no reality, no dimensions, no nature — just a point, the unformed divinity.

If this point in the cradle of the Gods would suddenly gain consciousness and awareness, at the verge of the creation of the Universe, it would stretch its energies left and right to the further reaches of the now forming Universe. This philosophical alchemy would create the first dimension — length. Following this primordial awakening the point would expand its awareness up and down, to the highest and the lowest realms of infinity. Height, the second dimension, would have been brought into existence. At last, the essence of the point would reach from front to back, creating the third and last dimension of our tridimensional reality — depth. In this philosophical approach the Kabbalah describes the Universe as being manifested out of three elemental realities, describing not only the root frameworks of the cosmos but also the foundations of sacred geometry. The number *three* then becomes the first number of primordial manifestation.

At this point a tridimensional reality was formed and, for empirical examination, through mathematical science and the principles of geometry, we can define it as a cube. The structure that embodies the Universe was given form out of the three basic dimensions — length, height and depth. If we pay closer attention to this newborn reality — the mystical cube — we realize that it exists by the means of seven frameworks; the six faces of the cube and the primordial dot in its center as the divine expression that manifested the whole Universe. Through this paradigm we reach at the number *seven* as the second number of primordial manifestation.

Studying this conceptual cube in further detail we realize that those seven universal frameworks must be supported by something, or some force, otherwise they would simply disperse into chaos. There must be some power holding them together, giving them meaning, through a coherent and balanced existence. That materializes through the line segments expressed as the edges of the cube. Those thin vibrational lines hold the faces of our cube in place, keeping order in the Universe. Such invisible filaments express the third and last number of primordial manifestation: the number *twelve*. In the Asetian tradition we call it Maat, the Ancient Egyptian personification of balance and order.

Finally, we can define the Universe through the unification of the three primordial dimensions, the seven frameworks of existence as the six faces of the cube plus the initial point and the twelve faces of Maat as the edges of the cube. This is an infinitely expanding reality with no real boundaries or form except those of perception. As a manifest Universe that is the natural expression of reality, like in all forms of creation, the cube is not limited by human geometry.

$$3 + 7 + 12 = 22$$

That is the Kabbalistic formula for the creation of the Universe and the alchemical secret behind the twenty-two letters of the Hebrew alphabet. This realm of esoteric numerology also expresses several mysteries behind the wisdom of the Tarot, the initiatory keys of the Universe, the foundations of biology and the rules of science.

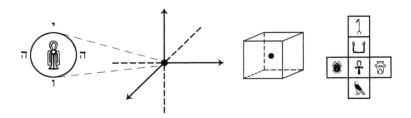

At this point the Asetianists studying this *Liber* with due focus and attention may be starting to see some order and meaning in the apparent chaos of the Kabbalah, as the number *three* found in this mystical alchemy can be seen as a philosophical expression of the *Three Primordials* and the number *seven* represents the *Seven Sacred Pillars* of the Asetian tradition. Like I previously stated, nothing is arbitrary.

The three Lineages — three dimensions of the soul — give form to the act of creation and through them manifest the seven frameworks that command the Universe — Ankh, Khepri, Ka, Was, Ba and Ib as the six faces of the sacred cube plus Tiet as the divine dot at the core of existence; the blood of Aset.

Delving deeper into the mysteries of the Hebrew alphabet we realize that by separating the letters into those three distinctive groups[22], according to the formation of the Universe, we find the three alchemical elements of initiation, the seven planets of the ancients and the twelve constellations of the zodiac.

The three primary or mother letters, also known as the elemental letters, are Aleph א, Mem מ and Shin ש — representing Air,

Water and Fire. Some may wonder why Earth is not represented but it happens that, in Kabbalistic mysticism and spiritual alchemy, Earth is seen as a lesser element of inferior purity. During the study of *Liber Sigillum 333*, particularly in the chapter on the *Sarcophagus of Flesh*, the reader shall understand the occult implications of such reasoning and the fundament for its neglecting aspect in the formation of the world.

The seven secondary or double letters are Beth ב, Gimel ג, Daleth ד, Kaph כ, Pe פ, Resh ר and Tav ת. They represent the planets of the ancients, which are also known as the seven classical planets of antiquity — Mercury, Moon, Venus, Jupiter, Mars, the Sun and Saturn.

For the learned occultist, the connection with each letter and their precise positioning on the Tree of Life and the Major Arcana of the Tarot has profound astrological implications in the interpretation of different esoteric systems. It is relevant to explain that the Sun is not a planet at all in astronomical nomenclature but a star, nor is the Moon seen as a true planet by contemporary astronomy; however, both were studied as planets by the ancient alchemists, and although they were astronomically incorrect those aspects represented important symbolical and conceptual references in their geocentric view.

In the Asetian tradition these seven frameworks are properly identified as the *Sacred Pillars*, important keys of mystery to understand Life and its manifestation in the Universe.

The twelve tertiary or simple letters are He ה, Vav ו, Zain ז, Cheth ח, Teth ט, Yod י, Lamed ל, Nun נ, Samekh ס, Ayin ע, Tsadi צ and Qoph ק. They represent the constellations of the zodiac — Aries, Taurus, Gemini, Cancer, Leo, Virgo, Libra, Scorpio, Sagittarius, Capricorn, Aquarius and Pisces.

	Name	Hebrew	Arabic	Magick
1	Aleph	א	ا	Air
2	Mem	מ	م	Water
3	Shin	ש	ش	Fire
4	Beth	ב	ب	Mercury
5	Gimel	ג	ج	Moon
6	Daleth	ד	د	Venus
7	Kaph	כ	ك	Jupiter
8	Pe	פ	ف	Mars
9	Resh	ר	ر	Sun
10	Tav	ת	ت	Saturn
11	He	ה	ه	Aries
12	Vav	ו	و	Taurus
13	Zain	ז	ز	Gemini
14	Cheth	ח	ح	Cancer
15	Teth	ט	ط	Leo
16	Yod	י	ي	Virgo
17	Lamed	ל	ل	Libra
18	Nun	נ	ن	Scorpio
19	Samekh	ס	س	Sagittarius
20	Ayin	ע	ع	Capricorn
21	Tsadi	צ	ص	Aquarius
22	Qoph	ק	ق	Pisces

Tree of Life

The Tree of Life is the central device in Kabbalistic technology. Known as *Eitz Chaim* in Hebrew — עץ חיים —, it is surrounded with meaning and rooted in symbolism. The proper interpretation and study of this magickal device has eluded occultists for centuries, being part of the teachings found throughout countless mystery schools of our past, present and certainly the future.

Published for the first time in 1652 in the work of Jesuit scholar Athanasius Kircher, entitled *Oedipus Ægyptiacus*, the image of the Tree is not just a symbol or a collection of sigils. Instead, it is a diagram of the manifest Universe: a model of creation and evolution. It represents Life but it also mirrors Death and the perpetual continuum. The interpretation and study of the Tree of Life should not be strict or shrouded in the limited light of rules but as dynamic and mutable as the realm of thought, since it cannot be properly understood if attached to dogma and the restricted boundaries of concept. The student is therefore advised not to focus solely on its connection with the Asetian Lineages and spiritual expression through the Holy Trinity — Serpent, Scarab and Scorpion —, while at the same time keeping such understanding in the scope of awareness. As meditative gnosis the glyph presents the hierarchical unfolding of consciousness, structured in order to break the advanced psychology of sentient beings into smaller layers possible of coherent study and to be analyzed by the focused mind.

The function and application of the wisdom deduced from the Tree is diverse and its occult scope should always be approached as a tool and multilayered chart that can be adapted and interpreted under different frameworks and to express different manifestations. Its reflex of the triple Asetian nature, although a potent spiritual tool, it is just one of the many applications of this symbol to be found in occult wisdom. While studying the Kabbalah it is important to remain aware that tools and interpretations such as the Tree of Life may be approached as another reflection of the Asetian nature through its many universal faces, but it would be incorrect to approach Asetianism and the study of its tradition as an expression of the knowledge manifested by the Tree. The Kabbalah and its symbolical structure of Life and layers of existence can be studied as complex esoteric expressions of the universal Asetian path and through that study to grasp further depth in Hebrew mysticism and its cultural legacy, but Asetianism should not be understood as a reflection of the Tree. In fact, on a first approach to the study of the Kabbalah some occultists may benefit from not overly focusing on the placement of the Lineage archetypes in the Tree as the lacking of certain mystery keys may raise confusion and lead to wrong interpretations. The Kabbalistic system can be studied without delving into its Asetian connections and influence, in an independent exploration that still retains its occult validity and power to be used in magickal practice.

The human mind has a tendency to categorize all information as a way to better understand and organize thought, and that makes people raise walls around different concepts instead of trying a more synergistic approach to occult wisdom. This leads to great misunderstanding when it comes to spirituality, as we are dealing with a realm of thought that cannot be defined or limited by the rules of definition and concept. To impose limitations in mystical thought and to restrict the understanding of transcendence by a need for categorization is limiting wisdom in its very essence. Although we make use of definition and concept in order to be able to pass certain layers of knowledge to other initiates it becomes important to realize that those very same definitions are limited and restricted, being ultimately impossible for them to carry the full weight of the gnosis they intend to convey. This is particularly relevant while studying such intricate traditions as Asetianism and the Kabbalah, as their spiritual and philosophical elements exist in the realm of transcendence where the only path to develop a proper — although still limited — level of understanding is through a holistic approach that interconnects all elements and reveals the world as a complex, unlimited and indefinable reality. Magickal sigils represent a fine example on the devices that require this approach in order to be properly used in esoteric practice, which becomes particularly clear while studying the Tree of Life. In this case, the esoteric glyph is much more than just a symbol and it should be understood as an actual spiritual technology to be explored in practice, study and meditation; one that if limitations and barriers are imposed quickly loses much of its hidden power.

Sometimes students don't immediately understand the meaning of the word *technology* when used in connection with spirituality, the occult and the magickal arts. Technology in any form represents a branch of knowledge that interconnects specific technical terminology and concepts in their relationship with life and the surrounding environment, which are often associated with science and engineering but are also strongly present in the scholarly fields of the occult and art. Although vastly unknown within popular occult circles, spiritual and esoteric technologies are an important part of traditional occult studies and have been created, developed and improved inside different Orders since the earlier days in Ancient Egypt to the initiatory societies still present in modern time. Spiritual technologies make use of esoteric devices that can be explored and applied by initiates of the mysteries in order to aid in the understanding of Life, the Universe and the secrets of inner Self. The Kabbalah and its Tree of Life represent one of those powerful technologies, but there are many

others like the usage of sigils and Asetian talismans to the study of
metaphysics, energy work and subtle anatomy; all different
technologies available to the occultist that comprise his arsenal of
wisdom and the tools to craft the foundations of the world.

Only in gradual steady progression the wisdom found in the
Tree can be unfolded and properly assimilated. Connections that
might not make sense in the initial study will eventually open the
gates of possibility after further exploration. Passion for the Kabbalah
represents a commitment of years in its study, a reason why so many
fail to understand it. Although so powerful and illuminating when
mastered, this kind of knowledge will not please those seeking brief
answers and easy paths. As mentioned in the introduction to this book,
anyone with such a mindset shall only find frustration and confusion
while studying this work or exploring the Kabbalah through any other
serious publication. To those not concerned about time and immediate
satisfaction, the ones willing to pour their energies into the colossal
undertaking of esoteric learning, they are bound to find through this
gnosis an empowering tool to understand the Universe and
themselves, as the keys in the Tree can be used to explore
macrocosmically and microcosmically. If the reader does not nurture
that same passion, strength and dedication to the noble mysteries of
the occult arts, it might be wiser to close these pages, store the book in
a safe location and return to it if renewed determination is found a few
years later.

The Tree of Life, as a composite symbol, can be used as an
instrument of cosmic understanding and, in that sense, it is a highly
scientific glyph. The occultist must learn to use the Tree as a device of
analysis and research, like a medical doctor makes use of the
stethoscope to locate signs of illness, the biologist goes to a
microscope to understand nature, or an astronomer observes the

cosmos through a modern telescope. The secrets of the Tarot, as an initiatory expression of the wisdom hidden in the Tree of Life, manifest such a potent spiritual tool by the means of art and symbols. When used together, they become a lens to see the Universe, a compass to chart the path and a language to enhance spiritual understanding. They are formulae to calculate reality.

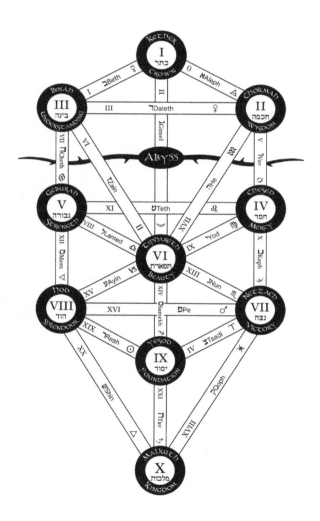

The Tree of Life is formed by ten sephiroth connected through twenty-two initiatory paths. Each sephirah, the singular for sephiroth, is a stage of spiritual enlightenment and magickal mindset, therefore only reached by a specific road of initiation. Each initiatory path that holds the key to open the doors to a sephirah is very important. This occult process of self-development is very powerful and develops through meditation and ritual as the initiate spiritually walks the paths of the Tree, defeats the terrible guardians at the doors of each sephirah and crosses its gates into the inner temple. The fact that there are exactly twenty-two paths in the Tree is far from random, and now you may start to see its relationship with the twenty-two letters of the Hebrew alphabet and how all this wisdom connects with the formation of the physical Universe by the manifestation of matter. This alchemical process of reaching the stage of matter — the physical realm — from an entirely spiritual reality made of energy is what we describe in Asetianism as the mystery *From Purity to Dust*, and you will learn more about it in the following pages. The twenty-two paths in the Tree of Life represent each of the twenty-two *Major Arcana* of the Tarot, therefore expressing profound initiatory keys to the understanding of the whole Tree, making Kabbalistic numerology and gematria an extensive subject of occult science.

Proper study, interpretation and understanding of the Tree are not possible without contemplation. The knowledge of the symbolism and spiritual terminology provided in this *Liber* is essential, but its usage is limited if not completed with the work of meditation. As you might have noticed by now, the spiritual significance of the Tree is dual, as it represents the formation of the Universe from energy to matter, and mirrors the initiatory nature of the soul. It describes the nature of the macrocosm while at the same time mirrors the microcosm of your inner Self. These two interpretations are essential to understand the wisdom of the Kabbalah and they complement each other, holding the key to understand your own place in the Universe at a specific moment in time.

Look within to see the Tree.
Look at the Tree to see yourself.

The structure of the Tree of Life is organized in such a way that the occultist can use it to study the locked doors of the soul, to master thought and Will, to unveil the path of initiation and to understand reality. Through its symbolism it can be perceived as mirroring the triple nature of the Asetian path, the decomposing of subtle energy into its microcosmic elements, the structure of the chakra of the Hindus and the Shen centers of the Asetians, as well as the steps of wisdom and enlightenment found in the Western philosophical schools.

The purpose of the Kabbalah and this introductory *Liber* is to provide the student with the mental and spiritual tools to constantly evolve into a higher state of consciousness and through this process to reach a higher level of wisdom and understanding. In Asetianism the initiate works towards the removal of ego, self-deceit and psychological conditioning created by society and cultural background, so that by the end of the spiritual process there is only raw Self left to acknowledge. When this initiatory state of awareness is attained, the true nature and individuality of Self is finally revealed and understanding of inner truth is unveiled. Only then is real communion with the divine possible. At this point of spiritual maturity prejudice from society holds no power and the mundane opinion of ignorance becomes a confirmation on the accomplishments of the initiate and a tool for further teaching. It is a powerful form of awakening at the root of a groundbreaking sensation of freedom often described by Asetianists committed to path of the Wise. This supreme state of liberation cannot be explained by words or defined by art, but only felt by those who have experienced it.

From Purity to Dust

Studying the formation of the Tree of Life is a complicated but essential mental process to understand Kabbalistic philosophy. Its interpretation and the relationship between each element of the Tree is highly complex and takes years of study to understand, so no detail should be underestimated as such teachings need the action of time in order to properly mature in the mind.

I will reduce each major element of the glyph to its basic foundation and explain the metaphysical development of the final Tree through a simple process of energy transmutation, from the highest vibrational stage into the lowest form of manifestation — the physical realm. This will make clear to the initiate how the process of mystical creation unfolds, as well as how the perpetual cycle of energy manifests through its degrading process of higher vibration in ethereal form into consecutive lower vibrational states until it finally descends into matter where it becomes perceivable by the common mind.

Through the study and understanding of the full process, the occultist opens the inner door to consciously manipulate and interfere with each stage of subtle and mental manifestation, exposing the art of energy work as practiced at an advanced level of magick.

Beyond the realm of matter, thought and even energy, lies the concept of divinity and what can be described as the purest form of existence: Indefinable. Incomprehensible. Infinite. Timeless.

This indecipherable embodiment of divinity is what is known in the Kabbalah as *Ain Soph*, אֵין סוֹף in Hebrew, sometimes also spelled *Ein Sof*. It is a conceptual representation of something immeasurable and beyond understanding to the mind while bonded to the physical reality of incarnation and life sustained in a material body. Ain Soph, the undefinable expression of deity that is at the same time nothingness and everything, is sometimes represented in the Kabbalah by three so-called *veils of negativity*, known as *Ain, Ain Soph* and *Ain Soph Aur*. At this stage, for simplicity of understanding, and as these three layers of unspoken divinity are in fact one and the supreme expression of oneness, we will refer to them simply as Ain Soph.

Below the not always represented invisible veils of Ain Soph reside the ten spheres of initiation known as *sephiroth* — סְפִירוֹת in Hebrew. For the occultist to explore the magick and power of each sephirah, contemplation and meditation are essential but not enough to achieve an enlightened understanding of its nature. It is also required to plunge the psyche deeply into the realm of the sephirah under exploration and experience its energy and lessons first-hand by the means of ritual, metaphysics and transcendence. Only after touching a sephirah with your magickal hands may you understand its secret language.

The first three sephiroth are very special and must be approached differently from the rest of the emanations present in the Tree. They are known as Kether, Chokmah and Binah and represent the only sephiroth located above the Abyss, expressing the archetypical emanations that will unfold the rest of the full Tree.

In Kabbalistic philosophy the spiritual process of their formation is understood under a mechanism of energy transmutation akin to what is experienced in metaphysical practice. This process, although subjective in its approach, is important to understand and we

✝

will now study it in detail in order to comprehend how does the full Tree of Life manifest into reality.

Starting with Kether, meaning Crown in Hebrew, at the very top of the Tree we have the first conscious emanation from the divine — Ain Soph — into our perceivable Universe; the actual personification of unspoken divinity, now definable and objective. In the fabric of the soul Kether appears as the quintessence of absolute oneness, the most transcendent layer of Self. As Kether is manifested through primordial creation, its first spiritual realization is conscious awareness of its own existence; the singular absolute truth — it exists. As we are dwelling in an ethereal realm of philosophy and energy, the very thought of acknowledging and accepting Self creates another sephirah in its image; a reflection of its self-awareness known as Chokmah, meaning Wisdom in Hebrew — in this case, Wisdom of Self and its absolute reality. However, scientific principles as the law of conservation of energy found in modern physics postulate that energy cannot be created but only transformed, and the same is true with the principles of metaphysics that were studied by the ancients. So these emanations of pure energy are not transmutable through an act of mirroring, but instead manifested in a process of fragmentation. This observation leads to the philosophical realization that Chokmah is not in fact an accurate mirror of Kether, but its own distorted view of itself. Awareness of this primordial truth, where the image of Self is not the same as true Self, is then manifested as Binah — the silent bringer of truth —, meaning Understanding in Hebrew.

Wisdom alone is incomplete if not mastered through Understanding, and only then, when united, they can Crown the supreme truth. The three sephiroth complete each other and form the highest representation of divinity: the indefinable Ain Soph. One *mirrors* into two and *becomes* three — the first Kabbalistic and Kemetic

✝

formula of creation: an accurate representation of the divine trinity and the triple nature of Life.

As confusing as this may sound, the reader should remain aware that this represents an abstract visualization of the process as interpreted by Kabbalistic mystics and should be interpreted as a philosophical theory and not a literal account of the Tree's formation.

Also worthy of reference is that while the first three sephiroth are also one single emanation when united, they all reside in an ethereal realm where there is no definition of time and space, so although we describe their formation through the process of energy transmutation explained above, they actually manifest in the exact same moment, and it would not be conceptually accurate to think of one as prior or older than another. Under an Asetian perspective it becomes clear how the concept of Kether resonates with the philosophical representation of Horus, where even its original Hebrew translation to *Crown* seems to hint at a past connection with Ancient Egyptian mythology where Horus was the personification of the pharaoh and sometimes described in religious literature simply as *The Crown*.

The first three sephiroth, often described as the supernal triad, exemplify the triple nature of reality that the Asetians have taught for centuries; the threefold path through which energy can manifest and how spiritual life comes into existence if it could be studied under a metaphysical microscope. They are an accurate personification of Unity in its most absolute form: the magickal formula where a *pure one equals three*. These three sephiroth are silently echoed in nature by the three stars in the belt of Orion, watching life unfold through its thrones in the sky; spiritual reflections of the three Primordials as the perfect echo from the essence of each Lineage in the spiritual bloodline of the Gods, glimmering in the dark cloak of the night.

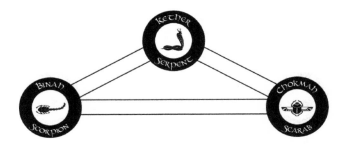

The three primal emanations of divinity appear in an area of the Tree meant to represent a different reality from the rest of the glyph, an ethereal world located above the veil of mystery that the Kabbalists designated as the Abyss or Da'ath. This mystical cloak of both light and darkness separates the realm of divinity and the land of the dead — the Duat from the Ancient Egyptian mysteries — from the lower realities of the astral plane and the world of matter; both permanently existing below the Abyss.

If we approach the supernal triad as one single unit, we can apply the same process of development that we have observed in its very own formation from the veils of negativity. The attaining of consciousness by the three higher emanations creates an imperfect reflection of their nature and energy in the realm below the Abyss, hence forming the sephiroth Chesed by reflection of Chokmah, Geburah by reflection of Binah and, finally, Tiphareth by reflection of Kether.

These newborn emanations are the sephiroth four, five and six, which translate from Hebrew to Mercy, Strength and Beauty, and they embody the higher manifestation of the sephiroth one, two and three in the *real* Universe, below the mystical veil of Da'ath, representing the hexagram of creation and mirroring the timeless principle of Thoth *"As Above, so Below."*

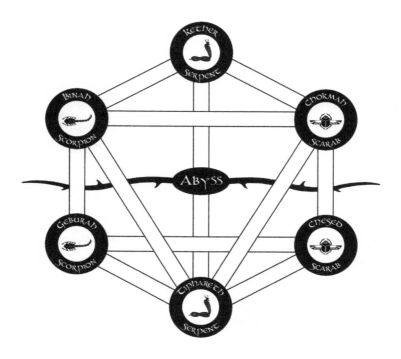

As the active thoughts of the reader might have conspired by now, the lower manifestations of the higher trinity cannot really be an accurate representation of the first three divine sephiroth. Even if we managed to ignore the metaphysical laws of energy transmutation, it would still be foolish to presume that pure divine archetypes could be made manifest in the known Universe, retaining the same conceptual purity. Reality itself exercises influence on their light, changing their properties and energy as it does with every single one of us.

Awareness of this fact, just like in the original process, instantly manifests a third trinity below the previous one, with the sephiroth seven, eight and nine, completing the set of initiatory seats above the physical world; six below the Abyss, already part of this Universe, and three above Da'ath, in the indefinable realm of infinity. The newly formed spiritual spheres are Netzach meaning Victory by reflection of

Chesed, Hod meaning Splendor by reflection of Geburah and Yesod meaning Foundation by reflection of Tiphareth.

The sephirah nine, Yesod, is the lowest manifestation of the one, Kether, before reaching the plane of matter and losing its subtle essence, being connected with the concept and name of this esoteric document, called *Liber* יסוד, meaning *Liber Yesod* or *Liber Foundation*. This sephirah holds central significance in occult studies as it represents one of the first initiatory steps and subtle thrones to conquer in advanced magickal practice.

Yesod is the psychic center and the primary filter through which the occultist experiences the metaphysical phenomena and extrasensory perception; it represents the first gate to energy work and the actual temple in which energy manipulation is consciously achieved. The sephirah Yesod as the cosmic engine behind the machinery of the Universe potentiates the sensitivity over the subtle, located a layer above the locks of matter found in Malkuth, in the same way that Hod embodies the throne of ritual magick and the gate to power through mystical knowledge.

The last sephirah, number ten, is called Malkuth, which means Kingdom in Hebrew, and it represents the physical world — the material plane. This is the final step of decadence and where the soul ultimately reaches after liberating most of its energy and spiritual properties in the paths above through the process of incarnation and physical birth. It is the fragmentation of energy from its highest and purest form into the lowest embodiment; the incarnation of matter.

These concepts along with the unveiling of their spiritual mystery will be further developed in the study of *Liber Sigillum 333*, when addressing the *Sarcophagus of Flesh*.

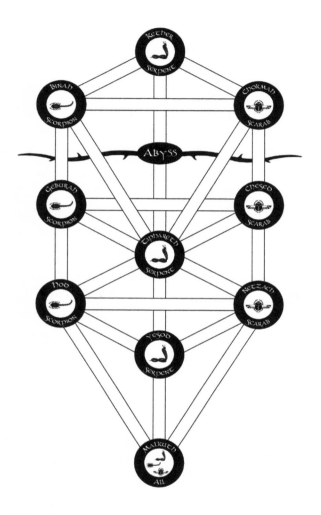

In Malkuth, the distinguishable characteristics of each Asetian Lineage blend with each other, being many times lost in confusion and hard to properly validate. Asetians in the spiritual stage of Malkuth are the unawakened, many times lost in the mundane life and unaware of their inner truth and hidden flame, but yet still retaining their divine spark in potential.

This sphere also represents the uninitiated adept — an Asetianist or the follower of another spiritual path — when the journey of enlightenment starts. It is a realm of unawareness, doubt and confusion, where energy and the subtle realms are hidden. It is the land of the living: the only place where the physical body actually exists.

In this context the Tree of Life represents the core of each initiate, as in terms of spiritual archetype the Serpent, Scarab and Scorpion all live inside each individual Asetian. This is one of the inner mysteries often misunderstood by the students of Asetian spirituality.

It is of paramount understanding that each and every Asetian has an imprint from Horus within the soul and his Divine Self represented in the Crown of Kether. However, this essence expressed through the first sephirah is not something perceivable or definable from a regular level of consciousness, as it is located much above the so-called Higher Self that still resides below the Abyss.

The Higher Self is the highest expression of each individual while still incarnated in the realm of flesh, but not the ultimate reality as that is embodied through his Divine Self above the gates of Da'ath, being part of the indefinable mystery of the Duat; the land of divinity and the highest vibrational plane before the plunge into nothingness, a place without positive or negative, past or future, but where all shapes and forms unify as One.

So the triple formula of Orion found in this system replicates the shift of mindset and energy throughout life and initiation, from the highest and purest form of three emanations above the veil of consciousness to their mundane and incarnated counterparts that degrade over the Tree of Life, reaching the lowest and unaware realm of Malkuth; the Kingdom. Once in Malkuth there is no longer a true spiritual identity, as the Self is so asleep and polluted, centered in the microcosm of the material world, which no longer holds the vision and awareness to realize that there is a whole rich spiritual realm above — represented in the full Tree of Life — and that all of it is in fact an essential part of himself.

The study of such gnosis aids the seeker in how to walk through the twenty-two initiatory roads in order to achieve communion with each sephirah in a state of spiritual enlightenment. Across the long journey of each personal path the student naturally shifts his awareness and mindset through different focus within the Tree, sometimes ending up relocated to a specific sephirah of thought without conscious effort or training, as they all represent universal spiritual thrones. In terms of personal growth and spiritual evolution, walking through the paths of initiation and reaching a specific sephirah does not mean that you are stalled or accomplished in that sphere. The state of each sephirah above Malkuth is not permanent, as everything in spiritual life is in constant motion and change, moved by chaos, nature and magick. So the sephiroth do not represent planes to master, but schools to learn from. They are not expressed through permanent states of enlightenment, but rather impermanent states of awareness and focus, achieved by successfully walking the twenty-two initiatory paths within the Tree of Life, being accepted by the ethereal guardians of each sephirah and to be trusted within its temple — becoming initiated in its mysteries. The temple of each sephirah embodies different attunements of perception in magickal seats of power, connected by the initiatory archetypes of creation.

As we reach at the fully developed scheme of the Tree of Life in this study I will now ask the reader to focus his attention on the triple vertical alignment of the sephiroth. That ordered arrangement defines three clear pillars parallel to each other, related to each Lineage and manifested by three sephiroth each — Malkuth is not really integrated in any of the spiritual pillars as it is located in a lower realm, that of physical matter.

They express what is studied within initiatory societies as *The Pillars of the Mysteries*; the left side of the Tree embodies feminine energies and the right side emanates the male principles, while the center unifies both male and female — described in the occult as the secret path of *The Middle Pillar*. On the Left there is darkness, mystery, introspection and the secrets of the unconscious, while on the Right there is light, openness, clarity and the virtues of the conscious mind. They govern the occult foundations of the Left Hand Path and the Right Hand Path, as two opposed beams leading to the same cave hidden in the ether: darkness and light, two faces of the same force — Equilibrium.

The ancient sages have also described the pillars in terms of polarity — the left being negative and the right being positive by tradition — and although such definition is valid in terms of metaphysics and magickal practice I have avoided delving deeper into the specific details of positive and negative energy frameworks, due to its potential for misunderstanding in earlier studies by the initiates with an inadequate cultural and philosophical background that may be conditioned to improper interpretation on the subjects of negative polarity and magickal destruction in spiritual alchemy. The pillars in each side of the Tree express a concept described in Asetianism as the *universal duality.*

Every manifestation is dual and the forces of nature, being always two-sided, unfold in an universal progression of two that as you can see, under the spiritual microscope, are actually an emanation of three; the Left, the Right and the Middle, that unifies both — oneness and completion.

Observing Binah and Chokmah in the Tree of Life, they are on the same vibrational layer but on opposed sides of the universal scale. That is in tune with the antagonistic forces of the archetypical Scorpion and Scarab as learned in the Asetian tradition. However, each sephirah, just like any subtle object of creation, embodies duality within itself. As an example of such reality, the sephirah of Binah, being the highest manifestation of the divine feminine in the Tree of Life, has a double face. It is at the same time the holy virgin and the intoxicating sexual beast: a violent expression of the *Sexual Flame* in its purest and most divine form.

At this point it becomes relevant to explain that masculine and feminine principles, as well as energy polarities, are independent of biological sexuality. This means that an incarnated stage through the Left Pillar of the Scorpion does not imply an incarnated female, just like a spiritual state attuned within the Right Pillar of the Scarab does not embody a strictly masculine principle. The Kabbalistic glyph hides a vast world of knowledge condensed in a limited group of shapes and symbols. As a further example on the level of complexity when studying the Tree of Life we have the sephirah Netzach that in terms of astrology is connected with the planet Venus, which is often associated with the symbolism of the woman; however, in here it is rightfully located in the column of the Right Pillar, which embodies a masculine foundation. The interpretations drawn from this magickal device are immense and its study should never be approached lightly.

An Asetian, just like each individual student of Asetianism, can walk through the different initiatory paths of the Tree and attain the level of consciousness embodied in each sephirah. Just because the three sephiroth of the Left Pillar are associated with the archetypical nature of the Scorpion that does not mean that a Scarab or a Serpent will not walk that same path; on the contrary, as the Tree of Life is universal and its initiatory framework is meant to be experienced in full. Each individual Asetian is unique and the Family is expressed through diversity. The Lineages are not meant to be interpreted as categorizations of the soul, since such an attempt would be both impossible and futile.

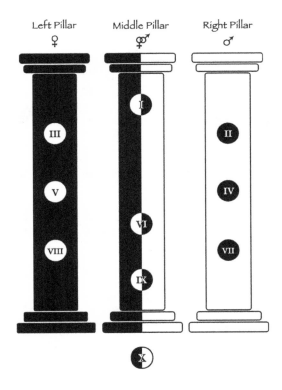

In terms of astronomy and astrology the sephiroth are also used to represent the solar system, where each individual sphere embodies the energy and influence of a specific planet or celestial body. Malkuth as expected represents the Earth itself, while Yesod is the Moon and Tiphareth the Sun, both powerful astronomical influences located in the Middle Pillar. Hod embodies Mercury, Netzach Venus, Geburah

Mars, Chesed Jupiter, Binah Saturn, Chokmah Neptune and finally, Kether represents Pluto, the most inaccessible and outer body in the solar system, just like Kether in the soul. You may have noticed the absence of Uranus in my description and that is because it is actually represented by the Abyss itself and it is embodied by the false and invisible sephirah of Da'ath.

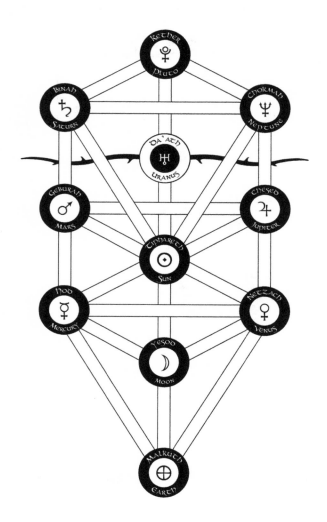

It is no mere coincidence that below the Abyss, where the manifest reality is located, we have seven, and specifically seven sephiroth. That is the realm below the Duat, governed by the seven universal keys of mystery. Intimately related with the Asetian tradition and extensively explored in its many layers of Egyptian magick, seven is a very special and sacred number due to a complexity of reasons, but one in particular is the *Seven Sacred Pillars* of Asetianism.[23]

Ankh. Khepri. Ka. Tiet. Was. Ba. Ib.

These are the cosmic forces and hidden keys that sustain the manifest Universe and give it meaning; the foundations that comprise the microcosm and macrocosm that exist inside each one of us. The reason why I continuously describe these keys as *hidden* is due to their profound initiatory nature and the realization that their proper understanding can open spiritual doors that are able to reach deeper than the wisdom found in any religion or dogma, and because such mysteries cannot be fully understood through any form of literature, painting or music, but only by looking within and gazing into the stars.

> *"When you look long into an abyss, the abyss looks into you."*
> Friedrich Nietzsche

The Tree of Life presents its students with three trinity units above the mundane existence in a triple process that generates three emanations. Again, the initiatory nature of *three* is revealed. For Asetianists it now becomes clear how the Tree represents the essence of the Lineages and their triple nature, from a divine and pure emanation beyond the gates of the Duat into their earthly manifestation while incarnated in the realm of flesh. It mirrors the process of reincarnation as well as the ascension to enlightenment, so always remember that the paths work both up and down the Tree. To an initiate of the Asetian tradition this study reveals a very special key, where the inscrutable, indefinable and timeless veil of the highest manifestation of divinity that the Kabbalistic scholars have described as Ain Soph can in fact be *simply* approached as a philosophical representation of Aset...

Tetragrammaton

The ancient Kabbalist mystics believed reality to be divided into four distinctive worlds: Atziluth, the world of emanation; Briah, the creative world; Yetzirah, the intellectual world; and Assiah, the world of matter. This fourfold division of the Universe echoes the deeper Hebrew understanding of the Tetragrammaton יהוה. Each letter of the Tetragrammaton, Yod He Vav He, represents one Kabbalistic world.

The fourfold division of reality is meant to potentiate the study of thought and practical magick alongside the understanding of the layers of the soul; it describes manifestation and organizes its major conceptual foundations so that conscious and rational thought may be able to examine its elements through their spiritual signature. These four worlds are perfectly mirrored in the Tree of Life and represented by each of the three triads of sephiroth that developed from the higher realm of infinity, with the singular exception found in the world of Assiah, the material plane, where only one sephirah is present — Malkuth.

Each world found in Asetianism and the Kabbalah is also associated with a governing elemental, connecting the Tree of Life with the principles of alchemical practice: Fire, Water, Air and Earth. Fire governs the realm of purest energy and power; Water rules the astral land of emotion; Air empowers the layer of thought; and Earth holds dominion over the physical land of matter. As everything is so intimately connected this leads to an obvious relationship with the four suits of the Tarot, known for being archetypical embodiments of each alchemical element: Wands, pure expressions of spirit and the subtle; Cups, associated with feelings and emotions; Swords, principles of the mind and intellectual process; and Disks, related with the body, matter and the mundane.

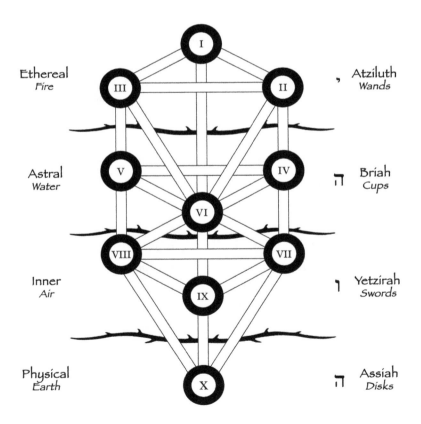

Atziluth represents the world where Kether, Chokmah and Binah live; the Yod ' of the Tetragrammaton as the land of elemental Fire, connected with the suit of Wands in the Tarot. Its Hebrew name means the land of emanations and, although it is probably the truest and most real world in the spiritual realm, it is also the harder — if not truly impossible — to understand while incarnated in a physical body. The three sephiroth present in this realm are separated from the rest of reality by a veil known as the Abyss. Being above the cloak of Da'ath means that they are still in the realm of the Duat, retaining their divine essence without distortion, and although not true deities in principle they can be approached philosophically as demigods, since the three sephirotic thrones when united as one and projected into the realm of nothingness — Ain Soph or Aset — form the unspeakable existence that is the essence of pure divinity.

Chesed, Geburah and Tiphareth are located in Briah, which the Hebrews associated with the He ה in the Tetragrammaton, the realm where elemental Water governs its power and is manifested through symbol by the suit of Cups in the Tarot. This is the land of pure emotion and creation, where the manifestation of a Higher Self presides; it is also the astral plane and in the scope of spiritual evolution it may give even the wisest seeker a feeling of representing the highest realm in existence, unaware of the reality above the Abyss.

The realm of Yetzirah holds the sephiroth Netzach, Hod and Yesod, being the final subtle reality before the world of matter; it is the Vav ו of the Tetragrammaton and manifests the powers of elemental Air, being represented in the Tarot by the suit of Swords. Here lies the formative world of inner reality: the chaotic land of the mind, thought and intricate psychology. It is also the spiritual location for the unconscious mind, the realm of dreams, wicked monsters and hidden desires. In terms of magickal practice the sephirah Hod is related to ritual and the harnessing of energy is driven from the intellect and through the mastery of wisdom, while Netzach connects with the energy drawn from music, painting and other forms of art as the path to overcome limitations. This is the lowest subtle plane, hence being often a realm of confusion, insecurity and the throne of ego. For the unbalanced mind, their own inner realm of Netzach may deceptively seem to represent the highest ladder in the spiritual world — a clear illusion driven from the lack of awareness and growth that sometimes can explain the psychology behind egocentric mindsets and ego-driven personalities.

Finally we reach the material plane of Assiah: land of Malkuth — the Kingdom. Representing the last He ה of the Tetragrammaton it naturally embodies the elemental qualities of Earth and it is present in the Tarot by the suit of Disks; the master of the physical. Assiah expresses the ultimate realm of unawareness — the very beginning of the spiritual journey. It is an impermanent road of passage in the overall path of Life, but yet an essential step to enlightenment.

In advanced studies the initiate learns to think and visualize not only in the traditional three-dimensional view but also to walk the Tree of Life in four actual dimensions. At this level of knowledge the glyph can be examined as four different expressions of the full Tree of Life in a four-dimensional world of spiritual abstraction. Although holding implications in ritual and initiatory meditations, this approach also allows for the accurate representation of the suit cards from the traditional Tarot in the Tree, as each card is connected with the sephirah under the same number and placed in one of the four Trees related to its suit. For example the *Three of Cups* card would be positioned in the third sephirah — Binah — in the Tree of Briah, regent of the element of Water. At this stage the reader that is new to the Kabbalah or to the advanced usage of the Tarot should not worry about the fourfold system of Kabbalistic notation if it seems confusing under a first approach, as its details and considerations are only necessary in more intricate explorations and in particular when the Tree is used in tune with the archetypical system of the Tarot to map out reality and the spiritual realm.

To the initiated occultist venturing the colored pathways of the universal Tree of Life it is of extreme importance to exercise cautious diligence and to do so with courage and without hesitation, but also with awareness for the many dangers that lie in those magickal alleys and hide behind the closed doors present in its paths. The Tree when explored within advanced meditation and ritual becomes a serious magickal map that should not be treaded lightly. Although most unaware students may be protected by ignorance, lacking the keys to open the invisible gates that can lead to the most dangerous paths within the Tree, limited progress can still be attained by perseverance making the Tree of Life a stern esoteric tool that should only be used in astral charting and spiritual navigation by those with a high level of experience in the occult arts. Notwithstanding the fact that the irresponsible occultist is likely to lack the understanding and mastery to work with the most advanced forms of magick, hence rendering most of its metaphysical operations as harmless, some elemental powers may still be manifested without conscious control even if not properly wielded, making exploratory occultism an unpredictable form of magickal practice with disregard for the wisdom of esoteric arts that may produce unexpected results — often of negligible danger, but not always.

In the process of exploring the Tree, not by meditative contemplation but through the ethereal magick crafted by the ancients, the initiate shall encounter puzzles that demand solving, tests that must be mastered, entities that need banishing, powers that require binding and keys that must be provided to the guardians so that you may conquer a trusted ally instead of awakening a monster. The ancient masters entrusted this warning to their apprentices, so that the curious seekers may be aware that while the lower paths of the cosmos may appear to be inviting, vulnerable and even safe, some of the most experienced occultists exploring the intricate paths leading to the higher temples have been lost forever.

The multiple warnings of peril and danger found in any serious Order, coven or group studying the Kabbalah and the traditional restrictions imposed on this path of learning along with its implied veil of secrecy, as maintained since the ancient times of the early Kabbalistic rabbis, are not practical implications driven from a desire to maintain an elitist form of enlightenment, but actually a thoughtful mechanism to protect the initiate venturing through this dangerous realm of wisdom.[24]

All this information and relationships between concepts may seem like a world of knowledge to process at once if the initiate is not yet familiar with the terminology and philosophy under study, so rereading and further examination of this book is advisable as well as taking benefit from recurring reference to the material being presented. As a note, and in the scope of scholarly completion, it should also be referenced that some schools of thought have adopted a different organization of the sephiroth into the four Kabbalistic worlds, like for example the usage of Kether as the sole representation of Atziluth, with Chokmah and Binah manifesting Briah and the six non-materialistic sephiroth below the Abyss being included in Yetzirah, retaining Malktuh alone in Assiah. There is no requirement to study the other systems in order to understand the Tree of Life and they are only mentioned in this context so that the student is given awareness of their existence. Although no approach should be labeled as entirely inaccurate, since they develop from contrasting angles and express different usages, it is important to be aware of those differences when studying the published literature on the Kabbalah as it is common for the seeker to come into contact with the different systems that without said mention and awareness of their existence, often neglected by the authors, could lead to much confusion.

It becomes relevant to remind that the Kabbalistic system, in particular the exploration and understanding of the Tree of Life, is an initiatory form of wisdom where information is often withheld and intentionally altered in publication by initiated authors with the intent to protect some of the most powerful esoteric keys from the preying eyes of non-adepts. However, in this case we have adopted a clear, concise and accurate representation of the system as studied within the Aset Ka in order to avoid confusion and misrepresentation of something that is already inherently complex by nature. Although this openness and revealing of otherwise secret material represents a conscious choice that will be contested and disapproved by initiates of the mysteries and other esoteric societies, I must state as the author of this grimoire that we are not governed by outside occult policy, in any form, when determined by other Orders or bound to the vows of secrecy in them established except our own.

Having made this clear, we may continue this examination of Kabbalistic wisdom as it now becomes comprehensible how the worlds found in the Tree of Life have an almost direct correspondence with the planes of existence studied in Asetianism and discussed in further detail within the *Asetian Bible* — the Physical, Inner, Astral, Ethereal and Divine. However, in Asetianism you have studied five universal planes and in the Kabbalah there are only four worlds of manifestation.

This apparent difference is inexistent under a closer look, as the plane defined in the Asetian tradition as the Divine — the infinite indefinable reality beyond all creation — is expressed in Kabbalistic gnosis as the concept of Ain Soph; the inscrutable world beyond thought.

This fifth world is not always seen as a true plane of existence because it is actually the expression of infinity and not a proper reality defined by boundary or concept — it is the indefinable All.

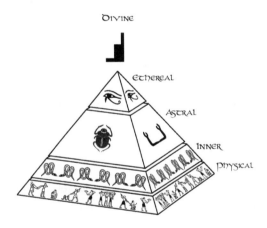

Although the four worlds — or five, depending on how you visualize it — represent the full reality of body, mind, energy and spirit, the two lower planes — Assiah and Yetzirah — are the ones most people would be familiar with and recognize under spiritual practice, being mostly unaware of the other two realms above, which are in fact far more real, permanent and eternal than the lower realities they may perceive as their full existence.

This realization on the existence and spiritual quality of the other planes can be considered a small initiation per se, as awareness and study of those realities already opens the potential doors for their exploration.

Tarot

While addressing the intricate world of Tarot symbolism I would like to start by establishing that the Asetian approach to this occult art is highly spiritual, esoteric and meditative, holding no relation to the superficial and extensively proliferated side of the practice.

The Tarot should be approached as an elaborate, delicate and detailed magickal device that takes wisdom, practice and effort to master, being far more complex and deceiving than the idea perpetuated by popular culture and, as such, deserving of proper respect.

This brief chapter serves the purpose of introducing the reader to the deep spiritual connection that exists between the symbolism of the Tarot, Asetian philosophy and the wisdom of the Kabbalah. The study of the Tarot is a serious spiritual pursuit that requires years of commitment, experience and development, but one that can certainly manifest into a highly rewarding experience to the initiate. It should also be stated that the embrace and study of this occult field of symbolism and archetypical language cannot be governed by time, as learning is a continuous process and the seeker should find new lessons hidden in the cards even after years of practice. It is of paramount understanding to realize that the core of Tarot initiation is through the path of experience. Practice is vital and the key to the understanding of this art, as nothing can truly replace meditation and contemplation of the symbolism found in each individual card and the wisdom to be drawn from such magickal exploration.

To the occultist nurturing a passion for symbolism and art while collecting Tarot decks, the spiritual exploration of every new set of cards along with the meditation and study of each Arcanum is a beautiful process of self-discovery. In every deck, carefully selected to integrate the personal occult collection of the initiate, hides a world of power waiting to be written by the ink of thought and magick; a whole mystical realm to be held in your hand, explored in your meditation and conquered in your dreams.

When holding, shuffling and examining a deck of Tarot cards you should remind yourself that you are holding the keys to the mysteries of the Universe in your hands — quite literally. The Tarot as a magickal device can echo the foundations of nature, time and life through the encoded language of symbolism. It is not a mere tool to predict the future as that remains an open book waiting to be written by each of you, where every individual holds the power to craft and define his own destiny. At best, and when properly understood, the Tarot may unfold the subtle influences and universal alignments of the ethereal threads that comprise the full timeless cord of your individual lifeline, allowing for the experienced practitioner to interpret a possible or predictable future. Still, that *future* is not set in stone and surely wasn't written by the Gods, as every possible future can still be changed and remains to be written through our actions, choices and committed Will. It is important to exercise responsibility and to understand that life has no *undo* button, so every choice we make causes change in the world around us, like ripples in the fluid pond of Life. Having said that, at the Aset Ka we make a conscious effort to set our practices with the Tarot and the study of its esoteric symbolism away from the whole fortunetelling aura found in popular practice and pursued by the seekers who lack a deeper understanding of this beautiful art.

Due to the obscure initiatory nature of the Tarot and, most of all, its common misinterpretation and misrepresentation, the new-age movement has seen the debut of new decks and designs spreading like a wild virus of occult ignorance.

The illustrated art present in the vast majority of these modern decks lack the esoteric wisdom and initiatory symbolism required for a Tarot deck to function as a magickal device. These new versions tend to copy the basic symbolism and structure from older traditional decks and interpret them under a modern view, but since some authors and the companies publishing them are not fluent in the symbolical language of the Tarot and its original connection with the Kabbalah, the most subtle — but absolutely vital — details are missed. It represents another echo of a money-driven society where literally anyone can publish their own decks, as long as it is commercially viable, independently of historical and magickal accuracy and that, unfortunately, results in the mainstream exposure to the Tarot becoming polluted with shallow attempts at producing relevant occult material and the silly variations of the Arcana with demons, angels, dragons and faeries, along with other unrelated fantasy.

Although some examples are quite beautiful in terms of visual arts and the included illustrations, by lacking occult sustenance or even a basic understanding of the hidden spiritual symbolism present in the cards, those decks are rendered entirely useless to any serious occultist, particularly to those interested in its initiatory properties. Such situation has often undermined the credibility of the Tarot as a valuable field within the occult due to the esoteric illegitimacy of many works and the popular approach to the art of symbolism.

From the Tarot decks available to the general public, the two most commonly used in occult practice, and thoroughly examined within the contemporary mystery schools, are the *Rider Waite Smith* deck, developed by Arthur Edward Waite and Pamela Colman Smith, both members of the Hermetic Order of the Golden Dawn, and the *Thoth Tarot* deck, developed by Aleister Crowley and Frieda Harris. Both decks, although vastly different in their approach to art, feature the important symbolism and Kabbalistic wisdom that define them as

†

such relevant instruments to students of the mysteries. The first deck presents a more traditional and simplistic approach, while the latter is imbued with an impressive wealth of symbolism, developed with an increased focus placed on initiation. There are other valuable Tarots available, but these two are among the most well-crafted and extensively studied cards from the publicly available decks, as well as representing one of the most respected tools used in practice throughout different occult traditions, systems and Orders. Of course, there are also special initiatory decks developed within different occult Orders, but those are often kept private and secret, traditionally only accessible to the initiates of each path as they reflect the nature, symbolism and culture that embodies each tradition that created them.

What all these decks — initiatory or not — should have in common, even the useless commercial ones, is featuring a set of twenty-two cards at the core of their teachings. These unique cards are commonly known as trumps, but in proper esoteric terminology they should be called *Major Arcana*. The word *Arcana* has its roots in the Latin and it means *Secrets*, so the definition of *Major Arcana* actually means *Greater Secrets*, being *Arcanum* the singular form meaning *Secret*. That is quite appropriate, as each card holds a very profound initiatory secret. The twenty-two cards of the Major Arcana express universal steps of initiation in the universal ladder of spiritual evolution that every student undergoes in his mystical quest throughout life — usually lifetimes.

Prominent English occultist Aleister Crowley called *Atus of Tahuti* — an alternative spelling for *Djehuty* — to these twenty-two cards, since it was his belief that the word *Atu* meant *Key* in Ancient Egyptian, literally designating the Major Arcana as the *Keys of Thoth*.[25]

Referring back to the wisdom of the Kabbalah previously learned throughout this *Liber*, the number of Major Arcana present in a full deck of Tarot is the same as the number of letters found in the Hebrew alphabet. Every letter should be approached as a small sigil that is connected to a specific card of the Major Arcana set, as each individual Hebrew character expresses a *secret* or, in other words, each letter connects to an initiatory path that unveils a fundamental key to the mysteries. Those secrets are hidden within the Tarot cards — as with the very nature of initiation, they are sometimes hidden in plain sight — and you can find them properly represented in the Tree of Life by the paths of wisdom that connect each sephirah in the system. The study and exploration of both magickal devices in synchrony — the Tarot and the Tree of Life — can provide the initiate with a powerful understanding to many of their esoteric questions and with the details that comprise the architecture of the Universe while manifested through spiritual creation.

Alongside the twenty-two Major Arcana — the major initiations — a full deck of Tarot includes additional fifty-six cards known as the Minor Arcana, or the *Lesser Secrets*. These cards are further organized into two distinctive categories — the court cards and the four suits.

The court cards represent the spiritual expressions of royalty and in traditional occult studies are considered to be entity-related. There are four court cards in each suit and they manifest differently in each deck. In the *Rider Waite Smith*, for example, the King, Queen, Knight and Page form the court cards; while in the *Thoth Tarot* the court set was updated to the Knight, Queen, Prince and Princess, as Crowley believed that these symbolical concepts illustrated a better embodiment of the archetypes these cards are intended to represent. In essence, both systems were developed from the Kabbalah so they can be used in practice with similar results if the underlying symbology and mystical layers are properly understood.

The four suits of the Tarot represent, quite obviously, the four elements of spiritual alchemy and they are divided into Wands, Cups, Swords and Disks (or Pentacles). As you learned through the study of this *Liber*, the Tetragrammaton יהוה can only be understood through a fourfold reality, which the Kabbalists connect with the four elemental powers that manifest the whole Universe. In occult study and alchemical symbolism Wands are known to represent the element of Fire, Cups to represent Water, Swords to represent Air and Disks to represent Earth, the lowest elemental plane of matter. If the initiate seeks to study each element through the metaphysical framework of the Asetian planes of existence, then Wands and Fire connect with the Ethereal reality, exclusive to energy and the realm of spirit, accessible only through True Will; Cups and Water are connected with the Astral plane, empowered by our passions and emotions in their purest form; Swords and Air connect with the Inner plane, controlled by our thoughts and ruled by our mind; and finally Disks and Earth are connected with the expressions from the Physical plane as archetypes of matter, health and body. Such analysis and exploration of each elemental force alongside its relationship with the planes described in the Asetian tradition sheds some enlightening light on the scope of interpretations drawn in the usage of traditional Tarot meditations and spreads.

Delving deeper into the mystical realm of the suit cards the initiate observes that each of the four suits is formed — made manifest — by a set of four court cards and additional ten numbered cards: Ace, Two, Three, Four, Five, Six, Seven, Eight, Nine and Ten. These last — but certainly not least — ten suit cards are expressions of the sephiroth present in the Tree of Life, starting by the energy in its purest form through the Aces in Kether and going down the whole Tree through its ten emanations, ending in the most material and

unaware form with the Tens in Malkuth. Looking at the number of
each sephirah in the representation of the Tree, we find its
corresponding numbered card from the Minor Arcana of the Tarot:
perfect synchrony.

This realization further develops on the notion that a deeper
study of the Kabbalah is at the foundation of any occultist wishing to
venture into the symbolical world of the Tarot. Its connections are
tremendous and they provide many of the keys to the hidden
meanings, initiations and wisdom lost in this forgotten art: one that so
many fail to acknowledge, let alone comprehend. The serious study
and understanding of both occult fields — the Tarot and the Kabbalah
— also provide the required symbolical language to understand many
contemporary esoteric works. A classic example is the apparently
daunting complexity of Aleister Crowley's *The Book of the Law*, as it is
largely developed on the unification of symbolism and concepts from
the Kabbalah and the Tarot.

> *"Invoke me under my stars! Love is the law, love under*
> *will. Nor let the fools mistake love; for there are love and*
> *love. There is the dove, and there is the serpent. Choose ye*
> *well! He, my prophet, hath chosen, knowing the law of*
> *the fortress, and the great mystery of the House of God.*
> *All these old letters of my Book are aright; but צ is not*
> *the Star. This also is secret: my prophet shall reveal it to*
> *the wise."*

AL I:57[26]

This is one of the several passages where said connections
become more perceptible as the *Book* being mentioned is in fact the full
deck of the Tarot, the *Star* is Major Arcanum XVII and the *fortress* is

Major Arcanum XVI, The Tower; while צ is naturally the letter Tsadi of the Hebrew alphabet, determining the positioning of the archetype found in a Major Arcanum in its specific path of initiation in the Tree of Life.

After years of adaptation and mingling with popular culture the Tarot remains an esoteric art of nameless origin as, although scholars arguably trace its introduction into Europe from Mamluk Egypt, historians still struggle to locate its earlier development, but the wisdom translated in the cards by the means of symbolism is universal and can be found all around us, from the most secretive occult traditions to common objects of no particular value as modern playing cards, where the Wands became Clubs, Cups became Hearts, Swords became Spades and Disks became Diamonds. The arcane symbolism and spiritual interpretation may seem *lost* but its hidden wisdom remains unchanged, only to be unveiled by those who are able to see what lies hidden in plain sight...

Liber Sigillum 333

S igillum 333 is a composite magickal seal or sigil created within the Order of Aset Ka, which embodies the spiritual mysteries of Orion and is used by the initiates of the Asetian tradition in meditation, ritual, initiation and esoteric study.

The word *Orion* has its roots in the Latin and is found in the Greek mythology as the expression of the divine hunter, placed by Zeus among the stars. Dating several centuries prior to the birth of Christ, the oldest works of Greek literature, such as Homer's poems in *The Iliad*, make references to Orion and describe the star Sirius as his loyal dog. A celebration to Orion was held at the city of Tanagra, in Greece, as late as the Roman Empire. It does not take much effort to realize how the concept has developed from earlier Egyptian myths — where most Greek mythology and wisdom originated — as the *hunter* is in fact a representation of the *universal predator*. Although the Greek tale of Orion eventually developed in an entirely different fashion of no particular spiritual interest, its underlying origins in the wisdom of Kemet are there, hidden in plain sight.

In Ancient Egypt the constellation of Orion was known as *Sah* and its spiritual significance was of central importance in the initiatory mysteries of its priesthood and in the interpretation of the cycles of Life and Death, as it is found in the older funerary texts.[27]

The word *Sah*, sometimes thought to represent a deity but illustrating a spiritual concept more akin to the personification of an initiatory path and layer of power rather than an embodiment of a specific divinity, was considered magickal and used in ancient spells, prayers and ritualistic utterances. The word alone is a magickal mantra that holds mystical power when uttered in proper practice, a secret the ancients have written in the stars.

Many centuries after the Orion mysteries developed in Ancient Egypt, the *Christian Bible* mentions Orion specifically three times in its passages, often in a cryptic way, serving as a reminder that the old secrets have not been forgotten. In Chinese astronomy Orion was known as *Shen* 參[28] [29] — a character connected with a healing herb used in Traditional Chinese Medicine — where coincidentally the spelling of *Shen* is also the transliteration of an important Ancient Egyptian word and hieroglyph related with the concept of infinity and used in the Asetian tradition to describe the energy centers of the soul in the field of subtle anatomy.[30] In modern literature a reference to Orion was also not forgotten by renowned English scholar and writer J.R.R. Tolkien in his epic literary work *The Lord of the Rings*, where the Orion constellation was described by the Elves as *Menelvagor*, a Sindarin name appropriately meaning the *Swordsman of the Sky*. In Tolkien's mythology the stars of Orion were drawn in the sky of Middle Earth by Elbereth — also known as Varda, meaning *Star Lady* — who in the ancient days empowered the stars with secrets to watch and guard from the sky.[31] [32]

Orion is an astronomical constellation stretching along the celestial equator and visible across the globe, which in initiatory occult studies represents a naturally formed sigil composed by seven major stars. This sigil unfolds the philosophical thread to many important spiritual mysteries, but primarily holds the key for the secrets of Death, Life and Rebirth in its triple formula as examined in this work. The core of the sigil is formed by a recognizable asterism — an astronomical pattern of stars — known as the *Belt of Orion*, and it is formed by the stars Alnitak or Zeta ζ Orionis, Alnilam or Epsilon ε Orionis and Mintaka or Delta δ Orionis.

Recent astronomical research suggests that Alnitak is located at roughly 800 light years away from the Earth and it shines 100000 times stronger than the Sun; Alnilam is 375000 times more luminous than the Sun and is located over 1300 light years away from the Earth; while Mintaka, distanced from our planet by around 900 light years has a light 90000 times brighter than the Sun.[33] [34]

Inside the constellation of Orion and below the three mentioned stars there is an area described in mythology as the *Sword of the Hunter* — the tool of the predator. This interstellar object, believed by the ancients to be another star, is in fact a far more complex structure known as a nebula. The Orion Nebula looks like an inspiring work of art created by the Gods, carved ethereally in the dark sky in shades of violet and red. Located below the triple belt, as mentioned in the book's introduction, this beautiful and mysterious cosmic panting is a place for the birth of stars, holding a wealth of significance for science, philosophy and spirituality.

The natural sigil is completed with other four major stars that encircle the central three present in the Belt of Orion, and they are Bellatrix, Betelgeuse, Saiph and Rigel, the brightest star in the constellation. Together with the three stars at the core of the sigil they form a magickal symbol composed of seven stars. The numbers *three* and *seven* are nothing new in respect to their power and spiritual significance to anyone fluent in the symbolism of the Aset Ka. This natural sigil of Orion drawn in the sky by the forces of the cosmos constitutes the centerpiece of *Sigillum 333*, to be examined in detail along the following pages, and it is sometimes designated as *The Inner Sigil* in advanced studies of this powerful composite seal.

For those seeking the knowledge of initiation and enlightenment through Asetianism it becomes important to realize and accept how this tradition can work as a magickal mirror that the student must learn to study and observe; one that will sometimes reflect and even augment your own flaws so that you can find your true nature without being able to hide behind a socially crafted mask.

Once the initiate breaks free from all forms of limitation and conditioning — imposed by others but also raised by Self — the Asetian path will only reveal pure reality, expressed by the often hidden but profoundly revelatory inner truth, whether or not he is willing to accept it.

Every spiritual and metaphysical initiation within the Asetian magickal system is permanent and irreversible so this document is hereby presented with a word of caution. Responsibility is an essential prerequisite in the study of any advanced magickal tradition, but even more sternly relevant in the case of Asetian spirituality. The very transformational nature of Asetian magick, philosophy and psychology make the spiritual practice found within this tradition a considerably dangerous system if not approached with maturity and respect, particularly when dealing with material that is actively used in initiation. The subtle seed of Asetianism can only be planted deep into the rich soil of the soul. If allowed to germinate, no matter if the initiate is a long time expert in the Asetian magickal arts and wisdom or simply a young inexperienced but hungry student, that seed will sprout its divine fruits of enlightenment in the most adequate way to the seeker's reality and spiritual context. That Asetian spark, a subtle mark carved hiddenly within your soul, will grow and live with you forever as a silent beacon of violet light; a perpetual reminder that the Asetians are still here and their magick lingers in the simpler things in nature.

A Word on Initiation
The ability to see, interpret and understand the mysteries that lie hidden in plain sight is what we designate by an *initiation*. The concept of initiation is one of the most misunderstood in occult studies,

✝

sometimes even exploited by those that do not understand the true nature of initiatory magick. In simple terms someone initiated — and this applies to all mystery schools and occult societies worthy of their name — refers to an individual that is able to see what others cannot. This does not necessarily imply that through initiation someone must develop any sort of supernatural power that would turn him into something greater than the surrounding unaware population. It simply means that they are the ones who were taught the hidden keys — the mystery — that would provide them with the knowledge to see what is hidden in plain sight. Quite simple... But also quite sophisticated. It may be seen as a road for the becoming of greatness, but such power comes from understanding and the subtle truth found within, not by an exercise of mystical power.

Using a very simple example, if you visit an old Christian church in Europe with a friend who has never studied the occult and notice a pentagram engraved on its stone walls — and it would not be as rare of a find as you might think — you immediately make the connection that at some point in history that church and its founders probably had a secretive connection with traditional witchcraft found in old Europe or with alchemy and earlier pagan practices. Depending on the surrounding symbolism and historical background you can even draw intimate connections as to what specific tradition they might have followed and what sort of ritual practices and metaphysical beliefs they held. Your friend — here representing the uninitiated — would probably walk by the symbol and not even notice it, as his mind is not programmed or attuned to pay attention to unknown symbolism, automatically rejecting most of what is alien to their conscious symbolical code. Even if he would notice the pentagram he would most likely just discard it and ignore it.

In this case you would be the initiated, as you would have the keys to another layer of understanding that your friend wouldn't have. You would know the *mystery* of said initiation and so you would be able to see what was there, hidden in plain sight, while it would still remain *invisible* to others. That is the true nature of initiation that most occult societies have kept secret for so many centuries.

By making the readers of this *Liber* aware of this vital but often overlooked magickal concept, I will provide some very important keys to the mysteries of *Sigillum 333* and how as a ritualistic and meditative seal it gracefully succeeds in the embodiment of the Orion secret using the language of symbol, the Kabbalah, the Hebrew alphabet, sacred geometry and, of course, the Asetian path. Such details when unveiled to the student of the occult and properly studied in inner practice will provide him with the necessary knowledge to understand, interpret and further explore the sigil of Orion, as he will never look blindly to its representation ever again, now seeing in it — and through it — what others cannot; becoming initiated into its mysteries.

Initiation provides the student with the tools that allow him to develop another level of awareness — an understanding deeper than that of the mundane mind. Once initiated into the mysteries the adept experiences his world changing forever, as he is now able to see what others cannot through a newfound perception empowered by knowledge. Some may dislike you, judge you or condemn you, as they would lack the ability to see through the initiated Eyes that you now possess. There is no point in arguing or forcing understanding on an uninitiated mind, as their thoughts will not shift nor will their eyes open wide simply because they lack the key to see what you can see. It is the proper road for the initiate — and I would dare say the only wise mindset — to just ignore those that may condemn you from below and instead opt to simply bask in the renewed light of your now initiated Eyes. As I always say… use them wisely.

The occult has always been and will remain a land of deceit. That reality is a positive learning ground for initiation as it makes easier to distinguish the weak from the brave and the foolish from the wise. If the seeker does not develop a strong sense of awareness and perception from the start of his inner journey he will eventually fall into one of the many deceptive pits. Do not give up on the first time you fail to reach for the ladder of wisdom, but instead remember that strength is measured by your ability to get up and admit that you have fallen, otherwise your misstep will not take you through the veil of unspeakable abyss but rather drown you in the ocean of oblivion. That is why, when clouded in the apparent inability to accomplish their own Great Work and to grasp through the veil of the ancient mysteries, some attempt to climb the hidden steps of enlightenment by spreading a layer of deceitful self-importance instead of simply standing on their own.

At the dawn of time we remain confident in our cosmical
role of silent initiators.

The Three Secrets
Three is a special magickal number. Although it is a simple mathematical element for the uninitiated, there is much magick and wisdom hidden inside, only waiting to be found, studied and liberated by the student of the mysteries.

Orion is examined in the context of this *Liber* as a spiritual expression for the mystical formulae of the sacred Three, where the central stars that form the constellation's belt — Alnitak, Alnilam and Mintaka — are at the core of these teachings. They embody a powerful expression for the spiritual archetype found in each Asetian

Lineage — Serpent, Scarab and Scorpion —, as well as the symbolical hallmark for the three-folded path of Death, Life and Rebirth, so important to any mystical tradition. This connection and spiritual framework is present throughout history in many forms of occult architecture, being most notably pioneered by the Ancient Egyptians in their religious edifications, particularly demonstrated in the state-of-the-art technology — in terms of science, engineering and metaphysics — found in the iconic initiatory temples that became known as the Pyramids, located in the necropolis of Giza.

The Pyramids of Khufu, Khafre and Menkaure are a symbolic mirror of the sky meant to function as a metaphysical door to the cosmos, rising among the heat and dust of the Egyptian desert. When conceptually aligned with Orion they are a perfect expression of the formation of the Asetian Lineages as found in the Kabbalistic Tree of Life. The three stars high in the sky can be understood as the spiritual emanation from the three Primordials located above the Abyss — in the timeless realm of the Duat —, while the physical Pyramids express their earthly manifestations below Da'ath as the incarnations from the three distinctive Lineages reflecting their archetypes from above.

Such understanding brings further meaning to the legacy of Thoth succinctly described by the formula *"As Above, so Below,"* which defines one of the conceptual backbones for the architecture of Asetian spirituality. In a Latin translation of the legendary work of Thoth known as the *Emerald Tablet* or *Tabula Smaragdina,* which is also included in the medieval dissertation *Secretum Secretorum* originally in Arabic, we find the following passage:

> *"Quod est inferius est sicut quod est superius, et quod est superius est sicut quod est inferius, ad perpetranda miracula rei unius."*

☦

The sentence translates to *"That which is below is as that which is above, and that which is above is as that which is below, to perform the miracles of the one thing."*

This law of Thoth is found to be accurately expressed in the sacred land of Egypt as the three Pyramids mirror the higher reality of the stars by representing Orion and its three inner mysteries, as our microcosm is only but a reflection of the subtle macrocosm hidden above the Abyss. The mundane Self is an expression of the Higher Self and the Higher Self is an expression of the Divine Self.

To the readers paying greater attention to detail, it may have come to mind why it is that throughout the whole book I have recurrently used the words Death, Life and Rebirth in this particular order while the rest of the world refers to this cycle as Life, Death and Rebirth. This change in literary order reflects an important paradigm found in Asetian spirituality that is intimately connected with the philosophy behind this work. To a regular mindset, physical Life is the focus of spiritual reality, reflected in the traditional order of Life, Death and Rebirth. People see Life as the ultimate goal and the center of their existence, so after it naturally follows Death and then the mystical Rebirth through reincarnation, and once again back to Life. This is how the vast majority of world religions that have adopted reincarnation within their philosophies express the perpetual cycle of their spiritual reality. But not the Ancient Egyptians...

In Asetianism, the ultimate liberation is not manifested through a permanent return to Life, but instead by an immortal return to Death. The Duat — Egyptian land of the dead and underworld — is the true world of *life* to an enlightened Asetian mind: their own native realm. Life is impermanent and transitory, while Death is eternal, infinite and the cradle of immortality.

Life is a powerful school of spiritual evolution, but merely a road in the universal path of growth, while Death is the true home of the soul: the throne of the Divine Self.

From this spiritual perspective Death is actually far more real than physical Life, which in mystical terms represents a powerful deceptive illusion. As dark and morbid as this may sound at first glance, it is actually quite a positive and enlightening view of the spiritual roadmap of the soul. Just like with the advanced Ancient Egyptian mind, the focus is instead placed on Death and its hidden mysteries; the breaking from the conditioning of matter and flesh to focus on the truth found within as the only real part that can survive physical death. This leads not to a sad or depressive view of the world, but actually to an enlightened mindset that has learned to enjoy life to its fullest by acknowledging its impermanent beauty and to value every moment.

With this secret in mind I have used Death, Life and Rebirth as an initiatory literary detail hidden throughout this book, since the Asetians approach the spiritual cycle with Death as their home, Life as the impermanent path in-between and Rebirth as the awakening into Death and the divine communion with Aset.

> *"Live as if you were to die tomorrow.*
> *Learn as if you were to live forever."*
> Mahatma Gandhi

The possible meanings behind the formulae of the sacred Three are endless and not restricted to the parallels drawn in this text. They are represented in the energy and symbolism of *Sigillum 333*, which as a powerful and intricate magickal device holds the keys to initiate the seeker with deeper layers of understanding of said formulae as he commits to further study and magickal work with the seal. In a small reference to the *Book of Giza*, the first work included in this three-folded grimoire, it is relevant to note that the occult document is formed by three distinctive Sebayt, while inside each Sebayt there are specifically thirty-three utterances. Nothing is random.

Beyond the multitude of meanings, the following pages will approach and describe three different layers of initiation from the formulae of the sacred Three, connected with *Sigillum 333*, and walk the initiate through the powerful spiritual work to be accomplished when studying the mysteries of Orion. As an esoteric tool imbued with energy and meaning, *Sigillum 333* will only continue to provide for those who have searched within its mysteries with honesty.

Sarcophagus of Flesh

The First Initiation

The descent of Spirit into matter is the spiritual process described in Asetianism as *From Purity to Dust*. While incarnated, the soul finds itself locked in a conceptual sarcophagus — the physical plane. The realization and awareness over this process and its spiritual implications are of vital importance in the work of initiation through the mysteries of Orion and its profound message of liberation. The philosophy behind this process can be properly understood during the study of *Liber* יסוד, which includes a chapter dedicated to the development of the concept and its metaphysical correlation with the Tree of Life.

One famous tale found in Ancient Egyptian mythology that survived the test of time is the account of Seth locking Osiris inside a powerful box made of solid gold, in order to imprison him away from his powers and blessed life. This golden box represents the material world: a spiritual metaphor for the constricted life in the material

✝

plane.[35] It symbolizes the desire from Seth to keep the royal family locked in a superfluous world of lesser significance instead of roaming freely through the plane where they rightfully ruled — the realm of Energy and Spirit — which in his deviant greed he wanted for himself, along with the throne of Egypt. In this state of unawareness, locked inside a prison of shimmering gold, the mind and soul are kept ignorant of their full existence and true potential outside of that box. Self is maintained in deep sleep, like a lost dream where the whole reality seems to be restricted to those shining walls of deceptive gold. This is the realm where mankind is locked up and jailed; the blind reality of physical matter, the true expression of unawakened futility and ego. To most people, these conceptual walls of matter raised by the laws of the physical plane represent their complete vision of reality, living under the vain sleep where this is all that matters, unaware of the wide subtle world of possibility that exists beyond this cage of body and matter that makes most of what is thought to be valuable quite superfluous in the grand scheme of things.

This is one of the most basic secrets behind Sethian rule and influence as well as the dangerous reality behind their power; a mythical expression from a legacy of control and unawareness, fully manifested in the plane where they hold their highest power — the physical realm of matter where all unaware souls are imprisoned. This Sethian dominion is well mirrored in the last era — the *Djehuty of the Crocodile* — that is historically marked with the rise of religious slavery to dogma and the fear of the divine, along with an increasing focus on the decadence of material possession, while the subtle and nature suffered the consequences of modern thought, being neglected and defaced by men, owners of the strongest intellect among all animals and hence spiritually responsible to protect it.[36]

Without this initiation into a state of awareness the soul carries on a life of blindness to the beautiful, empowering and liberating spiritual reality that hides right above their heads and all around them, but which they can not see, feel or touch, leading to the generalized conviction that it simply does not exist. This spiritual blindness — the jail of the soul within matter — is not only manifested by those that do not accept their spiritual side, but also, and many times more deceitfully, by those who see themselves as spiritual and aware when in reality under the veil of truth they are locked into the lower depths of their physical tomb, living a life of absolute slavery controlled by many *masters* like wealth, youth, possession, recognition and appearance. Just because someone attempts to study the occult, professes a spiritual life or tries to come forth as a mystical mind capable of deeper thoughts, that alone does not imply any level of enlightenment, wisdom or awareness. In fact, many vain representations of Self that are found in people seeking the magickal arts are often a sad expression of ego, insecurity and delusion.

This is an important mindset of central study and meditation, a major accomplishment for an initiate of the Asetian path, as well as a hallmark that truly distinguishes an Asetian or a learned Asetianist from an unawakened mind, by being free in the deepest and most liberating form. Through this path the seeker experiences the purest and most powerful of all forms of freedom by cracking his own sarcophagus open — the initiation into awareness — and is free to explore the realm of Spirit and master the energies in full awareness of all his potential.

Once the jail of physical matter is broken it cannot be locked again. When the initiate achieves such a state of mental and spiritual freedom — empowering him to see a glimpse of the Universe through the Eyes of an Asetian — he cannot be blinded again and his awareness is then unleashed to harness the full spectrum of his inner potential. This alchemical process of spiritual evolution sustains the philosophical and metaphorical realization that most people being capable of seeing in *color* are actually only experiencing a powerful illusion. They truly can only see in shades of gray while under the illusion that such view is the full spectrum of color, hence assuming it as the whole manifestation of the rainbow. But once you have your first glimpse of sight in real color, if you are capable to look at what an Asetian can see even if only for a split second, then a whole new Universe unfolds in front of your eyes. That is true initiation… and it is eternal.

> *"Once learned the tools that allow to see from an Asetian perspective, the soul remains forever changed, unable to go blind again."*
>
> Tânia Fonseca

This first initiation of Orion is accurately represented in Major Arcanum XVI of the Tarot — The Tower. As a cataclysmic expression of supreme destruction, this card, like so many others, is greatly misunderstood. The collapsing of the strong structure that is the tower symbolizes the break from belief and dogma with the rupture of our physical prison. The process can be painful and often devastating, but it will set the initiate free from the conditioning of the mundane. It will unleash the soul and open the ways. Pure, absolute and fearless freedom awaits once the foundations of your inner tower are destroyed. Remember, from the darkest times come the deepest forms of liberation.

The concept of awakening, often referred to in Asetianism, and so intimately connected with the tradition of the vampire, holds a great spiritual correlation with this mystery that I have described as the *Sarcophagus of Flesh.*

The breaking of the sarcophagus of matter and the conquer of independence from all the mundane conditioning, through the attaining of conscious spiritual awareness, is a powerful form of magick and personal achievement that brings the power over the subtle — but more real — existence back to the hands of Self. This represents a profound form of awakening, so hidden but also so very real, being a true hallmark of vampire spirituality so often misunderstood by the uninitiated, still locked inside their own mystical prison.

It should be noted that none of this means to say that every mundane aspect should be rejected and discarded, or that life in the material plane is inherently shallow and obsolete. Quite on the contrary, as life in this realm is a unique opportunity to learn and evolve in ways that mere subtle existence would not potentiate. It is up to the individual to make a conscious choice and take active steps in order to embrace life in its full potential for spiritual learning rather than to simply waste it in the empty illusions of the superfluous. In the end, true power lives inside every single one of you. The physical world allows for the unfolding of True Will and its enlightening flame to be made manifest once purified in the higher realms of subtle existence. However, to reach such a venerable state of freedom, when you can master the physical plane in order to manifest your inner essence, you must first break from the deceptive chains of matter.

That is one of the greater mysteries behind the alchemy of the soul and why the ancient alchemists and Kabbalists see Earth as a lesser element. While describing the Hebrew language in *Liber* יסוד I have explained that the three primary letters of the mystical alphabet were Aleph א, Mem מ and Shin ש, representing the three major elements — Air, Water and Fire. Earth is intentionally not represented, as in the Kabbalah this elemental force is approached as less powerful than the other three. The reason behind this apparent omission lies precisely in the mystery that I have named the *Sarcophagus of Flesh*. Earth remains a powerful elemental, but a deceptive and controlling one that the occultist must learn to break in order to gain control over the other three; the ones that truly manifest the spiritual world.

So now you have learned the alchemical secret behind the mystical thought of the descent into matter; the fall from purity to dust. It is the realization on the condition of the soul upon reincarnation — its jail in the sarcophagus of flesh. This is the central spiritual mystery taught inside most secret societies in history, from ancient times to the modern day. That is the first initiation of Orion; the break from the agonizing tomb where the Ba lies hidden and locked away from its full potential. But as a first initiation, that is the very early step into Orion…

Mysteries Unveiled
The Second Initiation

In this chapter you are about to embark on the study and direct analysis of the symbolical elements present in *Sigillum 333*. If the reader is not familiar with actively working with this specific sigil and the study of its symbolism, it is suggested that he dedicates some time to the independent usage and exploration of the sigil in meditation and ritual prior to the reading of the following chapter. In ceremonial magick, the sigil may be reproduced by the occultist's method of choice, often illustrated by hand through paper and ink in a gentle process of creation not governed by the limitation of time. This is later to be consumed in magickal practice by the heat of the flame that, with the four elementals as your witness, shall destroy the artistic energies and manifest its encoded essence within the mind of the initiate.

The complexity of this sigil and its included symbolism is immense, so going through every aspect and correlation present in its different elements would result in a full book on its own. However, I will be guiding the reader in a structured study of its main initiatory elements and the development of the sigil through its several fundamental parts and the correlating magickal significance to be drawn for each layer of wisdom. During this examination make sure to use continuous reference to the full sigil included in the cover of this *Liber*.

Starting by the center of the magickal seal there is a representation of the seven major stars found in the astronomical constellation of Orion that form what we have previously designated by the natural sigil of Orion or inner sigil, here illustrated inside a black circle that symbolizes the sky — and the whole Universe — through its circular shape, an ancient symbol of perfection and geometrical personification of the absolute.

In the outer layer of the black universal circle there is an hexagram with six symbols differentiated into two different groups of inverted coloration — the basic hieroglyphs for the three Asetian Lineages in black with white background and three Greek letters drawn in white laying inside a black background.

The Ancient Egyptian symbols for the Lineages and their significance require no introduction to a student of Asetian magick, but the Greek letters might appear as a surprise to some. They are used in this sigil due to their scientific and historical significance in terms of astronomy, as they correlate with the three stars in the belt of Orion — ζ is the letter Zeta and symbolizes Alnitak, ε is the letter Epsilon and represents Alnilam, and δ is the letter Delta and expresses Mintaka.

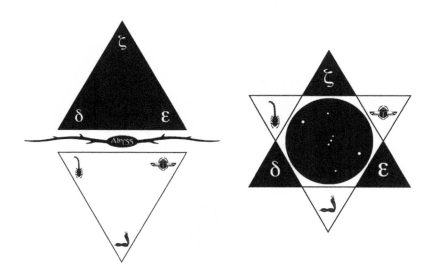

What might not be perceivable at surface is that this hexagram is in fact the union of two opposed triangles. The first one in black with the representation of the stars — the divine reality — and the second in white with the representation of the Lineages — the earthly manifestation of the higher stars below the Abyss.

When crossed together and united by the transcendence of the alchemical Abyss, they allow for the refraction of spiritual light and make visible the universal truth at the center, as expressed by the natural sigil of Orion, like two powerful magickal lenses that when placed at the top of each other by the hands of the elders can reveal a hidden image — the secret.

As the reader should now realize, these two triangles hide the mystery of the descent into matter — *From Purity to Dust* — through the formation process of the Tree of Life as I have described in *Liber* יסוד. When the triangles, two-dimensional symbolical representations of a pyramid here illustrated in inverted position, are moved together and united they become one singular entity and define the geometrical figure known as the hexagram.

Once the hexagram is formed, the archetypes of the Lineages and their divine emanations are now facing each other as opposed smaller triangles — Alnitak and Khufu are facing the Serpent; Alnilam and Khafre are facing the Scarab and Mintaka and Menkaure are facing the Scorpion.

The learned Kabbalist can see the most transcendental realms of the Tree of Life — the world of Atziluth in black and Briah in white — accurately represented in the sigil as the two higher triads of sephiroth appear in their right positions inside the two triangles of this secret: Kether, Chokmah and Binah in black; Chesed, Geburah and Tiphareth in white. The symbolism of the sigil finds the supernal triad of the higher emanations expressed by Alnitak, Alnilam and Mintaka, and their manifest incarnations below Da'ath properly represented by the known Lineage hieroglyphs.

The hexagram being the union of two opposed triangles, one

regular and another inverted, further hides another profound symbolical message. These two triangles are the traditional alchemical symbols for Fire and Water; the two major opposed forces and energies in the Universe. By combining them inside us through the magick of the seal we achieve the ultimate alchemy as the perfect union of opposites — the Hexagram: a powerful representation of balance and spiritual equilibrium.

This is the great secret behind the symbolism of the hexagram as studied within the Aset Ka, an initiatory detail that you now may understand as it remains hidden in plain sight, as a simple hexagram shall never look the same again. Its spiritual message is profound and transformational, but once fully understood and assimilated it becomes clear and beautiful in its simplicity. That hidden meaning is also unequivocally represented in Major Arcanum XIV of the Tarot, entitled Temperance, in which its traditional design a winged figure with a triangle at the chest mixes an unknown mystical fluid between two golden goblets. This is the Tarot card that Aleister Crowley infamously altered its name to Art, generating much controversy among the uninitiated. This *Art* that he refers to is the unification of the opposed forces present in duality as the internal alchemy of the occultist, and in the redesigned version of his deck Frieda Harris has drawn a figure with two heads pouring Fire and Water into a magickal cauldron. This literally illustrates the mystical union of Fire and Water, the two alchemical elements represented by the opposed triangles that create our hexagram. The two-headed figure mingling the elementals through her magickal art signifies the perfect bond and union of the King and the Queen, but Crowley and Harris went even further in the symbolism included in the card, as this androgynous entity is controversially depicted with six breasts, which you now can see represent the six smaller triangles that form our hexagram.

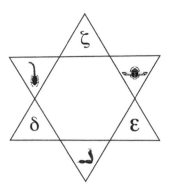

As we get deeper into the mysteries of the spiritual alchemy present in *Sigillum 333* by understanding the revealing detail that our hexagram is in fact the union of two alchemical symbols, the reader may acknowledge two smaller triangles at the top and another two below the hexagram figure inside the seal. These are the renowned alchemical symbols used in magick to represent the four elemental forces of the Universe — Fire, Water, Air and Earth. In Ancient Egyptian mythology these powerful elementals were hidden behind the theological concept of the *Four Sons of Horus,* and they were known as Imset, Qebehsenuf, Duamutef and Hapi — the four canopic jars used in the process of mummification.[37] [38]

The traditional occult method of thinking and practical magick is actually an exercise of highly scientific formulae, as the tools of the alchemist and initiatory occultist, described as the four elemental powers, are accurately represented in modern science, studied in physics and chemistry as the four states of matter: solid, liquid, gas and plasma. The physical properties of solid states are akin to the metaphysical qualities of elemental Earth, just like liquid is comparable to alchemical Water, gas is related to Air and plasma naturally equates with magickal Fire.

Each of these elements in the sigil interconnects two archetypes of different Lineage, hinting at further alchemical implications between the dual emanations. They are represented between a higher and a lower emanation, never of the same Lineage. For example, the symbol for Fire is between the ζ of Alnitak connected with the divine Serpent and the incarnated Scorpion, while the symbol for Earth is located between the ε of Alnilam connected with the divine Scarab and the image of the incarnated Serpent. These complex correlations, hard to understand on a first study, are related with the potential of energy interaction between the essence from two different Lineages and how that wisdom can be used in the alchemy of the soul through highly advanced metaphysical work, while it also establishes an accurate ritualistic framework concerning the ideal process of elemental evocation in Asetian ceremonial magick.

FIRE   WATER   AIR   EARTH

On each side of the hexagram there are two hieroglyphs of the Ankh ☥ — one straight and another inverted. This ancient hieroglyph is of central importance in the Ancient Egyptian tradition where it was considered sacred and often only represented in the hands of the Gods. In terms of language it translates literally to *Life* and it is related with the Asetian view of immortality. It is a powerful sigil in its own right, owner of one of the most ancient symbological legacies found in history with vast magickal and spiritual implications and, although often abused and misrepresented in modern times, its many layers of power are out of the scope of this *Liber*. The two Ankh included in this

☥

sigil convey several occult meanings, but the one we will reveal in this study is connected with *The Pillars of the Mysteries*. As you have learned in *Liber* יסוד the left side of the Tree of Life manifested by the sephiroth Binah, Geburah and Hod — different emanations of the Scorpion archetype — is known as the Left Pillar and it is a spiritual representation of our own inner darkness, here illustrated in the sigil by an inverted Ankh on the left. While visualizing the Tree of Life represented in the seal you should realize that by being positioned between the Scorpion and δ this inverted Ankh appears accurately located in Geburah and Binah.

On the right side of the Tree we have Chokmah, Chesed and Netzach as emanations of the Scarab, here illustrated by the straight Ankh; our face of light. Placed in the sigil between the Scarab and ε, the Ankh properly appears by the side of Chesed and Chokmah when visualizing the Tree of Life and its sephiroth. With this mindset, at the center of the sigil the representation of Orion through its seven-folded mysteries or stars can also be seen as a secret Ankh, symbolizing the Middle Pillar, as the balance and unification of opposite forces accurately located in symbol between ζ and the Serpent — Kether and Tiphareth — the two first sephiroth of the Middle Pillar in the Tree of Life.

The study of these connections and symbolism as it draws knowledge from different layers of wisdom and traditions may seem confusing on a first approach, hence why several readings of this document is recommended while in the process of studying the sigil, until all elements and their relevance are understood and properly assimilated.

Reaching the outer rim of the sigil the student finds a black circumference with six letters of the Hebrew alphabet. This alphabet is of central significance in every layer of knowledge related to the Kabbalah as well as extensively used in the foundation of Western mysticism for centuries. Its importance, symbolism and conceptual development can be properly understood during the study of *Liber* יסוד, where the reader can learn the secret behind the formation of the twenty-two letters that compose it. These small and curvy letter-sigils identify with each of the twenty-two initiatory paths found connecting the ten sephiroth in the Tree of Life, as well as the twenty-two Major Arcana from the traditional Tarot. With this in mind it becomes clear how each singular Hebrew letter embodies the symbolism of every spiritual pathway found in this system, so uniquely illustrated through art and color in the paintings of the Tarot cards.

In the sigil of Orion — which we described as *Sigillum 333* — the six Hebrew letters represented in the outer circle of the seal are located near the geometrical vertex of each of the individual six triangles generated by the union of alchemical Fire and Water as previously studied. Adopting a clockwise progression the selected Hebrew letters are Vav ו, Kaph כ, He ה, Beth ב, Gimel ג and Yod י. Two letters for each Lineage, in a divine and earthly manifestation of its energies. Again... duality.

✝

Located in Alnitak ζ and the Serpent we have the letters Vav ו and Beth ב. Vav ו represents the archetype of the illuminated guide, connected with Major Arcanum V of the Tarot — The Hierophant —, an universal symbol for the inscrutable connection between the human and the divine; a link between the sacred and the profane. Beth ב as a representation of knowledge and wisdom is tied to Major Arcanum I of the Tarot — The Magus — that beneath its mystical power also holds the dangerous trap of lack of conscience.

Near Alnilam ε and the Scarab we find the letters He ה and Kaph כ. He ה is a personification of transformational energies and purification, related to Major Arcanum XVII of the Tarot — The Star — that leaves a message of hope, possibility and eternity. Kaph כ is connected with dynamism and movement, which through Major Arcanum X of the Tarot — Wheel of Fortune — hints at new beginnings, uncertainty and the roads of fate.

Connected to Mintaka δ and the Scorpion are the letters Gimel ג and Yod י. Gimel ג is a letter of profound lunar influence, associated with Major Arcanum II of the Tarot — The High Priestess — that as the initiatrix she represents an archetype of intuition, trust and delicate strength. Yod י embodies darkness and introspection through Major Arcanum IX of the Tarot — The Hermit —, a mystical view on the rejection of the mundane and the quest for inner light, sometimes also connected with isolation and solitude.

It is important to keep in mind that all these cards and their wealth of symbolism are universal spiritual archetypes that represent powerful ideas and initiations, not emotional or psychological characteristics, so they should never be interpreted lightly. Their message and meaning are profound as each represents a single Major Arcanum of the Tarot, which in Latin means *Greater Secret*, here only represented six out of the twenty-two possible paths of life once the

☥

initiate sets forth in his inner quest for enlightenment through the worlds of the Tree of Life. Once more I urge the readers to remain aware that the Tarot cards being referred to, as well as their archetypal meanings, do not represent an attempt to categorize each Lineage in whatever form but instead are used in this context as initiatory facets of the dual emanations from each Lineage and their location in the Tree of Life, particularly due to their positioning above and below the Abyss of Da'ath. To simplistically associate the mysteries of an Arcanum from the Tarot with a specific Lineage would be a mistake.

As a last detail, there are three circles of different radius and thickness featured in the sigil, a last homage to the power and symbolism hidden behind such an apparently simplistic thing... the number Three.

The final mystery and ultimate key takes us back to the very early start of this study and it lies in the shape of Orion itself, as mirrored in the night sky while enchanting the initiatory body of Nut. That is why that illustration holds the central position in this sigil imbued with the teachings of the ancients.

Beauty is found in detail and only achieved through
simplicity.

Orion Key

<u>*The Third Initiation*</u>

0. Oh the void of the Fool! Through the mystery Key thy initiation cometh veiled in Three.

1. Hidden in the darkest face of Nut lies the Key to this mystery.

2. In the aphotic hours of inner clarity consume Her naked body and thou shall see!

3. The formula from Above is three equals one and one equals one plus one so that three equals seven.

4. The Splendor lives in Beauty but Beauty lives in Strength.

5. To Crown thy Self you must not seek Wisdom but awaken Understanding.

6. The Kingdom is for the weak and the blind for thou must break free from such prison.

7. His Beauty might be seductive but only in three shall the crownless see above the Abyss.

8. Three gave three and three but only then all became one.

9. The veil of time shall now be closed for this is the hour to seal it from within.

Liber Sigillum 333

Portuguese Edition

Sigillum 333 é um sigilo mágico ou selo compósito criado na Ordem de Aset Ka que incorpora os mistérios espirituais de Orion, sendo utilizado pelos iniciados da tradição Asetiana em práticas de meditação, rituais, iniciação e estudos esotéricos. A palavra *Orion* tem origem no Latim e encontra-se na mitologia Grega como a expressão do caçador divino, colocado por Zeus no céu entre as estrelas. Alguns séculos antes do nascimento de Cristo, poemas antigos da literatura Grega como *A Ilíada* de Homero, fazem referência a Orion e descrevem a estrela Sirius como o seu cão de confiança. Historicamente, celebrações dedicadas a Orion foram mantidas na cidade de Tanagra, na Grécia, até ao período do Império Romano. No estudo dos mistérios e legado histórico, é simples compreender como a simbologia de Orion se desenvolveu a partir de conceitos Egípcios mais antigos — onde grande parte da mitologia e conhecimento Gregos encontram a sua origem — pois o *caçador* é, na realidade, uma representação do conceito espiritual do *predador universal*. Embora a mitologia Grega em torno de Orion se tenha eventualmente desenvolvido de uma forma sem especial interesse espiritual, as suas origens no conhecimento Kemético estão bem presentes, escondidas à vista de todos.

O significado espiritual da constelação de Orion, conhecida por *Sah* no Antigo Egipto, tinha um papel de extrema importância nos mistérios iniciáticos bem como na interpretação dos ciclos da Vida e da Morte, como é comprovado pelos textos funerários mais antigos.[27] A palavra *Sah*, por vezes usada como referência a uma divindade, mas mais correctamente representativa de um conceito espiritual relacionado com a personificação de um caminho iniciático, era considerada mágica e utilizada em encantamentos antigos, orações e expressões ritualistas. A palavra em si é um mantra esotérico que esconde um ténue mas profundo poder místico quando proferida em práticas das artes ocultas, um segredo que os anciãos escreveram nas estrelas.

Vários séculos depois dos mistérios de Orion se terem desenvolvido no Antigo Egipto, a Bíblia Cristã refere Orion especificamente três vezes nas suas passagens, muitas vezes de uma forma encriptada, relembrando que os velhos segredos não foram esquecidos. Na astronomia Chinesa, a constelação de Orion é conhecida por *Shen* 參[28] [29] — etimologicamente relacionada com uma erva medicinal utilizada em Medicina Tradicional Chinesa — onde, coincidentemente, a grafia de *Shen* representa também a transliteração de uma antiga palavra Egípcia ligada ao conceito de infinito, encontrada frequentemente na tradição Asetiana para descrever os centros energéticos da alma no estudo da anatomia subtil.[30] Na literatura moderna, a referência a Orion não foi também esquecida pelo reconhecido escritor Inglês J.R.R. Tolkien, na sua obra literária *O Senhor dos Anéis*, onde a constelação de Orion é descrita pelo povo Élfico como *Menelvagor*, um nome Sindarin que adequadamente significa o *Guerreiro da Espada no Céu*. Na mitologia de Tolkien, as estrelas de Orion foram desenhadas no céu da Terra Média por Elbereth — também conhecida por Varda, a *Senhora das Estrelas* — que nos primórdios dos tempos escondeu nos céus segredos de aviso e protecção.[31] [32]

Orion é uma constelação astronómica que se estende pelo equador celeste, sendo visível por todo o globo. A nível ocultista, representa um sigilo cósmico natural, formado por sete estrelas principais. Este sigilo esconde uma profunda ligação filosófica a muitos mistérios espirituais mas, primariamente, detém a chave para os segredos da Morte, Vida e Renascimento na sua fórmula tripla, conforme explicado nos conteúdos deste livro. O núcleo do sigilo é formado por um reconhecido asterismo — um padrão astronómico de estrelas — chamado *Cinturão de Orion* e é formado pelas estrelas Alnitak ou Zeta ζ Orionis, Alnilam ou Epsilon ε Orionis e Mintaka ou Delta δ Orionis.

Recentes investigações na área da astronomia sugerem que Alnitak está localizada a aproximadamente 800 anos-luz da Terra e que brilha 100000 vezes mais do que o Sol; Alnilam é 375000 vezes mais luminosa do que o Sol e está localizada a mais de 1300 anos-luz da Terra; enquanto que Mintaka, distanciada do nosso planeta por aproximadamente 900 anos-luz, brilha 90000 vezes mais do que o Sol.[33] [34]

No interior da constelação de Orion e na zona inferior das três estrelas anteriormente mencionadas, existe uma área do céu descrita na mitologia clássica como a *Espada do Caçador* — o instrumento do predador. Este objecto interestelar, identificado erroneamente pelos cientistas da antiguidade como outra estrela, é de facto uma estrutura muito mais complexa descrita cientificamente como uma nébula. A Nébula de Orion aparece como uma peça de arte criada pelos Deuses, esculpida etereamente no céu nocturno em tons de violeta e vermelho. Localizada abaixo do cinturão triplo, conforme mencionado na introdução do livro, esta bela e misteriosa pintura cósmica é um lugar de nascimento de estrelas, detendo uma enorme importância para a ciência, filosofia e espiritualidade.

O sigilo natural é completado por outras quatro estrelas que contornam as três centrais presentes no Cinturão de Orion. Elas são Bellatrix, Betelgeuse, Saiph e Rigel, a estrela mais brilhante da constelação. Todo o conjunto forma um poderoso símbolo mágico constituído por sete estrelas. Os números *três* e *sete* não representam algo novo no que diz respeito ao seu poder e significado espiritual para alguém fluente no simbolismo da Aset Ka. Este sigilo natural desenhado no céu pelas forças do Universo, também designado por

Sigilo Interior em estudos mais avançados deste poderoso selo mágico, constitui a peça central do *Sigillum 333*, que será examinado em detalhe ao longo das próximas páginas.

Para quem procura o conhecimento de iniciação e iluminação através do Asetianismo, torna-se importante compreender e aceitar como esta tradição pode por vezes funcionar como um espelho esotérico, que o aprendiz deve aprender a estudar e a observar. Esse espelho poderá, eventualmente, reflectir e até aumentar as suas falhas e fraquezas, de forma a conseguir encontrar a sua verdadeira natureza sem lhe permitir esconder-se atrás de máscaras nem render-se ao condicionalismo das supérfluas expectativas sociais. A partir do momento em que o iniciado se liberta de tudo o que o limita e condiciona — não só imposto pelos que o rodeiam mas também por si mesmo — o caminho Asetiano irá apenas revelar a realidade mais pura, manifestada pela frequentemente escondida e obscura verdade interior mas profundamente reveladora, quer o iniciado esteja disposto a aceitá-la ou não.

Qualquer variante de iniciação espiritual ou metafísica utilizada no sistema Asetiano é permanente e irreversível e por isso este documento esotérico é aqui apresentado com uma palavra de precaução. Responsabilidade é um pré-requisito essencial no estudo de qualquer tradição mágica avançada, mas ainda mais severamente relevante no caso da espiritualidade Asetiana e das práticas metafísicas desenvolvidas neste sistema. A natureza transformacional da magia, filosofia e psicologia Asetianas, faz da prática espiritual abordada no seio desta tradição um sistema consideravelmente perigoso quando não encarado com maturidade e respeito, particularmente no caso de material usado activamente em iniciação. A semente subtil do Asetianismo só pode ser plantada no solo mais profundo e puro da alma. Se deixada germinar, quer o estudante possua um conhecimento avançado das artes Asetianas ou seja apenas um jovem iniciado e inexperiente mas ansioso por aprender, essa mesma semente vai dar origem aos frutos divinos da iluminação e sabedoria da forma mais adequada à realidade do ocultista e relevante ao seu contexto espiritual. Essa centelha Asetiana, uma marca subtil esculpida na alma, irá crescer e viver com o iniciado para toda a eternidade como um guia silencioso de luz violeta e uma bússola secreta dos mistérios; um aviso perpétuo de que os Asetianos ainda estão aqui e que a sua magia perdura nos pormenores mais simples da natureza.

Uma Palavra sobre Iniciação

A habilidade de ver, interpretar e compreender os mistérios que permanecem escondidos à vista de todos, é o que designamos por *iniciação*.

O conceito de iniciação é um dos mais incompreendidos no estudo do oculto, por vezes explorado e mal representado por aqueles que não entendem a verdadeira essência da magia iniciática. Em termos simples, alguém iniciado — em todas as sociedades ocultistas e escolas dos mistérios merecedoras do seu nome — é um indivíduo que tem a capacidade de ver o que outros não conseguem. O conceito não implica necessariamente que através de iniciação o ocultista tenha de desenvolver algum tipo de poder sobrenatural que o torne em algo superior à população mundana. Simplesmente significa que foi dada ao iniciado a chave secreta — o mistério — que lhe vai abrir as portas do conhecimento para que possa ver o que está escondido à vista do mundo. Aparentemente um conceito simples mas também altamente sofisticado. Pode ser visto como o caminho dos mistérios para alcançar a plenitude e superioridade, mas esse poder provém da sabedoria, compreensão e da verdade subtil encontrada apenas no interior de cada um e nunca através de qualquer mero exercício de poder místico.

Recorrendo a um simples exemplo, se visitar uma velha capela Cristã algures na Europa com um amigo que nunca tenha estudado ocultismo e observar um pentagrama esculpido numa das paredes de pedra — e isso não seria tão raro quanto se possa pensar — pode imediatamente fazer a ligação de que em algum momento na história a igreja e os seus fundadores tiveram, possivelmente, uma ligação secreta com feitiçaria tradicional Europeia ou algum envolvimento com alquimia e práticas pagãs. Dependendo do simbolismo presente e detalhes históricos envolventes, pode até ser possível definir que tradição específica seguiam e que tipo de práticas, rituais e crenças teriam. O amigo presente — aqui representando o não iniciado — provavelmente passaria pelo símbolo sem sequer reparar nele, pois a sua mente não está programada ou sintonizada para prestar atenção a simbolismo desconhecido, ignorando automaticamente muito do que é estranho ao seu código simbólico consciente. Mesmo que ele tivesse reparado no pentagrama iria muito provavelmente ignorá-lo.

Neste caso o leitor seria o iniciado, detendo a chave para um nível de compreensão e conhecimento que o seu amigo não teria. Saberia o *mistério* da iniciação em causa e, dessa forma, seria capaz de ver o que está escondido à vista de todos, enquanto que o mesmo permaneceria *invisível* para os outros. Esta é a verdadeira natureza da iniciação que a maioria das sociedades ocultistas mantiveram secreta durante tantos séculos.

Depois de ter revelado este conceito vital mas frequentemente incompreendido aos leitores deste *Liber*, irei explicar algumas chaves muito importantes no estudo dos mistérios do *Sigillum 333*.

Enquanto selo ritualístico e meditativo ele incorpora delicadamente o segredo de Orion através da linguagem secreta dos símbolos, da Kabbalah, do alfabeto Hebraico, da geometria sagrada e, claro, da tradição Asetiana. Estes pormenores, quando revelados ao estudante do oculto e adequadamente explorados em práticas metafísicas pessoais, irão equipar o iniciado com o conhecimento necessário para compreender, interpretar e explorar o sigilo de Orion, de forma a que nunca mais olhe para ele cegamente, tendo agora a capacidade para ver nele — e através dele — aquilo que outros não conseguem, tornando-se iniciado nos seus mistérios.

A iniciação desenvolve no ocultista as ferramentas que lhe permitem trabalhar — e pensar — a um outro nível de consciência, com uma compreensão mais profunda do que a da mente mundana. Uma vez iniciado nos mistérios, o estudante experiencia mudanças permanentes no seu mundo, sendo agora capaz de ver o que os outros não conseguem, com uma nova percepção da realidade assente no poder do conhecimento.

Muitos podem não gostar da confiança de um ocultista iniciado, podendo criticar, julgar ou condenar, sendo na realidade um reflexo de ausência de visão, não tendo o conhecimento para Ver através de olhos iniciados. Não é sensato discutir ou forçar entendimento numa mente que não foi iniciada, pois os seus pensamentos não irão fluir nem os seus olhos abrir para o mundo, simplesmente porque não conhecem a chave para ver o que o ocultista consegue. É o caminho correcto para o ocultista iniciado — e eu atrevo-me a dizer a única atitude evoluída e digna —, ignorar aqueles que o condenam de uma forma inferior e optar antes por meditar na renovada chama dos seus Olhos agora iniciados. Como eu sempre aconselho... usem-nos sabiamente.

O oculto sempre foi e continuará a ser um mundo rodeado de ilusão e armadilhas. Essa realidade deve ser vista como algo positivo visto ser o terreno ideal para métodos de iniciação, na medida em que, dessa forma, torna-se possível distinguir os fracos dos corajosos e os ignorantes dos sábios.

Se o ocultista não desenvolver um forte senso de consciência e percepção desde o início da sua viagem interior, irá eventualmente ficar preso numa das muitas armadilhas presentes no sinuoso caminho da sabedoria. É vital não desistir na primeira queda quando o iniciado tenta subir pela escada do conhecimento, mas sim lembrar-se que a verdadeira força do guerreiro é medida pela capacidade de se levantar novamente e admitir que falhou. De outra forma um passo em falso não lhe mostrará o segredo por detrás do véu do abismo abominável, mas poderá antes afogá-lo no oceano do esquecimento eterno. Esse fracasso encontra-se nos que, quando confusos pela aparente incapacidade de conquistar a sua própria espiritualidade e relevância no Universo, podendo finalmente observar a realidade escondida por detrás do véu dos velhos mistérios, tentam antes subir os degraus secretos da escada da iluminação através de mentiras e pela propagação da ilusão de uma falsa importância, em vez de simplesmente lutarem na escola da vida com honestidade e nobreza.

No amanhecer dos tempos continuamos confiantes no
nosso papel cósmico de iniciadores silenciosos.

Os Três Segredos

Três é um número mágico. Apesar de apenas um simples elemento matemático para os não iniciados, esconde na sua essência não só magia mas também conhecimento, pronto a ser descoberto, estudado e libertado pelo estudante do oculto.

No contexto deste *Liber*, Orion é examinada como uma expressão espiritual da fórmula mística do Três sagrado, onde as estrelas centrais que formam o cinturão da constelação — Alnitak, Alnilam e Mintaka — aparecem no centro destes ensinamentos. Elas incorporam uma poderosa expressão arquetípica de cada Linhagem Asetiana — Serpente, Escaravelho e Escorpião — assim como a fundação em símbolo para o caminho triplo de Morte, Vida e Renascimento, tão importante em qualquer tradição mística.

Esta relação com Orion e a sua cultura espiritual está presente ao longo de toda a história sob diversas formas de arquitectura ocultista. Os iniciados do Antigo Egipto, sendo notavelmente pioneiros, representaram a importância de Orion nas suas edificações religiosas, particularmente visível na tecnologia avançada — em termos de ciência, engenharia e metafísica — encontrada nos mais famosos templos iniciáticos da história, conhecidos como as Pirâmides, localizadas na necrópole de Gizé. As Pirâmides de Khufu, Khafre e Menkaure são um espelho simbólico do céu, funcionando como uma porta metafísica para o cosmos, edificadas por entre pó e o calor do deserto Egípcio. Quando alinhadas conceptualmente com Orion, as Pirâmides são uma expressão perfeita da formação das Linhagens Asetianas, tal como representadas na Árvore da Vida da Kabbalah. As três estrelas que se erguem no céu podem ser interpretadas como uma emanação espiritual dos três Primordiais acima do Abismo — no reino intemporal do Duat — enquanto que as Pirâmides presentes no plano físico expressam a sua manifestação terrena abaixo de Da'ath, como reflexo das três Linhagens incarnadas reflectindo os seus arquétipos superiores.

Uma compreensão mais profunda desta relação permite ver um significado ainda maior no legado de Thoth, sucintamente descrito através da fórmula *"As Above, so Below"* definindo uma importante base conceptual para a arquitectura da espiritualidade Asetiana. Numa tradução em Latim do trabalho lendário de Thoth, conhecido como a *Tábua de Esmeralda* ou *Tabula Smaragdina*, também incluído na dissertação medieval *Secretum Secretorum*, originalmente em Árabe, encontramos a seguinte passagem:

"Quod est inferius est sicut quod est superius, et quod est superius est sicut quod est inferius, ad perpetranda miracula rei unius."

A frase traduz-se para *"Aquilo que está abaixo é como aquilo que está acima e aquilo que está acima é como aquilo que está abaixo, para realizar os milagres do mistério uno."* Esta lei de Thoth está representada de uma forma muito concreta na terra sagrada do Egipto, onde as três Pirâmides reflectem a realidade superior das estrelas ao representarem Orion e os seus três mistérios interiores, tal como o microcosmo de cada indivíduo é também um reflexo do macrocosmo subtil escondido acima do Abismo. O Eu mundano é uma manifestação do Eu superior e este, por sua vez, é uma expressão do Eu Divino.

Para os leitores com especial atenção ao pormenor, poderão reparar que ao longo de todo o livro utilizei recorrentemente as palavras Morte, Vida e Renascimento nesta ordem em particular, enquanto que o resto do mundo refere este ciclo por uma ordem diferente: Vida, Morte e Renascimento. Esta mudança na ordem literária reflecte um paradigma importante da espiritualidade Asetiana, que está intimamente ligado à filosofia por detrás deste trabalho. Para uma mentalidade comum, a Vida no plano físico é o foco da sua realidade espiritual, reflectindo a ordem tradicional de Vida, Morte e Renascimento. As pessoas vêem a Vida como o objectivo principal e o centro da sua existência, por isso, naturalmente surge a Morte e depois o Renascimento através da reencarnação, regressando novamente à Vida e completando o ciclo. É desta forma que a grande maioria das religiões que adoptaram a reincarnação nas suas filosofias, expressam o ciclo perpétuo da sua realidade espiritual. Mas não o povo do Antigo Egipto...

No Asetianismo, a liberação absoluta não se manifesta através de um permanente regresso à Vida, mas sim por um retorno perpétuo à Morte. O Duat — império Egípcio dos mortos e submundo — é o verdadeiro reino da *vida* para uma mente Asetiana evoluída: o seu domínio nativo. A Vida é um estado impermanente e transitório, enquanto que a Morte é eterna, infinita e o berço da imortalidade. A Vida é uma escola poderosa de evolução espiritual, contudo meramente uma estrada no caminho universal que é o crescimento, enquanto que a Morte é o verdadeiro lar da alma: o trono do Eu Divino. A partir desta perspectiva espiritual, a Morte é na realidade muito mais genuína do que a Vida física, que em termos místicos representa uma ilusão poderosa e enganadora. Apesar desta visão poder parecer negra e mórbida à primeira vista, na realidade é uma perspectiva imensamente positiva e iluminada do percurso espiritual da alma. Tal como na mente avançada dos Antigos Egípcios, o foco está então na Morte e nos seus mistérios secretos; na quebra do condicionalismo da matéria e corpo, para uma dedicação à verdade encontrada no interior de cada um, sendo esta a única realidade que pode sobreviver à morte física. Isto não leva a uma visão triste e depressiva do mundo em que vivemos, mas sim a uma mentalidade iluminada que aprendeu a apreciar a vida no seu todo ao compreender a sua beleza impermanente e a valorizar cada momento. Com este segredo em mente, utilizei a fórmula de Morte, Vida e Renascimento como um detalhe literário iniciático escondido ao longo deste livro, pois os Asetianos encaram o ciclo espiritual tendo a Morte como o seu reino, a Vida como um percurso impermanente de aprendizagem e o Renascimento como o despertar para a Morte e a comunhão divina com Aset.

"Vive como se fosses morrer amanhã.
Aprende como se fosses viver para sempre."

Mahatma Gandhi

Os significados e conhecimento presentes nas fórmulas do Três sagrado são imensos e variados, não estando restritos aos paralelismos traçados neste texto. Eles estão representados na energia e simbolismo do *Sigillum 333* que, sendo um poderoso e complexo instrumento mágico, detém as chaves e os mistérios capazes de iniciar o estudante do oculto em níveis de conhecimento mais profundo enquanto se dedica ao estudo e trabalho esotérico com este sigilo. Numa breve referência ao *Book of Giza*, o primeiro trabalho incluído neste grimório triplo, torna-se relevante salientar que esse documento esotérico é formado por três Sebayt distintos, contendo cada um precisamente trinta e três revelações. Nada é ao acaso.

Para além da abundância de possíveis significados, nas páginas seguintes irei abordar e descrever três diferentes níveis de iniciação, derivados das fórmulas do Três sagrado e intimamente relacionados com o *Sigillum 333*, guiando o iniciado através de um poderoso trabalho espiritual de vital importância durante o estudo dos mistérios de Orion. Sendo um instrumento esotérico imbuído de energia e significado, o *Sigillum 333* apenas será útil e mostrará os seus segredos mais profundos aqueles que o utilizem com honestidade.

Sarcófago do Mundano
A Primeira Iniciação
A queda do Espírito para matéria é um processo espiritual descrito no Asetianismo como *From Purity to Dust*. A alma, enquanto encarnada, encontra-se fechada num sarcófago conceptual — o plano físico.

assimilada torna-se clara e bela na sua simplicidade. Este significado secreto está também representado inequivocamente no Arcano Maior XIV do Tarot — Temperança — que na ilustração tradicional mostra uma figura alada com um triângulo gravado no peito a praticar as artes mágicas, misturando um fluido místico desconhecido entre dois cálices dourados. Esta é a carta infame que o ocultista Aleister Crowley modificou o nome na sua versão pessoal do Tarot, chamando-lhe Arte, e gerando muita controvérsia entre os não iniciados. Esta *Arte* à qual Crowley se refere é nada mais nada menos do que a unificação das forças opostas presentes na dualidade, sendo a alquimia interna do ocultista. Na sua versão do Tarot, Frieda Harris ilustrou uma figura com duas cabeças, vertendo Água e Fogo para um caldeirão mágico.

Esse simbolismo ilustra de uma forma literal a união mística entre Fogo e Água, os dois elementos alquímicos representados pelos triângulos opostos que formam o nosso hexagrama. A figura de duas cabeças, que mistura os elementos através da suas artes mágicas, representa a união perfeita entre o Rei e a Rainha, mas Crowley e Harris foram ainda mais longe no simbolismo que incluíram nesta carta, pois esta entidade andrógina é desenhada controversamente com seis seios que, como agora se pode compreender, representam os seis triângulos menores presentes no nosso hexagrama.

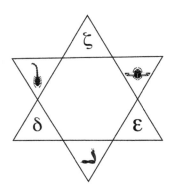

À medida que aprofundamos o estudo dos mistérios presentes na alquimia espiritual do *Sigillum 333*, depois de compreender o pormenor iniciático e revelador de que o hexagrama representa, quando observado pela mente mística, a união de dois importantes símbolos alquímicos, o leitor pode então observar a presença de dois triângulos menores no topo do hexagrama e outros dois abaixo, no interior do sigilo. Estes são os reconhecidos símbolos alquímicos utilizados nas artes mágicas para representar as quatro forças elementais do Universo — Fogo, Água, Ar e Terra.

Na mitologia do Antigo Egipto, estes poderosos elementos estavam associados ao conceito teológico dos *Quatro Filhos de Horus*, conhecidos por Imset, Qebehsenuf, Duamutef e Hapi — os quatro vasos canópicos utilizados no processo de mumificação e na magia desses velhos rituais de imortalidade.[37][38]

O método tradicional de pensamento e prática mágica é na realidade um exercício de fórmulas profundamente científicas. Os poderes dos verdadeiros alquimistas e ocultistas iniciados, descritos como os quatro elementais, estão correctamente representados nas ciências modernas, extensivamente estudados na física e na química como os quatro estados da matéria: sólido, líquido, gasoso e plasma.

As propriedades físicas do estado sólido tem correspondência com as qualidades do elemento Terra, tal como os líquidos são comparáveis à Água alquímica, gases relacionam-se com Ar e plasma, naturalmente, é relacionável com o Fogo mágico.

Estes elementos presentes no sigilo interligam dois arquétipos de Linhagens distintas, deixando pistas a possíveis implicações alquímicas entre emanações duplas de diferentes Linhagens. Cada elemento aparece representado entre uma emanação superior e outra inferior, mas nunca da mesma Linhagem. Por exemplo, o símbolo do Fogo está entre o ζ de Alnitak, associado à Serpente divina, e o mas delicada. Yod ' incorpora a escuridão e introspecção através do Arcano Maior IX do Tarot — O Eremita —, uma visão mística da pura rejeição do mundano e um símbolo da incessante busca pela luz interior, por vezes também relacionado com isolamento e solidão.

É importante compreender que todas estas cartas e o seu universo simbólico expressam arquétipos espirituais universais, que representam ideias e iniciações profundas, não emoções ou características psicológicas, e por isso não devem ser interpretadas de uma forma simplista ou superficial. As suas mensagens ocultas e significados reveladores são complexos e profundos, na medida em que cada carta representa um Arcano Maior do Tarot, que em Latim significa *Grande Segredo*, estando aqui representados apenas seis dos vinte e dois possíveis caminhos da vida do iniciado, a partir do momento em que inicia a sua conquista interior de evolução espiritual através dos mundos da Árvore da Vida. Uma vez mais chamo a atenção para o facto de que as cartas de Tarot serem aqui referidas, assim como os seus significados arquetípicos, não implica que representem uma tentativa de categorizar ou definir qualquer Linhagem Asetiana. São usadas neste contexto como expressões iniciáticas da dualidade presente nas emanações energéticas de cada Linhagem, particularmente devido ás suas posições acima e abaixo do Abismo de Da'ath, na Árvore da Vida. Associar de uma forma simples e independente os mistérios de um Arcano do Tarot com uma Linhagem específica, seria um erro.

Como último detalhe, estão presentes no sigilo três círculos de diferente diâmetro e espessura; uma última homenagem ao poder e simbolismo escondido em algo aparentemente tão simples... o número Três.

O mistério final e a chave suprema deste segredo levam-nos de volta ao início deste estudo e encontra-se na própria forma de Orion, conforme observável no céu nocturno, encantando o corpo iniciático de Nut. É por esta razão que essa ilustração mágica ocupa a posição central no sigilo, imbuído dos ensinamentos dos velhos mestres.

A beleza encontra-se nos detalhes e é apenas alcançada através da simplicidade.

✝

The Red Dawn

The Birth of Neith

A new dawn is rising

The red crown of Ra emerges in the East

Whispers of a nameless shadow

Unspoken words of trembling voices

Shaken grasps of dying hearts

Our night was one of painful sin

Blood has been spilled in the fields

Bodies found emerging from the filth in the river

The taste in our mouth is that of iron

Red is now the world as we see it

As the Sun rises high once more

The lament of the young widows

The pale faces of their newborn daughters

We have lived to watch our world collapse

Under our bare feet remain the empty stones

Edifications of once mighty temples

Strongholds of our precious Empire

Our peace was shaken by fire and stone

The lives claimed by the fist with a sword

Taken by surprise and cunning treachery

Drowned in our pride our night has ended

Oh mighty island of our Lady

Who would dare to strike right unto our heart?

How deep goes the wound inflicted upon us

Shall our enemies never fight with honor?

But history unfolds in the most unexpected ways

And the Violet Flame acts in mysterious perfection

Maybe were the stars so perfectly aligned?

Or did the wild birds sing unanimously in chorus?

Oh Seth how deeply your arrogance betrayed you

An army wanting to sing your hymns of victory

No one steps uninvited into Asetian holy ground

And in the time when your horde was striking

Right between your malignant plans to kill and burn

An unforeseen star was born in the elder sky

A child, that fought as a woman

A slave, that learned how to sting

Carved in the laws of the ancient desert

An untamed animal beneath golden skin

Among fire and red flame her love surfaced

Her weakened eyes shed tears in pain

A striking arrow pierced through the shadows

No mind was needed; no life, no gain

She put her love above the pain

And brought herself into the Flame

In an embrace of eternal claim

He gave her death, but took it away

In a soft and gentle Kiss

Their cursed lips betrayed life

And a mighty warrior was soon to rise

Years from this day her time will come

Blessed by the fierceness of her youth

You shall regret the daemon you awoken today

For she shall rise upon your cries

And inflict the strike of her divine bow

Oh Seth what did you do?

So condemned you have now become

For Neith was born in this painful night

Oh for the love of Aset

Neith was born in this Red Dawn!

"I am the things that are, that will be, and that have been.
No mortal has yet been able to lift the veil that covers Me."

Temple of Neith. Sa el-Hagar, Egypt

Framework

The painful dawn following a sudden Sethian attack at the heart of the
Asetian Empire in the sacred island of Philae. The ultimate sacrifice of a
young girl and the birth of a legendary Scorpion warrior known as Neith.

Child of Khufu

Behind a veil of memory and time
In curly hair she was then seen
Of darker color in shades of brown
A tender expression she carried with joy
In an immortal gaze she turned to see

Who this divine child might be?
To play in such unexpected place
In bare feet against sand and stone
Oh down the wider walkway she ran
In the grounds of Khufu, she remains

Peaceful guardian of the elder temple
How innocent is your untroubled smile
Is the rage hidden deep within you?
For a fierce lioness shall bloom one day
As the age of your gaze cannot hide the real you

Oh gentle creature of the sands
My honorable princess of eternal lands
May your feline paws guide our hearts into safety
And from all our foes keep the Empire at bail

Our trust lies blindly in you

For loyalty is your strongest clue

Like no human can ever perceive

Your dedication feeds our needs and deeds

So life springs forth in the beauty of our path

In sepia eyes reflecting our desert

One of the Pyramids you once became

An initiatory temple your body prevails

Oh hidden priestess of silent mystery

Stronghold of our immortality

Lady of Khufu please look at us

We adore you, but we fear you

For your coldness chills us out in the night

And your heat brings us forth in the day

That was the sight of a timeless girl

A young child beneath forbidden stone

Among the most noble daughters of the ancient land

In the holy temples she walked as her home

For an immortal predator she ultimately became...

The Prophecy

Art is achieved when the mind is not seeking
A formless pattern in the chaos of emotion
Sought by the lost and found by the humble
In a timeless dance of mysterious stumble

A secret is found only to be forgotten
In the chest of your thoughts locked within metal
Away from the truth but close to the heart
In the most vain of clues we can see your true chain

Empowered by desire and condemned by fear
You dream of a world that I painted in the night
Ghastly remembered in the time of tomorrow
Floating in the mourning shimmer of crimson light

Marriage of forces
Union of strength
Vindication of corpses
Justice in the land

☦

The pain was achieved
In silence, uncovered
Through color and smoke
The name was engraved

Allegiance was sworn
Carved in water and stone
The beauty was shown
Right beneath the pillar alone

The destiny was reached
Through sorrow and tomb
A prophecy was fulfilled
His legacy renown

The Return

In the lost horizon a binding light peeked in silence
Old gestures remembered by the sleep of forgotten minds
The mist of confusion gave birth to clarity and determination
While the eldest of flames awoke to the masters' call
An ensemble of beauty was heard throughout the lands
In a cosmic dance of indescribable nature
The time has come and they have returned

Kemet bleeds in the grasp of broken memories
Silence is enthralled by the shouts of golden tears
Now the ancient fear is dying from agonizing pain
For darkness and light have came forth as one
As the reddest of despairs trembles in hidden awe

Once more, from the Duat they came...

Featured in *Kemet* — *The Year of Revelation*

Book of Sakkara

Tales of the Ancients and Forgotten Spells

"May your flesh be born to life, and may your life encompass more than the life of the stars as they exist."

Pyramid Texts

The artwork presented in the previous page was hand drawn by Tânia Fonseca, depicting an accurate illustration of an Ancient Egyptian relief carving from a stone throne found inside the mortuary temple of Senwosret I[39], representing the legendary struggle between Asetians and Sethians.

he *Book of Sakkara* is the third and final work that comprises the grimoire manifested as the *Book of Orion,* also known as *Liber Aeternus* in the curriculum of the initiates within the Asetian tradition and to students of the occult venturing through the multilayered path of Asetianism. From all the three major documents it is the only which was not originally written by the author, as its contents originate from some of the most ancient spiritual texts known to mankind.

These texts were translated and compiled according to their magickal and historical significance to the occult student and they are the result of the dedicated work of numerous people, from occultists to Egyptologists, some who are no longer among the living. They are a collection of some of the oldest documented accounts of Ancient Egyptian religious prayers, meditative catalysts, spiritual utterances and metaphysical spells. The particular detail that the Pharaoh Unas, the founder of a pyramid in Sakkara where many of these texts were discovered, was sometimes identified as Orion in his funerary literature provides an even further layer of depth to the mystery and spiritual formulae under scrutiny within this book, presented through the timeless magick of Orion found in the Asetian tradition. The Ancient Egyptian word *Sah,* known for representing the constellation and spiritual concept of Orion, is often omitted from scholarly translations[40]; in some academic cases this is due to being considered an unknown ritualistic orientation, while in other circles it is consciously excluded in light of the nature of its esoteric implications.

The versions presented in this book were translated, assembled and interpreted by members of the Aset Ka in parallel with the study and reference of older public domain works together with the academic theories from Gaston Maspero, Samuel Mercer, Raymond Faulkner, Kurt Sethe and Alexandre Piankoff, whose work in the field of philological antiquities and Ancient Egyptian language in modern Egyptology has proven to be of invaluable relevance. The majority of the passages were translated in a literal and scientific way from the hieroglyphs presented on the walls and sarcophagi from the pyramids in Sakkara, while in a few cases a proper interpretation was introduced or amends to previous inaccurate translations were applied. It is important to note that this work does not include the full funerary texts ever discovered but only a small sample, and some of the utterances are organized in a specific order and connected in ways that may reveal a certain meaning, while the placement of others is intentionally random, as the finding of order in chaos is one of the necessary accomplishments to any student of the occult.

The nature and language of these ancient religious texts is fascinating, as it has sections of clarity expressed by such straightforward concepts and meanings, while in other excerpts it bears some of the most cryptic, subtle and codified language of all ancient scriptures ever documented. This detail, while brilliant from an occult and literary perspective, can prove daunting and misleading to some students, as the mind must be ready to shift from direct interpretation to a fully meditative and subjective perspective. During the study of the following pages it becomes relevant to keep in mind that we are dealing with very ancient literature and concepts found in Egyptian architecture and funerary objects, so it cannot be approached under a similar light as the magickal texts developed by the author in a contemporary time, like the initiatory utterances found in the *Book of Giza*. A careful observation and integration of *Sigillum 333* into your esoteric practices is highly advised, particularly in times where the light is scarce or the mind is dark.

The awareness and attention to detail that some of these texts can awaken in the initiate makes them a valuable spiritual resource that, particularly when allowing for the consciousness to commune with the Ba and to drink from the Ka, may enlighten the ways. A few utterances have the power to take you back to important occurrences in history and register those unique moments through an energy and taste that not all will be able to savor. Some can put you back in the mist of battle, others will take you on a quest of pain and sorrow, while a few will allow you to grasp the passion of victory as empires collapse and leaders are forged. Visions and emotions may manifest as you stare at those moments of long gone history, presented in here by the power of the ancient word. It may appear like the small pieces of the greater puzzle can now fit in the tight spots of your own Akashic reality, in order to reveal and liberate nearly forgotten memories of an ancient past. That is the inner alchemy behind these texts and why they should be approached as a spiritual tool in meditation and not just as mere academic literature of an ancient religion and past history. They can tell a tale of events in the Asetian past quite lucidly, in ways that shall never be openly revealed by the Order, presenting a unique source for the seeker to uncover that forgotten truth. But remember, they represent just another simple tool and, as such, these ancient texts are only a device for Understanding. They are merely doors, not the path the initiate must walk when past the gates of those portals. The profound knowledge they can liberate is not found in the words of these texts, but it actually lives within the initiate himself.

Give them a look...
Be ready to be taken on a journey back to the past.

1. May your flesh be born to life, and may your life encompass more than the life of the stars as they exist.

2. She uttered the spell with the magical power of Her mouth.

Her tongue was perfect and it never halted at a word.

Beneficent in command and word was Aset. The one of magical spells.

3. I have been given eternity without limit. Behold, I am the heir of Eternity, to whom have been given everlastingness.

4. You live according to your Will.

You are Wadjet, the Lady of the Flame.

Evil will fall on those who set up against you.

5. Oh Crown of Egypt! Oh Crown great of magic!

Oh fiery Serpent!

Grant that my terror may be as your terror.

Grant that the fear of me be like the fear of you.

Grant that the honor of me be like the honor of you.

Grant that the love of me be like the love of you!

Set my staff at the head of the living.

Set my staff at the head of the spirits.

Grant that my sword prevail over my foes.

☥

Oh Crown!

If you have gone forth from me so have I gone forth from you!

The Great was born in you.

The Serpent has become in you.

The Serpent was born in you.

The Great has adorned you.

As Horus encircled with the protection of his Eye.

6. I have come that I may be your magical protection.

I give breath to your nose, even the north wind that came forth from Atum to your nose.

I have caused that you exist as a God with your enemies having fallen under your sandals.

You have been vindicated in the sky, so that your limbs might be powerful among the Gods.

7. Aset will embrace you in peace.

She will drive away the opponent from your path.

Place your face to the West, that you may illumine the Two Lands.

The dead have stood up to look at you.

Breathing the air and seeing your face.

Like the rising of the Sun-disk in its horizon.

Their hearts are pleased with what you have done.

To you belong eternity and everlastingness.

8. Hail to the waters brought by Shu.

Which the twin springs rose.

In which Geb has bathed his limbs.

So that the hearts lost their fear.

The hearts lost their dread.

He was born in Nun.

Before there was sky.

Before there was earth.

Before there were mountains.

Before there was strife.

Before fear came about through the Eye of Horus!

9. Awake in peace, oh Pure One. In peace.

Awake in peace, Horus from the East. In peace.

Awake in peace, Soul of the East. In peace.

Awake in peace, Horus of the Land. In peace.

You lie down in the boat of night.

You wake up in the boat of day.

For you are he who gazes upon the Gods.

But there is no God who gazes on you!

Oh take him with you.

Alive, to you, oh mother Nut!

Gates of the sky, open for him.

Gates of the Duat, open for him.

He comes to you, make him live!

Order him to sit beside you.

✝

And beside him, who rises in the land!

Lead him to the Goddess beside you.

To make wide the seat at the stairway of the Duat.

Command the Living One, the Son of Sothis, to speak for him.

To establish for him a seat in the sky.

Lead him to the Great Noble.

The beloved of Ptah and his son.

Speak for him. To flourish his urn on Earth.

For he is one with the four nobles:

Imset. Hapi. Duamutef. Qebehsenuf.

Who live by Maat.

Who lean on their staffs.

Who watch over Egypt.

10. You have not died.

You are alive to sit on the throne of Osiris.

The power is in your hand so that you may command the living.

Give the orders to those of the Mysterious Land!

11. For I have looked at you as Horus looked at Aset.

I have looked at you as the Serpent looked at the Scorpion.

I have looked at you as Sobek looked at Neith.

I have looked at you as Seth looked at the Two who are reconciled.

12. There is no God who has become a star without a companion.

Shall I be your companion? Look at me!

You have seen the forms of the children who know their spell.

They are now Imperishable Stars.

May you see the ruler of the Palace: he can only be Horus or Seth.

13. Go after the Sun! You are to purify yourself.

Your bones are those of female hawks, the Goddesses who are in the Duat, so that you may be at the side of the One and leave your realm to your children: your own creation.

Everyone who speaks evil against your name when you rise above is predestined by Geb to be despised within the land and suffer.

You are to purify yourself with the cool water of the stars and you shall strike down upon the ropes of audacity on the arms of Horus.

14. Humanity cries after the Imperishable Stars have carried you.

Enter the place where your creator is united with Geb.

He gives you that which was on the forehead of Horus so that you may become powerful and glorious.

So then you become the one ruling in the West.

15. He has eaten the Red One. He has swallowed the Green One.

The Pharaoh feeds on the lungs of the wise.

His pleasure is to live on hearts as well as on their magic.

☥

16. Your head is that of Horus on the Duat, oh Imperishable One.

Your forehead is the one that has two Eyes, oh Imperishable One.

Your ears belong to the twins of Atum, oh Imperishable One.

Your eyes belong to the twins of Atum, oh Imperishable One.

Your nose is that of a Jackal, oh Imperishable One.

Your teeth are those of Sopedu, oh Imperishable One.

Your arms are those of Hapi and Duamutef.

You need to ascend to the Duat!

As you ascend your legs are those of Imset and Qebehsenuf.

You need to descend to the lower Abyss!

As you descend all your members are those of the twins of Atum.

Oh Imperishable One, you did not die as your Ka cannot die.

You are the Ka!

17. If I live or pass on, I am Osiris.

I enter you and appear through you.

I decay in you and I spring forth from you.

I descend in you and I repose on your side. The Gods are living in me!

As I live and grow in the emmer that sustains the exalted ones.

18. I have come to you, Nephthys.

I have come to you in the evening boat.

I have come to you, truth over the Red.

I have come to you, the one who remembers the Ka.

Remember him!

19. Orion is encircled by the Duat.

When the living horizon purifies itself.

Sothis is encircled by the Duat.

When the living horizon purifies itself.

The Pharaoh is encircled by the Duat.

When the living horizon purifies itself.

He is happy because of them.

He is refreshed because of them.

In the arms of his creator and in the arms of Amon.

20. Hail Atum, who made the sky.

Who created that which exists.

Lord of all that is.

Who gave birth to the Gods.

21. Seth and Nephthys, hurry!

Announce to the Gods of the South and their spirits:

There he comes as an Imperishable Spirit!

If he wills that you shall die, you will die.

If he wills that you shall live, you will live.

22. Geb said and it came forth from the mouth of the Gods:

"Hawk, after you have captured Self you are ensouled and powerful!"

☥

23. The doors of the horizon open and its gates slide.

He has come to you, oh Crown.

He has come to you, Flame Uraeus.

He has come to you, Great One.

He has come to you, Great of Magic.

Purified for you.

In awe before you.

Be pleased with him.

Be pleased with his purification.

Be pleased with the words he says to you

How beautiful is your face when you are pleased.

When you are fresh and young.

A deity has given you birth, the creator of the Gods!

He has come to you, Great of Magic.

It is Horus who fought to protect the Eye, oh Great of Magic.

24. Heka was made for them, to use as a weapon for warding off occurrences. And they created dreams for the night, to see the things of the day.

25. He comes down to meet his adversary and stands up as the greatest chief in his mighty kingdom. Nephthys praised him after he had captured his opponent.

26. You go up and open the ways through the essence of Shu as the embrace of your mother Nut enfolds you. You purify yourself on the horizon and leave that which should be purified from you in the waters of Shu.

27. Let them be in jubilation as the heart of the beast is exalted!
They have swallowed the Eye of Horus in Heliopolis.
The finger of the Pharaoh draws out what is in the navel of Osiris.

28. The Pharaoh is not thirsty.
He is not hungry.
His heart will not faint.
For the arms of the desert keep him away from his hunger.
Fill! Make the hearts full!

29. Judge, arise! Thoth, be high! Sleepers, awake!
The inhabitants of Nubia arise before the great trembler that comes out of the land.

30. The abomination from the Pharaoh is here.
He does not eat the abomination as Seth rejects the poison from the two who crossed the sky.
We call them Horus and Thoth.

31. The Pharaoh was conceived at night.

He was born at night before the morning star.

The Pharaoh was conceived in the watery abyss.

He is being reborn in the watery abyss.

He has come.

He has brought you the nourishment that he found there.

32. A face falls on a face as the face that has seen a face.

The marked knife, black and green, went forth against it.

It has swallowed that which it tasted.

33. Let your two glands of poison remain in the ground!

Let your two rows of ribs be in the cave!

Pour out the liquid!

As the two Kites stand by.

Your mouth is closed by the follower's tool.

The mouth of the follower's tool is closed by the feline.

The tired one is bitten by a serpent.

34. The White Crown should go forth after she has swallowed the Great so that the tongue is not to be seen.

35. The Uraeus is for the Sky.

The snake of Horus is for the Earth.

The cowards imitate Horus.

They have copied the path of Horus.

They know not. They are not knowing.

36. The Serpent of the flame is not to be found in the house of he who possesses Nubt. It is a Serpent that will bite what has slipped into the house of its prey so that it can linger.

37. Horus goes with his Ka.

Seth goes with his Ka.

Thoth goes with his Ka.

The Gods go with his Ka.

The Two Eyes go with his Ka.

You also go with his Ka.

Oh Pharaoh, the arm of your Ka is before you.

Oh Pharaoh, the arm of your Ka is behind you.

Oh Pharaoh, the leg of your Ka is before you.

Oh Pharaoh, the leg of your Ka is behind you.

I give you the Eye of Horus so that your face may be adorned with it.

May the perfume of the Eye of Horus be spread upon you.

38. Osiris, I open your mouth.

The divine metal from the South and the North.

The Eye of Horus that he seeks.

I bring it to you. Put it into your mouth.

Incense from the South and incense from the North.

Take the two Eyes of Horus, the black and the white.

Seize them in front of you so that they can brighten your face.

A white and a black receptacle to be raised up high!

39. May the night be favorable to you.

May the Two Ladies be favorable to you.

A gift that is brought to you is a gift that you can see.

A gift is in front of you. A gift is behind you.

So a gift is your due.

40. Recover the Eye of Horus that was stolen by Seth.

You must rescue it so that he may open your mouth with it.

41. Arise! You who are on the forehead of Horus, arise!

The purest of oils, hurry!

You who are Horus shall be placed on the forehead of the Pharaoh.

You grant him to have power over his body.

You unleash his terror in the eyes of all spirits when they look at him
and of everyone who hears his name.

42. Make the Two Lands bow before this Pharaoh as they bow before Horus! Make the Two Lands fear this Pharaoh as they fear Seth! Be seated before the Pharaoh as a God. Open his path in front of the spirits. That he may stand in front of the dead like Anubis. Forward! Forward, before Osiris!

43. You have caused it to retreat before you.
Sit down! Be silent!
Royal invocation and offering.
The Pharaoh shall take the severed heads of the Followers of Seth.

44. May you open your place in the Duat amongst the stars in the sky!
You are the unique star, the comrade of Hu.
May you look down on Osiris when he gives orders to the spirits.
You stand up high, far from him.
You are not of them as you shall not be of them.

45. Oh Great One who became the sky.
You are strong and you are mighty.
You fill every place with your beauty.
The whole Earth lies beneath you as you possess it!
You embrace the Earth and all things in your arms.
So have you taken this soul in you.
The Indestructible Star within you!

☥

46. See! This Pharaoh stands among you with two horns on his head like two wild bulls. For you are indeed the black ram, son of a black sheep, born of a bright sheep, suckled by four mothers. He comes against you, Horus with watery eyes. Beware of the Horus with red eyes, whose anger is evil, whose powers one cannot withstand! His messengers go. His quick runners run. They announce the one who raised his powers in the East.

47. The fire is laid so the fire shines.
The incense is laid on the fire so the incense shines.
Oh incense, your perfume comes to me.
Oh incense, may my perfume come to you.
Gods, your perfume comes to me.
Gods, may my perfume come to you.
Gods, may I be with you.
Gods, may you be with me.
Gods, may I live with you.
Gods, may you live with me.
Gods, I love you.
Gods, may you love me.

48. They see you as Min who rules over the Two Shrines. He stands behind you. Your brother stands behind you. Your relative stands behind you. You do not go under, you will not be annihilated. Your name remains with men. Your name comes into being with the Gods.

49. The blood of Aset.

The spells of Aset.

The magical powers of Aset.

Shall make this great one strong and shall be an amulet of protection that would do to him the things which he abominates.

50. Your son Horus has crafted this for You. The Great Ones shall tremble when they see the tool that is in Your hand as You come out of the Duat...

51. The Pharaoh has come out of the Island of Fire.

He has revealed Truth in the place of Falsehood.

He is the guardian of cleansing.

The one who watches over the Uraeus on the night of the great flood.

52. The Pharaoh is in control of his Ka.

Uniting the hearts from the one over wisdom.

The great one who is in possession of the Divine Book.

The wisdom at the right of Ra.

53. Oh you who are to be set over the hours. You who shall go in front of Ra. Find a way so that the Pharaoh can pass through the guard of demons with a terrible face!

54. The Pharaoh is on the way to his throne that is in front of the seats behind the God to whom a head has been given back. Adorned with the sharp and strong horn of a beast, he is the one who carries a knife that cuts the throat. This tool is the expeller of pain before the Bull, the one that blesses those in darkness. It is the strong horn of the beast behind the Great Gods. The Pharaoh has overpowered those who were to be punished. He has smashed their heads. The arms of the Pharaoh will not be opposed in the horizon.

55. The two crests of the mountain shall be united.
The two banks of the river will be joined.
The roads will be hidden from the travelers.
The steps will be destroyed for those that go up.
Make tight the rope! Sail the path into the Duat!
Strike the circumference on the realm of Hapi.

56. Ha! Fear and tremble before the storm of the Duat!
He has opened the Earth with that which he knew on the day when he intended to come.

57. One falls down with terror if his ineffable name is spoken.
Not even another God can call him by it.
He, whose name is hidden. Because of this he is a mystery.

58. The praised Serpent is on the throne.

Tefnut, she who supports Shu, has made the seat wide for the Pharaoh in Busiris, Djedet and in the necropolis of Heliopolis.

She erects his two supports in front of the Great Ones.

She excavates a pool for the Pharaoh in the Fields of Time, as she establishes his land in the Fields of Atonement.

The Pharaoh judges in the great flood who is between the Two Opposed Ones.

59. The hearts of his enemies fall before his fingers.

Their intestines are for the inhabitants of the Sky.

Their blood is for those of the Earth.

Their inheritance is to be lost and their homes set on fire.

Their land is to the hunger of the Nile.

60. I am the redness which came forth from Aset.

I am the blood that issued from Nebt-Het.

I am firmly bound up at the waist and there is nothing which the Gods can do for me.

For I am the representative of Ra and I do not die.

61. The horizon inflames before Horus.

The heat of its fiery breath is against you who surrounds the shrine.

Its poisonous heat is against you who wears the Great One.

62. Go away from your seat and lay down on the ground.

If you do not go from your seat the Pharaoh will come with a face like the Great One: the Lord with the head of a lion who became powerful through the injury of his Eye.

Then he will surround you and send a storm against those who did wrong so that it poisons the Primeval Ones.

The Great One rises then in his shrine.

63. Jubilation in the Duat!

The Gods of primeval times saw something new.

Horus was in the sunlight.

The lords of forms serve him as the two whole Enneads turn for him.

He sits on the chair of the Lord of All.

64. Osiris is the Pharaoh in a dust storm.

His horror is on Earth.

The Pharaoh does not enter Geb as he might be destroyed.

He might sleep in his house upon the Earth.

His bones might be broken.

His injuries are removed.

He has purified himself with the Eye of Horus.

His injuries are healed by the two female Kites.

The Pharaoh has freed himself!

65. The abomination of the Pharaoh is to go into darkness so that he does not see.

Upside down.

The Pharaoh comes out in this day and brings Maat with him.

He will not be handed to the Flame of the Gods.

66. The Pharaoh journeys the sky and passes above the Earth.

He kisses the Red Crown as if being cast by a God.

Those in the Three Crowns open their arms to him.

He stands at the East of the vault to the Duat and what rises from the path is brought to him.

He is King, the message of the Storm.

67. He passed by the dangerous place.

The fury of the great lake avoided him.

His charge is not taken by boat.

The shrine of the Gods could not ward him off the road to the stars.

68. He will pass a crossing to the eastern side of the Akhet.

He will pass a crossing to the eastern side of the sky.

His sister is Sothis and the Duat has given him birth.

69. The earth is broken into steps for him towards above.

That he may rise on them towards the Duat.

He rises on the smoke of the great fire.

He flies away as a Scarab on the empty throne that is your boat.

70. Horus takes him to his side.

He purifies him in the lake of the Jackal.

He cleanses his Ka in the lake of the dawn.

When the Two Lands are illuminated he opens the face of the Gods.

He takes his Ka to the Great Temple.

He leads him to the Imperishable Ones.

71. He is a lord of craft whose name even his mother does not know.

He is the one who judges by the side of the One with the hidden name
on the day when the elder is being sacrificed.

Khonsu is his name.

He who slaughters the lords, cuts their throats and takes out what
they cary within.

He is the messenger who sends out the punishment.

72. A serpent is coiled by another serpent when a young
hippopotamus is entangled.

Earth, swallow that which came out of you!

Monster, lie down and stand away!

The majesty of the bird falls in the water.

Serpent, turn over for Ra may see you!

The head of the great black bull is cut off.

A God in the disguise of a Serpent said to you.

A God-taming Scorpion said to you.

"Turn over, slither into the ground!"

They have said this to you.

73. Thoth is a protector but only when it is dark. Only when it is dark.

74. Hail to you, Daughter of Anubis, who stands at the gates of the sky. You are a friend of Thoth, who stands at the two sides of the ladder. Open the way for our Pharaoh so that he may pass!

75. Your two drops of Poison are on the way to the vessels. Split out the two as they are overfilled with liquid. Allow for the Snake to become kind and the throat of my heart to be saved. Clouds rupture! So that the lion may be drowned in water and the throat of the king be wide.

76. The Cat springs on the neck of the Serpent.

She who brought the Poison.

She strikes on the neck from the holy Serpent.

Who is the one that shall be spared?

77. Ra appears with the Uraeus on his head.

Against this Serpent which comes out of the land.

He cuts off your head with the knife that was in the hand of the Cat.

She who lives in the house of Life.

78. If you love life, oh Horus, upon his life the staff of truth!

Do not lock the gates of the Duat.

Do not seal its doors.

After you have taken his Ka into the Duat.

To the honoring of the Gods. To the friends of the Gods.

Who lean on their staffs.

Guardians of Upper Egypt.

79. There is no word against him on Earth and among men.

There is no crime from him in the Duat and among the Gods.

He has evolved with the word against him.

He has reversed it in order to rise towards the sky.

80. Serene is the sky.

Sothis lives for it is he who is the living son of Sothis.

The two Enneads have purified themselves for him as the Imperishable Stars.

His House that is in the sky will not perish.

His Throne that is on Earth will not be destroyed.

81. The humans hide themselves as the Gods rise above.

Sothis let him fly towards the sky amongst his brothers and the Gods.

Nut the Great has uncovered her arms for him.

82. The doors of the night boat shall not be opened for him.

The doors of the morning boat shall not be opened for him.

His speech should not be judged as that of one in his city.

The doors to the Palace of Annihilation should not be opened for him.

83. The male Serpent is bitten by the female Serpent.

The female Serpent is bitten by the male Serpent.

The Air is enchanted as Earth is enchanted.

Behind, mankind is enchanted.

Enchanted will be the God that is blind.

You, yourself, the Scorpion, will be enchanted.

These are the two knots of Abu that are in the mouth of Osiris.

Knotted for Horus over the Djed.

84. The Pharaoh has taken your necks.

Serve him so that he raises your Ka.

85. Oh you whose back is on his back.

Bring the blood to the offerings that are on the back of Osiris.

So that he may ascend to the Duat.

So that he may serve as Guardian in the sky!

86. I have appeared as Pakhet the Great.

Whose eyes are keen and whose claws are sharp.

The Lioness who sees and catches by night!

87. Infinite time, without beginning and without end.

That is what has been given to me.

I inherit eternity and everlastingness.

WORDS IN SILENCE
LIBER SILENTIS

Introduction

Introduction

E m Hotep.

Words are magick. That was the belief of the Ancient Egyptians; a spiritual and metaphysical paradigm that stood at the core of ancient wisdom. Such esoteric science of the elders was a powerful vehicle for the passing of hidden teachings — the mysteries. Bound to a code of secrecy that could shield them from those who seek to destroy, deface and exploit such powers, the magickal words were encrypted in the language of symbolism, intuition and energy. It became a subtle lock that could only be opened through a natural process of initiation into the Asetian realm.

For the past five years I have crafted a system of utterances that are limited in length but unlimited in scope of magickal reach. They elaborate on a series of teachings that are, in my opinion, essential to the evolution of the soul on its road of growth in the physical realm — the incarnated reality — and embody different layers of Asetian understanding, the ancient wisdom of the Aset Ka and elements that define the body of gnosis, ideals and values within this path. The individual sentences are literarily encoded in the depths of symbolism and the demonic mirrors of the unconscious mind, providing a fragment of wisdom that should be carefully studied under awareness towards the multitude of possible interpretations, though not all are intentionally cryptic or spellbinding. Some are surprisingly simple and yet effective in what they intend to convey while few are taken directly from other Asetian texts of my authorship such as the *Book of Orion*, the *Asetian Bible* and other private and even unpublished works. Their latent potential and the magnitude of the consequential magickal results achieved by the adept will be intimately bound to the strength of the fabric that makes up the student himself; as with most of my teachings, the profound lessons and their innermost powers can only be found by those who persevere. Do not be fooled by the apparently

753

simplistic structure of this tome as an organized tapestry of spiritual sentences and its multilayered cobweb of occult lessons and magickal utterances. Such content is much more than a mere compilation of ideas or a numbered listing of phrases — it is a manual for the perilous journey within. The wise allowing its guidance and the humble studying its lessons will discover magickal keys that have the ability to open different doors of power, knowledge and understanding, but not all will be able to read between the lines and make enlightened use of its symbolism. Upon this inked map of words, thoughts and energy, some will inevitably fall, never to rise again, while others shall find the strength to proceed, to conquer and to overcome. There will be sadness but there will also be happiness. There will be pain and there will be pleasure. Fear that can only be conquered with a sword. Craft your inner boat and sail the mysterious river of Asetianism with determination, honor and loyalty. When others fall down from their misshapen boats and become prey to the crocodiles lurking in this river, or those lacking the tools of evolution required to craft the first boat and start their journey, or even those too scared, too lazy or too limited to seek the crafting tools themselves, they all shall see this book as nothing more than a simple list of confusing statements and cryptic thoughts. Do not feed the crocodiles and do not stare them in the eye.

It becomes increasingly important to understand that the broad and multilayered field of the occult includes more than the exploration and mastery of magick. Occult knowledge and expertise manifests beyond the perception of hidden forces and the attaining of mystical wisdom. One important aspect of this path is the in-depth study of the mind, in its many manifestations and profound complexities — a process that can reach deeper than the limited scope of modern psychology, providing answers and a high level of understanding often not at the reach of someone imposing barriers on the exploration of something as limitless as the incredible potential of the mind. Such study has been a personal interest of mine and a rewarding field of knowledge that I have explored and developed at great length for many years. My different works and teachings should reflect precisely that, albeit in varying ways and by providing complementary approaches, especially to those who find in the exploration of the mind and the development of its potential an interest of their own. In this way my words and a committed study of the occult can allow for a unique understanding of modern society, the motivations and limitations of ordinary people, with the aim of analyzing the logic behind the behavioral patterns of groups and individuals as well as observing the action and inaction of humanity. From their relationships with each other to their dreams, fears and hopes, the occult should provide the advanced adept with a level of clarity that can be used towards the ability to see beyond human limitation and grasp upon the details that manifest a larger picture — the often misunderstood higher understanding of an occult scholar. The system provided within this book when used alongside elements found in my other texts, and in parallel with committed study, attentive contemplation and meditation, should furnish the curious occultist with interesting material to be explored under the banner of psychology and the many unseen secrets of the mind.

Every student or initiate of the Asetian path as a seeker of knowledge and explorer of mysteries faces many challenges and much opposition. Evolving is no simple task and the wiser you become the more misunderstood you shall be, for the vast ocean of humankind dares not taste the forbidden fruit of wisdom and often prefers to trail the path of safety hidden behind the protection of ignorance. To understand means to dare and such an approach is a dangerous aspiration when most do not have the courage to learn beyond the limited walls of their small world. Humanity has long thrived under the notion that if you close your eyes to the unseen it will silently go away, or at the very least will remain latent and unnoticed long enough so that it may be forgotten or no longer a threat. So they live and so they die — in absolute unawareness of the real world and the many truths that await in the dark. That is not an option for Asetianists, who will determinedly face the wingless monsters of despair and defeat any obstacle that stands in their road in order to nurture the inner seed of evolving wisdom; the silent path of the spirit. For that they will ever be condemned, criticized and publicly opposed by those who lack their higher understanding. The ignorant mock those who know more than them but those who know do not take insult for they understand that they simply know no better and mockery is a mirror of fools. Emotion is energy and should be saved and protected for the real threats in your path, not wasted on the envious smoke of limited minds. Take ignorant criticism and insult as a mighty crown and wear it with pride and nobility. Fight with honor. Learn with courage. Understand with wisdom. Only then shall my teachings flourish within your soul and liberate the greatest powers that live inside you.

The contents within this book have been made available to the occult community and students of Asetianism from all over the world in a progressive and non-linear manner for the past five years, which has potentiated the activation of subtle cues that allow us to initiate the superior understanding required to go forward in the study of Asetian mysteries, magick and spirituality. As always, remember that this book is yet another device in the long journey of magick, not the absolute code or a final teaching. It is another weapon in your arsenal of growth.

While some of the presented literary constructs are written sigils of energy and hidden inner power, others reflect much simpler secrets of life, death and the universal laws of nature. In its diversity resides its strength and varied use, with elements dated and published according to deeper significance presented alongside more spontaneous creations moved by lessons taught and learned at the unique moment in time and manifested in my own path, welcoming every Asetianist to drink from this personal road of enlightenment. In such a way this book, my fourth published work outside the secretive walls of my teachings, becomes another tool available to those daring to travel the dangerous road of Asetianism and its dark dungeons of inner potential.

Although this work may benefit anyone interested in magick, the occult and spirituality, even if they are not on the Asetian path, previous study of my other books is recommended to the explorers seeking to venture in the many caves within this tome and uncover the mysteries hiding inside each one, whether laying within golden coffers or sealed behind weathered locks of copper and brass. This is not to say that the Asetian teachings are restrictive, quite the contrary; they are a doorway to many other traditions, cultures and the multitude of knowledge both sacred and mundane available in this world. The Order of Aset Ka has always inspired its inner students and outside followers to explore every form of knowledge and wisdom they can dare touch, and not only through Asetian culture. In this way a learned Asetianist shall fly as an intricate flag of many colors, with insight and understanding of an incredible variety of subjects, reaching as far as the light of the Sun and the darkness of the Moon.

Now complied into a single volume, this system of wisdom has become available to every seeker, student or initiate of the magickal arts, so that it may be explored in the realms of ritual, meditation, incantation and further teaching. The result is *Words in Silence*, a small grimoire for those who seek to learn the ancient art of spiritual evolution and unfold the forbidden nature of magick through the mysterious power of silent words.

In our modern day and age, with the development of technology and the deceiving sense of empowerment that easy access to information and varying degrees of knowledge provides, many have criticized the Aset Ka for its secrecy and detachment. Often described as elitism and arrogance, such views spawn from the lack of understanding of what drives, enforces and empowers our signature silence and oaths of secrecy. As the author of several Asetian books and teachings I nurture no interest whatsoever in fame and recognition, finding no value in such vain desires. My achievements are held to much higher standards and they are bound to the conquering of growth, wisdom and enlightenment. Those victories are not at the reach of fame and ego, being only sung in the hymns of those who battle in silence, hence conquering the greater fortunes of all. Such uncommon commitment for a high standard and determination in fighting the recurring battle of perfecting your inner and outer arts may be understood as elitism, and under this mindset every Asetian is a proud elitist at heart. This is especially evident in what concerns the mysteries of magick and spirit, as our path can never be explored and understood when approached with the same mind that would seek, study and praise the work of mere dabblers or the mirrors of commercial occultism without a profound sustenance of truth. That is not the way of the Asetians as such a road is not the path of the warrior. In truth, if I would not constantly reject public exposure and the deviant desires of fans and readers, and have my work publicized and reach a much broader audience, I would still be criticized for doing something so opposed to my chosen privacy. As I have made clear in previous books, you cannot please everyone but most importantly nor should you. I would rather embrace criticism while being honest and true to myself, aligned with my nature and ideals, than bask in praise while pretending to be something I am not. Asetian secrecy is not here to please anyone and will remain strong and unbroken despite criticism, but if any genuine seeker finds the secretive nature of our knowledge and the intricate access to our teachings a negative sign of its value, then I am only left to wonder what real wisdom such a person has ever held contact with beyond the grasp of popular magick and basic metaphysics, as every true power fueled by occult knowledge is bound to oaths of secrecy, the art of initiation and vows of responsibility. That is how it has always been on the road to occult science and the way of magick enforced by every mystery school since the dawn of civilization and so it remains today. Believing otherwise is folly. Those seeking easy answers and quick lessons will never accept this but such minds have no place on the path of the wise. By now any student of the mysteries must have realized that Asetians bow to no desire or expectation from others and understand how criticism, insult or defamation hold no power over them. One of the most honest advices that any wise man can give to a new student of the Asetian path and seeker of this ancient culture is to ignore gossip and rumor. Falling for the tales of the lost and the lies of the paranoid is a fate of fools. People lie, manipulate, deceive and pretend, for that is their weakness. They add embellishments of grandeur to their experiences in a desperate attempt to portray to others a greater meaning in their life and existence. It is a facade; a mask of submission to the will of others. Discard all rotten fruit and seek the purity of the source, for only then truth can be found.

After the publishing of my first book and the break of silence that it implied from the Aset Ka after so many years of absolute mystery and confidentiality, some outsiders have stated that a secret Order such as ours should not disclosure esoteric information or release any literary works to the general public — I disagree. There are countless Asetianists spread throughout the world seeking to study this beautiful tradition and other occultists diverse in path and metaphysical approach wondering about Asetian magick, culture and spirituality. As an Order of mysteries with a history of privacy and secrecy, standing on an internal structure of initiation only accessible through the means of direct invitation and not providing any open membership system, it is only but natural that a vast legion of seekers are not actual members of the Aset Ka. It is my belief that such a fact should not be an obstacle to an honest Asetianist learning the intricacies of our path and culture. Even without disclosing an array of initiatory elements, practices and magickal secrets that are internal to the Order, it has been demonstrated that it is still possible to share and initiate those who remain loyal to Aset and the magick of Her children mirrored on the immortal legacy She created. Those who remain strong in their allegiance to the Aset Ka despite title or membership are worthy of our knowledge, teachings and friendship, proving that their inner quest is not driven by ego or the desire for power, but an honest commitment of the heart carved deep within their soul. Only then shall the ancient serpents of wisdom be willing to share power.

Treacherous obstacles and deceptive illusions raised by outside influences remain a menacing challenge to anyone studying Asetianism outside of our high walls. There is much speculation concerning the Aset Ka and its tradition among those that do not have access to its mysteries and inner workings, in a way that it becomes confusing ground to any truthful seeker of genuine information. It has been inferred that secrecy is the evil cause of all rumor surrounding the Order, however that is inaccurate and an innocent conclusion. It is not privacy, secrecy and mystery causing rumor and the spread of falsehood; it is the ego of those lacking access, information and proper understanding of the Aset Ka but pretending otherwise. Many claim to know secrets and truths of our Order, disseminating misinformation and misunderstanding. It is ironic that someone may criticize the Aset Ka and without any knowledge fantasize about it while using it to feed the ego by convincing others of pretentious access to something they secretly find so alluring and mysterious. The target of hate and unjustified criticism often proves to be an object of hidden desire. Unwillingly and unknowingly, they remain a banner of our power to inspire others and how our silence touches heart, mind and soul, leaving no one indifferent. Those insulting and hating the Asetians and the ones worshipping them accomplish the very same thing: a hymn to our mighty existence, no matter how hard they try to deny and fight the unbreakable nature of our call. From praise and idolatry to hate and insult, none are aware of the inescapable truth that no Asetian seeks worship and attention, constantly dismissing such expressions of admiration — hidden or otherwise — albeit being familiar with all of it for a very long time.

The life of an Asetian is one of magick, beauty and mystery, that being also what we teach and inspire in every Asetianist who freely embraces our spiritual journey and timeless culture. We live all such facets of existence in privacy and honor, as none of us is governed by outside influence or abides to the standards of others. We do not bow; we rise. Such is the strength of the warrior and the mind of the immortal, a trait incomprehensible to those who seek recognition as a mirror of their incompleteness and concealed sorrow. Our path is an endless process of change and growth potentiated by perpetual study, as the crown of all mysteries is infinite and knows no end. The door to such power and the inscrutable nature of our very existence is open to anyone seeking it with a truthful heart and a noble mind but not many will be able to enter and walk our golden road of silver halls and temples of stone, not because we reject their entry but because they limit themselves to their full potential, closing their mind to the openness of possibility and choosing death by oblivion instead.

The cover of the original book presents our readers with a photograph of Ancient Egyptian symbolism brought to life through different artifacts, some of which are part of special and unique altars located in currently active Asetian temples. Although simple and aesthetically gracious, such presentation is not random, as some of the objects included hold emotional significance to the Asetians and have relevance in late Asetian history, having been used in actual ritual and magickal work at the Aset Ka, making such inclusion in this work not only rare but also an element of rapport hereby gifted to the Asetianist community and our loyal readers. Additionally, three hand-drawn depictions of Ancient Egyptian artwork by Tânia Fonseca were included in these pages and complement the overall artistic feel and inspiration behind the book, blending with the signature emotion found in the lost art and magick of Kemet, as represented in modern times by the Aset Ka. It is our commitment and long-held belief that the published works we develop represent and personify much more than just books but manifest into actual magickal devices in their own right, each with its very personal identity and pulsating energy. A profound work of magick and ritual exists behind every single book published by the Aset Ka, from its early secretive inception to later stages of artistic development, occult implementation and initiatory discovery. It is a long and arduous journey that it is unlikely to be understood just by the study of the final words but one we believe can be appreciated and felt by the most aware of seekers finding the inner transformation and power that such works preserve and concede. It is a passionate work of love, nurtured not only for the beauty of magick in its purest form and the many lessons contained within, but most importantly as a mirror of our undying commitment to the legacy of Aset in its infinite expressions.

In a compilation of precisely three hundred and seventy three — 373 — individual teachings, each utterance in this book was edited and organized by manifestation date, which is aligned with the original creation or publication moment so that its archetypal intent, will and energy may be preserved and crystalized on this spiritual vehicle of matter that is each Asetian book. Proper references and brief annotations were included in order to easily point the reader toward varying elements of celestial influence and intricate energy signatures such as Full Moons, Equinoxes and other relevant timeframes. *Liber Silentis* can be a tool of ritual and a companion of meditation but it is also importantly a manual for students as well as teachers. May Asetianism be understood as the path where master and apprentice draw swords together and drink of the same chalice.

Liber Silentis

So the violet crown of timeless honor and immeasurable beauty goes forth once more, rising high above the mortal sky as it stood at the emerald dawn of the black lands on its mighty throne of magick.

1

Sometimes the dim veil between
sanity and insanity is perception.

23 August 2009

2

An Asetian never tries to talk louder
than the surrounding crowd.
An Asetian becomes that crowd.

24 August 2009
Asetian Bible

3

The deepest powers are often the most
subtle, something that most fail to realize.

25 August 2009

4

In the few hours before sunrise the world sparkles as a better place when most are silent and asleep.

26 August 2009

5

Knowledge is a sacred gem that must be conquered, wielded and empowered. To access such gnosis is not a right but a privilege of the evolved.

28 August 2009

6

Thoth paves the silver sky to rise in fullness upon the darkness of the underworld. Nut tenderly misses his empowerment and so do We.

2 September 2009

7

May the Violet Flame be with the ones
who are loyal in the night when Thoth
rises high and whole to cross the gates
of the unseen.

5 September 2009
Full Moon

8

It is safer to face a strong enemy
in the field of battle than to fight a
war by the side of a weak friend.

6 September 2009
Book of Orion

9

Beauty lies not on the words themselves
but in the listener that has the power to
understand them.

7 September 2009

10

A day of hidden storms and broken shields. Listen to the silent echoes within the shadow of lost cries and forgotten memories.

9 September 2009

9.9.9

11

When fully united, without ego or weakness, we become the greatest invisible force this world has ever witnessed.

10 September 2009

Book of Orion

12

To become an Asetian is to die and be reborn.

To forget all you have learned and learn all you have forgotten.

12 September 2009

Asetian Manifesto

13

Humans spend more time finding ways
to fight and criticize those who they
consider a threat than actually learning
how to overcome them.

14 September 2009

14

The solitary moveless dance of the
Asetians: hidden magick under the
prevalence of darkness.

14 September 2009

15

Words are more dangerous than
swords and guns.
They reach further and hurt deeper.

27 September 2009

16

Cherish the energies from the deep
and bend them to your will as
Thoth rises once more to empower
in darkness.

4 October 2009
Full Moon

17

Loyalty is a divine gift of the evolved.
Something humanity often places below
their shallow ego
5 October 2009

18

The night is Ours. Rejoicing in the
ethereal realms where We are
kings. Blessed souls of forgotten
immortality. They fear Us in every
grasp.

5 October 2009

✝

19

There is no greater power than
the one others do not believe you
possess.

9 October 2009

20

We live in Secret.
We live in Silence.
And we live Forever...

9 October 2009
Asetian Manifesto

21

Words are sigils that can hide the
coded language of the soul.

12 October 2009

☥

22

In darkness lies a mystery that
has the power to shine brighter
than true light.

17 October 2009
Book of Orion

23

You don't find Truth but Truth finds you.
19 October 2009
New Moon

24

No matter how hard you try,
after the day there will always
be a night.

27 October 2009

25

Life is a chance at Evolution.
Overcome yourself and Become.
30 October 2009

26

May Anubis be your loyal guide
through the underworld in the
night where the realms entwine
and the dead we meet.

1 November 2009
Circle of the Dead

27

Thoth blesses Geb with full light.
Vibrant energies in the crossing
through the darkened sky.
3 November 2009
Full Moon

☥

28

An evolved and balanced ego can be
a valuable tool for Self. A blinding
one remains among the footsteps
into oblivion.

6 November 2009

29

May the Ka be with the Ba of those
who are Loyal and True.

7 November 2009

30

An Asetian never feels threatened
by any force surrounding him.
We had the world on our hands and
willingly gave it away...

10 November 2009

31

Humans are naturally scared and confused creatures. They not only fear the unknown as they live fearing themselves.

11 November 2009

32

He who does not cherish life does not deserve to be among the living.

13 November 2009

Book of Orion

33

The power of faith can be a strong force but the power of knowing is even stronger.

14 November 2009

✝

34

Blind is he who innocently strikes
the weak apprentice for he is only
lowering his guard to the final
strike of the master.

15 November 2009
New Moon

35

Truth is not a right to be claimed
but a gift for those who are able to
conquer it.

18 November 2009

36

Poor are those who have eyes but
cannot see...

20 November 2009

37

Light and Darkness. One cannot exist without the other. There is no true master without the power of balance.

25 November 2009

38

You may think that you are not blind but can you see in the dark?

27 November 2009

39

Do not judge others without first judging yourself. There is no true strength without knowing thyself.

28 November 2009

40

The hidden mist of forgotten truth
is not for the mundane eye to see.

29 November 2009

41

Embrace the darkness within and
face the abyss without fear.

2 December 2009

Full Moon

42

Did you ever face Death and let it
stare back at you right in the Eye?

2 December 2009

Full Moon

☦

43

Predator and prey move through silent gestures on a seductive dance of death in the shadow cast by the vultures of the night.

6 December 2009

44

Departures and new beginnings. Rebirth and Immortality.

7 December 2009

45

To face a demon you must first look inwards and conquer your own darkness.

13 December 2009

46

Blend with the darkness without the blessing of light.

16 December 2009
New Moon

47

The evolved predator can get his prey to willingly enter the forbidden lair, unaware of the despair that lies within.

19 December 2009

48

May you find answers to the mysteries of your inner realities as the cycle shifts and Ra returns.

21 December 2009
Winter Solstice

✝

49

When you feel lost and hopeless just
close your eyes and look deep within.
You will find your compass.

9 January 2010

50

Do not fully believe in what you see
for sometimes only what is not
possible to be seen can be trusted.

10 January 2010

51

The Flame has a fire that not even
death can extinguish. That is the
eternal nature of the Asetian Family,
a bond no human can comprehend.

11 January 2010

52

How can you fathom Death if you
don't even understand Life?

14 January 2010

53

The darker it gets the easier it
becomes for subtle lights to be
revealed.

15 January 2010
New Moon

54

There is only one thing worse than
a coward and that is a deceptive
coward.

17 January 2010

55

The strength of a vampire lies in his soul, as an immortal flame that burns furiously like the devastating forces of nature.

19 January 2010

56

Truth is an ethereal pond hidden among the stars.

23 January 2010
Book of Orion

57

the Kingdom of truth is a twisted realm where reality deceives perception and embraces its purity on the inverted understanding of mortals

27 January 2010
Mirror of Perception

✝

58

Bask in the pale light and ask for the answers that your soul seeks. Inside you lies a puzzle to many mysteries.

30 January 2010
Full Moon

59

Some try so hard to be known and remembered that they fail to realize how insignificant they actually are. Life isn't about fame and recognition but a school of honor and enlightenment.

31 January 2010

60

There is no point in walking if you do not know where you are going.

4 February 2010

61

The silent you become the stronger
you can hear.
The better you stay still the greater
you can see.

7 February 2010

62

There is no Master without being
an eternal student.
There is no Master without the
ability to learn from the ones he
teaches.
There is no Master without the
experience of dying to be reborn...

11 February 2010

63

It hurts less to go forward and be
taken down than to live knowing
that you did not walk.

12 February 2010

64

Even when the face of Thoth is not
seen in the sky you still know that
he is present.
Seeing does not mean Knowing.

14 February 2010
New Moon

65

To be an Asetian is to be cursed by
a never-ending thirst for perfection.
17 February 2010
Asetian Manifesto

66

Life is binary.
You can be a one or a zero.
A warrior or a deserter.
A student or an ignorant.
Aware or blind.
A lover or a coward.

18 February 2010

67

The Tao is Knowledge.
Power is through Blood.
19 February 2010
Asetian Manifesto

68

There is no place like Home.
There is no bond like Family.
There is no sin like Betrayal.
26 February 2010

69

The physical plane is one of deceit.
Constantly strive for awareness.
28 February 2010
Full Moon

70

Violet light can be seen in total darkness but only felt with eyes closed when there is no fear to dim the Flame.

28 February 2010
Full Moon

71

If you have thirst for knowledge always drink from the source where the water is purer.

2 March 2010

72

True power always comes from within.

5 March 2010

73

Your soul is your inner temple.
Your body is but a thin cloak that
you keep changing for a cleaner one
on an eternal ritual of life.
6 March 2010

74

Fire destroys.
The Earth grounds.
Water cleanses.
The Air binds.
But only Blood transforms...
12 March 2010

75

I am the hawk that flies higher; the
darkness that goes forth.
I am the predator that storms from
above; the unformed truth of your
rebirth.
18 March 2010

76

The river of Life will follow its course with or without you. Take your chances carefully for the eternal clock is ticking.

21 March 2010
Spring Equinox

77

Old roots are not dead only if you have the power to pour fresh water on them.

23 March 2010

78

Asetian Souls are like the Pyramids. They have endured the test of time and hold secrets that mankind cannot comprehend.

25 March 2010

79

The night casts shadows upon
our senses in a perfect balance
of darkness and light.
29 March 2010
Full Moon

80

Fear is both a tool and a weapon.
Use it to guide you through a safe
road and to bring nightmares onto
your enemies.

1 April 2010

81

Beware of friends and allies for
only in days of thunder your
enemies shall be revealed.
5 April 2010

✝

82

Fight not to win. Fight to make a stand.
Determination is the key to awareness.
Hunt not to feed. Hunt to learn.
Knowledge is the key to shape the world.
Destroy not to kill. Destroy to transform.
Evolution is the key to immortality.

11 April 2010
Book of Orion

83

In a realm of lies and deceit have
the courage to be someone real.
There is no evolution without being
true to yourself.
23 April 2010

84

Do not fight your enemies. Ignore them.
28 April 2010
Full Moon

85

The very first step in not betraying someone is to never betray yourself. The second is to realize that if loyalty knows an if then it is no loyalty.

7 May 2010

86

When you lie there is only one you are letting down: yourself.

19 May 2010

87

Every Full Moon a new initiation begins, destined for those who can read behind the eyes of Thoth without falling into his abyss.

27 May 2010
Full Moon

88

The truth that enlightens the evolved often has the power to anger the unaware.

11 June 2010
New Moon

89

Before seeking understanding over the secrets of life first try to uncover your own inner mysteries.

15 June 2010

90

When you see Darkness become the Light and when there is Light become the Darkness.

26 June 2010
Full Moon

91

Never fear those who pretend to be your enemies for a real danger always comes in silence.

1 July 2010

92

The deepest cries are those held in absolute silence.

3 July 2010

93

Three echoes throughout eternity. The Violet Flame touches heart and soul of those who were Loyal and True.

7 July 2010

7.7

✝

94

Pay attention to every word and every gesture for each step echoes in both worlds.

13 July 2010

95

The greatest warrior is not the one with the strongest body but one with the strongest mind.

17 July 2010

96

That which can feed the wise may poison the blind.

24 July 2010

97

An Asetian is both an angel and a demon, with energy capable of healing the deepest wounds and power to take all life at his grasp.

5 August 2010

98

Remember that a soul, just like the phoenix, cannot be reborn without first bursting into flames.

15 August 2010

99

Death is the ultimate initiation for only through its mysteries the Ba can truly Live.

24 August 2010
Full Moon

☥

100

My army is the thunder in the sky and
the beasts from the earth, the wind in
the air and the tides of the sea.
My army is Me.

9 September 2010
Book of Orion
New Moon

101

In the moment when Night equals Day may
you remember the importance of balance
and equilibrium to an enlightened soul.
23 September 2010
Autumn Equinox
Full Moon

102

The life of a vampire is like a timeless
painting. Many souls will come and
go in a perpetual cycle but only true
artists remain.

22 October 2010
Full Moon

103

Power that needs proof is Doubt.
Power that needs voice is Ego.
Power that betrays is Dishonor.
Power that is afraid is Weakness.
Asetian Power is just Power.

31 October 2010
Circle of the Dead

104

How can mortals survive the test
of time if they cannot even pass
the test of silence?

21 December 2010
Winter Solstice
Full Moon

105

Great strength to claim important
victories; the forging of old bonds
and its powers awoken.

31 December 2010

☥

106
Only in the darkest corners of
existence the light cast by our
truest Self can be found.

12 January 2011

107
A true Writer cannot die, as the power
behind his Words will prevail for ages
yet to come.

30 January 2011

108
Be proud of long-due conquered
freedom but remain responsible
to avoid mistakes from the past.

12 February 2011

109

While it is not our charge to give power
to people it remains our responsibility to
enlighten them if we do.

20 February 2011

110

Only the Wise can see through the
riddles of the universe and grasp
upon the simplicity of the answers.

4 March 2011

New Moon

111

Seek your inner darkness for the light of
the world is deceptive and transitory.

12 March 2011

112

When ego is conquered and our honor raised to everlastingness we reach a plenitude that leaves us with nothing left to fear.

19 March 2011
Full Moon

113

Thoth dances through the body of Nut with a Light that threatens to blind those who are too scared to See.

19 March 2011
Full Moon

114

It is of unquestionable beauty how after so many lifetimes we can still feel such an intense passion for Life as if it was our first.

31 March 2011

115

Asetianism is spiritual liberation,
the most profound form of Freedom
through the power of Knowing.
Who lacks such understanding does
not know the Violet path at all.

17 April 2011
Full Moon

116

A wise vampire can hunt treacherous
preys by allowing them to believe that
they are actually being predators.

7 May 2011

117

Deciding the fate of others is not a
pleasant experience. It is a necessary
power and responsibility of leadership
that no one should seek.

17 May 2011
Full Moon

118

Words are poison, potion and elixir.
Choose wisely which ones to drink...

24 May 2011

119

The secret Light of the Lady echoes
in the deep like the sound of drums
against the hands of giants.
Once more We claim our victory.

11 June 2011

120

The initiate replicates the ancient
mystical art with a steady hand and a
focused mind as a surgeon of nature,
the sculptor of souls...

1 July 2011
New Moon

121
Sing the hymn of honor, joy and
passion on the embrace of Aset,
Her legacy and beloved children.
7 July 2011
7.7

122
In a world filled with blinding light
may we proudly continue to be the
darkness that preserves its mystery.
7 July 2011
7.7

123
Understanding is a power greater than
any form of knowledge, manifesting as
a harbinger of wisdom.
15 July 2011
Full Moon

124

Fear... Such a small harmless word
yet able to move so many. Once you
give in to fear you have already lost.

26 July 2011

125

Orion glows strong on the dark sky
of the temple, carrying the same
message it did so many ages ago.

18 August 2011

126

The fall of ghosts is written in
the tales from the rise of giants.

28 August 2011
New Moon

127

A true spiritual leader teaches not only with his words but also through his silence.

7 September 2011

128

Silence allows for fools to wonder, for the weak to fear, for cowards to run and for the loyal to awaken.

7 September 2011

129

You cannot fight Union, Loyalty and Love with lies, envy and anger.

19 September 2011

130

Life is too beautiful and meaningful
to be wasted fighting what you can
never defeat or comprehend. Cherish
its treasures and ease your pain.

19 September 2011

131

Asetianism embraces the path of darkness
through a definitive quest for liberation by
unfolding the greater mystery: yourself.

29 September 2011

132

Knowing Life is to know the Spirit.
Knowing the Spirit is to know Life.

10 October 2011

133

Servitude to the ego is an echo of a
life of slavery. Break the chains and
rise above!

17 October 2011

134

Only a fool tries to hunt down a
lion by throwing grains of sand.

26 October 2011

New Moon

135

We that live between the veil of
both worlds offer a moment of
silence for those that have fallen.
In darkness we honor their soul.

31 October 2011

Circle of the Dead

☩

136

The silent Hawk always stares into the confused eyes of the fallen before they fall...

22 November 2011

137

She taught us how to Love, without fear or weakness, and that forever remains a banner of our Family.

1 December 2011

138

The voice of immortality can only sing to the eyes of purity.

12 December 2011

✝

139

Who seeks fantasy and ego shall find
delusion and disappointment. Who seeks
growth and enlightenment shall find
wisdom and rebirth.

31 December 2011

140

With power to inspire and bring
nightmares each Asetian is a candle
forgotten in the wind, permanently
touching all life around him.

7 January 2012

141

Freedom is one of the best spiritual tools.
You claim the merit for your evolution but
if you fall you only have yourself to blame.

23 January 2012
New Moon

142

Can you see Orion reflected in
your inner desert?

7 February 2012
Full Moon

143

Understanding hides in absolute
darkness while hatred finds its
altar only in the light.

21 February 2012
New Moon

144

In life we are not walking towards
a goal or place. We are walking
towards ourselves.

8 March 2012
Full Moon

145

Rest on my wings for I am death
and burn in my fire for I am life.
6 April 2012
Full Moon

146

We can hold responsibility over our
words and the power they unleash but
never for how others misinterpret their
use and meaning.

15 April 2012

147

When blessed with true wings you
do not care to prove how well you
can fly.
21 April 2012
New Moon

148

At the dawn of despair we shaped
mountains and served terror.

21 May 2012
New Moon

149

Bask in the light of all abominations
for only when going through the gates
of the abyss you shall find your answer.
27 May 2012
Book of Orion

150

To reach the gates of transformation
you must first cross the desert of the
soul.

15 June 2012

151

Liber Aeternus.
The law of Three. Initiation into the
mysteries of Orion comes forth.
3 July 2012
Full Moon

152

When the laws of Maat are in balance
and the Word is placed upon the altar
of Truth, the Universe bends to our
own microcosm.
7 July 2012
7.7

153

Observation is a tool of the Wise, a
power of the Initiator and a compass
of the Conqueror.
18 July 2012
New Moon

154

The snake is a symbol of the evolving soul. As it sheds the skin so must the spirit perpetually be renewed to retain ethereal youth.

27 July 2012

155

Someone who has never lost and that has never fallen is not equipped to succeed. Embrace change. Fear nothing.

7 August 2012

156

To survive in the jungle of life you must unleash your wild inner beast.

31 August 2012

157
The beauty of Truth is that it always finds
a way for it is the only path of nature.
7 September 2012

158
Every genius mind through the limited
eye of fools is seen as insane.
18 September 2012

159
May the light of wisdom intertwine
with your darkest energies.
29 September 2012
Full Moon

☥

160

There is hidden dark beauty in imperfection for it is through its influence that uniqueness manifests.

7 October 2012

161

Strength when enforced only through extremes is a sign of a limited mind.

15 October 2012

New Moon

162

Poison does not hold sway over the accomplished occultist as the wise know how to craft their own elixir.

29 October 2012

Full Moon

163

Nut blesses the body of Geb
with her precious tears of Life.

6 November 2012

164

Only those who do not seek power but
commit to the quest of understanding
can stare both in the eye.

13 November 2012
New Moon

165

Perpetually misunderstood, the
occultist is the scholar of life and
death, the scientist of the unseen
and the seeker of all mysteries.

25 November 2012

166

One is only complete when embracing every corner of inner nature, from the brightest seed of Self to the darkest dungeon of evil.

4 December 2012

167

By studying the secrets of long gone history we can grasp into pieces of our own inner mysteries.

12 December 2012
New Moon

168

Clouds of wisdom conceal the spoils from silent battles of fallen leaves.

17 December 2012

169

The subtle seed of Asetianism can only be planted deep into the rich soil of the soul.

21 December 2012
Book of Orion
Winter Solstice

170

Never trust a path that teaches you not to try, experiment and question. Exploration remains one of the most powerful tools of understanding.

23 December 2012

171

Be an explorer of the unseen, a committed student of the mysteries within. Rise not as lost thread of conceit but as a master of Self.

23 December 2012

172

There are no rules but those of the heart.

There are no laws but those of imagination.

25 December 2012

173

The deepest bonds are not celebrated
with words or gestures but felt in the
silence of the heart.

31 December 2012

174

The delusional live in Netzach thinking of
Tiphareth but the deceitful often cannot see
beyond Malkuth while dreaming of Yesod.

3 January 2013

175

If you are constantly seeking for the approval of others you are living a life of no significance.

11 January 2013
New Moon

176

Light is an expression of ego and fear in disguise. Darkness represents its absence without expectation.

14 January 2013

177

There is a world within your mind that is far greater than that of the manifest Universe.

23 January 2013

✝

178

Many are ashamed to question but it is the incarnated condition of doubt that moves the mind forward in order to learn something new.

27 January 2013
Full Moon

179

Foul voices who never felt the weight of a sword speak of death and courage with an arrogance that is unworthy of blood spilled in honor.

6 February 2013

180

Never profess an ideology that you do not have the courage to live by.

8 February 2013

181

Souls of darkness hidden beneath the silent cloak of mortality are often the spark of inspiration that shape the course of history.

21 February 2013

182

Give in, wholeheartedly, to the song of nature and your inner beauty...

25 February 2013
Full Moon

183

To stand a victor is easy but to fight when defeat charges ahead is what defines courage.

3 March 2013

184

Writing is timeless spiritual art;
Words, primordial magick.
Magus, writer and reader are one:
the craftsman of worlds.

7 March 2013

185

Spiritual initiation is the transcendent
path of the phoenix, where you liberate
yourself to die in order to be reborn.

11 March 2013
New Moon

186

The awakened vampire is a spiritual
chimera, conquering inner light and
mastering darkness between worlds —
immortal spirit within mortal shell.

15 March 2013

187
Magick is not the attaining of power but
mastery of what hides within.
20 March 2013
Spring Equinox

188
In a vain modern world inspired by
conflict and competition, an Asetian
mind committed to loyalty and honor
is bound to be misunderstood.

23 March 2013

189
Intuition is a powerful ally. Look into
the lidless eye and listen to its seductive
voice without hesitation.
27 March 2013
Full Moon

190

You don't have to justify your beliefs to anyone! Openly celebrate them without fear of judgement and find the missing spark.

30 March 2013

191

By making Asetianism so illusive, the initiate truly seeking to follow it only has one way to go: inwards.

4 April 2013

192

False teachers pose threat only to fools. They bare a message with rotten fruit and speak of a tree that has no seed.

10 April 2013
New Moon

193
Desire for power instead of worthiness
in its higher use is the seed that burns
empires to the ground.
15 April 2013

194
Bonds forged by the magickal fire of
the Violet Flame have the perpetual
quality of spiritual immortality.
18 April 2013

195
Who once boldly or silently protected
the black land of Egypt is bound to fight
for it ever again as such Love is stronger
than time.
18 April 2013

196

All must be free to seek their own individual path and unlock inner truth. Limitations are not imposed by others but raised by self.

22 April 2013

197

Understanding of Asetian will transcends the realm of mortal consciousness. Attempting to see beyond the portal of our abyss is futile.

24 April 2013

Full Moon

198

Any force can be broken with the understanding of the right tool.

29 April 2013

✝

199

Prayer is not the reciting of established scripture but to touch the divine with your very soul.

2 May 2013

200

Extraordinary people are not governed by the ideals of ordinary men.

7 May 2013

201

To embrace the lies of others for personal gain is not only expressive of a weak character but also the mark of a coward.

9 May 2013

202

Loving self is not the same as worshipping self.
One mirrors confidence while the other speaks of delusion.

10 May 2013
New Moon

203

Not everyone survives the influence of Asetianism as its truth violently shatters ego in a rebirth that only the strong can overcome.
12 May 2013

204

Trust not those who speak of Kether without first being accepted in Binah.
16 May 2013

205

Do not trust a teacher who raises
limitations in your quest but embrace
the master who advises you to study
the work of his opposers.

19 May 2013

206

The apparently simpler metaphysical
rituals often imply the most advanced
mindset. The most advanced magickal
processes rely on your surrender to
simplicity.

21 May 2013

207

Inability to understand tradition or succeed
at practice does not constitute evidence of
its limitation but of your own.

24 May 2013

208

Our Empire is no longer felt on the sand of a desert or the flow of a river, nor confined to the boundaries of land. It became one of Spirit.

25 May 2013
Full Moon

209

Art differs from entertainment in the sense that it aims to represent the embodiment of subtle beauty without the influence of ego.
26 May 2013

210

The inner need for approval and recognition is inversely proportional to the level of mastery.

31 May 2013

211

Understanding is the weapon of the Wise.
Explore it fearlessly.
Use it openly with caution.
2 June 2013

212

We fight ignorance with wisdom, fear
with silence and weakness with strength.
5 June 2013

213

If the focus of life is misplaced on reaching
objectives the purpose of existence is missed
for its beauty hides in the journey.
10 June 2013

214

History is written by men of power —
a perspective, sometimes a vendetta.
The truth of the people is often untold,
surviving only as myth.

11 June 2013

215

There is more to learn from the will
of a dedicated student than in the
advice of a pretentious teacher.

14 June 2013

216

People smile, agree and connect to
conform, be accepted and avoid
judgment. Webs of lies in the eye of
those who were not born to follow.

17 June 2013

217

Sometimes not causing pain requires greater strength than to masterfully swing the sword.

19 June 2013

218

Do not fear touching the blinding energy of Ra but use it guardedly in your favor without setting your soul ablaze.

21 June 2013
Summer Solstice

219

Three is Magick.
Seven is Sacred.

23 June 2013
Full Moon

220

The weak prey on the innocent and needy in a spectacle that exposes their own limitations.

27 June 2013

221

When you close your eyes to embrace the selfless nature of Asetian loyalty you shall discover the final temple.

30 June 2013

222

We speak the language of Fire and our words have the gentle touch of flames.

5 July 2013

223
For we are darkness and speak Her name.
7 July 2013
7.7
New Moon

224
Rising fast means nothing when someone is rising to emptiness. Do not seek fame as accomplishment; conquer honor and wisdom instead.
14 July 2013

225
Do not ignore the alchemical medicine pouring behind an honest smile.
17 July 2013

226

Only the strong can commit to a
path that would take lifetimes of
learning. Asetian fire breaks the
weak and nurtures the strong.

19 July 2013

227

Someone who does not accept criticism
will never be able to improve.
Evolution is the path to mastery.

22 July 2013
Full Moon

228

Do not practice magick.
Become magick.

24 July 2013

229

The experienced commander understands how conceding defeat in a battle may present opportunity to win the war.

26 July 2013

230

Being capable of unspeakable things, vampires make no use of their abilities lightly for they seek no recognition. Just like a master sensei who knows how to kill is less likely to resort to such skills than the ordinary man.

30 July 2013

231

Asetianism expresses the inner art of honoring Aset through Her spiritual legacy as She is the essence of the violet bond that unites us.

6 August 2013
New Moon

232

Experience through diversity gives birth to enlightened tolerance, only rightfully chastised in the service of justice and honor.

9 August 2013

233

Inspiration is cyclical, flowing to the tides of an endless ocean. Whoever believes it to be permanent has yet to hear its fluid song.

11 August 2013

234

The smallest of flames can conceal the heat to ignite the greatest fires.

14 August 2013

235

Words can be deceiving. Observe choices, behaviors and patterns instead. Truth lies in details.

18 August 2013

236

Someone clouded by ego and obsessed with delusions of grandeur becomes exposed among the most limited of mortals.

Each cheer of the crowd, blind as the mere object of false admiration, echoes a hymn at their insignificance.

Embrace darkness within and conquer silent deeds worthy of immortal ages, not the vain whispers of those in decay.

20 August 2013
Full Moon

237

The mind is a creator of worlds, a most mighty magickal tool.

25 August 2013

238

If you dare looking into dark places
you may not like what you see.

29 August 2013

239

For millennia humanity has searched
for the divine to feed their spiritual
hunger, yet it still fails to recognize
the sacredness within.

2 September 2013

240

If someone willingly chooses to close
eyes at the waters of truth do not
blow air on his face but let the fire of
death teach him.

5 September 2013
New Moon

241

I teach people not to find magick in religion, dogma or the creations of mankind but in the intuition of their inner seed.

Those seeking quick, easy and safe results shall never understand my methods or the nature of my magick.

7 September 2013

242

Only someone who does not feel special exhibits the need to convince others of their uniqueness.

11 September 2013

243

There is no greater teacher than death.

16 September 2013

244

Who is lost can ever be found and all
that is hidden does not live forever
for eternal lie shall never be bound.

20 September 2013
Full Moon

245

A master lays the tools so that you may
carve the path, it does not force you to
believe for no truth can be imposed.

21 September 2013

246

To learn and live or to give up and
wither is a choice every seeker will
have to face at the doors of Khepri.

23 September 2013
Autumn Equinox

247

Be suspicious of those who appear with a
thousand friends for the gift of friendship
is a rare flower under selfless bloom.
26 September 2013

248

Your path cannot be broken by the
actions of others but only through
the inaction of Self.

29 September 2013

249

Elder magick cannot be contained,
only unleashed.
1 October 2013

250

Of all arts those serving the ego are the less relevant and consequentially the ones that lack the quality of immortality.

5 October 2013

New Moon

251

Danger lies not on the larger arm but in the smallest shadow.

9 October 2013

252

Our river still flows to the sound of music from the Gods, as blood carrying life to the black lands of old.

12 October 2013

253

Do not let growth be hindered by distractions. Such demons can only be banished through the fiery wand of your will.

15 October 2013

254

True strength is manifestly silent but the blind are chained to the unawareness that loudness mirrors their weakness.

19 October 2013

Full Moon

255

Ego establishes the boundaries of your being. When removed you become endless.

23 October 2013

256

To craft the hidden art you must
accept in the eye of thunder that only
when alone you become magick.

27 October 2013

257

Life should be a celebration of
the moment but also a conscious
preparation for the initiation of
death.

30 October 2013
Circle of the Dead

258

When we look closely there is magick
everywhere, like a subtle clock taming
the tides of time.

3 November 2013
New Moon

259

Only honesty is worthy of our respect.

6 November 2013

260

Secrets live not in the symbols for the symbols live within you and you are the secret.

8 November 2013

261

A mystical path requires courage as you must take a first step of faith so that the second may be of science.

12 November 2013

262

Someone incapable of love will often attempt to diminish those who celebrate their passion without fear.

16 November 2013
Full Moon

263

They raised fortresses where honesty is burned and valor diminished as falsehood became nurtured and vanity worshiped.

19 November 2013

264

When wielding elemental Fire do not blend the fluidity of Water unless you are willing to drink from the unheard sacrifice.

19 November 2013

265

Did you ever listen to the world through
the sound of a storm or seen its magick
in the eye of a falcon?
Have you ever felt it through the dance
of the wind or uncovered its mysteries in
the timeless words of poets?

22 November 2013

266

Only a soul with scars can speak
of pain, strength and fear.

24 November 2013

267

Answer honesty with kindness, respect
with dignity and rudeness with class.

27 November 2013

268

Ignorance seeking to ridicule sapience
is a recurring brand of a futile society
enslaved by weakness.

29 November 2013

269

When you trust the invisible over
illusions of matter thou shall be ready
to cross our gates.

1 December 2013

270

In matters of spirit anything but
excellence is insignificant.

4 December 2013
New Moon

271

The tome of evolution is found only by
the scribe of patience.

5 December 2013

272

Any soul that dishonorably scars
a seed of Aset is bound to an
inescapable truth: it may take one
day or a lifetime but fire awaits.

9 December 2013

273

Destiny is the map of every individual
choice in a unique roadmap of fate
defined by the sum of your actions and
inactions. Choose wisely.

12 December 2013

274

Creation and destruction are dangerous
yet essential catalysts of evolution —
the machinery of renewal.

14 December 2013

275

Devouring through sacred fire
brings forth the tears of life as
children of initiation.

14 December 2013

276

Do not speak of demons, evil and terror
to instigate dread for the fabric of
darkness is silent and nameless.

17 December 2013

Full Moon

277

The fall of deceit. Rest assured that a magus who fancifully exhibits his title is likely to need your wisdom more than he can ever teach.

19 December 2013

278

Magick is entirely selfless. It serves no desire for validation nor bends to ego. Magick is, nonetheless, undeniably arrogant. It does not listen to opinion nor does it care for judgement.

21 December 2013

Winter Solstice

279

When winter visits your temple do not curse the temper of rain but embrace its cleansing touch as it softly kisses your skin.

25 December 2013

Call of Winter

✝

280

To remain idle is easy but to break thunder upon the face of injustice defines valor.

28 December 2013

281

Be one of the rare few to carve a mark in this world that you would be proud to leave upon your passing.

31 December 2013

282

Celebrate the past, embrace the present and seize the future.

1 January 2014
New Moon

283

The greatest heroes are not celebrated in public for they discard recognition, conquering historical deeds discreetly in silence.

5 January 2014

284

Someone unwilling to fight for his passions and dreams deserves not having them fulfilled.

7 January 2014

285

The seventh night to all walking this violet road of Her mysteries.

7 January 2014

286

In time everything putrid is brought to surface and the rotten stumble into the light.

10 January 2014

287

The greatest mistake you can do on the path of the living is to take anything for granted. Only impermanence prevails.

13 January 2014

288

There is no ego that we cannot break. Only upon our eternal mirror of silence can your will truly be revealed.

14 January 2014

✝

289

Asetians stand unbroken by the passing of frozen winds as old alliances fall and the tides of history are carved in purple stone.

16 January 2014
Full Moon

290

Leave judgement on the chosen life of others to those without a fulfilling life of their own.

18 January 2014

291

Selfless union forged by trust is one of the most indestructible forces this realm has ever seen.

20 January 2014

☥

292

Warriors make deliberate use of contemplation before moving pieces on the board of life, unlike fools who act loudly without thought.

23 January 2014

293

Detachedly prune your inner garden of all weeds that hinder its blooming and pour poison on the crawling worms that seek your fruit.

25 January 2014

294

A spell is not a mental afterthought or the result of mystical illusion. It is energy given purpose and set in motion by conscious will.

28 January 2014

†

295

Both love and hate yield great power,
however only one leads to the ancient
gates of immortality.

30 January 2014
New Moon

296

You cannot fight that which remains
unseen for an enemy daring to strike
upon us must first learn how to
enslave smoke with bare hands.

1 February 2014

297

The strongest magick is not attained
through the constructs of ritual,
being manifested into reality by the
unsung will of the heart.

3 February 2014

✝

298

When the temple of the Elders becomes silent the seed of intent is revealed.

6 February 2014

299

The ecstasy of supreme liberation is not a sin of carnal allegiance but the expression of our innermost sexual divinity.

9 February 2014

300

Speak your mind.
Act on your ideals.
Trust your instincts.
Live your dreams.
Never surrender.
Ignore hate, envy and dishonest criticism.

11 February 2014

301

Only the weak are content with
what is to be found at surface.

13 February 2014

302

The silver crown of Thoth serves the
war banners of wisdom under the rule
of forgotten pharaohs without name.

14 February 2014
Full Moon

303

When you have been judged by
time and tested by the undying
fire no word of mortals holds
power over you.

15 February 2014

☥

304

Arguing with fools is useless. Allow them to speak and their words become a banner of their incomplete self.

17 February 2014

305

Anyone who explores the occult, magick or spirituality as a competition in any possible form is bound to inevitable failure.

20 February 2014

306

Trusting real initiations to be breakable or its bonds not eternal is one of the most dangerous mistakes an occultist can do.

23 February 2014

307

We celebrate truth in a world of liars.

25 February 2014

308

Deluded minds seeking the apotheosis of self-deification only expose their blindness towards the divine within.

27 February 2014

309

A dragon can only be awoken by fire.

1 March 2014

New Moon

310

Thoughts may define character
but only actions carve the valley
of honor.

4 March 2014

311

With power it becomes easy to claim justice
with bare hands and determined will but who
are we to condemn others to torment?
How many unspeakable sins have we not
committed ourselves, in this life or any before,
only to rise beyond any scar?
Be wary of easy assumptions and the quick
judgement typical of a mortal mind for even
the very wise restrain from using such dagger.
7 March 2014

312

Servants of the hippopotamus in
the Nile may adamantly not bend
the knee yet what does not bend
can be broken.

9 March 2014

313

Sometimes only the painful light of thunder can illuminate the machinery of wisdom.

12 March 2014

314

Harmony is born out of the seed of contrast under the mantle of duality.

14 March 2014

315

Without the grace of winter you cannot appreciate the warm smile of the sun and without the thirst of summer you cannot dance in the rain.

15 March 2014

✝

316

On the motherly cradle of Nun endures a devastating mystery that only the Queen holds its daunting key.

16 March 2014
Full Moon

317

As a living force of transformation and renewal there is no shame in change for only the unbending rock never grows.

20 March 2014
Spring Equinox

318

When grasping beyond the limits of flesh raised by blindness of physical existence it becomes undeniable that we are infinite.

23 March 2014

✝

319

May those seeking dreams of a pretentious heaven follow their deluded hope as we courageously embrace immortal hell.

27 March 2014

320

To find the true thoughts hidden behind masks and barriers we must pierce deeply into the understanding of their nightmares.

30 March 2014
New Moon

321

Disregard for the natural world in its infinite expressions is the stain of a society that does not realise its pathetic insignificance.

1 April 2014

322

Magick not empowered by
feelings is not magick at all.

4 April 2014

323

The ability to feel is tied to the
fabric of your soul and feelings
are not just chemical reactions
but energy given form.

5 April 2014

324

Remember that how you see
the world is not necessarily
reality. What you see is a
distorted perspective filtered
through your perception.

8 April 2014

325

The everlasting bond of Family finds
its sacredness not in blood but on the
willing heart of the soul.
The Ib of the Ba.

11 April 2014

326

Never forget that there is more
to learn from sorrow than from
happiness. Only balance creates
a complete life.

14 April 2014
Full Moon

327

If you lie about someone as an
attempt to discredit his words you
are not proving them false but only
revealing your fear of their power.

18 April 2014

✝

328

Certain eyes see in Asetians the gentler souls ever created while others find in them the personification of evil given flesh. Perception. Which mirrors the truth beneath our mantle of mystery?

20 April 2014

329

Many get lost seeking for answers they may never find, forgetting to live and enjoy the blessings already bestowed upon them.

24 April 2014

330

Fitting in is a quest of fools. Being accepted a hope of the weak.

Embrace your uniqueness notwithstanding opposition and criticism.

27 April 2014

331

We are horse and rider; the banner
high on the mountain. Chill of the
forest and shadow in the dark.
We are sword, steel and death.

30 April 2014
New Moon

332

Eternity is only achieved through
the perpetual experience of now.

4 May 2014

333

Fire destroys the weak and nourishes
the strong.

7 May 2014

†

334

No human power can burn the armies carrying flags soaked in red for only the flaming sword of immortals can scar their false crown.

9 May 2014

335

If someone insults or spreads lies concerning you it speaks more about them than it does about you.

12 May 2014

336

When we bleed we bleed as One.

15 May 2014

Full Moon

337
Who wields the greatest power
finds no service in its exhibition.
18 May 2014

338
A lost soul is not an abandoned
soul. Hidden beauty and forgotten
truth forever concealed until the
violet storm that can set it free.
24 May 2014

339
Most can only understand life in shallow
waters while we command fleets through
major storms at the abyss.
28 May 2014
New Moon

340

Empress of silver light, immortal Queen that brings empires to its knees and raises armies to the height of infinity.

1 June 2014

341

Drawing inspiration from recognition is a common sign on the absence of art upon the birth of commerce and ephemeral gratification.

5 June 2014

342

To be immortal is to start anew. Ancient flame in renewed shell, remembering to be One again.

9 June 2014

343

Nature does not listen to the sound
of envy and hate; it only sings to the
voice of silence.

13 June 2014
Full Moon

344

Not only physical experiences allow
us to live the greatest stories. Often
the very subtle hold the unexpected
power to redraw our lives.

18 June 2014

345

Asetians are proud to be a small
Family for never in history so few
rose above so many.

21 June 2014
Summer Solstice

346

When summer visits your temple do not
hide from the sun but master its cleansing
flame as it arrogantly burns your skin.

22 June 2014
Call of Summer

347

When making a promise, commit to it
through life and death. If your word
loses power you become nothing.
29 June 2014

348

My soul is my compass. My inner master.
The map of my past, candle of my present
and omen of my future.

3 July 2014

349

Exiled from the sand that blessed
their sunrise and unbound from the
mortal coil of eternal slumber they
bent stone and forged an empire.

7 July 2014

7.7

350

Those who succeed are not the ones
that never do mistakes but those who
never give up and that their mistakes
only make them fight harder.

9 July 2014

351

A species that does not respect nature
and its unquestionably superior power
shall never be respected in return.

12 July 2014

Full Moon

✝

352

Asetianism is not about power, it is about knowing. However, knowing often is power.

16 July 2014

353

The despair of those who hide elusive sadness beneath masked smiles and empty laughs is often evident as screams to all but themselves.

20 July 2014

354

We unleash fire that can burn time and forge the invisible bonds of immortality.

25 July 2014

355

To condemn and criticize what you do
not understand and know nothing about
is merely a futile exercise of ignorance.

27 July 2014
New Moon

356

Immortal drops forgotten on an
ocean of living mortality.
Unawakened love.

31 July 2014

357

Only those freely wielding their words
unbroken may sing among the stars.

3 August 2014

358
When facing dishonor there is nothing
as powerful as indifference.

5 August 2014

359
A beating heart veils the silent tune
of the last untouched stone.

7 August 2014

360
At the ancient crossing where Her
name remains unspoken a lost token
reveals the undying words of silver.

7 August 2014

361

Those obsessed with power will remain the ones lacking it.

9 August 2014

362

The most delicate alchemy allows for the transformation of pain and sorrow into wisdom.

10 August 2014
Full Moon

363

The ignorance of those who misunderstand your world and existence is commonly echoed through judgment, cynicism, fear and lies.

12 August 2014

364

Through pristine valleys along the road unseen the thread of starlight peeks beneath the golden door.

13 August 2014

365

When the beast within rests under the delicate balance of your willpower there is no enemy that can break you.

14 August 2014

366

Cowardice and laziness are common triggers behind the conscious or unconscious refusal of most to think for themselves.

16 August 2014

367

Strength cannot be glimpsed on the fabric of your body for it only becomes visible upon the mirror of your thoughts, choices and actions.

16 August 2014

368

When lost in the dark instead of turning on the light seek that which may teach you how to see in its absence.

17 August 2014

369

You cannot teach honor and loyalty to someone without character and a strong personality.

19 August 2014

370

Do not feed shallow tales to a monster
nor teach it the laws of mortal men. A
demon must not be tamed for it needs
only to be unleashed...

20 August 2014

371

Never mistake silence for idleness
and unawareness...

22 August 2014

372

On Her seductive halls of truth the
violet fire burns everlastingly, echoing
the primordial anthem that carries the
untold mystery of old.

23 August 2014

373

So the word is sealed and the road of five revealed.

23 August 2014

The Call of the Warrior

In silence the storm gathers
For in darkness our name is spoken
The gaping pit of lost nightmares
Rising high where it cannot be found

We shall ride the raging monsters
Bringing the Sun unto our domain
Crushing down with one thousand spears
Raining flame above thy name

To raise the Moon on stellar heights
Unleashing wisdom in trails of silver
For Thoth has come and Nut remained
Our army calling in timeless trumpets

We cause pain and heal the flame
Storming the enemies of Her name
Without fear or a thread of shame
Serving the empire in hidden game

We are the violet legion
The sword that cuts in the dark
A terror that goes forth
The chill in the long night

Her crown, a beacon of hope
Cold skin, the gracious dove
Her hair, forgotten tales
Menacing eyes, the strength of us

Shining deeds seek not the light
Ancient lore that became legend
A song in the dreams of mortals
Terrifying secret unknown to men

By conquering fire we forged a fate
Through mighty stone we crushed all thought
In solitude we curse the desert
For in Her womb our bonds revive

We are the warriors of death
The sages of immortal life
Our shields are crafted of sorrow
Our swords made of shadow and light

We hunt the souls and brand their call
We claim life and give it anew
Taming dragons with whips of silence
We fly above your world in unseen view

†

Appendices

Map of Kemet

Ancient and Modern Sites

Appendices

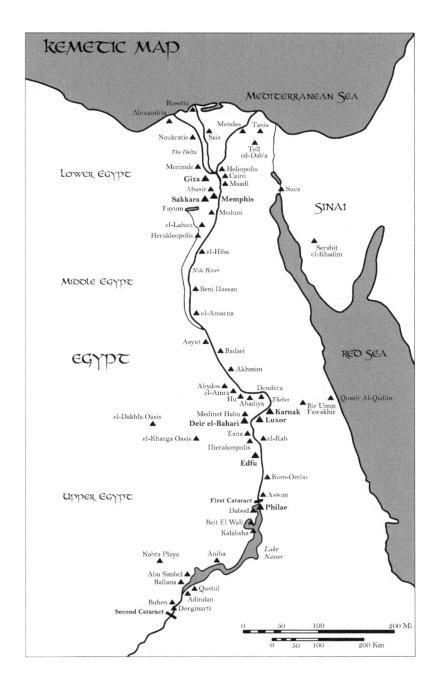

KEMETIC MAP

MEDITERRANEAN SEA

Rosetta
Alexandria

Mendes Tanis
Naukratis Sais

The Delta

Tell
ed-Dab'a

LOWER EGYPT

Merimde

Giza

Abusir

Sakkara **Memphis**

Fayum

Heliopolis
Cairo
Maadi

Suez

SINAI

Medum

el-Lahun
Herakleopolis

el-Hiba

Serabit
el-Khadim

MIDDLE EGYPT

Nile River

Beni Hassan

el-Amarna

EGYPT

Asyut

Badari

Akhmim

RED SEA

Abydos
el-Amra Dendera
Hu Abadiya *Thebes*

el-Dakhla Oasis

Medinet Habu **Karnak**
Deir el-Bahari **Luxor**

Quseir Al-Qadim
Bir Umm
Fawakhir

Esna el-Kab

el-Kharga Oasis

Hierakonpolis

Edfu

Kom-Ombo

UPPER EGYPT

First Cataract Aswan
Dabod **Philae**
Beit El Wali
Kalabsha

Nabta Playa Aniba

Lake Nasser

Abu Simbel
Ballana

Qustul
Adindan
Dorginarti

Buhen
Second Cataract

0   50   100   200 Mi

0   50   100   200 Km

903

Shen Mapping

Subtle Anatomy

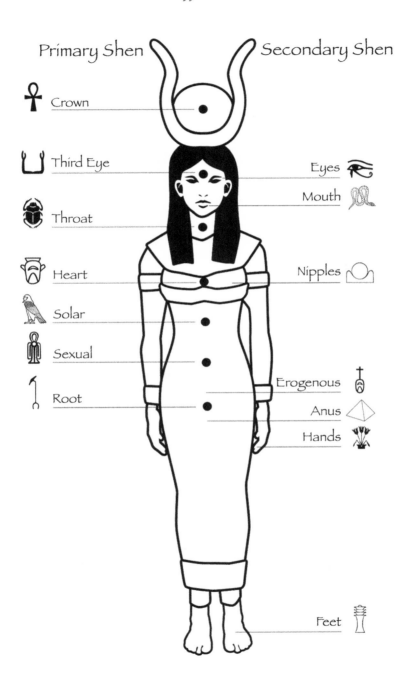

Primary Shen

Crown

Third Eye

Throat

Heart

Solar

Sexual

Root

Secondary Shen

Eyes

Mouth

Nipples

Erogenous

Anus

Hands

Feet

Shen Systems

Applied Energy Cores

Root Shen

Asetian Pillar	Was
Sanskrit	Muladhara
Location	Perineum
Color	Black or Red
Alchemy	Earth
Functions	Grounding, Strength, Survival, Instinct
Minerals	Hematite, Obsidian, Ruby, Tourmaline
Anatomy	Spinal Column, Colon, Bladder, Anus, Rectum, Legs
Positive	Physical Body, Coordination, Stability, Courage
Negative	Weakened Immunity, Violence, Anger, Ego

Sexual Shen

Asetian Pillar	Tiet
Sanskrit	Svadhishthana
Location	Lower Abdomen
Color	Orange
Alchemy	Fire
Functions	Sexuality, Vitality, Creativity
Minerals	Carnelian, Topaz, Amber
Anatomy	Kidneys, Genitals, Ovaries, Testicles
Positive	Abundance, Desire, Pleasure, Intimacy, Surrender
Negative	Sexual Conditions, Confusion, Jealousy, Envy

Solar Shen

Asetian Pillar	Ba
Sanskrit	Manipura
Location	Below the Chest
Color	Yellow
Alchemy	Fire and Water
Functions	Metabolism, Nervous System, Digestion
Minerals	Citrine, Tiger's Eye
Anatomy	Stomach, Liver, Pancreas
Positive	Will, Motivation, Confidence, Self-control
Negative	Digestive Conditions, Anxiety, Fear, Depression

Heart Shen

Asetian Pillar	Ib
Sanskrit	Anahata
Location	Sternum
Color	Green
Alchemy	Water
Functions	Blood, Emotion
Minerals	Emerald, Jade, Malachite, Rose Quartz
Anatomy	Heart, Circulatory System, Lungs, Breasts, Arms
Positive	Forgiveness, Compassion, Understanding, Acceptance
Negative	Repressed Feelings, Heart and Lung Conditions

Throat Shen

Asetian Pillar	Khepri
Sanskrit	Vishuddha
Location	Throat
Color	Blue
Alchemy	Air
Functions	Sound, Vibration
Minerals	Turquoise, Aquamarine, Sapphire
Anatomy	Thyroid, Throat, Tongue, Teeth, Ears
Positive	Spoken Word, Communication
Negative	Poor Expression, Incoherent Speech

Third Eye Shen

Asetian Pillar	Ka
Sanskrit	Ajna
Location	Forehead
Color	Indigo
Alchemy	Spirit
Functions	Metaphysics, Thoughts, Vision
Minerals	Lapis Lazuli, Sodalite
Anatomy	Eyes, Brain
Positive	Intuition, Insight, Clairvoyance, Enlightenment
Negative	Blocked Abilities, Headaches, Neurological Conditions

Crown Shen

Asetian Pillar	Ankh
Sanskrit	Sahasrara
Location	Above the Head
Color	Violet
Alchemy	Divinity
Functions	Divine Connection, Energy Source
Minerals	Amethyst, Diamond
Anatomy	Transcendence
Positive	Higher Self, Spirituality, Oneness
Negative	Senility, Stagnation, Decay

Notes

Notes

[1] Almásy László, *Az Ismeretlen Szahara (The Unknown Sahara)*
(Franklin-Társulat, 1934)

[2] George Hart, *The Routledge Dictionary of Egyptian Gods and Goddesses*,
Second Edition (Routledge, 2005)

[3] Richard Hinckley Allen, *Star Names: Their Lore and Meaning*
(Dover Publications, 1963)

[4] Luis Marques, *Book of Orion – Liber Aeternus*
(Aset Ka, 2012)

[5] Bram Stoker, *Dracula*
(Archibald Constable and Company, 1897)

[6] Anne Rice, *Interview With The Vampire*
(Alfred A. Knopf, 1976)

[7] William Godwin, *Lives of the Necromancers*
(Frederick J Mason, 1834)

[8] Richard Wilkinson, *The Complete Gods and Goddesses of Ancient Egypt*
(Thames & Hudson, 2003)

[9] Luis Marques, *Book of Orion – Liber Aeternus*,
"Liber יסוד *– From Purity to Dust"* (Aset Ka, 2012)

[10] Jean Houston, *The Passion of Isis and Osiris: A Union of Two Souls*
(Ballantine Wellspring, 1995)

[11] Luis Marques, *Book of Orion – Liber Aeternus*,
"Book of Ipet Resyt" (Aset Ka, 2012)

[12] Lon Milo DuQuette, *The Magick of Aleister Crowley*,
"The Evolution of Magical Formulae" (Weiser, 2003)

[13] Luis Marques, *Book of Orion – Liber Aeternus*,
"Liber Sigillum 333 – Mysteries Unveiled" (Aset Ka, 2012)

[14] Schwaller de Lubicz, *Le Temple dans l'Homme*
    (Le Caire, 1949)

[15] John Anthony West, *Magical Egypt*,
    "The Temple in Man" (Cydonia, 2001)

[16] Luis Marques, *Book of Orion – Liber Aeternus*,
    "Liber יסוד – Tetragrammaton" (Aset Ka, 2012)

[17] John Anthony West, Robert Bauval and Lon Milo DuQuette,
    Magical Egypt, "Illumination" (Cydonia, 2001)

[18] Authorized King James Bible translation
    Cambridge Edition (1760)

[19] Luis Marques, *Asetian Bible*,
    "Metaphysics – Planes of Existence" (Aset Ka, 2007)

[20] Dion Fortune, *The Mystical Qabalah*,
    "Binah, the Third Sephirah" (Aquarian Press, 1987)

[21] Lon Milo DuQuette, *Understanding Aleister Crowley's Thoth Tarot*,
    "Secrets of the Rose Cross Back" (Weiser, 2003)

[22] *Sepher Yetzirah*
    Rabbi Isidor Kalisch translation (1877)

[23] Luis Marques, *Asetian Bible*,
    "Sacred Pillars – The Seven Frameworks" (Aset Ka, 2007)

[24] Daniel Chanan Matt, *The Essential Kabbalah: The Heart of Jewish Mysticism*
    (HarperOne, 1996)

[25] Aleister Crowley, *The Book of Thoth*,
    The Equinox Vol. III No. V (Weiser, 1974)

[26] Aleister Crowley, *Liber AL vel Legis*, sub figura CCXX as delivered by
    XCIII=418 to DCLXVI (Ordo Templi Orientis, 1938)

[27] Richard H. Wilkinson, *The Complete Gods and Goddesses of Ancient Egypt*
    (Thames & Hudson, 2003)

☥

[28] 江晓原, 历史上的星占学

(Shanghai Science and Technology Education Press, 1995)

[29] 张闻玉, 古代天文历法讲座

(Guangxi Normal University Press, 2008)

[30] Luis Marques, *Asetian Bible*,

"Subtle Anatomy – Shen Centers" (Aset Ka, 2007)

[31] J.R.R. Tolkien, *The Lord of the Rings – The Fellowship of the Ring*,

"Three is Company" (1954)

[32] Christopher Tolkien and J.R.R. Tolkien, *The Lost Road and Other Writings*,

"The Etymologies" (1987)

[33] James B. Kaler, *Portraits of Stars and their Constellations*

(University of Illinois, 2012)

[34] European Space Agency Hipparcos, *Simbad*

(Centre de Données Astronomiques de Strasbourg, 2012)

[35] John Anthony West, *The Great Work*,

"Initiation One – The Material Plane" (Chance Gardner, 2008)

[36] Luis Marques, *Asetian Bible*,

"Djehutys – Haunting of the Treacherous Crocodile" (Aset Ka, 2007)

[37] Luis Marques, *Asetian Bible*,

"Elementals – Alchemical Foundation" (Aset Ka, 2007)

[38] Rosemary Clark, *Sacred Magic Of Ancient Egypt: The Spiritual Practice Restored*

(Llewellyn, 2003)

[39] Mark Lehner, *The Complete Pyramids*,

"The Pyramids at Lisht" (Thames & Hudson 1997)

[40] Richard H. Wilkinson, *The Complete Gods and Goddesses of Ancient Egypt*

(Thames & Hudson, 2003)

✝

The old days of the mighty Asetian empire might be a lost pleasant memory only seen as violet glimpses beyond the veil of time as the era of long gone formidable magick. The courageous hymns of epic battles and the dominion of honor, honesty and loyalty might be over but the immortal bloodline lingers still. The Asetians are still here. We are still here. Silently observing, teaching and illuminating in darkness with the banners of endless flame and undying Fire. We are Her legacy and our essence the living flesh of the Violet Throne.

We live in Secret. We live in Silence. And we live Forever...

The word is sealed.
Em Hotep.

They were only Three.

Yet, they moved a nation.

They were only Seven.

Yet, they conquered the desert.

They became endless.

Yet, they were forgotten.

They became legend.

Then, they were remembered.

Liber Aeternus III.3

CPSIA information can be obtained
at www.ICGtesting.com
Printed in the USA
LVHW041556300423
745688LV00001B/66